Studies in International Taxation

A National Bureau
of Economic Research
Project Report

Studies in International Taxation

Edited by   Alberto Giovannini,
R. Glenn Hubbard,
and Joel Slemrod

The University of Chicago Press

Chicago and London

ALBERTO GIOVANNINI is Jerome A. Chazen Professor of International Business at Columbia University, a research fellow at the Centre for Economic Research in London, and member and coordinator of the Council of Experts of the Italian Treasury Ministry. R. GLENN HUBBARD is professor of economics and finance at the Graduate School of Business, Columbia University, and former deputy assistant secretary (tax analysis), U.S. Department of the Treasury. JOEL SLEMROD is Jack D. Sparks Whirlpool Corporation Research Professor in Business Administration and professor of economics at the University of Michigan. All are research associates of the National Bureau of Economic Research.

The University of Chicago Press, Chicago 60637
The University of Chicago Press, Ltd., London

02 01 00 99 98 97 96 95 94 93 1 2 3 4 5

ISBN: 0-226-29701-2 (cloth)

Library of Congress Cataloging-in-Publication Data

Studies in international taxation / edited by Alberto Giovannini, R. Glenn Hubbard, Joel Slemrod.
  p.   cm.—(A National Bureau of Economic Research project report)
  Includes bibliographical references and index.
  1. International business enterprises—Taxation.   2. Income tax—Foreign income.   3. Investments, Foreign—Taxation.   4. Capital levy.   I. Giovannini, Alberto.   II. Hubbard, R. Glenn.   III. Slemrod, Joel.   IV. Series.
HJ2347.S78   1993
336.24′3—dc20   93-9797
                                                                          CIP

⊗The paper used in this publication meets the minimum requirements of the American National Standard for Information Sciences—Permanence of Paper for Printed Library Materials, ANSI Z39.48–1984.

Relation of the Directors to the
Work and Publications of the
National Bureau of Economic Research

1. The object of the National Bureau of Economic Research is to ascertain and to present to the public important economic facts and their interpretation in a scientific and impartial manner. The Board of Directors is charged with the responsibility of ensuring that the work of the National Bureau is carried on in strict conformity with this object.

2. The President of the National Bureau shall submit to the Board of Directors, or to its Executive Committee, for their formal adoption all specific proposals for research to be instituted.

3. No research report shall be published by the National Bureau until the President has sent each member of the Board a notice that a manuscript is recommended for publication and that in the President's opinion it is suitable for publication in accordance with the principles of the National Bureau. Such notification will include an abstract or summary of the manuscript's content and a response form for use by those Directors who desire a copy of the manuscript for review. Each manuscript shall contain a summary drawing attention to the nature and treatment of the problem studied, the character of the data and their utilization in the report, and the main conclusions reached.

4. For each manuscript so submitted, a special committee of the Directors (including Directors Emeriti) shall be appointed by majority agreement of the President and Vice Presidents (or by the Executive Committee in case of inability to decide on the part of the President and Vice Presidents), consisting of three Directors selected as nearly as may be one from each general division of the Board. The names of the special manuscript committee shall be stated to each Director when notice of the proposed publication is submitted to him. It shall be the duty of each member of the special manuscript commmittee to read the manuscript. If each member of the manuscript committee signifies his approval within thirty days of the transmittal of the manuscript, the report may be published. If at the end of that period any member of the manuscript committee withholds his approval, the President shall then notify each member of the Board, requesting approval or disapproval of publication, and thirty days additional shall be granted for this purpose. The manuscript shall then not be published unless at least a majority of the entire Board who shall have voted on the proposal within the time fixed for the receipt of votes shall have approved.

5. No manuscript may be published, though approved by each member of the special manuscript committee, until forty-five days have elapsed from the transmittal of the report in manuscript form. The interval is allowed for the receipt of any memorandum of dissent or reservation, together with a brief statement of his reasons, that any member may wish to express; and such memorandum of dissent or reservastion shall be published with the manuscript if he so desires. Publication does not, however, imply that each member of the Board has read the manuscript, or that either members of the Board in general or the special committee have passed on its validity in every detail.

6. Publications of the National Bureau issued for informational purposes concerning the work of the Bureau and its staff, or issued to inform the public of activities of Bureau staff, and volumes issued as a result of various conferences involving the National Bureau shall contain a specific disclaimer noting that such publication has not passed through the normal review procedures required in this resolution. The Executive Committee of the Board is charged with review of all such publications from time to time to ensure that they do not take on the character of formal research reports of the National Bureau, requiring formal Board approval.

7. Unless otherwise determined by the Board or exempted by the terms of paragraph 6, a copy of this resolution shall be printed in each National Bureau publication.

(Resolution adopted October 25, 1926, as revised through September 30, 1974)

Contents

Acknowledgments   ix

Introduction   1
Alberto Giovannini, R. Glenn Hubbard, and Joel
Slemrod

I. INTERNATIONAL FINANCIAL MANAGEMENT

1. **Taxes and the Form of Ownership of Foreign
   Corporate Equity**   13
   Roger H. Gordon and Joosung Jun
   Comment: Alberto Giovannini

2. **Impacts of Canadian and U.S. Tax Reform on
   the Financing of Canadian Subsidiaries of
   U.S. Parents**   47
   Roy D. Hogg and Jack M. Mintz
   Comment: Neil Bruce

3. **The Effects of U.S. Tax Policy on the Income
   Repatriation Patterns of U.S. Multinational
   Corporations**   77
   Rosanne Altshuler and T. Scott Newlon

II. INVESTMENT

4. **Taxation and Foreign Direct Investment in
   the United States: A Reconsideration of
   the Evidence**   119
   Alan J. Auerbach and Kevin Hassett
   Comment: James M. Poterba

5. **On the Sensitivity of R&D to Delicate Tax Changes: The Behavior of U.S. Multinationals in the 1980s**   149
James R. Hines, Jr.
Comment: Bronwyn H. Hall

6. **The Role of Taxes in Location and Sourcing Decisions**   195
G. Peter Wilson
Comment: R. Glenn Hubbard

III. INCOME SHIFTING

7. **Explaining the Low Taxable Income of Foreign-Controlled Companies in the United States**   237
Harry Grubert, Timothy Goodspeed, and Deborah Swenson
Comment: Jeffrey K. MacKie-Mason

8. **Income Shifting in U.S. Multinational Corporations**   277
David Harris, Randall Morck, Joel Slemrod, and Bernard Yeung
Comment: John Mutti

Contributors   309
Author Index   311
Subject Index   315

Acknowledgments

This volume includes nine papers that were prepared as part of a research project on international aspects of taxation, undertaken by the National Bureau of Economic Research. The authors present new empirical studies of effects of tax policy on decisions of multinational corporations in three areas: international financial management, investment, and income shifting. This research was the focus of a conference attended by academics, policymakers, and representatives of international organizations. The conference was held in New York on September 26–28, 1991.

The editors are grateful to the Ford Foundation and the Starr Foundation for financial support of this project. The success of the conference and the project also depended on the efforts of Robert Allison, Kirsten Foss Davis, Ilana Hardesty, and Jane Konkel of the National Bureau of Economic Research.

Alberto Giovannini, R. Glenn Hubbard, and Joel Slemrod

Introduction

Alberto Giovannini, R. Glenn Hubbard, and Joel Slemrod

In recent years, as multinational corporations have played a greater role in the global economy, interest in international aspects of capital income taxation has also rapidly increased. In the United States, discussions of problems of U.S. competitiveness and the position of the United States in the world economy have prompted public debate on international taxation issues. In Europe, policy discussions on capital income taxation have increased in the wake of the announcement that several European countries have liberalized capital flows, of the single European market, and of the Economic and Monetary Union. An experts' committee of the European Commission proposed, in early 1992, a substantial harmonization of corporate income tax structures. These developments raise the question of whether the existing structure of multinational taxation was viable only in the highly regulated international financial system and under the relative restrictive controls on international capital movements that characterized the world economy in the post–World War II period. Is the current system of taxing income—and multinationals in particular—inconsistent with the trend toward liberalized world financial flows and increased international commercial competition?

This question has begun to attract the attention of the academic community. Its answer depends on the effect of taxes on saving, on capital formation in different countries, on the pattern of international borrowing and lending, on international competitiveness, and on the opportunities for tax avoidance.

Alberto Giovannini is Jerome A. Chazen Professor of International Business at Columbia University, a research fellow at the Centre for Economic Research in London, and member and coordinator of the Council of Experts of the Italian Treasury Ministry. R. Glenn Hubbard is professor of economics and finance at the Graduate School of Business, Columbia University, and former deputy assistant secretary (tax analysis), U.S. Department of the Treasury. Joel Slemrod is Jack D. Sparks Whirlpool Corporation Research Professor in Business Administration and professor of economics at the University of Michigan. All are research associates of the National Bureau of Economic Research.

Much of the recent research in this area combines newly developed models in the fields of public finance and international economics.

At the same time, policymakers in the United States have indicated a willingness to reconsider the entire system of taxation of income from inbound and outbound investment. In July 1992, the House Ways and Means Committee held hearings on a comprehensive and controversial package of tax proposals affecting U.S. and non-U.S. multinational businesses (H.R. 5270, The Foreign Income Tax Rationalization and Simplification Act of 1992). The Bush administration signaled its interest in reform of the international tax system when then Secretary of the Treasury Nicholas Brady directed Treasury's Office of Tax Analysis to launch its own economic analysis.

Broad-based studies of the international taxation system will have to reconcile results of the simplest theoretical models with the complex world of business finance and investment decisions in the global economy. Conceptual analyses of capital income taxes in open economies have produced extremely simple and intuitive propositions on the desirability of alternative international tax regimes. Among these, the least controversial and the best known is the proposition on the superiority, from a global perspective, of residence-based capital income taxes, under which the domestic and foreign incomes of residents of any given country are taxed at the same rate, irrespective of origin. Residence-based taxation satisfies the criterion of capital-export neutrality, often referred to in informal discussions of international capital income taxation. For multinationals, it is implemented by taxing their worldwide income and allowing an unlimited credit for taxes paid to governments.

Despite the great intellectual appeal of this proposition and despite the fact that many industrial countries have officially adopted the residence principle of taxation of international income, capital-export neutrality is not achieved in practice by any country. There is significant tax discrimination between domestic- and foreign-source capital income, caused by limitations of tax credit on foreign taxes paid, by the possibility of deferring foreign-source income, by countries' differences in the degree of integration between the taxation of corporate and personal income, and by the differences in the definitions of tax bases—including how foreign-source and domestic-source income are delineated.

Even if these problems could be eliminated, it is unlikely that a pure residence-based system of capital income taxation could be put in place, because tax enforcement is by its very nature territorial. The enforcement of tax laws can seldom, and only with great difficulty, be extended outside the boundaries of a country. The territorial nature of tax enforcement and the difficulties of recovering taxes from overseas income have led countries to tax income produced by foreign residents in their own territory. Hence, the movement to a pure residence-based system would require relinquishing tax revenue from income produced by foreign investments, a reform that would encounter substantial political resistance.

Do observed deviations from capital-export neutrality give rise to significant losses of efficiency? More generally, how does the world allocation of productive capital, research and development facilities, and tax revenues respond to tax incentives? These questions have straightforward answers in simple theoretical models, but answers in practice are more difficult because of the complexity of real-world tax rules, financial management, and investment decisions. This difficulty is compounded by the fact that the answers to these questions have important implications for the appropriate direction of policy. For example, if cross-country differences in corporate tax rates would give rise to significant income shifting but little incentive to shift production facilities, then international coordination efforts ought to be focused on harmonizing corporate statutory tax rates. If, alternatively, income shifting were insignificant but real investment were very sensitive to taxation, then attention should be given to effective tax rates, which depend not only on statutory tax rates but also on the definition of the tax base.

The efficiency of factor allocation is not the only criterion by which international tax policy must be judged in practice. The distribution of tax revenues across countries is also a continuing concern, especially since some countries deliberately set their tax structure to make it attractive for the multinational corporation to shift taxable income into their jurisdiction. Attempts by other countries to limit the loss of revenue because of income shifting have contributed to the extreme complexity of the tax rules that apply to multinationals. This complexity exacts a resource cost not only through the expenses incurred in complying with the rules but also in the difficulty and uncertainty added to the long-term planning process. Although equity and simplicity of operation should be kept in mind as criteria for judging international tax policy, because of the difficulty of analyzing these issues most economic research has to this point focused on the incentive effects of taxation on factor allocation.

Some recent attempts to identify the tax incentives to international investments that account in a realistic way for the existing tax rules are the cost-of-capital calculations based on the methods developed by King and Fullerton (1984). Devereux and Pearson (1991) use the King-Fullerton techniques to compute the cost of capital of a number of cross-border investments and find that, at least for European countries, differences in the cost of capital for different types of cross-border investments are very large. This puzzling evidence adds to less systematic descriptions, typically found in publications of accounting firms, of the opportunities offered by the numerous loopholes created by international inconsistencies in national tax rules. Even the Devereux-Pearson calculations are based on very rudimentary assumptions about the details of how multinationals are taxed and the dimensions in which firms can adjust their financial and accounting behavior in response to taxes.

Very large differences in costs of capital and a bewildering variety of legal means that allow multinational corporations to significantly reduce their taxes paid have not been exploited fully; that is, such profit opportunities apparently have not been taken to the limit. This puzzle raises questions about the appropriateness of many models currently used in international taxation that predict the (often instantaneous) disappearance of these profit opportunities and on which welfare evaluations of alternative tax regimes are based. In other words, if apparent profit opportunities are not eliminated by arbitrage, existing models are likely not accounting for important factors that influence the finance and investment decisions of multinational corporations in the real world.

It is clear that the conceptual models that frame our understanding of international taxation policy have not caught up to the new realities of the financial and investment decisions in the global economy. Before building new models, however, we believe that it is important to examine the relevant empirical facts. That is the goal of this volume. The papers that follow exploit a variety of data sets, many of which are new, to provide evidence on three crucial aspects of multinational corporations' responses to international tax incentives: (1) international financial management, (2) international investment, and (3) international income shifting. Only with an understanding of these issues can we assess the likely impact of alternative tax regimes and evaluate these alternatives according to their economic impact, their simplicity of operation, and their distribution of tax revenues across countries.

International Financial Management

The first two papers are concerned with the effect of taxation on international financial management. Roger H. Gordon and Joosung Jun investigate the implications of the fact that the tax law treats differently the two ways individuals can buy equity in foreign firms—directly by purchasing these shares in the securities market (portfolio investment) or indirectly by investing in a domestic corporation that then uses the funds to invest in foreign firms (foreign direct investment). Either approach allows investors to take advantage of the potentially more favorable returns abroad and to diversify their portfolios. Of course, the relative importance of portfolio equity investment versus foreign direct investment will be affected by more than just tax factors. When corporations invest abroad, they acquire both ownership and control over the foreign firms, whereas portfolio investors merely acquire ownership. This makes corporate investments more attractive to the extent to which there are synergy gains from joint operations of the domestic and foreign firms. In addition, through use of capital controls, some countries attempt to discourage portfolio investment abroad.

Gordon and Jun analyze empirically how tax and nontax factors affect the relative importance of portfolio equity investments versus foreign direct investments, using aggregate data from ten foreign countries on the composition of portfolio and direct ownership of U.S. equity for the period 1980–89.

Their analysis of these data shows that the composition of equity flows does differ dramatically among these countries and that at least part of the explanation appears to be tax differences. However, behavior did not seem to change much during the 1980s, in spite of the many large changes in tax rates that occurred during that period. Part of the explanation for the lack of response appears to be the importance of capital controls in many of the sample countries. Another problem, making inference more difficult, is that tax policy itself appears to have been endogenous—countries in which investors could more easily invest abroad were more likely to have lower tax distortions and to impose capital controls. In principle, the increasing international integration of financial markets and the steady reduction of capital controls should lead to increasing responsiveness of the composition of international capital flows to tax distortions. As a result, countries will be under increasing pressure to reduce these tax distortions, and past behavior suggests that they will in fact respond to this pressure.

In the second paper, Roy D. Hogg and Jack M. Mintz examine the impact of U.S. and Canadian tax reforms on the financing of U.S. multinationals operating in Canada. They use a unique time-series data file, compiled by Arthur Andersen & Co., with information on twenty-eight U.S. companies operating in Canada.

After a thorough review of the tax reforms in the United States and Canada, the authors present three hypotheses about the impact of these reforms: (1) that U.S. subsidiaries in Canada would increase local debt financing, (2) that they would increase cross-border charges, and (3) that they would increase dividends paid out to the U.S. parent corporation. The authors conclude that in general these hypotheses are confirmed by the data although, they note, there are both tax and nontax explanations of the results. They find a dramatic increase both in the number of companies issuing dividends and in dividend payout ratios from the 1983–85 subperiod to the 1987–89 subperiod. In the latter subperiod, the average ratio of dividends paid to net income was close to 100 percent when companies chose to pay dividends.

Companies that tended to pay dividends also paid more of their income to U.S. parents in the form of cross-border charges. Hogg and Mintz found little change in aggregate debt-asset ratios over the two subperiods, but on a firm-by-firm basis the debt-asset ratios increased for a majority of companies and fell for the remainder; the increase in debt-asset ratios was found to be significant. They did not, however, find a significant increase in cross-border charges, as would have been expected after the Tax Reform Act of 1986.

A final way in which tax policy affects international financial management decisions of multinational corporations is its influence on dividend policy decisions within the multinational enterprise. Rosanne Altshuler and T. Scott Newlon, in chapter 3, use new data from 1986 corporate income tax returns to study effects of taxes on decisions by foreign subsidiaries to repatriate dividends to U.S. parent corporations. The authors stress three features of the treatment of foreign-source income under U.S. tax laws: (1) deferral (because U.S. tax on foreign-source income of U.S. firms is delayed until the income is remitted to the parent), (2) foreign tax credits (through which credit for foreign taxes paid on foreign-source income is allowed against U.S. tax liability), and (3) the overall limitation on foreign tax credits (restricting such credits so as not to exceed the U.S. tax otherwise payable on foreign-source income).

Altshuler and Newlon extend approaches taken in earlier studies using firm-level data by examining dynamic aspects of U.S. taxation of foreign-source income (in particular, the possibility that the overall credit position of the parent may change over time, affecting the tax consequences of dividend repatriation decisions). They find that changes in the tax price of dividend remittances have statistically significant and economically important effects on the level of dividend remittances from foreign subsidiaries to U.S. multinational parent corporations. Their results suggest that U.S. parent companies are able to alter the flows of income from their foreign subsidiaries in such a way as to reduce their worldwide tax paid by foreign-source income. Pursuing the Altshuler-Newlon analysis further will require more recent data, since the Tax Reform Act of 1986 changed incentives for dividend repatriation decisions in important ways. Such an extension may provide valuable evidence for policymakers analyzing the economic effects of changes in deferral or the foreign tax credit limitation.

Business Investment

A second area of multinational corporations' decisions potentially affected by tax policy encompass investment decisions. Three papers in the volume concentrate on investment decisions—in particular relating to tax incentives for (1) the level and location of research and development activities, (2) foreign direct investment, and (3) location and sourcing decisions generally.

Although most models of investment suggest that tax policy should affect foreign domestic investment, econometric studies of inbound (to the United States) foreign direct investment have generated few robust conclusions. In their paper, Alan J. Auerbach and Kevin Hassett argue that distinctions between financial flows and investment data and between investment in new capital (e.g., a start-up) versus investment in old capital (e.g., an acquisition) account for much of the confusion in the existing literature.

Auerbach and Hassett extend a simple model of investment to incorporate explicitly the different tax treatment accorded to old and new capital under U.S. law. This extension is important because, as the authors note, a substantial portion of the increase in foreign direct investment during the late 1980s came not from new investment but through foreign acquisitions of existing capital. They argue that, given the differences in tax treatment of new investment and acquisitions and the likely effects of the Tax Reform Act of 1986 on acquisitions, attributing the increase in foreign direct investment to tax changes is not likely to be correct. Simulations of their model do not corroborate some earlier studies' findings of strong tax effects on foreign direct investment generally and the relative increase in foreign direct investment from certain countries. Indeed, Auerbach's and Hassett's suggestive results indicate the importance of carefully specifying tax incentives for alternative forms of investment. Application of their approach to panel data on individual firms in future research will permit them to distinguish effects of tax factors from those of nontax factors—including exchange rate shifts and the liberalization of financial markets—on foreign direct investment decisions. The results will provide useful evidence for thinking about effects of future tax reforms on foreign direct and portfolio investment in the United States.

Over the past two decades, policymakers have been concerned about the way in which taxation can affect decisions by multinational corporations regarding the level and location of research and development (R&D) performed. The United States has attempted to stimulate R&D by U.S. companies, following the view of many economists that the social return to R&D exceeds the private return. After a particularly generous tax treatment in the Economic Recovery Tax Act of 1981 for R&D performed in the United States by certain multinational firms, Congress changed the tax laws pertaining to R&D on several occasions during the 1980s. Indeed, by the early 1990s, the United States had still not proposed a permanent policy toward the R&D activities of multinational corporations. In the summer of 1992, the Treasury Department extended the R&D expense allocation rules for eighteen months, with a view toward studying the appropriate long-run policy.

In chapter 5, James R. Hines, Jr., models the incentives provided in U.S. tax law for the level and location of R&D undertaken by multinationals. Using a special panel data set drawn from Compustat (with significant detail on foreign pretax earnings and foreign taxes paid that is not generally contained in Compustat), he estimated the effects of changes in the tax price of R&D on the level of R&D performed in the United States by U.S. firms. Hines is careful to consider the effect of a multinational's foreign tax credit position on the tax price of R&D and the effects of merger and acquisition activity on the characteristics of firms in the sample. He finds that changes in the after-tax price of R&D have a statistically significant effect on spending decisions of U.S. multinationals. The economic importance of this effect is, however, more difficult to gauge. As Hines notes, one would have to compare any externality benefits of domestically performed R&D with the costs of raising alternative revenue to fund more-generous tax incentives for R&D by multinational corporations.

Finally, tax policy can affect location and sourcing decisions generally. G. Peter Wilson's paper contains descriptive evidence from a careful field study of location (capacity expansion) and sourcing (capacity utilization) decisions in nine U.S. multinational manufacturing corporations. Wilson initiates a research agenda to identify and characterize nontax benefits and costs of particular strategies in order to formulate better economic models of location, investment, transfer pricing, and financial policy decisions. Wilson focuses on three categories of nontax factors: product- or industry-specific characteristics (e.g., the production process, importance of distance to market, economies of scale, and entry strategies), country-specific characteristics (encompassing regulation or infrastructure characteristics), and firm-specific characteristics (including intrafirm coordination issues, and information and incentive problems).

Wilson's interviews gathered information on the firms' location and sourcing decisions in twenty-five countries over the 1960s, 1970s, and 1980s. He concludes that nontax considerations are very important for manufacturing location decisions. In particular, part of the apparent insensitivity to tax considerations could reflect the link between taxes paid and the provision of important infrastructure (e.g., in education and transportation support). Second, where nontax considerations are not particularly important (e.g., for administrative or distribution centers), tax considerations are paramount. Third, the effectiveness of transfer pricing in reducing multinationals' worldwide tax burdens is limited by nontax factors. Interestingly, government restrictions dominate problems in intrafirm coordination in this respect. In principle, firms' use of transfer pricing for tax planning could be reduced by the need to evaluate managers for compensation or other purposes. Wilson finds that firms can effectively use information from multiple accounts to guide tax planning on the one hand and managerial evaluation and compensation on the other. Case studies such as Wilson's can help researchers identify nontax factors limiting the international tax arbitrate implied by some theoretical models.

Income Shifting

Multinational companies by definition operate in many different countries, all of which assert the right to tax income earned within their borders and some of which attempt to tax, with limited credit for taxes paid to foreign governments, the worldwide income of their resident multinationals. Because tax rates, bases, and rules differ across countries, it is generally not a matter of indifference to the companies where income is reported. Furthermore, there is some flexibility available to multinationals in reporting where the income is earned. For example, through the pricing of intercorporate transactions, taxable income can be shifted from one jurisdiction to another. Most countries have elaborate rules, often complex and always controversial, governing such transfer prices and other avenues for income shifting. The final two papers in the volume attempt to measure the quantitative significance of income shifting in two different settings: foreign-controlled companies operating in the United States and U.S.-resident multinationals.

In chapter 7, Harry Grubert, Timothy Goodspeed, and Deborah Swenson address an issue that has attracted much recent attention in the press and in congressional hearings—that foreign-controlled companies in the United States report on average a much lower rate of return, and therefore pay lower taxes for a given level of assets, than domestically controlled companies. This has led to speculation that these companies are engaged in income shifting by means of abusive transfer pricing or other methods. Alternative explanations have been suggested—for example, that the foreign affiliates are newer companies that have not yet achieved profitability. (Congressional concern has been severe enough to prompt a proposal in H.R. 5270 to impose a formulary standard for foreign firms operating in the United States.)

Unlike previous examinations of this issue, this analysis makes use of several firm-level data files, including the actual tax returns filed by foreign-controlled companies. This allows the authors to separate the impact of determinants of profitability such as the newness of the operation. They find that about half of the initial foreign-domestic taxable income differential is attributable to the special characteristics of foreign-controlled companies and not to transfer pricing per se. First, the revaluation of the book value of assets following acquisitions can distort the comparison of the ratio of taxable income to assets. Second, a maturation process is indicated by the fact that the profitability of foreign-controlled manufacturing companies rises over time relative to comparable domestically controlled firms. Foreign investors may, therefore, accept initially lower returns in exchange for high long-run profits. Third, relative to their domestically controlled counterparts, the taxable income of foreign-controlled wholesale companies is found to rise as the real value of the dollar increases relative to other currencies. In particular, the large drop in the dollar since 1985 has depressed recent returns of foreign investors in wholesaling.

Other commonly suggested reasons for the foreign-domestic differential have less explanatory power. High debt-asset ratios and earnings stripping do not appear to be major reasons for the low taxable income of foreign-controlled companies. Although such companies have an apparent preference for operations with rising profit profiles, there is not much evidence that any advantage in the cost of equity capital explains the foreign income differential. Neither parent size nor whether a parent is from a capital-exporting country is important. Furthermore, foreign parents seem in general to be more profitable than the typical U.S. company. Finally, the evidence does not support the hypothesis that foreign firms tend to acquire relatively unprofitable firms. Another interesting result is that low profitability is a characteristic of foreign-controlled companies, irrespective of their country of origin; it is not restricted to companies based in only a few countries or operating in a narrow range of industries. The Goodspeed, Grubert, and Swenson analysis will no doubt lead to future studies of income shifting.

U.S.-resident multinationals are faced with incentives and constraints regarding income shifting that are similar to those faced by foreign-resident firms. In the paper that concludes the volume, David Harris, Randall Morck, Joel Slemrod, and Bernard Yeung attempt to assess quantitatively the importance of income shifting of U.S. multinationals.

Although firm-level anecdotal evidence and studies of highly aggregated data suggest that significant income shifting occurs, surprisingly little evidence based on firm-level data is available. This paper makes use of Compustat data for 1984 through 1988, supplemented by information from firms' annual reports and by data on the geographical location of operations, for a sample of 200 U.S. manufacturing firms. The basic strategy is to ascertain whether taxes paid to the U.S. government, as a ratio of either U.S. sales or U.S. assets, are related to the location of foreign operations, holding constant other determinants of profitability. To the extent that shifting occurs, the U.S. tax ratio should be lower than otherwise if the multinational operates in low-tax countries such as Ireland and higher than otherwise if it operates in high-tax countries such as Germany, reflecting the incentive to shift income into Ireland and out of Germany.

The authors find evidence that is consistent with tax-motivated income shifting. Having a subsidiary in a tax haven, Ireland, or in one of the "four dragon" Asian countries (all jurisdictions with low tax rates) was during this period associated with lower U.S. tax ratios. Furthermore, having a subsidiary in a high region generally was associated with a higher tax ratio. The income shifting that is consistent with this pattern of behavior reduces U.S. taxes substantially only for firms with an extensive multinational structure. For U.S. multinationals as a whole, income shifting leads to a moderate—and imprecisely estimated—reduction in U.S. tax payments, between 3 percent and 22 percent of total tax liability.

To summarize, the eight papers in this volume present new empirical contributions to the analysis of the effects of international taxation on financial management, business investment, and income shifting. Further empirical research in these areas should guide the development of new theoretical models in public finance and international economics, as well as inform the ongoing policy debate on reforming the taxation of multinational businesses in the United States and abroad.

References

Devereux, M., and M. Pearson. 1991. Corporate tax harmonization and economic efficiency. Report Series no. 35. London: Institute for Fiscal Studies.
King, M., and D. Fullerton. 1984. *The taxation of income from capital: A comparative study of the U.S., U.K., Sweden, and West Germany.* Chicago: University of Chicago Press.

I International Financial Management

1 Taxes and the Form of Ownership of Foreign Corporate Equity

Roger H. Gordon and Joosung Jun

Investors in risky corporate capital face strong economic incentives to diversify their holdings not only across firms within their own country but also across firms in other countries.[1] The most commonly discussed method of such international diversification involves investing in multinational firms based in the home country that then invest throughout the world. The tax treatment of investment abroad by multinational firms is extremely complicated and has appropriately been the subject of substantial research.[2]

Foreign direct investment is not the only means through which investors in one country can acquire ownership of equity in another country. The obvious alternative is for them simply to purchase shares in foreign equity in the securities market or to buy shares in a mutual fund that invests in foreign equity. These alternatives, known as portfolio investment, face a very different statutory tax treatment than foreign direct investment. In addition, while tax enforcement is always a problem with investments abroad, enforcement problems are likely to be far worse with portfolio investments than with foreign direct investments, to the point that portfolio investments abroad are often referred to as capital flight.

Our objective in this paper is to estimate the degree to which differences in the tax treatment of portfolio investments versus foreign direct investments

Roger Gordon is professor of economics at the University of Michigan and a research associate of the National Bureau of Economic Research. Joosung Jun is assistant professor of economics at Yale University and a faculty research fellow of the National Bureau of Economic Research.

The authors would like to thank Smith W. Allnut III, Chris Gohrband, and Harlan King, all of the Bureau of Economic Analysis, for helping obtain data on the composition of foreign equity holdings. They also would like to thank conference participants for comments on an earlier draft of this paper.

1. See Adler and Dumas (1983) or French and Poterba (1991) for evidence on the substantial diversification achieved through purchase of foreign equity.

2. Many of the other papers in this volume, for example, as well as those in Razin and Slemrod (1990) analyze the tax treatment of foreign direct investment.

have affected empirically the relative use of these alternative routes through which investors can purchase foreign equity. Our data set consists of aggregate information, much of it previously unpublished, on both portfolio and foreign direct investments in U.S. equity made by investors from each of ten other countries during the period 1980–89.

The relative importance of portfolio equity investment versus foreign direct investment will be affected by more than just tax factors. When corporations invest abroad, for example, they acquire both ownership of and control over the foreign firms, whereas portfolio investors merely acquire ownership. This makes corporate investments more attractive to the extent to which there are synergy gains from joint operations of the domestic and foreign firms. In addition, through use of capital controls, some countries discourage portfolio investment abroad. In the empirical work, we attempt to control for the effects of these nontax factors on the relative importance of portfolio versus foreign direct investment.

The principle conclusions of the study are as follows. First, portfolio investment is quantitatively important. In spite of the presence of capital controls (which restrict portfolio investments abroad) in half of the countries in our sample, portfolio investment in U.S. equity from our sample countries was still on average about two-thirds the size of foreign direct investment from these countries. Yet most studies of the taxation of international equity flows have confined their attention solely to foreign direct investment, thereby missing an important component of these equity flows.

Not surprisingly, portfolio investment plays a much more limited role among investors from countries with important capital controls. This is true even though these countries generally have much higher personal tax rates on dividends, a fact that in itself makes portfolio investment much more attractive, given the ease with which domestic personal taxes can be evaded on portfolio investments abroad. Apparently, these capital controls are effective enough that the countries can impose high taxes on dividends without inducing much capital flight, making such taxes much more attractive. It is not surprising, therefore, that the countries that eased capital controls during our sample period also tended at about the same time to lower their personal tax rates on dividend income. Given the substantial easing of capital controls in recent years and therefore the greater ease of capital flight, we would forecast both an increasing importance of portfolio investment in the future and further cuts in the personal income taxation of dividend income.

By focusing our study narrowly on the form of ownership of foreign equity, we avoided a number of complications that normally arise in any study of international portfolio holdings. For example, Adler and Dumas (1983) and French and Poterba (1991) both emphasize the puzzling lack of international diversification of equity portfolios. In our study, we take as given the total holdings of foreign equity and focus solely on the form in which this foreign equity is owned. Implicitly, we assume that the factors that explain the lack of international diversification of equity portfolios do not also affect the relative attractiveness of the two alternative forms of ownership of foreign equity. In addition, many complicated factors can affect the degrees to which international capital flows take the form of debt versus equity. We take as given the degree to which equity is used and focus solely on how this equity is purchased.

The organization of the paper is as follows: In section 1.1, we analyze how taxes distort the relative attractiveness of portfolio versus direct investment. Nontax factors are summarized in section 1.2. In section 1.3, we describe the measurement of the various data series used in the empirical work, and the empirical results are given in section 1.4.

1.1   Tax Distortions

In order to assess how taxes affect the relative attractiveness of portfolio equity investment versus foreign direct investment, we compare the tax treatment of each type of capital flow.

1.1.1   Tax Treatment of Portfolio Investment

We begin by analyzing the tax implications when an investor living in country i buys directly a share of equity costing a dollar in firm f in country c. Assume that this firm earns pretax economic income, per share, of x_{cf}. Based on the tax code in country c, firm f has taxable income per share of x_{cf}^c and faces a statutory corporate income tax rate of τ_c^s,[3] resulting in corporate tax payments of $\tau_c^s x_{cf}^c$.[4] The firm's income net of corporate taxes is therefore $x_{cf} - \tau_c^s x_{cf}^c = x_{cf}(1 - \rho_{cc}\tau_c^s)$. Here, $\rho_{cc} \equiv x_{cf}^c/x_{cf}$ measures the ratio between taxable income and economic income for firms in country c, based on the tax law in country c. For simplicity of notation, let $\tau_c \equiv \rho_{cc}\tau_c^s$.

Assume that the firm pays out the fraction d of this net income as dividends each period. If the shareowner lives in country i, then this dividend is subject to a withholding tax in country c at rate ω_{ci}.[5] Individuals therefore receive income net of foreign taxes of $x_{cf}(1 - \tau_c)(1 - d\omega_{ci})$.

In principle, shareowners still owe personal income taxes on this income. However, it is extremely difficult for a government to enforce a tax on foreign-source income. In general, taxes on individual investors are primarily enforced either by requiring financial intermediaries to report directly to the government the income earned by domestic residents or by withholding at

---

3. For simplicity, we ignore variations in effective tax rates by firm. See Swenson (1990) for a comparison, across U.S. industries, of effective tax rates versus the amount of foreign direct investment in the industry.

4. If the marginal tax rate varies with income, we adjust the measure of income here to produce the correct estimate of corporate tax payments.

5. In practice, this rate need not necessarily equal the statutory rate applying to capital flows between country c and country i. Investing through a financial intermediary in a third country may result in a lower withholding tax rate. We ignore these complications in the empirical work

source. When individuals invest in foreign corporations through domestic financial intermediaries, these intermediaries can also be required to report the resulting income of each investor to the government, making enforcement straightforward.[6] However, when residents invest abroad through foreign financial intermediaries, neither approach is feasible—these intermediaries cannot be required to withhold taxes for another government or report information to another government.[7] Since the home government has little ability to detect evasion in these circumstances, investors have little incentive to pay domestic taxes on such income. If they do evade domestic taxes, then their net income is simply $x_{cf}(1 - \tau_c)(1 - d\omega_{ci})$.

If individuals invest abroad through domestic financial intermediaries, however, then the government should be able to monitor their earnings, forcing the payment of domestic taxes on this income.[8] Under standard double-taxation conventions, such individuals are taxed at home on their pre-withholding-tax dividends, $dx_{cf}(1 - \tau_c)$, but receive a credit up to the amount of any domestic taxes owed for the withholding taxes paid abroad. If the typical personal tax rate in country i on dividend income is m_i, then the net receipts of shareholders equal

$$(1) \qquad x_{cf}(1 - \tau_c)[1 - d\max(m_i, \omega_{ci})].$$

In addition, the investors receive capital gains and may owe capital gains taxes if they sell shares. For simplicity, however, we ignore capital gains taxes. We will use expression (1) to describe the net receipts of portfolio investors even when investors evade personal taxes. When evasion is assumed, m_i, will simply be set equal to zero.

1.1.2 Tax Treatment of Foreign Direct Investment

If individuals invest abroad instead by investing further in a domestic firm that then uses these funds to buy a dollar of equity in the same firm f in country c, the tax treatment becomes much more complicated. To begin with, the tax treatment varies depending on the fraction of shares in the foreign firm purchased by the domestic corporation. The United States, for example, requires that a domestic firm own at least 10 percent of the shares in a foreign firm to qualify for a credit for taxes paid abroad and at least 50 percent to be able to pool earnings from this firm with those from other majority-owned firms

6. Not all countries require this reporting by financial intermediaries. Without it, even taxes on earnings from domestic financial assets are difficult to enforce except through withholding at source.
7. Some countries have information-sharing agreements with each other. These agreements, however, do not involve automatic transfers of information but cover only transfers of information about specific accounts which the home government learned about independently. But acquiring this independent information is a large part of the problem.
8. The convenience of using a domestic financial intermediary may outweigh the extra tax burden. In principle, the net return given evasion should be reduced to reflect the inconvenience of using foreign financial intermediaries.

abroad. The tax treatment also varies depending on whether the foreign firm is organized as a subsidiary or as a branch of the domestic firm. In the former case, domestic taxes are due only when profits are repatriated; in the latter, domestic taxes are owed each year on the entire profits.[9] For simplicity, we focused on the dominant case, that of a subsidiary in which at least 50 percent of the shares are owned by the foreign parent.

The pretax income per share, x_{cf}, of this subsidiary is, as before, subject to corporate income taxes at an effective rate τ_c. Dividend payments remain subject to withholding taxes in country c. If the parent is based on country i,[10] then the withholding tax rate is denoted by ω^*_{ci}. Commonly, $\omega^*_{ci} < \omega_{ci}$, in itself giving a tax advantage to foreign direct investment. If the dividend payout rate is d, then income net of taxes in country c equals $x_{cf}(1 - \tau_c)(1 - d\omega^*_{ci})$.

Corporate and personal taxes may be owed in country i on the dividends received from this foreign subsidiary. In countries with a territorial tax system, such as the Netherlands, corporations do not owe tax on foreign-source income. Other countries (e.g., Canada and Germany) exempt from domestic corporate taxes any foreign-source income earned in countries with which they have signed tax treaties. In these cases, the only additional taxes owed are personal taxes on the dividend income. In order to equate the dividend payout rate in the case of individual portfolio investment versus corporate direct investment, we assume that all net-of-tax dividends received from abroad are then distributed to individual investors. If we denote by m^*_i the personal tax rate on this income, then the final net income equals[11]

$$(2a) \qquad x_{cf}(1 - \tau_c)\{1 - d[\omega^*_{ci} + (1 - \omega^*_{ci})m^*_i]\} .$$

Most countries, however, tax the pretax income needed to finance the dividends received by domestic corporations from foreign subsidiaries but allow corporations a credit for any corporate and withholding taxes paid abroad. These credits can reduce or eliminate taxes due on the foreign-source income but cannot reduce taxes due on any domestic-source income. Consider first the case of a multinational based in country i which invests only in firm f in country c. This multinational receives dividends per share from abroad equal to $dx_{cf}(1 - \tau_c)(1 - \omega^*_{ci})$. Under standard double-taxation conventions, it owes domestic corporate taxes on the corporate income, before both corporate and withholding taxes, needed to finance these dividends but receives a credit up to the domestic corporate taxes owed for all taxes paid abroad on this income. In particular, if the subsidiary's total income before any taxes, as defined

---

9. Withholding taxes are also normally owed on the entire net-of-foreign-tax profits of a branch but only on the dividends paid by a subsidiary.

10. For simplicity, we assume that the parent is located in the same country as the investor. In principle, the investor could own shares of a parent based in a third country, or the investment could be made through a subsidiary located in a third country, introducing further complications.

11. Note that credits for withholding taxes paid abroad are not passed through the domestic corporation to individual shareholders.

under the tax law of country i, is denoted by x^i_{cf}, then the parent owes domestic taxes at statutory rate τ^s_i on the fraction of this income equal to the ratio of its dividend receipts to the subsidiary's income net of corporate taxes paid to country c, and it receives a credit for the same fraction of the corporate taxes paid to country c, as well as for all withholding taxes paid. Net corporate taxes owed in country i on the dividend income $dx_{cf}(1 - \tau_c)(1 - \omega^*_{ci})$ therefore equal

$$\frac{dx_{cf}(1 - \tau_c)}{(x^i_{cf} - \tau_c x_{cf})} (\tau^s_i x^i_{cf} - \tau_c x_{cf}) - \omega^*_{ci} dx_{cf}(1 - \tau_c) ,$$

or zero, whichever is larger. If ρ_{ci} is defined to equal x^i_{cf}/x_{cf} and $\tau_{ci} \equiv \rho_{ci}\tau^s_i$, then the parent's dividend receipts net of domestic corporate taxes equal, after simple algebra, $dx_{cf}(1 - \tau_c)\min[(1 - \omega^*_{ci}),(\rho_{ci} - \tau_{ci})/(\rho_{ci} - \tau_c)]$, while the shareholders' income, including retained earnings but net of personal taxes, equals

$$(2b) \quad x_{cf}(1 - \tau_c) \left\{ (1 - d) + d\min\left[(1 - \omega^*_{ci}), \left(\frac{\rho_{ci} - \tau_{ci}}{\rho_{ci} - \tau_c}\right)\right](1 - m^*_i)\right\} .$$

The role of ρ_{ci} in this expression deserves some discussion. If $\rho_{ci} = 1$ and a corporate surtax is due on repatriated income, then this income is taxed on net at the same rate as domestic-source income; foreign taxes are fully rebated. If $\rho_{ci} < 1$, however, then the effective tax rate on repatriated income is higher than that on domestic-source income if $\tau_{ci} > \tau_c$, and conversely. The understatement of foreign-source income results in too large a fraction being taxed for a given amount of dividend repatriations, but it also results in a credit for too large a fraction of foreign tax payments. The net effect depends on whether the foreign or the domestic effective tax rate is larger.

When a multinational invests in several foreign countries, it is normally allowed to pool the income repatriated from all of these countries and to credit against the domestic taxes due on this income any corporate and withholding taxes paid abroad on this income. In doing so, it can use excess credits from operations in one country to reduce any domestic taxes due on operations in another country. If, in total, its credits are sufficient to wipe out its domestic tax liabilities on its foreign operations worldwide, then no domestic corporate taxes result in particular from its operations in country c. In this case, its final net income is the same as in the territorial case, as shown in equation (2a). If, in contrast, its credits are insufficient to wipe out all domestic taxes due on foreign-source income, then it can receive a credit for all corporate and withholding taxes paid in country c, even if these taxes exceed the domestic taxes due on repatriations from country c. In this case, its final net income equals

$$(2c) \quad x_{cf}(1 - \tau_c)\left[(1 - d) + d\left(\frac{\rho_{ci} - \tau_{ci}}{\rho_{ci} - \tau_c}\right)(1 - m^*_i)\right] .$$

Through careful allocation of its investments and timing of its repatriations, a corporation should normally be able to avoid domestic corporate taxation of its foreign operations.[12] Whenever it invests in a country with a low tax rate, where corporate and withholding taxes will be insufficient to offset domestic taxes, it can simultaneously invest in a country with a high tax rate. Repatriations should then occur simultaneously from each country, so that total tax payments abroad just equal total tax liabilities at home, precredit. Not all firms may find this tax planning worth the effort. Planning sufficient to wipe out domestic corporate taxes becomes more difficult, if not impossible, when the domestic corporate tax rate is high. Therefore, in general, when pooling is allowed, some firms will earn net income described by equation (2a), and some will earn net income described by equation (2c). The percentage facing equation (2c) should rise as τ_{ci} rises, where we denote the percentage facing equation (2c) by θ.[13] We therefore will use a weighted average of equation (2a) and (2c) to measure the net income from corporate investments, with weights $(1 - \theta)$ and θ. To capture the relation between τ_{ci} and θ, we let $\theta = a + b\tau_{ci}$. Theory suggests that $b > 0$ and that $\theta = 0$ for relatively low τ, implying that $a = -b\tau' < 0$ for some low τ'.

Since 1986, the United States has required that repatriations from subsidiaries that are not majority owned must each be put in a "separate basket," preventing this pooling of credits. If this applied to all firms, then net income would be measured by (2b). However, pooling of credits is still allowed among firms that are each majority owned. Therefore, for the United States, the new provisions should not change the incentives faced by most firms. We assume that pooling is the norm in the countries in our study which use a crediting system.

Two of the countries in our study use a hybrid system. In particular, France and Italy exempt a certain fraction, e, of repatriated foreign-source income from domestic corporate taxes.[14] On the remaining income, domestic taxes are due on the income received prior to withholding taxes paid abroad; the amounts paid in withholding taxes on the remaining income can then be claimed as a credit against domestic corporate taxes. Implicitly, foreign corporate tax payments are deductible from domestic taxable income. Net domestic corporate tax payments then equal $dx_{cf}(1 - \tau_c)(1 - e)(\tau_{ci} - \omega_{ci}^*)$. After taking into account personal income taxes, a firm's net income is

---

12. For supporting evidence, see Hines and Hubbard (1989).

13. Many other factors can affect the likelihood that a corporate surtax is due at repatriation. For one, economic and technological factors may cause multinationals based in one country to invest in a quite different set of host countries than do multinationals based in another country. In addition, some countries offer "tax sparing," which reduces the corporate surtax due on repatriations from selected countries. Funneling repatriations through these selected countries then reduces the corporate surtax due on investments in country c. We have not attempted to control for these other factors.

14. France exempts 95 percent of these repatriated earnings, while Italy exempts 60 percent.

(2d) $x_{cf}(1 - \tau_c)\{(1 - d) + d[1 - e\omega_{ci}^* - (1 - e)\tau_{ci}](1 - m_i^*)\}$.

What factors affect the personal tax rate m_i^*? To begin with, m_i^* should equal the value m_i would take ignoring evasion.[15] When dividend imputation schemes are available to domestic investors in domestic corporations, however, m_i^* but not m_i will be reduced. Under these schemes, an investor in country i receiving dividends of δ from a domestic corporation is imputed to have received dividends of $\delta/(1 - s_i)$ for some tax parameter s_i, which are then taxable under the personal income tax. However, the investor gets a tax credit of $s_i\delta/(1 - s_i)$. On net, therefore, the individual owes taxes of $(m_i - s_i)\delta/(1 - s_i)$, so that $m_i^* = (m_i - s_i)/(1 - s_i)$. Under a full imputation scheme, $s_i = \tau_i^s$. On net, m_i^* is always less than or equal to m_i.

Countries, do, however, try to restrict investors' ability to use the dividend imputation scheme on dividends from domestic corporations financed by earnings from abroad. Typically, countries require that dividends eligible for the dividend imputation scheme be less than the firm's after-tax profits from domestic operations. Unless a firm desires an abnormally high dividend payout rate, however, this restriction is unlikely to be binding. In the empirical work, we have assumed that these restrictions are not binding.

What about evasion of personal taxes? When individuals buy shares in domestic corporations, in principle the government can require that these corporations report to the government the dividends paid to all domestic residents, making the tax on dividends easily enforceable. Alternatively, the government can withhold taxes on dividends at source. Evasion cannot be ruled out, however. Some countries, for example, do not require firms to file such reports. Even if such reports are required, individuals can buy shares in domestic corporations through foreign financial intermediaries, making it difficult or impossible for the government to learn independently how much dividends these individuals receive.[16] To allow for the possibility of evasion, we will try replacing m_i^* by $\min(m_i^*, 0)$ in some of the regressions described below. We try this alternatively for all countries and for just the countries in continental Europe, where evasion seems to be more prevalent.

So far, we have assumed that the dividend payout rate is the same for corporate and portfolio investments. In general, dividend payments result in ex-

---

15. In principle, the two forms of investments may attract different clienteles. For example, if there are economies to scale in learning about foreign investment opportunities, only wealthy individuals will invest abroad directly. However, equity holdings are sufficiently concentrated in most countries that this is unlikely to make much difference. In addition, financial intermediaries such as insurance companies and pension plans may face restrictions concerning the amount of foreign securities they can invest in. Japan, for example, has had such restrictions, although they were eased somewhat in 1986. In principle, the composition of equity purchased outside of these intermediaries can be adjusted to offset the effects of such restrictions, but the offset is complete only if enough equity would be purchased outside of these plans.

16. In this case, however, the investor must pay the withholding taxes due on repatriations to the country of the foreign financial intermediary. Presumably, investors would seek out intermediaries in countries facing low withholding tax rates.

tra taxes, so firms should avoid dividend payments unless the nontax gains from these payments outweigh their tax cost. These nontax factors could include cash needs of the shareholders (as in Poterba and Summers 1985), the desire to limit agency costs (as in Easterbrook 1984), or the signaling role of dividends (as in Bhattacharya 1979). With portfolio investment, the foreign firm chooses the dividend payout rate, based presumably on the nontax factors affecting its domestic shareholders. With corporate direct investment, in contrast, the parent can choose separately the dividend payout rate from the subsidiary to the parent and the dividend payout rate from the parent to the shareholders, in each case based on considerations affecting shareholders in country i. To the extent that the firm gains from this extra flexibility, there is more of an advantage to corporate direct investment than is seen by comparing equations (2a) and (2c) with equation (1). Hines and Hubbard (1989), for example, show that subsidiaries appear to time their payouts to their parents so as to avoid surtaxes at repatriation, while Hines (1991) reports that parents have much higher payout rates to shareholders than do firms without foreign subsidiaries, perhaps because signaling is more important for firms with foreign operations. Firms therefore do seem to take advantage of the flexibility they have over dividend patterns.

Similarly, the above discussion assumes the same use of debt finance regardless of the form of ownership. In general, firms in countries with high corporate tax rates should borrow relatively more, using bonds denominated in the currencies of countries with high inflation rates.[17] Multinationals may have extra flexibility, however. For example, a multinational may face less risk of default, since it can pool relatively independent risks from its operations in two different countries and so be able to borrow more. In addition, if it can use its combined assets as collateral for loans, regardless of which firm does the borrowing, then it can concentrate its borrowing in the country where the deductions are more valuable. The gain from doing so would be greater the larger the difference in marginal tax rates applicable to interest deductions in the two countries. To the degree to which multinationals respond to these differences, there is more of an advantage to corporate direct investment in countries with extreme tax rates, both high and low, than is seen by comparing equations (2a) and (2c) with equation (1).

We have also ignored any flexibility multinationals have to shift taxable income toward countries with lower tax rates. They can do this not only through manipulation of the transfer prices used for goods and services traded between the subsidiary and the parent but also through such devices as the location of ownership of corporate patents. The gain from shifting a given amount of taxable income to the low-tax country is proportional to the absolute value of the difference in the marginal tax rates affecting income accruing in each country.

17. See Gordon (1986) for further discussion.

To try to capture the gains available to a multinational through reallocations of interest deductions, and taxable income more generally, we include in the regression the absolute value of the difference in the statutory corporate tax rates in the two countries, $\mathrm{abs}(\tau_c^s - \tau_i^s)$.[18] Harris et al. (ch. 8 in this volume) find that reported profits of U.S.-based multinationals vary as forecast with the corporate tax rates faced by their foreign subsidiaries, supporting this hypothesis.

1.1.3   Comparison of Net Tax Rates

How do the net tax rates compare on portfolio investments versus corporate direct investments? On portfolio investments, the investors' net income from an investment in firm f in country c equals $x_{cf}(1 - \tau_c)[1 - d\max(m_i, \omega_{ci})]$. On corporate direct investment by multinationals based in countries using the credit system, we have measured the net income from the same investment by a weighted average of equations (2a) and (2c) (with weights $[1 - \theta]$ and θ) plus the gain from transfer pricing of $\gamma\mathrm{abs}(\tau_c^s - \tau_i^s)$, where γ measures the relative importance of this term.

After some simplification, the net tax advantage of portfolio investment can be expressed by

$$
\begin{aligned}
(3) \quad & dx_{cf}(1 - \tau_c)[\omega_{ci}^* + (1 - \omega_{ci}^*)m_i^* - \max(m_i, \omega_{ci})] \\
& + \theta dx_{cf}(1 - m_i^*)\,[A_{ci}(\tau_{ci} - \tau_c) \\
& - \omega_{ci}^*(1 - \tau_c)] - \gamma\mathrm{abs}(\tau_c^s - \tau_i^s)\, ,
\end{aligned}
$$

where $A_{ci} \equiv (1 - \tau_c)/(\rho_{ci} - \tau_c)$. This expression consists of three terms. The first term describes the tax advantage if corporate investors owe no domestic corporate taxes when profits are repatriated. Corporate investors cannot claim a credit for withholding taxes against their personal tax liabilities, whereas portfolio investors can, giving an advantage to portfolio investments. Both withholding tax rates and personal tax rates tend to be lower, however, for corporate investments. The second term measures the extra tax burden corporate investors face if they are in a deficit-credit position and so pay at least some domestic corporate taxes on repatriated earnings. The third term measures the tax advantage corporate investors have through use of transfer pricing.

In sum, portfolio investors gain because they may be able to avoid domestic personal taxes on their foreign-source income and by construction they face no domestic corporate taxes at repatriation. If they do pay personal taxes, they can claim a credit for withholding taxes. Corporate investors, in contrast, may well owe domestic corporate taxes at repatriation. On their foreign operations as a whole, these domestic taxes are always nonnegative. However, by operating in a particular high–tax-rate country, they may reduce their domestic

---

18. The overall marginal tax rate on income accruing in each country may be more complicated due to the surtaxes when profits are repatriated.

corporate taxes by using excess credits from operations in that country to reduce domestic taxes due on other foreign operations, so that the second term in equation (3) can sometimes be negative. Corporate investors also often face lower withholding tax rates on their repatriations and can take advantage of transfer pricing. Even if their shareholders cannot evade personal income taxes, these personal tax obligations are reduced in countries that use a dividend imputation scheme. On net, the sign as well as the size of the net tax distortion will vary by country and over time.

For multinationals based in territorial countries, no corporate surtaxes are due at repatriation, so that the second term in equation (3) would be zero. For France and Italy, however, which use a hybrid system, this second term would equal the corporate taxes due at repatriation and so would equal $dx_{cf}(1 - \tau_c)$ $(1 - e)(1 - m_i^*)(\tau_{ci} - w_{ci}^*)$.

1.2   Nontax Factors

Many nontax factors also affect the relative importance of portfolio versus corporate investments abroad. One key difference between the two is that corporate investments abroad allow joint control and operation of production in the two countries, whereas portfolio investments just affect ownership of the firm's income. Consider, for example, the situation of a firm based on country i that owns a distinct product or technology that can profitably be manufactured in country c. This could occur because factor prices in country c are more favorable (e.g., wage rates are lower, and the firm's production is relatively labor intensive); it could occur because transportation costs make it cheaper to produce the good nearer the foreign customers (e.g., shipping the syrup for Coca-Cola is cheaper than shipping the bottled soda); it could occur because trade barriers prevent sales of the product to foreign customers unless the good is produced locally; or it could result from the greater ease of adjusting the product to accommodate local tastes if production occurs on site or if the distribution outlets are owned by the manufacturer.[19] These advantages may be sufficient to induce corporate investment in country c even if it is taxed less favorably than portfolio investment in country c. The greater the tax disadvantage of corporate investments, the more important these nontax advantages must be to justify the investments.

All of these pressures are based on the premise that firms in country i have some distinct products or technologies. The more this is the case, therefore, the greater these nontax pressures, everything else equal. We proxy the degree to which firms in a country own distinct products or technologies by a measure of the R&D effort in that country.[20]

---

19. For an extended discussion of nontax factors, see Dunning (1985).
20. Because we only examine the pattern of foreign investments made in one country, the United States, we cannot readily test the effects of variation in the characteristics of the host country, such as the severity of trade barriers.

When the nontax advantages of investing in country c are large, what options does a firm have to reduce or eliminate any tax disadvantages of this investment? One option would be to license use of the technology to firms in country c, thereby allowing the technology to be used there while limiting the extent to which tax-disadvantaged investment must occur in country c. While transferring the technology to a subsidiary may allow better control over use of the technology, better control over access to information about the technology, and better transfer of information about the detailed characteristics of the technology, taxes may outweigh these advantages of common ownership.

When the gains from joint operations arise from other sources, other types of contractual links may arise which allow the firm to avoid tax-disadvantaged capital flows. For example, if the gain from joint operation is simply common control over pricing, then cartels might be set up instead to coordinate pricing. Similarly, distribution outlets can be arranged through contractual links, as with chain stores, rather than through direct ownership.

If common ownership is essential for nontax reasons, then another option is to have the user of the technology in country c buy the owner of the technology in country i. Tax considerations would normally favor one direction of capital flow over the other. Ignoring withholding taxes and personal taxes, for example, the tax loss from corporate direct investment results from the corporate surtax that may be due when profits are repatriated to the parent corporation. When the multinational is operating in a high-tax and a low-tax country, then this surtax would be due if profits are repatriated from the low-tax to the high-tax country, but not conversely. In this case, therefore, joint ownership should occur through the firm in the low-tax country raising funds worldwide to finance the purchase of the firm in the high-tax country. If direct investment from country i to country c is tax disadvantaged, direct investment from country c to country i is likely not to be.

In certain cases, however, gains from joint operation may well require paying the extra taxes that result from a firm in a high-tax country taking over a firm in a low-tax country. For example, when operations of the potential multinational in one country are much larger than in the other countries, then it is much easier for this firm to acquire the other firms. If so, how large a capital flow is needed to acquire the gains from joint operation, and are further gains possible through larger capital flows? Everything else equal, the surtax paid will be proportional to the size of the capital flow, providing an incentive to minimize the amount of direct investment. This can be done by purchasing a smaller share of the equity in the subsidiary or by using relatively more debt in financing investments there. It might also be done by setting up a joint venture, in which most of the financing comes from the foreign partner. The share of the profits going to the firm in country i can be adjusted as needed to reflect the value of the technology it contributes to the joint venture. In each case, corporate direct investment from country i to country c is reduced or eliminated while the companies still maintain the economic advantages of joint operation.

A variety of other nontax factors could also prove to be important. One obvious one is the use of capital controls in a number of the countries in our sample. These controls can take a variety of forms. France, for example, had regulations from 1981 to 1986 which allowed the purchase of foreign assets only from other French residents, in principle preventing any increase in portfolio investment abroad. Italy, in contrast, required that residents deposit funds equal to 50 percent of the amount invested abroad in an interest-free account. We see no way to capture directly the effects of such diverse regulations on equity flows.

In order to test for the possible importance of capital controls, we simply included a dummy variable, denoted by C_{it}, which is set equal to one if significant restrictions exist in that country in that year on portfolio investment abroad. We experimented with alternative definitions of "significant." Countries with capital controls would be expected to have less portfolio investment abroad. We also tested to see whether controls make portfolio investment less responsive to changes in tax incentives.

1.3   Data on Relative Tax Rates and the Composition of Capital Flows

In order to test the sensitivity of the composition of international capital flows to these tax incentives, we collected data on the relative tax treatment of portfolio versus direct investment in the United States coming from each of ten other countries, and the composition of capital flows to the United States from each of these countries during the period 1980–89. The ten countries are Australia, Canada, France, West Germany, Italy, Japan, the Netherlands, Sweden, Switzerland, and the United Kingdom.[21]

1.3.1   Relative Tax Rates

In total, we needed data for m_i, m_i^*, ω_{ci}, ω_{ci}^*, τ_c, τ_{ci}, τ_i^s, A_{ci}, R&D intensity, and the dummy variable C_{it} measuring the presence of capital controls, yearly from 1980 to 1989.

m_i

To begin, we set m_i equal to the top marginal tax rate prevailing in country i in each year. Where appropriate, we took into account both federal and local tax schedules. Given the concentration of wealth holdings among investors in the top tax brackets and given the greater tendency among those in the highest

---

21. Data were also available for Bermuda and the Netherlands Antilles, but we decided not to include these data because the above theory was not designed to address the consequences of investing from country i to country c through some third country j.

tax brackets to invest in equity, this assumption seemed reasonable.[22] Data on these rates were taken from various issues of Coopers and Lybrand's *International Tax Summaries*.[23] The resulting tax rates for the period 1980–89 are reported in table 1.1. In most of the regressions, however, we set m_i equal to zero, on the presumption that individuals can easily evade domestic taxes on portfolio investments abroad.

m_i^*

To calculate m_i^*, we used our estimate of the top marginal tax rate along with information about the characteristics of any dividend imputation scheme available in country i in that year (Coopers and Lybrand).[24] The resulting tax rates are reported in table 1.2.

ω_i and ω_i^*

Here we simply used statutory rates for dividend payments from country c to country i in that year (Coopers and Lybrand). These withholding tax rates are reported in table 1.3. The figures ignore the possibility of firms routing dividend payments through a third country.[25]

τ_i^s and τ_c^s

In each case, we used the statutory rate that applied to the largest firms in that year (Coopers and Lybrand). When state or provincial governments in that country also taxed corporate profits, we used a combined tax rate.[26] This approach does not take into account the possibility that firms may have tax losses and so face a zero marginal tax rate or may be subject to supplementary taxes (e.g., an alternative minimum tax). When the statutory tax rate changed during the calendar year, we used a weighted average tax rate. The resulting tax rates are reported in table 1.4. A few of the countries in the sample use a split-rate system, taxing retained income at a different rate than that used for income paid out as dividends. For these countries, both rates are reported in table 1.4.

22. This ignores, however, purchases of equity by financial intermediaries (e.g., pension plans), which are subject to very different tax treatment. When we test for evasion of personal taxes on all purchases of equity setting $m_i = m_i^* = 0$, this also provides a test for the possibility that equity purchases mainly occur through pension plans.

23. Data from Australia and the United Kingdom were adjusted in certain years to take account of the difference between their fiscal year and the calendar year.

24. When tax changes occurred in midyear, we used a weighted average tax rate for that year.

25. This omission creates a problem only to the degree to which the opportunities differ by country or over time. But the size of the withholding tax to be avoided differs very little across countries or over time, as seen in table 1.3, whereas access to tax havens should be very similar. Therefore, our results should be robust to this omission.

26. Where possible, we attempted to duplicate the procedure for calculating the combined rate used in Pechman (1988). For Switzerland, the combined rate is the maximum rate payable by a corporation operating out of Zurich.

Table 1.1   **Top Individual Income Tax Rates (percentage)**

	1980	1981	1982	1983	1984	1985	1986	1987	1988	1989
Japan	80	80	80	80	78	78	78	76	76	65
Canada	63	63	50	50	50	50	55	52	46	47
France	60	60	65	65	65	65	58	57	57	57
West Germany	56	56	56	56	56	56	56	56	56	56
Netherlands	72	72	72	72	72	72	72	72	72	72
United Kingdom	60	60	60	60	60	60	60	60	45	40
Italy	72	72	72	65	65	62	62	62	62	50
Sweden	86	86	87	83	82	79	79	76	74	72
Switzerland	23	23	23	20	20	19	19	14	16	16
Australia	60	60	60	60	60	60	59	53	49	49

Source: Authors' calculations based on Coopers and Lybrand (1980–1989).

Notes: Combined federal and local rates are reported where applicable. When the tax rate changed during the calendar year, a weighted average tax rate is used.

Table 1.2   **Top Individual Income Tax Rates, Net of Divided Tax Credit (percentage)**

	1980	1981	1982	1983	1984	1985	1986	1987	1988	1989
Japan	75	75	75	75	73	73	73	70	70	56
Canada	50	52	36	36	36	36	42	43	38	39
France	40	40	48	48	48	48	37	36	36	36
West Germany	31	31	31	31	31	31	31	31	31	31
Netherlands	72	72	72	72	72	72	72	72	72	72
United Kingdom	43	43	43	43	43	43	44	45	26	20
Italy	63	63	63	53	45	41	41	41	41	22
Sweden	86	87	87	83	82	79	79	76	74	72
Switzerland	23	23	23	20	20	19	19	14	16	16
Australia	60	60	60	60	60	60	59	29	8	16

Source: Authors' calculations based on Coopers and Lybrand (1980–1989) and table 1.1.

Table 1.3   **Withholding Tax Rates on Dividends (percentage): Corporate Recipient/ Individual Recipient**

	1980	1981	1982	1983	1984	1985	1986	1987	1988	1989
Japan	10/15	10/15	10/15	10/15	10/15	10/15	10/15	10/15	10/15	10/15
Canada	15	15	15	15	15	10/15	10/15	10/15	10/15	10/15
France	5/15	5/15	5/15	5/15	5/15	5/15	5/15	5/15	5/15	5/15
West Germany	15	15	15	15	15	15	15	15	15	15
Netherlands	5/15	5/15	5/15	5/15	5/15	5/15	5/15	5/15	5/15	5/15
United Kingdom	5/15	5/15	5/15	5/15	5/15	5/15	5/15	5/15	5/15	5/15
Italy	5/15	5/15	5/15	5/15	5/15	5/15	5/15	5/15	5/15	5/15
Sweden	5/15	5/15	5/15	5/15	5/15	5/15	5/15	5/15	5/15	5/15
Switzerland	5/15	5/15	5/15	5/15	5/15	5/15	5/15	5/15	5/15	5/15
Australia	15	15	15	15	15	15	15	15	15	15

Source: Coopers and Lybrand (1980–1989).

Table 1.4   **Statutory Corporate Tax Rates (percentage)**

	1980	1981	1982	1983	1984	1985	1986	1987	1988	1989
Japan*	56/44	56/44	56/44	56/44	58/46	58/46	58/46	57/45	56/44	55/47
Canada	51	51	51	51	51	52	53	52	48	44
France	50	50	50	50	50	50	45	45	42	39/42
West Germany*	56/36	56/36	56/36	56/36	56/36	56/36	56/36	56/36	56/36	56/36
Netherlands	48	48	48	48	43	43	42	42	40	35
United Kingdom	52	52	52	51	46	41	36	35	35	35
Italy	36	36	41	41	46	46	46	46	46	46
Sweden	57	57	57	57	52	52	52	52	52	52
Switzerland	38	38	38	34	33	33	33	33	31	31
Australia	46	46	46	46	46	46	46	48	44	39
United States	51	51	51	51	51	51	51	45	39	39

Source: Authors' calculations based on Coopers and Lybrand (1980–1989).

Notes: Combined federal and local rates are reported where applicable. When the tax rate changed during the calendar year, a weighted average rate is reported.

*In a split-rate system, the first rate applies to retained earnings and the second to dividends.

τ_c, τ_{ci}, and A_{ci}

By definition, $\tau_c = (\tau_c^s x_{cf}^c)/x_{cf}$, and $\tau_{ci} = (\tau_i^s x_{cf}^i)/x_{cf}$. In each case, the numerator equals actual tax payments and the denominator equals economic income, so that the ratio measures an effective corporate tax rate. For τ_c, this is the effective corporate tax rate on foreign holdings in the United States. Most firms operating in the United States will have at least some foreign owners, though the fraction will vary by firm. We simply assumed that the effective tax rate on foreign holdings is the same as that on firms as a whole operating in the United States, regardless of ownership, so we measured τ_c by the ratio of actual corporate tax payments to a measure of economic income.[27] Specifically, we measured τ_c by the ratio of direct taxes on income to operating surplus less net interest paid for the U.S. nonfinancial corporate sector (as reported in OECD 1980–1989).

In measuring τ_{ci}, the appropriate definition was less clear, because existing data sources do not report directly the average tax rate on foreign-source income. As a result, we explored several alternative approaches. The first and simplest approach was to set τ_{ci} equal to τ_{ci}^s, the statutory tax rate. This definition would be appropriate if each country defined taxable foreign-source income based on some approximation to economic income—for example, it did not extend various subsidies such as investment credits or accelerated depreciation to capital invested abroad. This in fact approximates the U.S. law.

27. Grubert, Goodspeed, and Swenson (ch. 7 in this volume), however, found that the average tax rate paid by foreign subsidiaries in the United States was much less than that paid by other firms. We assume that this is due to financial arbitrage engaged in by these firms, measured in our theory by $\gamma \mathrm{abs}(\tau_i^s - \tau_c^s)$, rather than to differences in the tax treatment of foreign-owned firms.

Our second approach assumed implicitly that each country measures U.S.-source taxable income based on the U.S. tax rules, implying that firms do not in practice recalculate their taxable income when profits are repatriated. In this case, $\tau_{ci} = \tau_i^s(x_{cf}^c/x_{cf}) = \tau_i^s(\tau_c/\tau_c^s)$. Given this approach, $\tau_{ci} - \tau_c = \rho_{cc}(\tau_i^s - \tau_c^s)$ so that differences in effective tax rates are measured by differences in statutory tax rates, up to a multiplicative factor.

Our third approach assumed that foreign-source income is measured based on the domestic tax law in each of these countries, without modification due to its foreign source. As a first pass, the average tax rate on foreign-source income should then equal that on domestic-source income.[28]

Yet a fourth approach to measuring τ_{ci} would have been to infer the effective tax rate based on the user cost of capital in each year, constructed using detailed information about corporate tax provisions. This is the approach used, for example, in Slemrod (1990). As argued in Bradford and Fullerton (1981), this measure of the effective tax rate can be very sensitive to assumptions made about such things as the required rate of return. More important, if reported earnings are not coming primarily from the return to marginal capital, as argued in Gordon and Slemrod (1988), then an effective tax rate measure based on the user cost of capital will be very misleading. Instead, the statutory rate should become more important. This provides an alternative justification for our second approach to measuring τ_{ci}, which results in a comparison of statutory tax rates.

One complication for each of these definitions is the existence in some countries of a split-rate corporate tax system in which the tax rate on retained earnings is different than the tax rate on earnings paid out as dividends. As seen in equation (3), the only place that τ_{ci} enters relates to the tax treatment of dividend payments. Therefore, for the first two definitions of τ_{ci}, we used the statutory rate applied to earnings paid out as dividends in countries with a split-rate corporate tax system. Things are a little more complicated under the third definition. Here τ_{ci} refers to the average corporate tax rate for earnings paid out as dividends. We observed only the average tax rate on earnings, whether retained or paid out, which we denote by τ_{ci}^a. We estimated τ_{ci} by assuming that the average tax rate on retentions has the same relation to the statutory tax rate on retentions as the average tax rate on payouts has to that statutory tax rate.

Only the third definition for τ_{ci} required new data. We measured the average corporate tax rate in country i using the same procedure and data source used in measuring τ_c. There were missing data in these publications, however, for Canada, Switzerland, and the United Kingdom. For Canada, we found com-

---

28. The two average tax rates can still differ for various reasons. For example, given the lack of indexation for inflation in the definition of taxable income in any of these countries, the effective tax rate on foreign-source income should differ from that on domestic-source income due to any differences in the inflation rates in the two countries, for the reasons discussed in Feldstein (1980a, 1980b).

parable data in the *Corporate Financial Statistics* issued by Statistics Canada, which we used to calculate the Canadian rates. For Switzerland and the United Kingdom, however, we were not able to find even roughly comparable data, so we used instead the statutory corporate tax rate. The resulting measures of the average corporate tax rate are reported in table 1.5. These figures are surprisingly volatile, often changing substantially from one year to the next. In four cases, all during the early 1980s, the resulting tax rate exceeds 100 percent. The cause of this volatility is unclear. It could be caused, for example, by the importance of no loss-offset during the recession in the early 1980s. Alternatively, if investment credits on new investment or rapidly accelerated depreciation allowances are used to offset heavy future tax payments, then observed tax rates will be unusually high during periods of low investment, as in the early 1980s, and conversely. It seems unlikely that firms would respond much to these year-to-year fluctuations in incentives, even if the incentives were measured correctly—behavior should respond to a weighted average of expectations of future as well as current tax incentives. Given these problems, this measure seems much weaker than either of the first two measures. In practice, these first two definitions are very similar. In the empirical work, we focused on the second measure but report selected results using the other two measures for τ_{ci}.

We also needed to measure $A_{ci} = (1 - \tau_c)/(\rho_{ci} - \tau_c)$. Here we made use of the relation $\rho_{ci} = \tau_{ci}/\tau_i^s$ and substituted the appropriate measure of each of the tax variables.

R&D Intensity

We measured R&D intensity in year t by the average value in country i of R&D divided by gross domestic product (GDP) during years $t - 3$ to $t - 1$; we denote this average ratio by R_{it}.[29]

C_{it}

This variable was set equal to one for country i in those years in which there were substantial capital controls. Some important controls existed in Australia (1980–84), France (1981–86), Italy (1980–87), Japan (1980–86), and Sweden (1980–88). Our loosest definition of capital controls sets $C_{it} = 1$ during each of these years. The nature of these controls differed substantially by country and over time, however. For example, Italy during the period of controls required that residents deposit funds equal to 50 percent of the amount invested abroad in an interest-free account, thereby sharply discouraging open ownership of foreign equity. These controls were gradually phased out during 1983–87. In contrast, during 1981–86, France prevented investors from *pur-*

---

29. A one- to three-year lag between R&D expenditures and available technology is representative of the results found in empirical productivity studies, such as Griliches (1980).

Table 1.5   **Average Corporate Income Tax Rates (percentage)**

	1980	1981	1982	1983	1984	1985	1986	1987	1988	1989
Japan	49	51	50	48	46	46	42	44	45	53
Canada	Territorial									
France	8	14	18	17	14	13	7	7	5	5
West Germany	Territorial									
Netherlands	Territorial									
United Kingdom	Unavailable									
Italy	23	71	117	41	40	31	27	35	32	32
Sweden	88	125	52	51	33	30	30	45	42	67
Switzerland	Unavailable									
Australia	60	77	128	106	47	44	49	51	45	39
United States	43	37	33	30	28	26	29	31	31	32

Source: Authors' calculations based on OECD (1980–1989).
Note: See the text for an explanation of the tax rates larger than 100 percent.

chasing equity from abroad, but existing holdings of foreign equity could continue without penalty and be traded within France. As a result, the French provisions should not in themselves have lowered portfolio holdings abroad but would have prevented individuals from responding to any increase in incentives for further portfolio investment abroad. During 1980–86, the main restriction in Japan involved tight limits on the amount of foreign securities that financial intermediaries could purchase. Because Japanese investors directly own relatively little equity, these controls may well have affected aggregate portfolio investment in foreign equity even though they did not restrict direct purchases of foreign equity. Our strictest definition of capital controls assumed that the Japanese provisions did not affect equity flows, that the French regulations had no effect, and that Italy had effectively ended is capital controls during 1987. The third and main definition we focused on was an intermediate case in which we weakened this latter definition by assuming that the Japanese controls were binding through 1986.

What do these numbers imply for the differential tax treatment of portfolio versus direct investment from each of these ten countries into the United States? As seen in equation (3), the net tax advantage to portfolio investment consists of three terms, the first measuring the tax differences assuming no corporate surtax when profits are repatriated, the second measuring the corporate surtax assuming that firms are in a deficit-credit position, and the third measuring the potential gain from shifting taxable income between the two countries. Given the estimates of the various tax parameters reported in tables 1.1–1.5, we calculated each of these terms. The resulting values for the first tax term are reported in tables 1.6 and 1.7, making alternative assumptions about evasion; those for the second tax term are reported in table 1.8; those for the last term are reported in table 1.9.

Table 1.6   **Personal Tax Advantage to Portfolio Investment: No Evasion**

	1980	1981	1982	1983	1984	1985	1986	1987	1988	1989
Japan	−0.014	−0.016	−0.017	−0.018	−0.020	−0.020	−0.019	−0.021	−0.021	−0.030
Canada	−0.028	−0.024	−0.033	−0.035	−0.036	−0.060	−0.052	−0.026	−0.014	−0.013
France	−0.097	−0.107	−0.100	−0.104	−0.107	−0.110	−0.126	−0.126	−0.126	−0.125
West Germany	−0.082	−0.090	−0.097	−0.101	−0.103	−0.106	−0.102	−0.099	−0.099	−0.098
Netherlands	0.008	0.009	0.009	0.010	0.010	0.010	0.010	0.010	0.010	0.010
United Kingdom	−0.081	−0.089	−0.096	−0.010	−0.102	−0.105	−0.097	−0.086	−0.104	−0.109
Italy	−0.043	−0.047	−0.050	−0.066	−0.122	−0.136	−0.130	−0.127	−0.127	−0.165
Sweden	0.004	0.004	0.004	0.006	0.006	0.008	0.007	0.008	0.009	0.010
Switzerland	0.022	0.024	0.026	0.028	0.029	0.030	0.029	0.030	0.029	0.029
Australia	0.034	0.038	0.040	0.042	0.043	0.044	0.044	−0.092	−0.187	−0.138

Table 1.7   **Personal Tax Advantage to Portfolio Investment: Evasion**

	1980	1981	1982	1983	1984	1985	1986	1987	1988	1989
Japan	0.357	0.392	0.419	0.437	0.433	0.445	0.427	0.401	0.400	0.312
Canada	0.245	0.277	0.204	0.212	0.218	0.200	0.234	0.233	0.201	0.206
France	0.160	0.176	0.236	0.246	0.252	0.259	0.178	0.164	0.164	0.162
West Germany	0.152	0.167	0.179	0.186	0.191	0.196	0.188	0.184	0.184	0.182
Netherlands	0.334	0.367	0.392	0.409	0.419	0.431	0.413	0.404	0.403	0.399
United Kingdom	0.176	0.193	0.206	0.215	0.221	0.227	0.222	0.225	0.103	0.061
Italy	0.284	0.311	0.333	0.284	0.237	0.211	0.202	0.197	0.197	0.074
Sweden	0.410	0.450	0.487	0.482	0.488	0.480	0.461	0.430	0.416	0.399
Switzerland	0.067	0.072	0.077	0.061	0.065	0.056	0.054	0.023	0.039	0.034
Australia	0.292	0.320	0.342	0.357	0.366	0.376	0.352	0.170	0.048	0.091

The figures in table 1.6 report the value of $(1 - \tau_c)[w_{ci}^* + (1 - w_{ci}^*)m_i^* - \max(m_i, w_{ci})]$, assuming no evasion of personal income taxes. These figures suggest substantial variation across countries in the personal tax treatment of portfolio versus direct investment. Most of this variation is due to the effects of dividend imputation schemes. France, Germany, Italy, and the United Kingdom all have important imputation schemes, and Australia adopted such a system in 1987, as can be seen comparing the values of m_i versus m_i^* in tables 1.1 and 1.2. The result, as seen in table 1.6, is a substantial personal tax advantage to direct over portfolio investment in these countries. Canada and Japan have less important imputation schemes, yielding only a slight tax advantage to direct investment. Personal taxes made little difference in the other countries. If personal taxes on portfolio investments are evaded, then the results change dramatically, as seen in table 1.7, where this expression is reevaluated under the assumption that $m_i = 0$. Now there is a dramatic personal tax advantage to portfolio investment.

Table 1.8 reports the size of the corporate surtax, assuming that firms are in a deficit-credit position. For countries which exempt foreign-source income, the corporate surtax is zero. For Italy and France, which use a hybrid system, the corporate surtax term instead equals $(1 - \tau_c)(1 - m_i^*)(1 - e)(\tau_{ci} - w_{ci}^*)$. For countries using a crediting system, the term equals $(1 - m_i^*)[A_{ci}(\tau_{ci} - \tau_c) - w_{ci}^*(1 - \tau_c)]$. In the figures in table 1.8, τ_{ci} is set equal to $\tau_i^s(\tau_c/\tau_c^s)$.[30] These tax terms are generally smaller than those reported in table 1.6 and dramatically smaller than those in table 1.7, suggesting that differences in the personal tax treatment of portfolio versus direct investment are much more important.

The term measuring the potential gain from transfer pricing is reported in table 1.9. For countries with a split-rate corporate tax system, we use the tax rate applied to retained earnings.

---

30. The figures under the two alternative measures of τ_{ci} are qualitatively very similar.

Table 1.8   **Corporate Surtax at Repatriation**

	1980	1981	1982	1983	1984	1985	1986	1987	1988	1989
Japan	-0.035	-0.038	-0.041	-0.042	-0.042	-0.042	-0.040	-0.021	-0.002	0.011
Canada	0	0	0	0	0	0	0	0	0	0
France	0.006	0.006	0.005	0.004	0.004	0.004	0.004	0.006	0.006	0.006
West Germany	0	0	0	0	0	0	0	0	0	0
Netherlands	0	0	0	0	0	0	0	0	0	0
United Kingdom	-0.010	-0.011	-0.011	-0.024	-0.060	-0.104	-0.140	-0.088	-0.059	-0.063
Italy	0.022	0.020	0.022	0.025	0.032	0.033	0.036	0.044	0.052	0.070
Sweden	0.005	0.006	0.007	0.010	-0.055	-0.006	-0.005	0.012	0.028	0.030
Switzerland	-0.140	-0.158	-0.169	-0.224	-0.243	-0.255	-0.247	-0.165	-0.101	-0.100
Australia	-0.058	-0.063	-0.068	-0.071	-0.072	-0.074	-0.074	-0.051	-0.043	-0.086

Table 1.9   **Difference in Statutory Corporate Tax Rates**

	1980	1981	1982	1983	1984	1985	1986	1987	1988	1989
Japan	0.054	0.054	0.054	0.054	0.065	0.068	0.068	0.118	0.174	0.158
Canada	0.000	0.000	0.000	0.000	0.000	0.010	0.020	0.070	0.090	0.050
France	0.010	0.010	0.010	0.010	0.010	0.010	0.060	0.000	0.030	0.000
West Germany	0.050	0.050	0.050	0.050	0.050	0.050	0.050	0.110	0.170	0.170
Netherlands	0.030	0.030	0.030	0.030	0.080	0.080	0.090	0.030	0.013	0.040
United Kingdom	0.010	0.010	0.010	0.005	0.047	0.097	0.147	0.100	0.040	0.040
Italy	0.147	0.147	0.097	0.097	0.047	0.047	0.047	0.013	0.073	0.073
Sweden	0.058	0.058	0.064	0.064	0.007	0.007	0.007	0.067	0.127	0.127
Switzerland	0.131	0.135	0.135	0.171	0.183	0.183	0.185	0.125	0.076	0.076
Australia	0.050	0.050	0.050	0.050	0.050	0.050	0.050	0.025	0.050	0.000

1.3.2 Data on the Composition of Capital Flows

The initial source of data for direct versus portfolio investment by residents of country i in U.S. equity came from the *Survey of Current Business,* using data compiled by the Bureau of Economic Analysis. These accounts, however, report data on direct investment in equity only from Canada, Japan, the Netherlands, and the United Kingdom. Similarly, the published tables include data on portfolio investment in equity only for investors from Canada and Japan. Smith W. Allnut III of the Bureau of Economic Analysis kindly provided us with internal estimates of direct investment in U.S. equity for the other six countries in our sample, and Harlan King, also of the Bureau of Economic Analysis, provided us with estimates of portfolio equity investment in the United States for the remaining eight countries.

Inevitably, these data do not measure precisely what we want. To begin with, if a corporation investing in a foreign firm does not own at least 10 percent of the shares in this firm, then the investment is reported as portfolio investment. Similarly, if an individual investor purchases more than 10 percent of a foreign firm, then this purchase is reported as a direct investment. In addition, the book figures for direct investment becomes misleading due to inflation in the United States for the same reasons that book capital figures can be misleading for domestic firms. Fortunately, the direct investment in the United States tends to be quite recent, and the U.S. inflation rate during the 1980s was relatively low. Another complication is that the balance sheet figures are based on infrequent benchmark surveys, with updates based on reported flows derived from a more limited sample. If investors transfer funds to the United States through a third country, perhaps to avoid domestic or withholding taxes, then the reported flow figures but not the benchmark figures will attribute the capital flow to this third country.[31] For both reasons, the

---

31. The benchmark survey asks the ultimate beneficial owner of payments made to foreign investors.

reported values can accumulate errors between benchmark surveys, as argued by Slemrod (1990). We were not in a position to correct for any of these possible measurement errors, so we simply assumed that they are uncorrelated with the measures of the tax variables. If so, then the measurement errors lead to a larger standard error of the regression but do not bias the coefficients.

The resulting figures for the fraction of equity flows from each country to the United States that take the form of direct investment are reported in table 1.10. As seen in the table, these figures vary substantially across countries. On average, for example, 90.9 percent of the equity flows from Sweden to the United States take the form of direct investment, whereas the comparable figure for Switzerland is only 23.3 percent. This strikingly low figure for Switzerland suggests that portfolio investors from third countries, who route their investments through Swiss financial intermediaries to avoid domestic taxation, may form an important if not dominant component of the capital flows from Switzerland. Although in principle the U.S. data report the ultimate beneficial owner, Swiss banking regulations prevent the nationality of the ultimate owner from being revealed. Another country whose data might be suspect is the Netherlands. Due to the low withholding taxes on interest payments from the United States to the Netherlands and the territorial treatment of firms by the Netherlands, multinationals often found it attractive to funnel investments through the Netherlands. The high fraction of direct investment from the Netherlands, in spite of their lack of any capital controls, at least suggests that some of it was owned by investors in other countries, in spite of the U.S. attempt to trace the ultimate beneficial owner. Given our concerns with the data from these two countries, we test below the sensitivity of our results to the exclusion of these two countries.

One immediate observation from table 1.10 is that there is little systematic trend over the sample period or even substantial movement in the composition of equity flows, in spite of substantial changes in tax rates in these countries during the sample period. This tells us immediately that any tax effects, if found, must be subtle.

Table 1.10   **Direct Investment Relative to Total Equity Position (percentage)**

	1980	1981	1982	1983	1984	1985	1986	1987	1988	1989
Japan	85.0	88.2	87.8	85.5	88.9	87.0	76.0	62.3	67.7	64.9
Canada	45.0	43.9	40.5	35.6	43.6	41.3	39.1	43.5	42.4	40.4
France	33.1	41.0	38.7	36.2	40.5	38.8	40.1	44.7	47.7	51.3
West Germany	73.5	78.4	75.1	68.6	74.0	69.2	69.1	72.2	72.5	72.7
Netherlands	81.1	86.1	83.9	83.3	84.9	83.7	80.3	81.5	79.1	77.6
United Kingdom	46.9	51.3	52.6	48.1	48.9	45.0	43.0	50.8	55.7	52.3
Italy	39.4	78.2	80.5	77.4	75.3	62.3	57.3	64.9	60.8	56.9
Sweden	91.4	92.4	87.1	88.1	94.8	90.9	94.4	95.3	92.0	82.5
Switzerland	18.0	19.8	21.5	20.6	24.2	22.0	20.2	24.9	29.1	32.3
Australia	45.0	71.6	59.9	57.8	75.7	74.5	72.1	78.7	73.5	70.9

1.4   Estimation

1.4.1   Statistical Specification

The basic model for countries using a credit system assumes that the fraction of equity flows from country i to country c that takes the form of direct investment rather than portfolio investment is a function of the three tax terms in equation (3), where $\theta = a + b\tau_{ci}$. Substituting for θ gives four tax variables, denoted by T_p, T_c^a, T_c^b, and T_c^s, where

$$T_p = (1 - \tau_c)[w_{ci}^* + (1 + w_{ci}^*)m_i^* - \max(m_i, w_{ci})] ,$$

$$T_c^a = (1 - m_i^*)[A_{ci}(\tau_{ci} - \tau_c) - w_{ci}^*(1 - \tau_c)] ,$$

$$T_c^b = \tau_{ci}T_c^a , \text{ and}$$

$$T_c^s = \mathrm{abs}(\tau_c^s - \tau_i^s) .$$

For countries exempting foreign-source income, $T_c^a = T_c^b = 0$. For Italy and France, we defined a fifth tax term, $T_c^c = (1 - \tau_c)(1 - m_i^*)(1 - e)(\tau_{ci} - w_{ci}^*)$; its coefficient is allowed to differ from those of the other tax terms.

These five variables, plus R_{it} and C_{it}, will be used to forecast the value of the ratio of direct investment to direct plus portfolio investment. Denote this ratio by D_{it}. This ratio by definition is between zero and one. A linear regression with this ratio as the dependent variable would therefore suffer from the same problems that linear probability models do. We therefore decided to use a logit specification. Given that we observe the population outcome for the choice between the two forms of equity flows, we can estimate a logit model using the ordinary least squares (OLS) method, with the dependent variable being $\log[D_{it}/(1 - D_{it})]$.[32] We started out with the regression specification

$$
(4) \qquad \log\left(\frac{D_{it}}{1 - D_{it}}\right) = \beta_0 + \beta_1 T_p + \beta_2 T_c^a + \beta_3 T_c^b +
$$
$$
\beta_4 T_c^c + \beta_5 T_c^s + \beta_6 R_{it} + \beta_7 C_{it} + \varepsilon_{it} ,
$$

where ε_{it} captures the effects of factors omitted from the specification on the composition of equity flows. Based on the above discussion, the coefficients of T_c^a, T_c^s, R_{it}, and C_{it} should be positive, while those of T_p, T_c^b, and T_c^c should be negative.

1.4.2   Regression Results

In our initial specification, we started with the following measures of the above variables: First, in defining T_p, we assumed personal tax evasion on portfolio investments but not on direct investments.[33] Second, we set τ_{ci} equal

---

32. See, for example, Kmenta (1986) for a demonstration of this.

33. One striking and anomalous implication of this assumption is that the correlation of the resulting values of T_p with the dependent variable is .78, which is the highest pairwise correlation with the dependent variable found in the study. Note that the sign of this correlation is the opposite of that forecast by the theory, a finding returned to below.

to $\tau_i^s(\tau_c/\tau_c^s)$, which assumes that home governments rely on the U.S. definition of corporate taxable income when taxing repatriated earnings. Finally, we used our intermediate definition for C_{it}.

Using these variable definitions, we first estimated equation (4) using OLS. The resulting coefficient estimates are reported in column 1 of table 1.11, with t-statistics reported in parentheses.[34] The results are rather mixed. The coefficients of R&D and capital controls are both of the expected sign and statistically significant. The other statistically significant variable is T_p, but its coefficient is of the wrong sign. One hypothesis concerning the coefficient of T_p is that countries which are less threatened by capital flight are more inclined to impose high personal tax rates, implying a reverse causation. We return to this hypothesis below. Of the remaining coefficients, those of T_c^a and T_c^b have the expected signs, while those of T_c^c and T_c^s do not. All these coefficients are very small and statistically insignificant, however.

To test for delayed responses to changes in incentives, we tried instead using lagged values of each of the independent variables. Since we did not collect tax data for 1979, the regression had to be run with data from 1981–89. The resulting coefficients on these lagged terms appear in column 2 of table 1.11. The fit is slightly better statistically. The coefficients of T_c^c and T_c^s now have the expected signs, though they remain small and insignificant. Otherwise, any differences from the original specification are minor. We therefore chose to focus on use of contemporaneous data in order to avoid the loss of degrees of freedom.

Both of these regressions were estimated using OLS. Yet OLS is appropriate only if the error terms in the regression are homoscedastic and independent across observations. Given the panel nature of the sample, however, the error terms for a given country may be correlated over time, because of, for example, omitted random or fixed effects. Ignoring these correlations at least results in a bias in the estimates of the standard errors of the coefficients. If omitted country effects are correlated with the included independent variables, then the initial coefficient estimates are themselves biased.

To test for the importance of these possible problems, we reestimated the initial equation, using both a fixed-effects estimator and a random-effects estimator. The resulting coefficient estimates assuming fixed effects are reported in column 3 of table 1.11, whereas those assuming random effects appear in column 5.[35] As is apparent from the jump in the adjusted R^2, these country

---

34. As noted below, these t-statistics are biased at least because the residuals are not independent across observations due to country effects.

35. As shown in Fuller and Battese (1973), the random-effects estimator involves replacing the initial dependent variable, Y_{it}, and independent variables X_{it} with $Y_{it} - \lambda Y_i$ and $X_{it} - \lambda X_i$, respectively. Here Y_i and X_i are the mean values for country i over the full time period, and $\lambda = 1 - [\sigma^2/(\sigma^2 + T\sigma_r^2)]^{1/2}$, where σ_r^2 is the estimated variance of the random effects, σ^2 is the variance of the idiosyncratic component of the residual, and T is the number of years. As the estimate of λ approaches one, the random-effects estimator approaches the fixed-effects estimator. In this specification, the estimate of λ was 0.83, explaining the similarity of the coefficient estimates in the two cases.

Table 1.11   **Test of Statistical Specification (t-statistics in parentheses)**

	OLS (1)	Lag (2)	Fixed Effects (3)	Between Effects (4)	Random Effects (5)	Excluding Switzerland and the Netherlands (6)
Constant	−0.579	−0.472	—	−0.706	0.176	−0.609
	(−3.98)	(−3.20)		(−1.02)	(0.81)	(−3.75)
T_p	1.971	1.911	−0.281	2.302	0.162	1.013
	(5.77)	(5.49)	(−0.81)	(1.37)	(0.47)	(2.04)
T_c^a	2.436	2.534	−1.580	14.983	−1.317	5.782
	(1.21)	(1.28)	(−1.25)	(0.88)	(−0.98)	(1.15)
T_c^b	−2.520	−0.895	2.792	−46.354	7.280	−20.700
	(−0.29)	(−0.10)	(0.41)	(−0.65)	(1.06)	(−1.09)
T_c^c	1.709	−2.656	−7.588	−4.960	−3.685	1.515
	(0.54)	(−0.71)	(−1.99)	(−0.27)	(−1.04)	(0.46)
T_c^s	−0.084	0.855	−1.677	5.766	−1.473	0.528
	(−0.12)	(1.15)	(−3.39)	(1.01)	(−2.90)	(0.71)
R	15.486	9.059	7.439	5.364	5.866	23.808
	(2.93)	(1.70)	(0.86)	(0.18)	(0.75)	(4.03)
C	0.256	0.273	0.099	0.153	0.145	0.429
	(3.05)	(3.23)	(1.31)	(0.31)	(1.89)	(3.81)
Adjusted R^2	0.67	0.70	0.90	0.63	0.13	0.58

Note: The regression using lagged independent variables is based on ninety observations, 1981–1989, by ten countries; all others based on one hundred observations, 1980–1989, by ten countries.

effects are highly significant as a group.[36] If the country effects are uncorrelated with the other included variables, then a random-effects estimator would be appropriate. To test for this lack of correlation, we used the procedure described in Hausman (1978), which compares statistically the coefficient estimates from the fixed-effects and the random-effects regressions. The resulting Hausman test statistic is 32.9, which has a P-value of only 0.00003 under the approximate χ^2 distribution, and so strongly rejects the random-effects model. We therefore focus on the results from the fixed-effects procedure.

The coefficient estimates that result from the fixed-effects procedure differ substantially from those resulting from OLS, as is seen comparing column 1 with column 3. Comparing the fixed-effects coefficients with the forecasts from the theory, the results are again mixed. The coefficient of T_p is now of the expected sign but statistically insignificant. The coefficients of T_c^a and T_c^b have both changed sign, both contrary to theoretical forecasts. Given their relative sizes, however, the net effect of the corporate surtax ($\beta_2 + \beta_3\tau_{ci}$) is still negative, as expected, as long as $\tau_{ci} < .57$, which is satisfied for all the countries in our sample. What is surprising is that the effect is more negative for countries with a smaller value of τ_{ci}. The coefficient of T_c^c, describing the

---

36. The value of the F-test for omitting the country dummies in the fixed-effects procedure is 3.2, compared with a 5 percent significance level of about 1.35.

corporate tax surcharge in Italy and France, has also changed to the expected sign and is statistically significant. While the coefficients of the R&D and the capital-controls variables still have the expected signs, they are no longer significant.[37] The main inconsistency with the theory is the coefficient of T_c^s, which is not only of the wrong sign but highly significant. The economic effect implied by the coefficient is small, however. Given the logit specification for the dependent variable, $|\delta D_{it}/\delta \tau_i^s| = D_{it}(1 - D_{it})\beta_5 \leq .25\beta_5$, implying tiny effects of τ_i^s on D_{it}, given the various parameter values. Given the multiple ways in which tax rates enter the regression, and the small sample size, it is difficult to interpret each coefficient too strongly.

The estimates for the country dummies in the fixed-effects regression are reported in table 1.12. Of the six countries with positive coefficients, four had capital controls during at least some part of the sample period, and the data from one of the others (the Netherlands) are likely to overestimate the size of D_{it}. These coefficients rather than the capital-controls dummy would capture the effects of capital controls if these effects did not disappear quickly with the official end of capital controls. Learning lags could explain this slow response, suggesting stronger effects of capital controls than are captured by the capital-controls dummy. The only significant negative coefficient is that for Switzerland, where we also view the data with suspicion.

The differences between the fixed-effects results and the OLS results reflect the relative lack of time-series variation in the data but the substantial variation in average levels of D_{it} across countries. In order to highlight these conflicting aspects of the data, we also report results from a between-effects regression in column 4 of table 1.11, in which country averages of each variable over the ten-year period are used. The only coefficient whose sign is contrary to the theory is again T_p. Given the small number of countries in the sample, it is not surprising that t-statistics for the coefficient estimates are so low. Since it may be difficult to capture the *timing* of tax effects adequately in the fixed-effects regressions, these results do provide an important independent view of the nature of these tax effects.

Given our suspicions about the quality of the data from Switzerland and the Netherlands, we tried dropping these two countries from the sample. The last column in table 1.11 reports OLS results using the eight remaining countries. The main change is that the coefficients of T_c^a and T_c^b are now dramatically larger and still of the correct sign. The coefficients of R&D and capital controls are also much larger. T_p still has the wrong sign, however.

In table 1.13, we explore a variety of alternative definitions of the variables. Column 1 repeats the fixed-effects results from table 1.11. In column 2, we try the stricter definition of the capital-controls variable; little changes, except that the coefficient of C_{it} is now negative but insignificant. (Results with the

---

37. Our definition of R&D is likely to measure poorly the timing of effects of R&D, so that weaker estimated effects in the fixed-effects model should not be surprising.

Table 1.12   **Country Effects**

	Coefficient	t-statistic
Japan	0.612	2.24
Canada	−0.142	−0.99
France	−0.187	−0.95
West Germany	0.421	1.84
Netherlands	0.704	3.08
United Kingdom	−0.096	−0.40
Italy	0.611	2.84
Sweden	0.990	3.67
Switzerland	−0.634	−2.05
Australia	0.308	1.73

Table 1.13   **Test of Alternative Definitions of Variables (t-statistics in parentheses)**

	Fixed Effects (table 1.11) (1)	Capital Controls (strict) (2)	No Evasion (3)	τ_{ci} (average corporation rate) (4)	τ_{ci} (statutory corporation rate) (5)	2SLS* (without fixed effects) (6)
T_p	−0.281	−0.012	−0.750	−0.284	−0.309	−0.206
	(−0.81)	(−0.03)	(−1.26)	(−0.88)	(−0.84)	(−0.14)
T_c^a	−1.580	−1.281	−1.548	3.352	7.783	−5.209
	(−1.25)	(−1.00)	(−1.24)	(1.95)	(1.16)	(−0.77)
T_c^b	2.792	0.195	3.934	−7.241	−15.397	47.142
	(0.41)	(0.03)	(0.58)	(−2.49)	(−1.05)	(1.40)
T_c^c	−7.588	−10.417	−7.325	7.827	−6.956	−12.019
	(−1.99)	(−2.66)	(−1.98)	(4.22)	(−1.85)	(−1.38)
T_c^s	−1.677	−1.861	−1.529	−1.049	−1.557	0.233
	(−3.39)	(−3.93)	(−2.98)	(−2.70)	(−3.06)	(0.20)
R	7.439	4.347	6.094	1.434	4.652	12.760
	(0.86)	(0.50)	(0.70)	(0.20)	(0.56)	(1.70)
C	0.099	−0.073	0.119	0.178	0.113	0.857
	(1.31)	(−0.88)	(1.53)	(2.72)	(1.48)	(2.13)
Adjusted R^2	0.90	0.90	0.90	0.92	0.90	0.40

*2SLS = Two-stage least squares.

looser definition of C_{it} are very close to those in column 1.) We also tried alternative assumptions about personal tax evasion; again, little changes. The results assuming no evasion are reported in column 3. In columns 4 and 5, we measure τ_{ci}, using the two alternative definitions explored above. The coefficients of the corporate surtax terms do turn out to be very sensitive to the choice of this definition, although the other coefficients do not change much. When $\tau_{ci} = \tau_i^s$, all three of these coefficients are of the expected sign; when the average corporate tax rate is used, T_c^a and T_c^b have the expected signs, but

T_c^c flips to having the wrong sign.[38] Before the behavioral effects of this corporate surtax can be judged with any confidence, more work is needed to assess how foreign-source corporate income is measured in practice in these countries.

One complication in interpreting any of the above results is that government policy variables could well be endogenous, given the importance of tax evasion in many of these countries. To begin with, capital controls make it much easier to impose high personal tax rates, because evasion of these taxes through investing abroad would be discouraged by the capital controls. This merely suggests a correlation between the independent variables,[39] which does not create statistical bias. In addition, however, countries where investors can for institutional or geographic reasons more easily shift funds abroad and should find it more costly to impose high personal tax rates. In itself, this suggests a reverse effect of the dependent variable on m_i^*, biasing the coefficient estimates generally but primarily creating a positive bias in the coefficient of T_p. The very high positive correlation in the data between T_p and the dependent variable certainly suggests such a reverse causation. Countries facing more pressure from capital flight, everything else equal, should also be more likely to adopt capital controls in order to lessen these pressures. This suggests that the residual will also be negatively correlated with C_{it}. We therefore experimented with two-stage least squares (2SLS) estimation methods, treating C_{it} and m_i^* as endogenous. In particular, we collected data on the top marginal tax rate on wages[40] in each of these countries, and the ratio of tax revenue to GDP, to use as instruments. The higher the tax rates are on labor income and the higher the amount of revenue the government desires, everything else equal, the more likely the country is to raise revenue from taxes on financial income and to impose capital controls to facilitate this taxation of financial income. Although no aggregate variable will be entirely exogenous, any effects of the dependent variable on these series should be trivial, making them reasonable instruments. The variables T_p, T_c^a, T_c^b, and C_{it} were all treated as endogenous. Rather than using the two instruments directly, we included six variables constructed using them,[41] along with the remaining variables from the original regression, in each of the four auxiliary regressions. The results, without fixed effects, are reported in column 6 of table 1.13. These results ought to be compared with the OLS results in column 1 of table 1.11.

---

38. Because foreign direct investment and average tax rates can both be affected by cyclical factors, these coefficients must be judged with some caution.

39. The correlation between T_p and C_{it} in our sample is 0.56, very much supporting this hypothesis.

40. Given the equivalence in present value of value-added taxes and wage taxes, this variable captures the combined effects of both.

41. In particular, the six instruments were tax revenue/GDP, (tax revenue/GDP)^2, T_p with m_i^* replaced by the top marginal tax rate on labor, this variable squared, and both T_c^a and T_c^b with m_i^* replaced by the top marginal tax rate on labor.

As expected, the coefficient of T_p dropped substantially and now has the expected sign, while the coefficient of C_{it} became dramatically large. Reverse causation does appear to be an important factor. The coefficients of the remaining tax variables all change sign, still leaving two with the sign forecast by the theory. They all remain statistically insignificant, however.

Another possible complication is that capital controls may hinder any new portfolio flows but may not force investors to liquidate unreported investments they have already made abroad. Even though the U.S. government knows about the nationality of these portfolio investors, this does not imply that the home government is in a position to prosecute specific cases of tax evasion or evasion of controls. To test for this, we allowed capital controls to reduce the sensitivity of the dependent variable to tax distortions, as well as to change the mean value of the dependent variable. In particular, we multiplied each of the tax factors in equation (4) by $(1 - \alpha C_{it})$, then estimated α using a grid search.[42] Our expectation was that $0 \ll \alpha < 1$. The resulting estimate of α, starting from the original OLS specification, was -1.55. Surprisingly, behavior seemed *more* sensitive to tax rates in countries with capital controls, though tax effects are still small.

1.5 Conclusions

Existing tax structures in our sample countries have important effects on the relative attractiveness to individuals of buying foreign equity directly versus having a domestic firm they own buy these shares instead, particularly given the ease with which individuals appear able to evade domestic taxes on portfolio investments abroad. To what degree do these distortions change behavior? The composition of equity flows does differ dramatically among these countries, and at least part of the explanation appears to be tax differences. Behavior did not seem to change much during the 1980s, however, in spite of the many large changes in tax rates that occurred during this period. Part of the explanation appears to be the importance of capital controls in many of the sample countries. Another problem, making inference more difficult, is that tax policy itself seemed to be endogenous—countries where investors could more easily invest abroad were more likely to have lower tax distortions and to impose capital controls. In principle, the increasing international integration of financial markets and the steady reduction of capital controls should lead to increasing responsiveness of the composition of international capital flows to tax distortions. As a result, countries will be under increasing pressure to reduce these tax distortions, and past behavior suggests that they will in fact respond to this pressure.

---

42. In doing this, we used our loosest definition of C_{it}, because the controls in France should reduce the responsiveness of D_{it} to taxes even if they do not discourage ownership of foreign equity per se.

References

Adler, Michael, and Bernard Dumas. 1983. International portfolio choice and corporation finance: A synthesis. *Journal of Finance* 38:925–84.

Bhattacharya, Sudipto. 1979. Imperfect information, dividend policy, and the "bird in the hand" fallacy. *Bell Journal of Economics* 100:259–70.

Bradford, David F., and Don Fullerton. 1981. Pitfalls in the construction and use of effective tax rates. In *Depreciation, inflation, and the taxation of income from capital*, ed. C. R. Hulten. Washington, D.C.: Urban Institute Press.

Coopers and Lybrand International Tax Network. 1980–1989. *International tax summaries*. New York: Coopers and Lybrand.

Dunning, John H., ed. 1985. *Multinational enterprises, economic structure, and international competitiveness*. Chichester: Wiley.

Easterbrook, Frank H. 1984. Two agency-cost explanations of dividends. *American Economic Review* 74:650–59.

Feldstein, Martin S. 1980a. Inflation and the stock market. *American Economic Review* 70:839–47.

———. 1980b. Inflation, tax rules, and the stock market. *Journal of Monetary Economics* 3:309–31.

French, Kenneth R., and James M. Poterba. 1991. Investor diversification and international equity markets. NBER Working Paper no. 3609. Cambridge, Mass.: National Bureau of Economic Research.

Fuller, W. A., and G. E. Battese. 1973. Transformations for estimation of linear models with nested error structure. *Journal of the American Statistical Association* 68:626–32.

Gordon, Roger H. 1986. Taxation of investment and savings in a world economy. *American Economic Review* 76:1086–1102.

Gordon, Roger H., and Joel Slemrod. 1988. Do we collect any revenue from taxing capital income? *Tax Policy and the Economy* 2:89–130.

Griliches, Zvi. 1980. Returns to research and development expenditures in the private sector. In *New developments in productivity measurement and analysis*, ed. J. W. Kendrick and B. N. Vaccara. Chicago: University of Chicago Press.

Hausman, J. A. 1978. Specification tests in econometrics. *Econometrica* 46:1251–72.

Hines, James R., Jr. 1991. Dividends and profits: Some unsubtle foreign influences. Mimeograph.

Hines, James R., Jr., and R. Glenn Hubbard. 1989. Coming home to America: Dividend repatriations by U.S. multinationals. NBER Working Paper no. 2931. Cambridge, Mass.: National Bureau of Economic Research.

Kmenta, Jan. 1986. *Elements of econometrics*. New York: Macmillan.

Organization for Economic Cooperation and Development. 1980–1989. *National accounts*. Paris: OECD.

Pechman, Joseph A. 1988. *World tax reform: A progress report*. Washington, D.C.: Brookings Institution.

Poterba, James M., and Lawrence H. Summers. 1985. The economic effects of dividend taxation. In *Recent advances in corporate finance*, ed. Edward I. Altman and Marti G. Subrahmanyam. Homewood, Ill.: Irwin.

Razin, Assaf, and Joel Slemrod. 1990. *Taxation in the global economy*. Chicago: University of Chicago Press.

Slemrod, Joel 1990. Tax effects on foreign direct investment in the United States: Evidence from a cross-country comparison. In *Taxation in the global economy*, ed. A. Razin and J. Slemrod. Chicago: University of Chicago Press.

Swenson, Deborah L. 1990. The impact of U.S. tax reform on foreign direct investment in the U.S. Mimeograph.

Comment   Alberto Giovannini

This very careful study uses a new data set, compiled by the U.S. Bureau of Economic Analysis, to evaluate the effects of taxes on the composition of foreign investment (direct investment versus portfolio investment).

In a nutshell, the regression equations estimated by Gordon and Jun contain, on the left side, a measure of the ratio of portfolio investment flows over direct investment flows into the United States. The data are a cross section and time series from ten industrial countries. The explanatory variables are tax and nontax variables. The tax variables include a measure of the tax advantage of portfolio investment arising from the ability of individuals to claim credits on withholding taxes and a measure of the tax advantage of portfolio investment arising whenever corporations are in a deficit credit position. Corporate investment, however, is more attractive whenever transfer pricing allows a reduction of the total tax burden of the corporation: this effect is entered separately in the regressions. Gordon and Jun also include nontax variables, such as the presence of controls on portfolio investments by individuals, and R&D intensity (the latter is presumably a good proxy for the incentives to locate overseas that arise from ownership of distinct products or technologies).

The empirical analysis of international capital flows has a long tradition. Twenty years ago, the implications of the portfolio model for international capital flows were discovered, which led to substantial research with often disappointing results (see, for example, the essays in Machlup, Salant, and Tarshis 1972). Gordon and Jun pay little attention to the issues that inflamed researchers twenty years ago (stock versus flow equilibria) but concentrate on deriving consistent tax variables. Like many of their predecessors, they fail to establish convincing empirical evidence in favor of their own chosen model of international capital flows. Their results beg the question of why it is so difficult to explain observed capital flows data. I suggest a number of possible causes of this difficulty:

1. *The quality of capital flows data.* Gordon and Jun use data constructed by Bureau of Economic Analysis officials. The fact that the data are not published makes me suspect that the agency might regard them as not perfectly reliable. Although I do not think this is enough of a reason for economists to shy away from unpublished data, I suspect that in this case putting the data with errors on the left side of the regression equations might not be enough. As the International Monetary Fund (1987) study on the world current account discrepancy has shown, statistical errors in the data are often caused by underreporting, which is caused by tax evasion. Hence, tax variables are likely to be significantly correlated with errors in measurement of the dependent variable in Gordon and Jun's regressions.

Alberto Giovannini is Jerome A. Chazen Professor of International Business at Columbia University and a research associate of the National Bureau of Economic Research. He is also a research fellow at the Centre for Economic Research in London and member and coordinator of the Council of Experts of the Italian Treasury Ministry.

2. *The specification of the regression equations.* As I mentioned above, the innovation of the portfolio approach in international capital flows was to regress capital flows on *first differences* in interest rates. The assumption was that stock equilibrium holds at every point in time. Gordon and Jun regress capital flows on variables that represent their relative profitability. The basic problem of their regression is that they might have inconsistent long-run predictions. For example, they might predict a permanent increase in the share of portfolio investment in total capital *flows* in response to a given tax incentive: this is, of course, a prediction that does not produce constant steady-state portfolio shares.

3. *The choice of explanatory variables.* It is not clear that the tax variables constructed by Gordon and Jun represent the relevant variables faced by international investors. In international finance, the actual intermediate stops made by investments from country A to country B matter tremendously. Tax havens permit corporations and individuals to substantially lower taxes on foreign-source incomes. Tax havens are heavily used: for example, data from the Japanese Ministry of Finance (Annual Report of the International Finance Bureau, 1985) show that the share of direct investments out of Japan into tax havens was as high as 27 percent in 1983.

Suppose, for the sake of illustration, that a corporation in Italy wishing to invest in the United States finds that the cheapest way of doing so is through a subsidiary in the Netherlands Antilles. Under that hypothesis, the tax variables calculated by Gordon and Jun would not be the relevant variables faced by such corporation. At the same time, however, we would not observe any corporate investment flows from Italy to the United States. This discussion suggests that, to the extent that data on cross-border investments between the countries in the sample are observed, the investments might be motivated by factors other than the tax factors which are the focus of this paper, as the authors themselves acknowledge. The nontax factors used by Gordon and Jun are simply too few to provide enough explanatory power. In addition, even if these additional factors are orthogonal to the tax variables, one should not expect their coefficients to have signs consistent with the theory, as long as cheaper options to move investment funds from one country to another are available.

In summary, I found Gordon and Jun's paper to be both stimulating and careful. I suspect, however, that the problem they attack is still too big for the data and models currently at our disposal.

References

International Monetary Fund. 1987. *Report on the world current account discrepancy.* Washington, D.C.: IMF.

Machlup, F., W. S. Salant, and L. Tarshis, eds. 1972. *International mobility and movement of capital.* New York: Columbia University Press.

2   Impacts of Canadian and U.S. Tax Reform on the Financing of Canadian Subsidiaries of U.S. Parents

Roy D. Hogg and Jack M. Mintz

During the past decade, Canada and the United States undertook significant reforms that affected the income tax treatment of corporations in each country. Arguably, one of the most significant changes introduced by these reforms was with respect to the Canadian and U.S. tax treatment of U.S. multinationals operating in Canada.[1] In this paper, we examine the impact of U.S. and Canadian tax reforms on the financing of U.S. multinationals operating in Canada prior to and after Canadian and U.S. tax reform in the years 1986–87.

The data developed for this examination are based on a cross-section time-series file of twenty-eight companies for the years 1983–89 that was compiled by Arthur Andersen & Co. The virtue of this data set is that it is longitudinal, since current data are only one-year cross-section snapshots or aggregate time series. Also, we have been able to incorporate 1988 and 1989 data that would otherwise be unavailable at this time. However, the data are limited by the number of observations.[2] We cannot, therefore, vouch that the data are representative of all U.S. companies, although we have checked the comparability of our data with aggregate calculations found for all U.S. multinational companies operating in Canada. Aggregate 1980 data are reported in table 2.1.

Roy D. Hogg is tax practice director, Arthur Andersen & Co.—Canada. Jack M. Mintz is the Arthur Andersen Professor of Taxation, Faculty of Management, University of Toronto.

The authors are grateful to Sergio Traviza for his research assistance. Comments from Neil Bruce, Joel Slemrod, and two reviewers are gratefully acknowledged.

1. For a documentation of the U.S. treatment of foreign source income under the new tax reform law, see U.S. Congress, Joint Committee on Taxation (1987) and Ault and Bradford (1990). A review of Canadian tax reform measures and their impacts may be found in Canada, Department of Finance (1987), Bruce (1989), and Jog and Mintz (1989).

2. Total assets in 1984 equaled to $1.2 billion. This is approximately 1 percent of the 1984 assets of U.S. companies operating in Canada, as reported by Frisch and Goodspeed (1990) and in the Statistics Canada, CALURA no. 61-210.

Table 2.1   U.S.-Controlled Foreign Corporations in Canada, 1980: By Selected Industry of Incorporation in Canada (U.S.$ millions)

Industry	Percent of U.S. Corporations (1)	Percent of Foreign Corporations (2)	Total Assets (3)	Business Receipts (4)	Current Earnings or Profits before Tax (5)	Foreign Income Taxes (net, paid in Canada) (6)	Distributions		Payout Ratio (%) (8) ÷ (5)
							Total (7)	Out of Current Earnings or Profit (8)	
All industries	2,527	5,415	$90,044 (35.6)	$100,773 (39.9)	$8,285 (3.28)	$3,143 (1.24)	$1,988 (0.786)	$1,559 (0.617)	18.8%
Mining	139	240	7,605 (54.7)	4,309 (31.0)	1,212 (8.72)	416 (2.99)	252 (1.81)	202 (1.45)	16.7
Construction	74	114	1,092 (14.8)	2,387 (32.3)	85 (1.15)	32 (0.43)	27 (0.36)	8 (0.11)	9.4
Manufacturing	1,179	1,741	43,581 (37.0)	66,335 (56.3)	5,039 (4.27)	2,017 (1.71)	1,274 (1.08)	1,026 (0.87)	20.3
Transportation and public utilities	89	172	5,908 (66.4)	4,556 (51.2)	338 (3.80)	112 (1.37)	113 (1.27)	83 (0.93)	24.5
Wholesale trade	536	677	3,850 (7.18)	8,525 (15.9)	722 (1.34)	235 (0.44)	166 (0.31)	136 (0.25)	18.8
Retail trade	92	260	2,942 (32.0)	8,042 (87.4)	289 (3.14)	102 (1.11)	130 (1.41)	87 (0.95)	30.1

Note: Numbers in parentheses are, for each category, the average number of U.S. dollars per corporation.

These numbers roughly compare to the aggregate data of our sample for earlier years.

Section 2.1 of this paper describes the changes to Canadian and U.S. tax law during the period 1983–89. U.S. tax reform provisions began to apply to U.S. companies in 1987, while Canadian Phase I tax reform measures applied to Canadian companies in 1986, Phase II reforms in 1988.

Section 2.2 outlines various hypotheses that would be drawn from theory regarding the impact of Canadian and U.S. reforms. The hypotheses we are concerned with deal with changes in financial behavior: in particular, dividend payouts, cross-border charges (nondividend payments to the parent), and debt.

Section 2.3 presents data that are a preliminary confirmation or rejection of the hypotheses. The results are interesting, but we have to be cautious with respect to interpretation. Some of the trends that we notice may be explained by both tax and nontax factors. Only further data development and statistical testing would allow us to disentangle the factors that influence financial behavior.

Subject to this caution, we obtain the following main results:

- A dramatic increase took place both in the number of companies issuing dividends and in dividend payout ratios from the 1983–85 subperiod to the 1987–89 subperiod. In the latter, the average ratio of dividends paid to net income was close to 100 percent when companies chose to pay out dividends. The observed growth in dividend payments for this data set is consistent with the 50 percent real growth in dividends remitted abroad as reported on a national income accounts basis.[3] Both tax and nontax factors can explain this significant increase in dividend payouts.
- Companies that tended to pay dividends also paid more of their income to U.S. parents in the form of cross-border charges. As discussed below, this is consistent with a tax-minimizing strategy on the part of the parent and its subsidiary.
- Little change occurred in aggregate debt-asset ratios over the two subperiods. However, on a firm-by-firm basis, the debt-asset ratios increased for a majority of companies, falling for the remainder. The increase in debt-asset ratios was found to be significant. Both tax and nontax factors can explain these results.

2.1 Tax Changes during the Period 1983 to 1989

Since 1985 in Canada and 1984 in the United States, significant changes have occurred in the tax systems of both countries. The focus here is exclu-

---

3. Computed in table 2.2. During the 1975–82 period, dividends remitted abroad were, on average, $2.7 billion per year. During the years 1983–85, dividends remitted abroad were $3.7 billion per year. In the 1987–89 period, dividends remitted abroad were $6.4 billion per year. Corrected for inflation, the growth in dividends was 50 percent from 1983–85 to 1987–89.

Table 2.2   **Dividends Paid to Nonresidents and Canadian Exchange Rates, by Year**

Year	Dividends ($ billion)	Canadian Exchange Rate (U.S. Cents, Average Closing Prices)
1983	$2.5	80.4 cents
1984	3.9	75.7
1985	4.6	71.5
1986	5.8	72.4
1987	4.7	77.0
1988	8.5	83.9
1989	5.9	86.3

Source: Bank of Canada, 1990, *Review.*

sively on the provisions that affect wholly owned Canadian subsidiaries of U.S. parent companies.

2.1.1   Statutory Tax Rates

Table 2.3 shows the changes in the statutory rates of both countries between 1985 and 1989. For purposes of illustration and to make the table meaningful, both Canadian federal and provincial rates are combined, and both U.S. federal and state rates are shown, using the Canadian provinces of Quebec and Ontario and the U.S. states of Illinois and New York to illustrate the rate comparisons, in addition to reporting weighted average corporate tax rates. In Canada, the lower effective statutory tax rate on manufacturing, both federal and provincial, has been segregated. The rates of tax imposed by provinces other than Quebec are very close to the Ontario rates.

Prior to 1986, as table 2.3 indicates, statutory rates were generally lower in Canada than in the United States. Getting money "home" by way of dividends did not lead to additional taxes paid because the 10 percent Canadian rate of withholding on dividends was creditable against other taxes.[4] From a tax viewpoint, little attention was paid to cross-border charges, and therefore there was a limited focus on whether proper charges were made for such things as management and administration fees (particularly "specific expense reimbursements") and royalties, and transfer prices for goods. Attention had to be paid, however, to the provisions of the Internal Revenue Code of the United States (the "code"), and its regulations governing the deductibility of costs and expenses that may otherwise relate to the business of a subsidiary or related entity and be appropriately chargeable to that other entity.[5]

It is arguable that beginning in 1986, outside of Quebec, some tax incentive

4. Article X (2)(a) of the Canada–United States Income Tax Convention 1980 (the "treaty").
5. Section 482 of the code and the detailed rules found in regulations 1.482-1 and 1.482-2 to the code.

Table 2.3   **Comparative Tax Rates***

	United States			Canada				
Year	New York	Illinois	Average for All States†	Quebec	Ontario	M&P‡ Quebec	M&P‡ Ontario	Average for All Provinces and Industries†
1985	51.4%	49.51%	50.05%	42.41%	51.93%	36.26%	44.78%	46.69%
Rate including 10 percent dividend with-holding tax				48.17	56.74	42.63	50.30	53.02
1989	39.94	38.59	38.95	34.9	44.34	32.37	40.81	40.50
Rate including 10 percent dividend with-holding tax				41.41	49.91	39.13	46.73	45.45

*Rates, provided for comparative purposes only, may not be entirely accurate due to surtaxes or special taxes/credits for certain types of income or use of capital.

†Weighted average of state/provincial corporate tax rates, with the weights based on the distribution of corporate taxable income.

‡Manufacturing and processing credit applied.

exists to increase cross-border charges and transfer pricing so as to take advantage of the tax rate arbitrage that now exists in favor of the United States.

2.1.2 Statutory Changes in the System—Canada

For the most part, recent corporate tax reform in Canada was proposed in 1985, and implementation began in February 1986. Significant technical amendments have been introduced almost every year since, and presently Bill C-18, dated May 30, 1991, consolidates amendments released in draft form in July 1990 and again, after extensive consultation, in February 1991. The amendments proposed in Bill C-18, yet to be passed into law (i.e., given "royal assent"), relate not only to federal budget initiatives, the traditional ways of introducing tax changes in Canada, but also to various other initiatives introduced by Canada's minister of finance by way of press releases and other pronouncements.

The major statutory changes in the system in Canada in the period 1983 through 1989, as they might affect Canadian subsidiaries of U.S. parents, are as follows:

- Rates of tax (see table 2.3)
- Capital cost allowance (tax depreciation)
- Repeal of the inventory allowance
- Corporate surtaxes
- Increase in the effective statutory tax rate on manufacturing profits

- Investment tax credits
- Scientific research and experimental development tax credit
- Tax avoidance—general antiavoidance rule (GAAR)

Rates of Tax

As referred to earlier, table 2.3 indicates what happened to statutory rates of tax in Canada between 1985 and 1989. More important, however, the average rates of corporate income tax (tax divided by book profits) in Canada have increased as a result of a number of initiatives. These initiatives are discussed below.

Capital Cost Allowance

Capital cost allowance has been curtailed by way of reduced rates on specific categories of assets. For example, manufacturing and processing machinery and equipment, with certain exceptions, falls into a 25 percent declining balance class after tax reform, as opposed to the former 50 percent straight-line rule.

Repeal of the Inventory Allowance

In taxation years commencing before February 26, 1986, the Income Tax Act (the "act") provided for a deduction in computing income from business or property of an amount equal to 3 percent of tangible property held in inventory for sale and for the purposes of being processed, fabricated, manufactured, incorporated into, attached to, or otherwise converted into or used in the packaging of property for sale in the ordinary course of business. The inventory allowance, an effective rate reduction for taxpayers with inventories of tangible property was to compensate for inflation given the use of first-in, first-out accounting for tax purposes in Canada.

Corporate Surtaxes

Canada has a relatively long history of corporate surtax as a means of temporarily adjusting the statutory rate of corporate income tax as it applies to specific categories of taxpayers. Initially, the corporate surtax applied only to taxable production profits from a mineral resource and manufacturing and processing profits, to the extent that profits exceeded a percentage (30 percent) of the corporation's Canadian manufacturing and processing profits, at a rate of 10 percent of tax otherwise payable. For the year 1983, the rate of surtax was basically 2½ percent of tax otherwise payable.[6] For the year 1984, the rate of surtax was 5 percent.[7] In 1985 and 1986, Canada had a break from surtax, but in 1987, the corporate surtax was reintroduced for taxation years

---

6. Section 123.5 of the act, repealed by 1985, c.45, S.69(1).
7. Section 123.3 of the act, repealed by 1985, c.45, S.69(1).

ending after 1986 at a rate of 3 percent of tax otherwise payable.[8] That rate of surtax continues to be applicable.

Various provinces have also used a corporate surtax as a means of temporarily adjusting their effective rates of corporate income tax. Quebec for example, introduced a corporate surtax at a rate of 7.25 percent, beginning May 1, 1986.

Increase in the Effective Tax Rate on Manufacturing Profits

As an incentive to expanding manufacturing and processing in Canada, as opposed to the export of raw materials from Canada's rich natural resource base, Canada introduced in 1972 a favorable rate of tax on "Canadian manufacturing and processing profits" determined as part of income according to a formula set out in regulations to the act. Initially, the rate of reduction in the corporate tax rate otherwise applicable was 9 percent, reducing to 7 percent for taxation years ending after June 1987. (Canadian-controlled private corporations were permitted an even greater reduction.) After June 1988, the rate of reduction was reduced to 5 percent of Canadian manufacturing and processing profits.

Investment Tax Credits

Complex provisions have provided for investment tax credits in Canada since the mid-1970s as a means of encouraging capital investment. The rates in Canada vary according to region. The general rate of credit is 7 percent but can vary up to 60 percent (before 1989) and 45 percent (after 1988) for an "approved project property." To the extent of a taxpayer's "annual investment tax credit limit" (basically, for Canadian subsidiaries, the aggregate of $24,000 plus three-fourths of the tax otherwise payable in excess of $24,000), a taxpayer may deduct the investment tax credit from tax otherwise payable. Because of the variation in rates, regions, projects, and circumstances, any comparison of investment tax credits allowable in the years 1983–89 is difficult. Suffice it to say that rates of credit were declining in the period.

Scientific Research and Experimental Development Tax Credit

Canada permits an immediate deduction of both *current* expenditures on scientific research (as determined to be qualified according to detailed regulations) made both in and outside Canada and *capital* expenditures on scientific research made in Canada.[9]

In the period 1983–89, the rules with respect to what qualified as "scientific research and experimental development" were tightened several times. However, outside of the province of Quebec, the general statement can be made

---

8. Section 123.2 of the act.
9. Sections 37 and 37.1 of the act.

that Canada's rules do not provide sufficient tax incentive, relative to the U.S. rules on research and development, to shift major research projects and the costs and tax effects thereof from Canada to the United States.

Tax Avoidance—GAAR

The general antiavoidance rule, commonly referred to as the GAAR, is applicable with respect to transactions entered into on or after September 13, 1988, other than grandfathered transactions.[10] Much has been said and written about the GAAR, and no paper on corporate income taxation can be considered complete without at least some reference to its existence. Like most good antiavoidance provisions in any taxing statute, the GAAR does its job most effectively by just being there.

Specific transactions may be attacked by Canada using the GAAR, but the act has always had avoidance provisions[11] and provisions which specifically address transactions between persons not dealing with each other at arm's length.[12] Therefore, it does not appear likely that the GAAR will have any dramatic impact upon parent/subsidiary behavior from a tax viewpoint.

2.1.3   Nonstatutory Changes—Canada

Administrative procedures and assessing practices are becoming much more focused and efficient in terms of tax collection. In the area of transfer pricing of goods sold between parent and subsidiary or between any related nonresident entities and the Canadian subsidiary, Canada is considerably more active and diligent than in the past in reviewing the basis for the transfer pricing. Tax cases which, as a result of review of transfer pricing issues by Revenue Canada, Taxation, have proceeded to the courts evidence mixed results.[13] It is safe to say that taxpayers are much more aware of the need to adequately support transfer prices used in intercompany transactions, even though there is clearly a tax motivation (at least since 1986) to charge the Canadian subsidiary the highest price justifiable for the goods. To some degree, this tax motivation is countered by customs duties, payable on transaction value for the goods.

Our study makes no attempt to focus on the issue of transfer pricing.

Revenue Canada, Taxation, is also focusing more sharply in recent years on other cross-border charges such as interest, rents, royalties, and management and administration fees and charges that are supportable as reimbursement for specific costs and expenses incurred by the parent on behalf of and for the benefit of the Canadian subsidiary. Specific expense reimbursements are de-

---

10. Section 245 of the act.
11. Former subsections 245(1) and 245(2) of the act, amended by 1988, c.55, S.185(1).
12. For example, see section 69 of the act.
13. *The Queen* v. *Irving Oil Ltd.*, (1991) DTC 5106 (F.C.A.); *Dominion Bridge Co. Ltd.* v. *The Queen*, (1977) DTC 5367 (F.C.A.); *Spur Oil Ltd.* v. *The Queen*, (1981) DTC 5168 (F.C.A.); *Aluminum Co. of Canada Ltd.* v. *The Queen*, (1974) DTC 6408 (F.C.T.D.)

ductible in Canada and can be paid to nonresidents without any Canadian withholding tax being applied. (The income received by the parent is treated as U.S.-source income.) There is therefore a tax motivation for charging the Canadian subsidiary the maximum for such costs. During the period 1983–89, the rules in this regard remained unchanged except for the change in the treaty in 1985 which effectively removed the requirement that management fees be a reimbursement of costs and included such fees as part of business profits.

However, what might be referred to as the "tax tension" between Canada and the United States has increased significantly with respect to cross-border charges. Although Revenue Canada, Taxation, admittedly struggles at the assessing level to ascertain exactly what it should be asking for in the way of factual support for cross-border charges, it is nevertheless much more active in reviewing and questioning the deductibility of such costs. From a U.S. perspective, on the other hand, there may be a strong need in many cases to bring funds back to the United States (to repay high interest rate debt, to fund expansion in the United States and elsewhere, to eliminate exchange risks on potential devaluation of the Canadian dollar, etc.). In addition, the Internal Revenue Service (IRS) is equally becoming more diligent in applying the provisions of the code[14] to costs and expenses which from a U.S. tax standpoint are legitimately chargeable to the Canadian subsidiary.

Interest, rents, and royalties are fully deductible for tax purposes in Canada (assuming that reasonableness and capitalization tests are met) and subject only to Canadian nonresident withholding tax upon payment or credit (15 percent in the case of interest and 10 percent in the case of royalties when paid or credited to the United States).[15]

The discussion needs to be taken further. During the period studied, some U.S. parents that were substantially indebted as a result of leveraged buyout and other acquisition financing took steps to move some of the debt out of the United States and into Canada and other foreign subsidiaries. Arrangements were made with Canadian lenders, sometimes with the guarantee of the U.S. parent, to provide financing to the Canadian subsidiary. This allowed the subsidiary to repatriate more dividends or other funds to the U.S. parent.

In more recent years, acquisition debt has actually been arranged in Canada for the acquisition price related to the Canadian subsidiary. As a result, interest that might in previous years have been included in the total cross-border charges paid or credited by the Canadian subsidiary may now be directly paid to Canadian lenders and the statistics on cross-border charges affected accordingly. To what degree this has occurred can only be determined by more detailed analysis.

---

14. Section 482 of the code.

15. Paragraphs 212(1)(b) and 212(1)(d), respectively, and Article XI with respect to interest, Article VI with respect to rents, and Article XII with respect to royalties, of the treaty.

2.1.4 Statutory Changes in the System—United States

The United States experienced significant reform of its corporate income tax system in both 1984 and 1986. Those reforms affected not only domestic U.S. operations and income but also the determination of foreign-source income for U.S. purposes and the allowable foreign tax credits for income taxes paid outside the United States.

1984 Reforms

Prior to the reforms introduced in 1984, earnings and profits of a foreign corporation were generally classified and maintained on an overall basis. A U.S. corporation, in the determination of the foreign tax credit limitation, had the opportunity of averaging high- and low-taxed income in one overall foreign tax credit limitation calculation. Only certain interest income and dividends from domestic international sales corporation (DISC) required the calculation of separate foreign tax credit limitations.

In addition, prior to 1984, a U.S. taxpayer corporation could create foreign-source income simply by earning income through a foreign corporation. Interest income, otherwise subject to separate limitation, could be converted into income subject to the overall foreign tax credit limitation by earning the interest income through a foreign corporation.

The 1984 tax reform act introduced two very important changes with respect to the determination of U.S. foreign tax credits:

1. U.S.-source treatment was prescribed for certain income regardless of the fact that such income would otherwise be classified as foreign-source income (only for the purposes of the foreign tax credit limitation).

2. "Look-through" rules were introduced, which provided that interest income generated by certain foreign corporations retained its character as interest income upon an actual or deemed distribution or when paid out as interest. Foreign corporations could no longer be used as a vehicle for transforming into foreign-source income what would otherwise be U.S.-source income.

Interest retained its character as interest. Such interest income and associated foreign taxes, commonly referred to as "separate limitation interest," were subject to their own separate foreign tax credit limitation.

Separate "baskets," or pools, of foreign earnings, for purposes of determining the foreign tax credit limitation, were created for foreign sales corporation (FSC) dividends and for taxable income of an FSC attributable to foreign trade income.

1986 Reforms

The Tax Reform Act of 1986 (1986 TRA) maintained the basic principle of the overall (as opposed to separate-country) foreign tax credit limitation. However, the 1986 TRA added a number of separate baskets for determining the total foreign tax credit limitation. This expanded system of baskets was designed to prevent averaging of low-tax foreign-source income with high-tax foreign-source income. The foreign tax credit rules, as amended by the 1986 TRA, provide that deemed-paid foreign tax credits should be applied separately with respect to each foreign tax credit limitation basket. Five foreign tax credit limitation baskets were increased to at least nine by adding separate baskets for financial services income, shipping income, high withholding tax interest, and dividends from each noncontrolled code section 902 foreign corporation.

Look-through rules were expanded to ensure that the character of the earnings and profits and foreign taxes paid were preserved for purposes of determining the foreign tax credit.

In addition, foreign income taxes paid or accrued with respect to a separate category of income now include, under the amendments of the 1986 TRA, only those taxes that are "related" to income falling into a separate basket. For example, if foreign law exempted a particular type, or category, of income from tax, then no foreign income taxes would be allocable to that income.

The foreign tax credit limitation regulations, as amended in the 1986 TRA, prescribe detailed rules for the allocation of expenses, including interest, against income in each separate basket. Interest paid to related persons is first netted against foreign personal holding company income; the excess, along with other expenses, is allocated to the income included in each separate basket.

Under the law, as it existed prior to the 1986 TRA, taxpayers could minimize the expenses allocated against foreign-source income by applying the expense allocation regulations on a separate-company basis. Using this method, if the debt was incurred by a Canadian subsidiary that had only U.S. income or assets, the interest expense would be entirely allocable to U.S.-source income, regardless of the income or assets of other members of the group. The regulations, as they then existed, also allowed taxpayers to allocate interest expense on the basis of U.S. or foreign gross income relative to total gross income as an alternative to allocating expenses on the basis of U.S. or foreign assets relative to total assets.

It was a common practice for U.S. companies to hold all foreign subsidiaries in a U.S. holding company with no debt, so that all U.S. interest expense was allocated against U.S. income.

The 1986 TRA amended the law so that interest expense of an affiliated group of corporations must be apportioned between U.S. and foreign sources by taking into account all assets of the U.S.-affiliated group as if it were one corporation. The gross income method for computing the amount of interest expense that can be allocated to foreign and U.S. sources is no longer available.

This new rule for allocating interest applies to interest expenses incurred in tax years beginning after 1986, but only with regard to the interest associated with the increase in the aggregate amount of indebtedness outstanding on November 16, 1985. Specific phase-in rules apply to interest expense associated with the debt outstanding on or before November 16, 1985.

General and administrative expenses, which under prior law were allocable on a separate-company basis, under the 1986 TRA are also allocable by treating an affiliated group as one taxpayer.

Rents and royalties, however, are treated as income in a separate category to the extent that such rents or royalties are allocable to the income of a foreign corporation in the separate category.

Rules first published in 1977 with respect to the allocation of research and development expenditures but subject to a moratorium introduced in 1982 were reenacted by the 1986 TRA. Under these rules, most research and development expenses are allocated to U.S. foreign sources either on the basis of U.S. or foreign sales over total sales or under the optional gross income method. The new rules were applicable for the taxable year beginning after August 1, 1986, and on or before August 1, 1987.

The combination of the expansion of the number of pools, or baskets, and the allocation of expenses, including interest, to each separate pool of income generally resulted in U.S. corporate taxpayers with excess foreign tax credits in the active-income basket and excess limitations in the other separate baskets. Requiring earnings and profits and related foreign taxes to be maintained in separate pools based on income categories prevents taxpayers from taking advantage of varying effective rates of foreign tax on different types of income in order to maximize the foreign tax credit.

The 1986 TRA changed what was an elective method of computing earnings and profits (referred to as the "partial section 946 method") to a required method (functional currency method). The "functional" currency is the currency used for calculating subsidiary earnings and profits. After 1986, the functional currency method required assets and liabilities as well as profits to be maintained in foreign currency, except for currencies of hyperinflationary countries and contiguous countries. One new requirement, however, was added. Foreign taxes, under the 1986 TRA, are maintained in U.S. dollars rather than in local currency.

Maintaining earnings and profits in a functional currency and foreign income tax in U.S. dollars can have a significant impact on the effective foreign tax rate. When the Canadian dollar has appreciated vis-à-vis the U.S. dollar from the date the earnings were generated to the time the earnings were distributed or deemed distributed, then the effective tax rate on the earnings of the Canadian corporation decreases.[16] Table 2.2 shows the Canadian dollar exchange rates for the years 1983–89.

Prior to the 1986 TRA and effective for years prior to 1987, earnings and profits for purposes of the foreign tax credit limitation rules were determined on a year-by-year basis. Foreign taxes paid were also allocated year by year. It was possible for some taxpayers to structure effective foreign tax rates by

16. For example, assume that income earned in 1989, at a time when the Canadian dollar was at 80 cents (relative to the U.S. dollar), is repatriated by way of dividend to the U.S. percentage in 1991, when the Canadian dollar has appreciated to 90 cents. Assume further a Canadian federal and provincial income tax rate of 40 percent on the 1989 earnings of the Canadian subsidiary.

not claiming discretionary deductions in one year and maximizing discretionary deductions in another taxation year (sometimes referred to as the "rhythm method"). The discretionary deductions often used in Canada for such purposes were capital cost allowances (discretionary as opposed to the U.S. "claimed or claimable" rule) and specific reserves and allowances (e.g., allowance for doubtful accounts). Such discretionary deductions, determined according to U.S. rules, would reduce earnings and profits for U.S. purposes.

Rather than paying dividends, say, of equal amounts, in two successive taxation years, a dividend of the same aggregate amount might be paid in the year of higher Canadian taxes. When measured as a ratio of that year's earnings and profits, the aggregate dividend (the numerator in the foreign tax credit limitation formula) would represent a higher proportion of that year's foreign taxes paid and creditable according to the limitation formula. Because the deductions were discretionary, the only additional Canadian tax cost involved in the process would be the imputed interest cost of the timing difference of the deductions.

By replacing the year-by-year calculation of U.S. earnings and profits with an accumulation-of-years, or pooling, basis, the 1986 TRA eliminated any advantage of the use of the rhythm method in claiming foreign tax credits.

The 1986 TRA made other changes that had an indirect, if not direct, effect on foreign tax credit imitations. Effective July 1, 1987, the top rate of corporate income tax was reduced from 46 percent to 34 percent (for a calendar-year taxpayer, the rate for 1987 would be 40 percent). Although the rate of tax was reduced, a number of measures were adopted to broaden the base upon which tax was imposed. Some of the more significant amendments adopted were:

1. The replacement of the existing "add-on minimum tax" with a new corporate "*alternative* minimum tax," in an attempt to ensure that all corporations with financial statement income pay some tax currently on that income.

2. The revamping of the accelerated cost recovery system (ACRS) introduced in 1981. The new ACRS rules were designed to more evenly match

Year	Income of Canadian Subsidiary		Dividend Paid to U.S. Parent		Canadian Income Taxes Paid (40%)*		Effective Tax Rate Applicable to Dividend
	Canadian	U.S.	Canadian	U.S.	Canadian	U.S.	
1989	$1.00	$0.80			$0.40	$0.32	
1991			$1.00	$0.90			$0.32/$0.90 = 35.6%

*Not including Canadian withholding taxes on dividend to U.S. parent.

The Canadian income taxes paid, in U.S. dollars equal to 40 percent of $.80, or $.32, are measured relative to a dividend of U.S. $.90 in 1991, and the effective rate of Canadian income taxes, exclusive of applicable Canadian withholding taxes on the dividend, decreases from 40 percent to U.S. $.90 ÷ U.S. $.32, or 35.6 percent.

class lives with economic or useful lives of particular assets and were effective mainly for property placed in service after July 31, 1986. The new system of ACRS, generally speaking, is less generous than the combination of the old ACRS and the investment tax credits.

3. The introduction of new limitations on the use of net operating loss carryovers, effective where there is more than a 50 percent ownership change, by value, of a loss corporation.

4. The introduction of new rules with respect to the measurement and timing of taxable income (for example, new uniform cost capitalization rules).

2.1.5   Nonstatutory Changes—United States

In a mature tax environment such as the United States, it should not be surprising that tax collectors become more sophisticated, knowledgeable, and hence more aggressive. As expected, the IRS has focused considerable attention on costs and expenses allocable to the earning of income from Canadian subsidiaries and repatriated to the U.S. parent by way of dividends. Rules which have existed for a long time (e.g., the provisions of section 482 of the code) are now more consistently and more stringently applied. Audit teams are trained in the area of international operations, and sophisticated techniques such as functional analysis as being applied to the issue of transfer pricing. The capacity of the IRS is enhanced by the same technology available to private business, and the exchange-of-information provisions of various treaties form the basis for a joint audits of international operations and much more detailed knowledge of foreign subsidiaries of U.S. parents.

2.2   Predictions regarding Tax Reform Impacts

This section outlines the predicted responses in behavior of U.S. multinationals following the tax changes discussed in section 2.1.[17] The U.S. and Canadian reforms are expected to affect three financial variables: debt, cross-border charges, and dividends. We do not try to investigate the impact of tax reform on investment decisions.

Hypothesis 1: Tax Reform Measures Adopted in 1986–87 Favor Local Debt Finance of U.S. Subsidiaries in Canada

As cited in section 2.1, two tax factors would particularly encourage more debt being issued in Canada by U.S. subsidiaries. First, the higher statutory tax rate in Canada relative to the United States encourages debt finance in Canada, where nominal interest deductions have greater tax value to the

---

17. The discussion in this section refers to earlier theoretical work, particular that developed by Bruce (1989) and Leechor and Mintz (1990). See also Horst (1977), Jun (1990), Slemrod (1990), Grubert and Mutti (1989), and Hines and Hubbard (1990), who have tested the effects of tax policy on investment or financial variables.

firm.[18] Although particularly true for U.S. companies in an excess credit position, it also applies to companies in a deficient credit position.[19] Second, the new U.S. rules for the allocation of interest costs encourage debt to be issued by the Canadian subsidiary (and discourage debt to be issued by the parent to finance investments in Canada). As noted above, the 1986 U.S. reform requires parents to allocate U.S. borrowing costs to the subsidiary based on the allocation of assets of a corporate group.

Although these tax factors suggest that the Canadian and U.S. reforms encourage more debt finance taken in Canada rather than in the United States, there is at least one tax factor that would point to a reduction in the use of debt finance by both the subsidiary and the parent. Reform-induced lower statutory corporate tax rates in both countries encourage the parent and subsidiary to reduce leverage.[20] On the other hand, the broadening of tax bases in both the United States and Canada reduces the incidence of potential tax losses, thereby encouraging more leverage as interest deductions become more valuable to companies that were previously not paying taxes despite the reduction in statutory corporate tax rates.

Other economic factors also have affected leverage over this period. The 1981–82 recession in Canada led to a significant increase in debt ratios due to shortages of cash flow.[21] As a result, leverage ratios were high in 1983, falling over time as economic recovery took place. Also, the recession may have increased bankruptcy risk (captured by the past variance in rates of return on capital), thereby discouraging leverage by Canadian firms after 1982.

Hypothesis 2: Cross-Border Charges Would Increase as a Result of U.S. and Canadian Tax Reform in 1986–87. They Would Also Be Positively Correlated with Remitted Dividends Paid to the U.S. Parent as Parents Average Excess and Deficient Credits on Remitted Income to Reduce Canadian and U.S. Taxes Paid.

As remarked above, after U.S. and Canadian reforms, Canadian corporate tax rates were generally higher than U.S. rates. To take advantage of the

18. See Halpern and Mintz (1991) for specific calculations on the impact of the higher corporate tax rate in Canada on the cost of debt finance of U.S. multinationals. These calculations do not take into account Canadian "thin capitalization" rules that limit interest deductions of non-arm's-length debt held by foreign parents in their subsidiaries.

19. See Leechor and Mintz (1990) for a derivation of the cost of issuing debt when a company is in a deficient tax credit position. Additional debt taken in Canada could increase or reduce the rate of U.S. tax on remitted dividends, depending on the differences between the tax bases as well as between statutory rates of tax of the two countries.

20. See Bartholdy, Fisher, and Mintz (1989) and MacKie-Mason (1990) for evidence that a reduction in tax benefits of interest deductions from corporate taxable income reduces the incentive to issue debt. Of course, as remarked in section 2.1, the significant rise in leveraged buyout (LBO) debt in the United States had increased leverage there for many parents, including some in our sample. We are not able to investigate this matter because we do not have matching data for the parent companies.

21. Bartholdy, Fisher, and Mintz (1989), MacKie-Mason (1990), and readings in Hubbard (1990) confirm the importance of cash flow in reducing leverage.

higher Canadian corporate tax rate, there would have been an incentive to take deductions for interest, management fees, royalties, and specific expense reimbursements, especially those items that are not subject to withholding tax or are taxed at low withholding rates in Canada.

In addition, the U.S. reform did not broaden the tax base for the calculation of earnings and profits, but it did lower the corporate tax rate on earnings and profits. Thus, many parents found that they moved from a deficient to excess credit position. When companies are remitting income to the United States, excess credits are not desirable from a tax-minimizing point of view since they are not being applied to taxes on other forms of income earned by the parent. The tax cost of remitting dividend and other sources of income is the Canadian withholding tax, which cannot be credited when the parent is in an excess credit position. This tax could be more than U.S. tax (net of deemed-paid foreign tax credits) paid on remitted income when the parent is in a small deficient tax credit position.

To minimize excess tax credits on remitted income in Canada, the parent could try, by taking more deductions in Canada, to reduce taxes paid in Canada. If they qualify under U.S. basket rules, the remitted cross-border charges would also generate a deficient credit position on income taxed at the U.S. rate, soaking up any excess credits, particularly on dividends. This form of averaging reduces taxes paid in Canada without increasing the amount of taxes paid to the U.S. government on remitted income.

During this period, nonstatutory tax factors also affected the use of cross-border charges by multinationals. As remarked in section 2.1, administrative practices by tax authorities in Canada and the United States changed with respect to the auditing of U.S. parent and subsidiary accounts. Cross-border charges were particularly subject to diligent review by authorities, and companies were less apt to use them.

Hypothesis 3: Tax Reform in the Period 1986–87 Reduces the Incentive to Reinvest Earnings in Canada. Dividend Payouts Would Increase after Tax Reform.

The impact of tax reform on U.S. subsidiary dividend payouts is quite difficult to determine theoretically. In theory, the tax cost of remitting dividends is the Canadian withholding tax rate when the parent is in an excess credit position and the U.S. tax rate (net of foreign corporate and withholding credits) when the parent is in a deficient tax credit position. It is commonly accepted that the incentive for a subsidiary is to defer payment of taxes by reinvesting profits to avoid payment of taxes on remitted income.[22] However, the tax cost of paying dividends is zero when the deficient tax credit position is

---

22. This is due to Hartman (1985), who models the "new," or "trapped equity," view that dividends are simply surplus over investment needs. The result applies for the excess tax credit case only when host country corporate income and withholding taxes are solely paid on income

equal to withholding taxes payable on dividends.[23] In this case, the parent is indifferent to paying out dividends or to reinvesting earnings from a tax point of view. Thus, the tax deterrent to paying out dividends is minimized as long as the parent can average excess credits on some sources of income with deficient tax credits on other sources.

Prior to tax reform in Canada, many companies faced relatively low average corporate tax rates. Thus, the U.S. tax on remitted income could be quite high, significantly deterring repatriation of dividends to the U.S. parent. However, there were two important methods that could be used to minimize taxes paid on remitted earnings. First, parent companies could remit income from other sources (e.g., dividends from high-tax countries, cross-border charges) and virtually eliminate any U.S. tax on remitted earnings.[24] Second, when dividends were remitted, Canadian subsidiaries could delay claiming capital cost allowances, resource write-offs, and investment tax credits and push up their average tax rates, thereby eliminating any U.S. tax on remitted dividends (the so-called rhythm method).[25]

Canadian and U.S. tax reforms changed the tax positions of the subsidiary and parent in several ways. The increased Canadian corporate tax payments expected to result from Canadian tax reform (and reduced U.S. average tax rate on earnings and profits in Canada) reduced, if not eliminated, the difference between Canadian and U.S. average tax rates. This subsequently reduced the tax incentive to reinvest earnings in Canada.

On the other hand, as discussed in section 2.1, U.S. tax reform also restricted the ability of U.S. parent companies to minimize U.S. taxes on dividend repatriations by "basket clause" provisions and by the requirement to pool earnings over time. To the extent these provisions are effective, the incentive to reinvest earnings is increased. Although these limitations are important, the scope for averaging excess and deficient tax credits to eliminate U.S. taxes on foreign-source earnings has not been fully curtailed. However,

---

remitted to the parent. Hartman, however, modeled the multinational investment decision for a deficient tax credit position assuming that the U.S. tax rate minus the Canadian tax rate is exogenous. As Leechor and Mintz (1990) point out, this result only holds when tax bases are similar across countries. If the tax base in the host country is larger than in the home country, it may be optimal to finance investment with local debt and pay out dividends to the parent.

23. See Hines and Hubbard (1990) for a test of the effect of taxes on the dividend payout of U.S. subsidiary companies. They assume the tax price of remitted income to be zero when the parent is in an excess credit position. This is not correct because the true tax cost is the withholding tax imposed by the host country. In a similar way, the tax price for the deficient tax credit case is the U.S. tax, net of foreign tax credits, plus withholding tax paid on remitted dividends. If the amount of tax is negative (and credited against offset U.S. tax), the tax price of dividends may be less in the deficient tax credit position than in the excess credit position.

24. See Hines and Hubbard (1990) for evidence of this for 1984.

25. Indeed, in the year that the dividends are not remitted, the subsidiary could create a tax loss by claiming stored-up deductions and credits and carry back the loss without affecting its previous foreign tax credit for U.S. tax purposes.

the incentive to use the rhythm method described above has been virtually eliminated.

The above discussion suggests that tax reform only reduced the incentive to reinvest earnings, not eliminated it entirely. So why should dividend payouts increase? Two related answers are provided for this. First, companies may have had nontax reasons to remit dividends (Hines and Hubbard 1990). As discussed above, many U.S. parents faced cash flow shortages due to increased leverage (e.g., LBOs). Cash flow from foreign subsidiaries would alleviate the need to raise funds in the United States. Second, the interest allocation rules, discouraging leverage in the United States, induced U.S. parents to remit income from Canada to buy down U.S. debt.

Other nontax factors might explain changes in dividend payouts. Exchange rate risk, the increase in the value of the Canadian dollar (beginning in 1987), and perceived lower profitability in Canada would induce an outflow of dividends from Canada to the United States commensurate with a reduction in subsidiary investment in Canada.

In the following section, we provide some evidence on the impact of tax reform with respect to the above three hypotheses.

2.3   Data and Empirical Results

2.3.1   Description of Data

As remarked above, selected data were compiled for twenty-eight companies on a confidential basis. In some years, data were missing for ten of the twenty-eight companies.

Of the companies chosen, most were in manufacturing and resource industries. The companies also varied considerably by size. In 1989, two were in the range of $5 million to $10 million total assets, ten were in the range of $10 million to $25 million of assets, eight were between $25 million and $100 million, and eight had assets of more than $100 million.

Except for five companies, the U.S. parents of the Canadian subsidiaries were in an excess credit position for all years. We have not yet been able to determine the status of the other five over the whole period, although they were in a deficient tax credit position for the latter part of the period. In the past few years, three of the deficient tax credit companies were of the largest size. Three of the five companies issued dividends, and all five had cross-border charges in the past three years. Given the lack of data at this point regarding the deficient tax credit position, we are unable to do further analysis of this case.

With the data, we calculated several variables that are of particular interest in this paper:

1. DIV: Dividends remitted to the parent
2. CBC: Cross-border charges (royalties, management fees, interest, and specific expense reimbursements)

3. Z: After-tax book income prior to the deduction of cross-border charges

4. NI: Net income—after-tax book income net of cross-border charges

5. ATR: The average tax rate computed as federal and provincial corporate income taxes paid dividend by before-tax income

6. RE: The return to equity computed as after-tax book income divided by equity reserves plus minority interest

7. D/A: The debt-asset ratio computed as debt liabilities divided by total assets[26]

8. DIV/NI: The dividend payout ratio computed as dividends divided by net income

9. CBC/Z and DIV/Z: The cross-border charges and dividend ratios expressed as a proportion of net income prior to the deduction of cross-border charges

The data set also had other information related to tax information (e.g., investment tax and foreign tax credits), which is not reported below for the purposes of this paper.

2.3.2 Presentation of Aggregate Data for Companies

In tables 2.4 through 2.6, we provide some descriptive data indicating the financial behavior of the companies on an aggregate basis. For this purpose, we have dropped data in those years in which companies incurred a loss for book purposes (4 of 155 observations). Otherwise, some of the variables, particularly the dividend payout and cross-border charge ratios, would be negative in value. In terms of the aggregate value of ratios (DIV/NI, DIV/Z, and CBC/Z), the ratios are somewhat understated by eliminating the years in which companies had book losses.

Table 2.4 presents year-by-year and subperiod ratios for financial variables, aggregated across companies. We note that the dividend payout ratio from 1983 to 1989 more than doubled over the years, while the CBC and leverage ratios hardly changed. Somewhat surprising to us, Canadian average tax rates declined rather than increased after tax reform, and the rate of return to equity rose significantly. Results in this table seem to reject most of the hypotheses offered in the previous section. Only the dividend payout ratio increased. Certainly, the higher dividend payout ratio is not indicative of poor economic opportunities in Canada, given the high returns to equity.[27] Instead, it seems the U.S. parents needed to get money home, perhaps arising from the need to buy down debt issued by the parent.

Table 2.5 separates companies according to whether they paid dividends or

---

26. We also measured leverage as debt divided by fixed assets. There are few differences in these results, compared to that obtained below. Leverage ratios and rates of return to equity are not corrected for inflation.

27. We found that the unweighted mean growth rate in fixed assets during the 1987–89 period was close to 15 percent, 3.6 percent above the 1983–85 mean. The average growth in fixed assets of companies that paid dividends sometime in the years 1987–89 increased 3.9 percent over the 1983–85 time period. Only three companies reduced investments in Canada and remitted dividends.

Table 2.4   **Average Financial Ratios for All U.S.-Owned Companies Operating in Canada—1983–89 with Positive Net Income**

Year	Number of Companies	Dividend Payout Ratio (DIV/NI)	Cross-Border Charges (CBC)* Ratio	Leverage*	Average Tax Rate (ATR)	Return to Equity (RE)	Mean Asset Size ($ million)
83	18	.31	.18	.47	.31	.19	
84	20	.33	.16	.33	.35	.22	
85	22	.27	.12	.44	.30	.20	
86	24	.54	.14	.42	.32	.21	
87	24	.48	.17	.38	.37	.24	
88	23	.82	.17	.44	.27	.25	
89	20	.70	.17	.41	.17	.31	
83–85	60	.30	.15	.42	.32	.20	$72.9
87–89	67	.68	.17	.42	.27	.27	99.6
83–89	151	.56	.16	.42	.29	.24	88.2

Source: Authors' computations.

Note: See Sec. 2.3.1 of text for explanation of variables.

*Leverage = Debt-asset ratio, or D/A.

Table 2.5 Average Financial Ratios for Companies Paying Dividends or Not*

Financial Ratio	1983–85			1987–89			1983–89		
	DIV > 0	DIV = 0	DIV = 0 CBC = 0	DIV > 0	DIV = 0	DIV = 0 CBC = 0	DIV > 0	DIV = 0	DIV = 0 CBC = 0
Dividend payout (DIV/NI)	.75	0	0	1.00	0	0	.97	0	0
CBC/Z	.10	.18	0	.12	.26	0	.11	.22	0
DIV/Z	.67	0	0	.88	0	0	.87	0	0
Leverage (D/A)	.44	.42	.54	.44	.36	.70	.45	.39	.57
ATR	.36	.29	.22	.22	.35	.47	.27	.32	.26
RE†	.22	.19	.19	.28	.25	.21	.26	.21	.19
Percent of total number†	16.7	83.3	33.9	44.8	55.2	26.5	33.1	67.9	30.9
Percent of total assets†	34.7	65.3	19.5	68.9	31.1	56.4	53.3	46.7	14.8
Mean asset size ($ million)	$164.5	$54.7	$38.8	$153.3	$56.0	$17.0	$142.5	$61.3	$36.1

Source: Authors' computations.

Note: See Sec. 2.3.1 of text for explanation of variables.

*In years with positive net income.

†Percentage = Number or assets of firms issuing dividends, or net dividend ÷ Number or total assets of all firms in that period.

not. There are three interesting results to glean from this table. First, there was a substantial increase in the percentage of companies (both in number and weighted by assets) that issued dividends after 1986 compared to the earlier period. In fact, most companies did not remit dividends prior to 1986, while the majority began paying dividends afterward. We also note that dividend-paying firms tended to be more leveraged and larger in size, and their rate of return to equity was higher on average compared to non-dividend-paying companies.

Second, we note that dividend-paying firms, on average, relied less on cross-border charges than did non-dividend-paying firms in each period. This suggests that cross-border charges and dividend remissions were substitutes rather than complements, contradicting hypothesis 2.

Third, the average tax rate prior to 1986 was higher when companies paid dividends than when companies were non–dividend paying (36 percent versus 29 percent). This trend seems to confirm the use of the rhythm method. After tax reform, the situation reversed, and dividend-paying companies had lower average tax rates than non-dividend-paying companies.

In table 2.6, we compare ratios for companies that paid corporate income taxes to federal and provincial governments and those that did not. Most companies were taxpaying, although more tax-loss companies appeared in the prereform years compared to the period afterwards. We found that companies that did not pay income taxes did not remit dividends (although they remitted income through cross-border charges). The preference for cross-border charges arises from the lower withholding taxes on certain cross-border charges, particularly specific expense reimbursements.

These aggregate calculations (and the lack of statistical testing) do not provide the information needed to assess the impact of tax reform on financial variables. Given the small number of companies (twenty-eight), aggregate numbers are sensitive to just a few cases of firms switching categories (e.g., from non–dividend paying to dividend paying). For example, the fall in the average tax rate from the period 1983–85 to the period 1987–89 reflects just two large firms significantly lowering their taxes paid. Firm-by-firm statistical analysis is thus warranted.

2.3.2   Empirical Results

Below, we present some empirical results that test the three hypotheses presented in section 2.2. Table 2.7 provides correlation coefficients and tests of significance for various financial variables, using the individual company data. Several important results arise from this analysis.

First, when companies pay dividends, the correlation coefficient between DIV/Z and CBC/Z is positive (.53) and significant.[28] Unlike the aggregate

---

28. The correlation coefficients for DIV/Z and CBC/Z were .85 and .52 for the two subperiods 1983–85 and 1987–90, respectively.

Table 2.6   **Average Financial Ratios for U.S. Companies Operating in Canada, by Taxpaying Status in Canada***

	1983–85		1987–89		1983–89	
Financial Ratio	Tax > 0	Tax = 0	Tax > 0	Tax = 0	Tax > 0	Tax = 0
Dividend payout (DIV/NI)	.30	0	.69	0	.56	0
CBC/Z	.15	.22	.17	.26	.16	.23
DIV/Z	.25	0	.57	0	.47	0
Leverage (D/A)	.42	.67	.42	.35	.42	.57
ATR	.32	0	.27	0	.29	0
RE	.20	.13	.27	.07	.24	.10
Percent of total number†	90.0	10.0	98.5	1.5	94.7	5.3
Percent of assets†	98.4	1.6	99.1	0.9	98.5	1.5
Mean asset size ($ million)	$79.8	$11.6	$100.2	$55.4	$92.2	$17.7

Source: Authors' computations.

Note: See Sec. 2.3.1 of text for explanation of variables.

*In years with positive net income.

†Percentage = Number or assets of firms issuing dividends, or net dividend ÷ Number or total assets of all firms in that period.

time-series information presented in tables 2.4 and 2.5, this seems to indicate that companies that remit income to the United States view dividends and cross-border charges as complements rather than as substitutes. This evidence confirms hypothesis 2, that companies, when remitting income to the United States, average excess tax credits on dividends with deficient tax credits on cross-border charges to minimize U.S. tax payments.

Second, we find that the average tax rate is positively and significantly correlated with both dividend and cross-border charge ratios (for dividend-paying companies only). In addition to calculations shown in table 2.7, the correlation coefficients for ATR and DIV/Z and ATR and CBC/Z were also calculated for each subperiod. For ATR and DIV/Z, the correlation coefficients, also significant, were .56 and .53 for the 1983–85 and 1987–89 periods, respectively. For ATR and CBC/Z, the correlation coefficients were .57 and .24 for each period, respectively (both significant). In the earlier period, the positive correlations between DIV/Z and CBC/Z with ATR is consistent with a tax-minimizing strategy of using the rhythm method prior to tax reform. When companies remitted income, they increased both their Canadian taxes paid on dividends and the amount of cross-border charges to reduce U.S. taxes paid. After 1986, minimizing U.S. taxes or reducing Canadian excess credits on foreign-source income required companies to increase cross-border charges with remitted dividends, particularly if the companies were high-taxed firms.

These correlation coefficient results of table 2.7 contradict conclusions sug-

Table 2.7   **Correlation Coefficients of Selected Financial Ratios, 1983–1989†**

	D/A	DIV/Z	CBC/Z	ATR	RE
All companies					
D/A	1.0				
DIV/Z	−.01	1.0			
CBC/Z	−.08	.19	1.0		
ATR	.10	.31*	0.17	1.0	
RE	.46*	−.05	−.16	−.08	1.0
Companies with DIV > 0					
D/A	1.0				
DIV/Z	−.10				
CBC/Z	−.28*	.53*	1.0		
ATR	.12	.49*	.47*	1.0	
RE	.54*	−.19*	−.29*	−.21*	1.0
Companies with DIV = 0					
D/A	1.0				
DIV/Z	0	1.0			
CBC/Z	.01	0	1.0		
ATR	.07	0	.09	1.0	
RE	.41*	0	−.09	−.05	1.0

Source: Authors' computations.

Note: See Sec. 2.3.1 of text for explanation of variables.

*Significance of the 95 percent confidence level.

†For companies in years with positive net income.

gested by the aggregate calculations of table 2.5. Instead of average tax rates falling for dividend-paying firms after 1986, we find a positive correlation between the dividend ratio and average tax rate. Also, we find a positive correlation between cross-border charges and dividends, not the negative one suggested by the numbers of table 2.5.

The aggregate calculations of tables 2.4–2.6 also mask variation in the financial behavior of individual companies. Over the two subperiods, some companies increased certain types of financings, while others did not. To what extent has there been a significant change in financial behavior in the two subperiods 1983–85 and 1987–89? To answer this question, we calculated, for each company, the mean ratios of D/A, DIV/NI, CBC/Z, ATR, and RE for the two subperiods and subtracted the 1983–85 mean from the 1987–89 mean. A frequency distribution for each case was plotted (see the histographs in figs. 2.1–2.3)[29] and a t-test was performed to determine whether there was a significant increase or decrease in the level of each variable.[30] (The test was conducted on unweighted mean increases across all companies.)

29. The histographs are presented with a restriction that the change in the ratio lies between −1.0 and 1.0. (This eliminates certain outlying data points that would otherwise show a frequency distribution with most values falling in a small range.)

30. The t-test is based on all values that are computed except for the case of the dividend payout ratio that had two outlying values above or below 15.0 and −15.0, respectively.

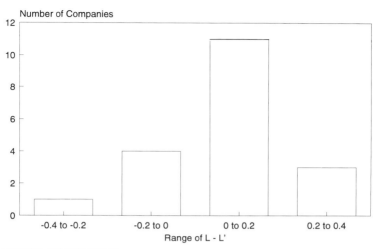

L is for 1987-89, and L' is for 1983-85.

Fig. 2.1   Changes in debt-asset ratios (L) pre- and postreform

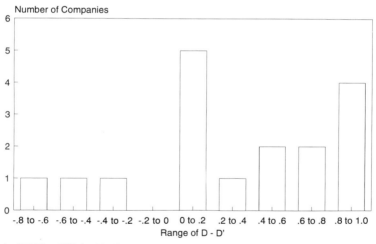

D is for 1987-89, and D' is for 1983-85.

Fig. 2.2   Changes in dividend payout ratios (D) pre- and postreform

The frequency distributions are presented below for the changes in the levels (pre- and post-1986) of debt-asset ratio (D/A), dividend payout ratio (DIV/NI), cross-border charge ratio (CBC/Z), average tax rate (ATR), and return to equity (RE). Tests on the mean change in the level of ratios were based on a 95 percent confidence test (one-tail test for value greater or less than zero). The following results were obtained:

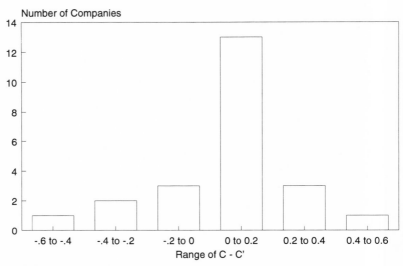

C is for 1987-89, and C' is for 1983-85.

Fig. 2.3   Changes in cross-border charge ratios (C) pre- and postreform

Hypothesis 1. The debt-asset ratio increased by .06 and for a majority of companies (about 70 percent). A one-tail t-test indicates that the mean average debt-asset ratio increased significantly (t-value of 2.27). This is consistent with hypothesis 1 that the debt-asset ratio of U.S. multinationals increased after 1986, given the higher statutory corporate tax rate in Canada relative to the United States and the effects of the new U.S. interest allocation rules.

Hypothesis 2. The cross-border ratio fell slightly, by less than .1 percent. Only 25 percent of the companies reduced their cross-border charge ratio. The decrease was found to be insignificant (t-ratio of $-.05$). This result is not consistent with hypothesis 2, which predicted an increase in cross-border charges. However, as discussed in section 2.1, there has been a change in the auditing practices of Canadian authorities that might have discouraged the use of cross-border charges to remit income.

Hypothesis 3. The dividend payout ratio was found to increase by .72 and for a majority of companies (55 percent increased the dividend payout ratio, 25 percent remained non–dividend paying throughout the period, and the remainder reduced their dividend payout ratio). A test that the dividend payout ratio increased was found to be significant (t-value of 5.1). This is consistent with the aggregate calculations shown in tables 2.4–2.6 and with hypothesis 3 that dividends remitted to U.S. parents would possibly increase, perhaps to pay down debt in the United States.

In addition, we calculated the mean increase in average tax rate and return to equity ratios. The average tax rate increased by .09 on average and was found to be significant (t-value of 2.0). The average profit rate increased .07 and was found to be significant (t-value of 2.0).

2.4 Conclusions

In summary, we find that the hypotheses seem to be confirmed by the data; in particular, the dividend payout ratio and, to a lesser extent, the debt-asset ratio of U.S. subsidiaries have increased. We also find a positive correlation between dividend and cross-border charges ratios, indicating that U.S. multinationals average excess and deficient tax credits on sources of income to minimize taxes paid to Canadian and U.S. authorities. We have not, however, found a significant increase in cross-border charges, which would have been expected after 1986 as Canadian companies restructure their payments to take advantage of the higher statutory corporate tax rate in Canada.

Much of the statistical testing in this paper was rudimentary. As discussed above, there are a number of tax and nontax factors that explain debt, dividend, and cross-border charge ratios. A full statistical analysis includes the modeling of the financial decisions of the companies so that the effects of exogenous factors, including tax reform, could be disentangled from each other. In future work, we intend to explore further this data set, as it is sufficiently rich to see how tax policy in Canada affects the financial and investment behavior of U.S. multinationals.

References

Ault, Hugh J., and David F. Bradford. 1990. Taxing international income: An analysis of the U.S. system and its economic premises. In *Taxation in the global economy,* ed., A. Razin and J. Slemrod. Chicago: University of Chicago Press.

Bartholdy, Jan, Gordon Fisher, and Jack Mintz. 1989. An empirical study of the impact of corporate taxation on debt policy of Canadian firms. Queen's University Discussion Paper no. 742. Kingston, Ont.

Bruce, Neil. 1989. The impact of tax reform on international capital flows and investment. In *Economic impacts of tax reform,* ed. J. M. Mintz and J. Whalley. Toronto: Canadian Tax Foundation.

Canada, Department of Finance. 1987. *Income tax reform.* Ottawa: Government of Canada.

Goodspeed, Timothy, and Daniel Frisch. 1989. U.S. tax policy and the overseas activities of U.S. multinational corporations: A quantitative assessment. Mimeograph.

Grubert, Harry, and John Mutti. 1989. Financial flows versus capital spending: Alternative measures of the U.S.-Canadian investment and trade in the analysis of taxes. Washington, D.C.: U.S. Department of the Treasury. Mimeograph.

Halpern, Paul, and Jack Mintz. 1991. Taxation and Canada-U.S. cross-border acquisitions. In *Corporate globalization through mergers and acquisitions*, ed. L. Waverman, Calgary: University of Calgary Press. 94.

Hartman, David. 1985. Tax policy and foreign direct investment. *Journal of Public Economics* 26:107–21.

Hines, James R., Jr., and R. Glenn Hubbard. 1990. Coming home to America: Dividend repatriations by U.S. multinationals. In *Taxation in the global economy*, ed. A. Razin and J. Slemrod. Chicago: University of Chicago Press.

Horst, Thomas. 1977. American taxation of multinational firms. *American Economic Review* 67:376–89.

Hubbard, R. Glenn. 1990. *Asymmetric information, corporate finance, and investment*. Chicago: University of Chicago Press.

Jog, Vijay, and Jack M. Mintz. 1989. Impact of Phase I corporate tax reform. In *Economic impacts of tax reform*, ed. J. M. Mintz and J. Whalley. Toronto: Canadian Tax Foundation.

Jun, Joosung. 1990. U.S. tax policy and direct investment abroad. In *Taxation in the global economy*, ed. A. Razin and J. Slemrod. Chicago: University of Chicago Press.

Leechor, Chad and Jack Mintz. 1990. On the taxation of multinational corporate investment when the deferral method is used by the capital exporting country. Toronto: University of Toronto. Mimeograph.

MacKie-Mason, Jeffrey. 1990. Do taxes affect corporate financing decisions? *Journal of Finance* 45:147–1493.

Sinn, Hans-Werner. 1987. *Capital income taxation and resource allocation*. Amsterdam: North Holland.

Slemrod, Joel. 1990. Tax effects on foreign direct investment in the United States: Evidence from a cross-country comparison. In *Taxation in the global economy*, ed. A. Razin and J. Slemrod. Chicago: University of Chicago Press.

U.S. Congress, Joint Committee on Taxation. 1987. *General explanation of the Tax Reform Act of 1986*, H.R. 3838, 99th Congress, Public Law 99-514. Washington, D.C.: U.S. Government Printing Office.

Comment   Neil Bruce

Ultimately, corporations investing abroad desire to repatriate the earnings of their investments. Tax considerations are likely to be an important influence both on the decision of how much to repatriate in a particular year and on the method—dividends, cross-border charges, and other—to be used. Hogg and Mintz make an important contribution to our knowledge of the importance of such tax considerations by examining the repatriation behavior of a select number of U.S. subsidiaries operating in Canada. They examine these firms over a time period that brackets some important tax reforms and changes that are likely, in theory, to have a substantial impact on repatriation behavior.

They begin by discussing in detail the changes in Canadian and U.S. tax law between 1984 and 1986 that would probably alter repatriation behavior.

Neil Bruce is professor of economics at the University of Washington.

Primarily, (1) U.S. statutory corporate tax rates declined relative to Canadian rates, reducing the overall foreign tax credit (FTC) limitation relative to FTCs generated; (2) additional separate limitations ('baskets') were introduced, limiting the ability to average high- and low-taxed foreign income; (3) in determining the deemed-paid FTC, foreign taxes and affiliate earnings were to be pooled over time, eliminating the advantage of the "rhythm method" of dividend repatriation; (4) sourcing and look-through rules were imposed and/or tightened to prevent U.S. parents from creating foreign income simply by redirecting passive income through foreign affiliates; and (5) U.S. parents effectively were required to allocate more expenses, particularly domestic interest expenses, to foreign income.

Hogg and Mintz proceed to formulate three hypotheses about the effect of these changes on financial and repatriation behavior: first, affiliates would be more likely to issue their own debt rather than to obtain such funds through the parent; second, cross-border charges (nondividend payments to U.S. parents) would increase; third, dividend repatriations would increase. The second and third hypotheses imply that total repatriations increase and that the firm would balance dividend and nondividend payments in order to minimize the tax liability generated.

Although no formal model of firm repatriation behavior is developed, the authors motivate their hypotheses by pointing to the changes in tax prices and tax arbitrage opportunities resulting from the tax changes. This is somewhat helpful, but I think it is instructive to consider the repatriation decision in more detail.

The decision to repatriate is a decision not so much of *whether* to repatriate but of *when* to repatriate. That is, the firm faces a choice whether to take the income home now or to reinvest its earnings in the host country for a period of time and take them home in the future. In this regard, anticipations about future tax rates become important, and observed repatriation levels may well reflect these anticipations rather than the level of taxes applying to repatriations. Although the 1986 changes probably reduced repatriation tax rates significantly, a firm need not be motivated to repatriate now if future tax rates are expected to be lower or, at least, no higher. The distinction is important because it bears on the question of whether the extraordinary increase in dividend repatriations that the authors observe in their sample can be expected to continue.

In other words, the empirical question is whether the increased repatriation levels observed occurred simply because existing tax rate levels on repatriations were lower after 1986, because firms prior to 1986 had anticipated the reduction in tax rates and postponed repatriations, or because firms believed the current tax rate applying to repatriations is abnormally low and could be expected to rise in the future, inducing them to repatriate now rather than wait. (This of course is similar to the problem faced when trying to determine how the *level* of the capital gains tax rate affects realizations.) I do not know that the Hogg and Mintz data set will be able to cast any light on this issue, but I believe it is worth examining.

Turning to the empirical part of their paper, I am struck by the fact that their results do not always relate to their hypotheses. As noted by the authors, the aggregate descriptive data seem to contradict the first and second hypotheses, with only the significant rise in dividend repatriations after 1986 supporting the hypothesis that tax changes motivated changes in repatriation behavior. The authors then report correlations of variables across firms paying dividends, a rather small sample (I believe nine firms), but they do not say whether these correlations are across pooled time-series and cross-section observations or across firms averaged over time. If the latter, the results do not directly test the hypotheses—which are about the 1984–86 changes' effects on firm behavior. The authors do report confirming evidence using *unweighted* average (across firms) values of the relevant variables over the two subperiods; but why should the unweighted averages be better than the weighted averages (i.e., aggregate data)? If one huge firm were to decrease its cross-border charges over the subperiods while two tiny firms increased theirs, I wouldn't necessarily see this as a confirming observation.

Finally, I would like to raise one concern about the representative nature of the sample. The authors state that the parent companies of twenty-three of the twenty-eight subsidiaries in their sample were in excess credit positions throughout the period studied. How representative is this? Deutsch and Jenkins (1982, 230) found that, in the 1970s, U.S. parents of Canadian subsidiaries were typically in excess limitation position, except in the petroleum and wholesale trade industries. I bring this up because companies that are in excess credit positions both before and after tax reform can be expected to respond less to the tax changes than do companies that are in excess limitation, and even less than companies that are switched from excess limitation to excess credit by the tax changes. Perhaps this contributes to the apparently contradictory nature of the aggregate data in the authors' sample.

Reference

Deutsch, Antal, and Glenn Jenkins. 1982. Tax incentives, revenue transfers, and the taxation of income from foreign investment. In *Tax policy options in the 1980s,* ed. W. R. Thirsk and J. Whalley. Toronto: Canadian Tax Foundation.

3　The Effects of U.S. Tax Policy on the Income Repatriation Patterns of U.S. Multinational Corporations

Rosanne Altshuler and T. Scott Newlon

U.S. corporations earn a substantial portion of their income from foreign sources. In 1986, the net foreign-source income reported by U.S. corporations on their U.S. tax returns was over $140 billion, which amounted to over 52 percent of their total net income.[1] Both the United States and the countries that are the source of this income generally assert the right to tax it. But U.S. tax policy attempts to some extent to balance the U.S. tax claim against a desire to prevent double taxation. This balance, and the overlapping tax claims that require it, complicates tax collection by the United States and can open various avenues for tax avoidance by U.S. multinational corporations. Such tax-avoiding behavior would reduce U.S. tax revenue and could distort international financial flows and the international allocation of investment by U.S. corporations. An important policy question is to what extent these incentives for tax avoidance actually affect the behavior of U.S. corporations and reduce tax revenue. In this paper, the authors attempt to address that question by examining the impact of tax incentives on the way in which U.S. corporations structure and coordinate remittances of income from their foreign subsidiaries.[2]

Rosanne Altshuler is assistant professor of economics at Rutgers University and a faculty research fellow of the National Bureau of Economic Research. T. Scott Newlon is an economist in the Office of Tax Analysis of the U.S. Department of the Treasury.

The authors are extremely grateful to Gordon Wilson for his assistance in using the Treasury tax data. For helpful discussions, comments, and suggestions, they thank Sheena McConnell, Joel Slemrod, Glenn Hubbard, Harry Grubert, Bill Randolph, Dan Frisch, Jim Poterba, the International Taxation Staff of the Office of Tax Analysis, and participants at the NBER Summer Institute Workshop on International Taxation. They are also grateful to Richard Wood and Rita Van Buren of Price Waterhouse for generously providing data. The conclusions expressed herein are those of the authors and do not necessarily represent the position of the U.S. Department of the Treasury.

1. These figures are from the latest tax return data available, as presented in Redmiles (1990).

2. The focus here is on the exploitation of opportunities for legal tax avoidance; we do not examine enforcement issues such as those relating to transfer pricing.

This study uses new data from 1986 U.S. corporate income tax returns to examine the effects of taxes on the patterns of remittances of income from foreign subsidiaries to their U.S. parent corporations. We focus on the behavioral effects of three important features of the U.S. tax treatment of foreign-source income: (1) the deferral of tax on the income of foreign subsidiaries of U.S. corporations until the income is remitted to the United States; (2) the credit allowed against U.S. tax for foreign taxes already paid on foreign-source income; and (3) the limitation of the foreign tax credit so that it does not exceed the U.S. tax otherwise payable on foreign-source income and therefore cannot reduce U.S. tax on domestic income. We are particularly interested in the effects on income repatriation patterns of the *global,* or *overall,* limitation that is allowed under U.S. tax law. The overall limitation allows the use of foreign tax credits generated from one source of income to offset the U.S. tax liability generated by other sources of foreign income.

Several previous studies have used aggregate data to investigate the effect of taxation on the income repatriation activity of multinationals. Kopits (1972) used U.S. tax data aggregated by country to estimate a dividend payout equation for payments from foreign subsidiaries to their U.S. parent corporations. In a subsequent study, Kopits (1976) used U.S. tax data aggregated by country and industry to estimate the effects of taxation on royalty remittances from foreign subsidiaries. Using aggregate data on U.S. foreign direct investment, Hartman (1981), Boskin and Gale (1987), Newlon (1987), Slemrod (1990b), and Jun (1990) all estimated tax effects on the retention of earnings by the foreign affiliates of U.S. companies and/or the U.S. affiliates of foreign companies. A fundamental problem with all of these studies is that the complex incentives provided by the tax system cannot necessarily be captured using aggregate data. For example, tax incentive effects on income repatriations from individual subsidiaries in the same country can vary depending upon the global tax situation of their respective parents.

Only a few studies have used microdata to examine the effect of taxes on income repatriation by multinational companies. Mutti (1981) appears to have done the earliest study. He used U.S. tax return data from 1972 to estimate the effect of tax costs on the choice of income remittance channels. Significant tax effects were found in estimates of a dividend equation using the underlying microdata. Using financial accounting data for the foreign affiliates of British companies, Alworth (1988) estimated dividend equations. He found significant effects of tax cost variables on dividend payout behavior. Both Goodspeed and Frisch (1989) and Hines and Hubbard (1990) used 1984 tax return data of a sample of U.S. corporations and their foreign subsidiaries to investigate tax effects on their income remittances. Goodspeed and Frisch matched data on parent corporations with country-specific information on their foreign subsidiaries in an attempt to quantify income repatriation incentives created by the U.S. tax system. By further disaggregating the 1984 tax return data,

Hines and Hubbard were able to study income repatriation behavior using a data set that matched foreign subsidiary–specific information to parent corporation data. Both studies found significant evidence of tax effects.

We improve on and extend the previous microdata studies in three respects. First, we use the most recently available tax return data for a large sample of U.S. corporations and their foreign subsidiaries. Second, our specification of the tax cost of income remittances from abroad more accurately reflects the tax incentives facing firms. For example, unlike Alworth (1988), we use actual company tax data to calculate the tax incentives facing firms. Whereas Goodspeed and Frisch (1989) employ foreign subsidiary data that is aggregated by country, we use a similar data set to Hines and Hubbard (1990), one that matches subsidiary-specific information with parent corporation tax information. Unlike Hines and Hubbard, when measuring tax incentives, we incorporate the withholding taxes most firms face on remittances of foreign income, and we account for some important variations in source-country corporate income tax systems. Finally, we investigate some of the dynamic aspects of the U.S. taxation of foreign-source income. We attempt to reflect these dynamics in our econometric estimates of dividend remittance equations.

The remainder of this paper is organized as follows. Section 3.1 describes the basic structure of the U.S. tax treatment of the foreign income of U.S. corporations and discusses the possible effects of this system on income repatriation incentives and the consequent policy concerns. Section 3.2 specifies the tax prices that U.S. multinational corporations pay for income remittances from their foreign subsidiaries. These tax prices measure the change in a multinational's tax liabilities caused by an incremental increase in income payments from its foreign subsidiary. Section 3.3 discusses the tax return data used in this study. Section 3.4 presents the results of our analysis of the income remittance patterns of the corporations in our sample. The final section attempts to draw some policy implications from the results.

3.1 U.S. Tax Policy Toward Foreign Income

When a U.S. corporation earns profits from its operations in a foreign country, the source country usually gets the first crack at those profits through its corporate income tax. The source country may also levy withholding taxes on remittances of income out of the country in the form of payments such as dividends, interest, rents, fees, and royalties. Like the United States, some countries also levy an additional tax, on top of the ordinary corporate income tax, on the profits of branches of foreign companies.[3]

---

3. The source country may also collect revenue through sales taxes or a value-added tax (VAT). Some of the burden of these taxes may be borne by the foreign operation of the U.S. company.

3.1.1 Deferral

The time at which the U.S. Treasury first taxes foreign profits depends on the way in which the foreign operation is organized. If it is organized as a *branch* of the U.S. corporation (i.e., it is not separately incorporated), then the United States taxes the profits as they accrue. If it is organized as a *subsidiary* (i.e., it is separately incorporated in the foreign country), then the profits are not generally taxed until they are remitted to the U.S. parent corporation. This delay in taxation until a subsidiary's profits are actually remitted to the United States is known as *deferral*.

The deferral of taxation on income earned by foreign subsidiaries is an important and controversial aspect of U.S. tax policy. Deferral gives firms an incentive to accumulate profits in low-tax jurisdictions rather than to repatriate them to the United States. Deferral is particularly relevant in this study because our data provide detailed information on the foreign subsidiaries of a sample of U.S. corporations. We do not have detailed information on their foreign branch operations.

Deferral has been attacked for allowing U.S. multinational corporations to avoid U.S. taxes on foreign income by retaining it abroad in low-tax, or tax haven, jurisdictions, in consequence favoring foreign direct investment over domestic investment. The tax code does contain restrictions that hamper the ability of multinationals to permanently avoid tax payments on overseas income held in subsidiaries. The subpart F provisions of the tax code restrict deferral on certain types of unrepatriated subsidiary income by treating it as if it was distributed as a dividend. In general, under subpart F, income that accrues from a subsidiary's passive ownership of assets (called *passive income*) is denied deferral and taxed immediately. On the other hand, income earned from the conduct of a business (called *active income*) is generally not subject to the subpart F rules and is allowed deferral.

3.1.2 Foreign Tax Credit

The United States attempts to reduce the possibility that foreign-source income could be taxed twice by allowing a credit against U.S. taxes for taxes levied by the source country. The foreign tax credit has two components. The first, called the *direct* credit, is a credit for foreign taxes paid directly on income as it is received by a U.S. taxpayer. Foreign taxes eligible for the direct credit include withholding taxes on remittances to the U.S. taxpayer, such as dividends, interest, and royalties, and also income taxes on foreign branch operations. The second component, called the *indirect,* or *deemed-paid,* credit, is a credit for foreign income taxes paid on the income out of which a distribution is made to the U.S. taxpayer. The deemed-paid credit is available to a foreign corporation's U.S. corporate shareholders who own at least 10 percent of the voting stock of the foreign corporation.

We will outline briefly how the deemed-paid credit works. Suppose subsidiary i makes a dividend payment, D_i, to its U.S. parent corporation. Since this is a distribution of profits after foreign tax, the United States considers the taxable income arising from this dividend to be the dividend *grossed up* by the foreign tax deemed paid on that dividend. The grossed-up dividend is

$$(1) \qquad\qquad D_i + T_i D_i / (Y_i - T_i) \, ,$$

where T_i denotes the total foreign income tax paid by subsidiary i and Y_i denotes the subsidiary's pretax income from the U.S. perspective, which is the subsidiary's book earnings and profits.[4] Equation (1) can be rewritten in a way that may be more familiar to economists as $D_i/(1 - \tau_i)$, where τ_i represents the average subsidiary tax rate, T_i/Y_i, on foreign earnings from the U.S. perspective. The U.S. tax on the dividend before the deemed-paid credit is $\tau D_i/(1 - \tau_i)$, where τ denotes the U.S. rate of tax. The United States considers that creditable foreign tax was paid on the dividend in the amount of $\tau_i D_i/(1 - \tau_i)$. The U.S. tax liability on the dividend payment is therefore $D_i(\tau - \tau_i)/(1 - \tau_i)$.

The amount of foreign tax credit that can actually be used is limited, however, to the amount of U.S. tax payable on foreign income. Therefore, if the foreign tax rate, τ_i, exceeds the U.S. tax rate, τ, *excess credits* are created in the amount of $D_i(\tau_i - \tau)/(1 - \tau_i)$. If the foreign tax rate is less than the U.S. tax rate, then a U.S. tax liability of $D_i(\tau - \tau_i)/(1 - \tau_i)$ accrues, and the remitted foreign income is said to be creating *excess limitation*.

3.1.3   Overall Limitation and Cross-Crediting

As noted earlier, the limitation on the foreign tax credit operates to some extent on an overall basis. This means that excess credits accruing from one source of foreign income can often be used to offset U.S. tax (excess limitation) on foreign income from another source.[5] We call this cross-crediting, or averaging of foreign income.

Cross-crediting can take three forms. First, U.S. taxpayers can cross-credit by receiving simultaneous dividend remittances from subsidiaries in high–tax rate and low–tax rate countries. Second, cross-crediting can occur between income types that tend to incur relatively high foreign taxes (dividends or branch income) and income types that incur lower foreign taxes (e.g., interest, rents, and royalties). Third, cross-crediting can occur over time using foreign tax credit carryovers. We will discuss the third type of cross-crediting in more detail below.

---

4. The U.S. tax base can differ from the tax base as defined by the host government for a variety of reasons. For example, the amount of interest deductions allowed, depreciation schedules, and inflation rates may differ in host and home countries. Hines (1989) and Leechor and Mintz (1990) show that these differences can have important incentive effects.

5. Until 1976, U.S. taxpayers could elect to apply their limitation either on a global basis or on a per country basis. The per country limitation was eliminated in 1976.

The ability to cross-credit can reduce U.S. tax revenue from foreign-source income. It may also affect the incentives for income repatriation and investment abroad. For example, if a U.S. corporation is in an excess limitation position—that is, the U.S. tax liability on its foreign-source income is greater than its supply of foreign tax credits—then any income it derives from a low-tax subsidiary faces additional U.S. tax. The total amount of tax paid is the same as would be paid on U.S.-source income. Consequently, the tax rate differential between the United States and the foreign country does not distort the allocation of capital by U.S. corporations in favor of the low-tax country (i.e., *capital-export neutrality* is preserved).[6] However, if the U.S. corporation is in excess credit, say because it has income derived from a high-tax country, the excess credits may offset any additional U.S. tax on the income from the low-tax country. In this case, capital-export neutrality may be violated because investment in the low-tax country will be tax favored over investment in the United States or in high-tax countries. On the other hand, cross-crediting may move the tax system *closer* to capital-export neutrality. This is because capital-export neutrality does not hold unless corporations that invest in high-tax countries receive refunds from the U.S. government for the difference between taxes paid at home and taxes paid to host countries with high average tax rates. With the overall limitation, firms that have the ability to average high- and low-taxed foreign-source income will be more willing to undertake investments in high-tax countries, all else equal, than they would be under a per country limitation where cross-crediting is only permitted for income derived from the same country. Therefore, under our current tax system, whether or not capital-export neutrality holds depends on the credit position or averaging potential of the multinational. Excess credit parents favor investments in low-tax locations over investments in high-tax locations (violating capital-export neutrality), while excess limitation parents face the same U.S. tax rate on foreign investment projects regardless of their location (preserving capital-export neutrality).[7]

Such revenue and efficiency considerations have made the appropriate form for the limitation on the foreign tax credit the subject of policy debate in the past. Prior to the Tax Reform Act of 1986, movement to a per country limitation was proposed in the Treasury tax reform proposal (U.S. Department of the Treasury 1984) and the president's tax reform proposal (U.S. Department of the Treasury 1985). But the desire to restrict cross-crediting has instead been pursued through the application of separate limitations to *baskets* of dif-

---

6. This ignores the possible effects of deferral in violating capital-export neutrality.

7. This discussion ignores the role of deferral. Taking deferral into account, Hartman (1985) argues that capital-export neutrality holds neither for excess limitation firms nor for excess credit firms. He argues that only the host country tax matters for foreign investment financed through foreign subsidiary retained earnings. His insight is that the taxes paid to the U.S. government upon repatriation of foreign earnings decrease both the opportunity cost of investment (reduced dividends in his case) and the return to investment by the same amount and are therefore irrelevant to marginal investment decisions.

ferent types of foreign income. Before the 1986 act, the period that our study covers, there were five separate baskets: (1) investment interest income, (2) domestic international sales corporation (DISC) dividend income,[8] (3) foreign trade income of a foreign sales corporation (FSC),[9] (4) distributions from a foreign sales corporation, and (5) all other foreign-source income, which we will call general limitation income. The 1986 act decreased the potential for cross-crediting further by increasing the number of separate limitation baskets to nine. Since then, various parties have argued for reductions in the number of baskets, generally on grounds of simplicity or competitiveness concerns.[10]

Taxpayers are permitted to carry excess foreign tax credits back up to two years or forward up to five years to offset U.S. tax on other foreign-source income. As noted above, these carryovers effectively allow taxpayers to cross-credit over time. They also mean that the "true" foreign tax credit position of a taxpayer—excess credit or excess limitation—in a given year, and consequently the tax effect of a remittance of foreign income in that year, may differ from what it appears to be. For example, if a taxpayer is currently in excess limitation, then it would appear that a dividend payment from a subsidiary in a low-tax (i.e., lower than U.S. tax rate) country would incur an additional U.S. tax. But if the U.S. taxpayer will move into excess credit next year, then the dividend payment may incur no additional U.S. tax,[11] because next year's excess credits can be carried back to offset taxes paid in the current year.

3.2   The Tax Price of Subsidiary Income Remittances

To measure the influence of taxation on income flows within U.S. multinational corporations, we derived *tax prices* for income remittances from subsidiaries to their U.S. parent corporations. We defined the tax price as the additional tax liability arising from an incremental dollar's worth of income remittance. The tax price of sending income back to the United States depends on the foreign tax credit position of the U.S. parent—whether it is in excess credit or excess limitation—and the channel used to remit the income. We can differentiate broadly between the dividend channel and channels, such as interest, royalties, and rents, for which the remittance is tax deductible in the source country. Although dividends are not tax deductible in the source country, they do get the deemed-paid foreign tax credit in the United States. This

---

8. A domestic international sales corporation is a corporation through which U.S. companies can generate export sales. DISCs were created in 1971 to provide a tax incentive to U.S. exporters. Companies that set up DISCs were allowed to defer a portion of the U.S. tax due on export income.

9. In 1984, Congress effectively replaced the DISC program with the foreign sales corporation rules. FSCs are a special class of corporations which are eligible to receive an exemption from U.S. taxation on a portion of export income.

10. See, for example, Price Waterhouse (1991) and Tillinghast (1990).

11. Except for the time value of the additional tax paid this year that will be offset by a reduction in tax next year.

section presents the tax prices first for dividend remittances and then for other forms of remittances.

3.2.1   Tax Price of Dividend Remittances

The tax price of remitting income through dividend payments depends not only on tax rates but also on the source country's system for taxing corporate income. Our specification of the tax price of dividend payments is similar to that of Alworth (1988)[12] and Hines and Hubbard (1990); however, as noted earlier, it differs in a few important respects. Unlike Alworth, we use actual tax return data to calculate the average tax rate for the deemed-paid credit. Unlike Hines and Hubbard, we incorporate withholding taxes, which can be significant in magnitude,[13] and we account for divergences from the classical system of corporate income taxation by some important countries in the sample, such as the United Kingdom, West Germany, and Japan.

For purposes of specifying a tax price for dividend remittances, the countries in our sample can be classified into three different categories on the basis of their corporate income tax systems: classical systems, split-rate systems, and imputation systems. We discuss the tax price of dividend remittances from subsidiaries under each of these systems.

Classical Systems

Under a classical corporate income tax system, the only source-country tax consequences of a dividend remittance arise from withholding taxes. The source-country tax liability for subsidiary i can be defined as

$$T_i = \tau_i Y_i + \omega_i D_i ,$$

where ω_i denotes the withholding tax rate in the subsidiary's country for dividends paid abroad and the other variables are as defined above. The foreign taxes creditable against U.S. tax liability are deemed-paid taxes plus withholding taxes, or

$$\tau_i D_i/(1 - \tau_i) + \omega_i D_i .$$

If the U.S. parent is in excess credit, any U.S. tax liability on the dividend is offset by excess credits, so

$$T_{US} = 0 .$$

And, of course, the U.S. tax price of a dividend remittance is simply

$$dT_{US}/dD_i = 0 .$$

---

12. Alworth expresses the tax cost of dividend remittances in the form of the opportunity cost of retained earnings.

13. For the countries in our sample, withholding tax rates on dividends range from 0 to 55 percent.

If the U.S. parent is in excess limitation, then the U.S. tax liability deriving from the dividend payment is

$$T_{US} = D_i\{(\tau - \tau_i)/(1 - \tau_i) - \omega_i\} .$$

The U.S. tax cost of remitting an additional dollar of dividend is

$$dT_{US}/dD_i = (\tau - \tau_i)/(1 - \tau_i) - \omega_i .$$

Note that this expression is negative if the source-country average tax rate exceeds the U.S. tax rate or if the amount by which the U.S. rate exceeds the foreign rate is more than offset by the effect of the withholding tax. In that case, a dividend payment actually reduces the firm's total U.S. tax liability because it creates excess credits that can be used to offset U.S. tax on other foreign income.

The global tax effects of a dividend remittance for the firm are simply the sum of its source country and U.S. tax effects:

$$T_G = T_{US} + \omega_i D_i .$$

If the parent is in excess credit, this expression reduces to

$$T_G = \omega_i D_i$$

because the payment of source-country withholding tax does not result in any offsetting reduction in U.S. taxes. The tax price is simply

$$dT_G/dD_i = \omega_i .$$

If the parent is in excess limitation, the global tax effect is

$$T_G = D_i(\tau - \tau_i)/(1 - \tau_i) ,$$

and the tax price of an additional dollar of dividend remittance is

$$dT_G/dD_i = (\tau - \tau_i)/(1 - \tau_i) .$$

This expression is negative if the source-country tax rate exceeds the U.S. tax rate, because the additional credits created by the dividend remittance are used to reduce U.S. tax on other foreign income. The withholding tax has no net effect because the extra withholding tax paid on the remittance is offset by a reduction in U.S. tax of an equal amount. For reference, the tax prices we have derived are summarized in table 3.1.

We have ignored the effect of the foreign tax credit carryover in the derivation of these tax prices. If the parent firm's foreign tax credit position changes during the period over which foreign tax credits can be carried forward or back, then the true credit position differs from the position on the books. This means that it may be more appropriate to specify the tax price as an *expected* price that incorporates the probability of changing credit position. Table 3.1 indicates the direction of the potential error introduced by ignoring the carryover potential of foreign tax credits.

Table 3.1   **Tax Price of Dividend Repatriations**

Tax System	U.S. Tax Price	Global Tax Price
Classical		
Excess limitation parent	$(\tau - \tau_i)/(1 - \tau_i) - \omega_i$	$(\tau - \tau_i)/(1 - \tau_i)$
Excess credit parent	0	ω_i
Split-rate		
Excess limitation parent	$(\tau - \tau_i)/(1 - \tau_i) - \omega_i +$ $(D_i/Y_i)(\tau_u - \tau_d)(1 - \tau)/(1 - \tau_i)^2$	$(\tau - \tau_i)/(1 - \tau_i) + \tau_d - \tau_u +$ $(D_i/Y_i)(\tau_u - \tau_d)(1 - \tau)/(1 - \tau_i)^2$
Excess credit parent	0	$\tau_d - \tau_u + \omega_i$
Imputation		
Excess limitation parent	$(1 + \theta_i)[(\tau - \tau_i)/(1 - \tau_i) - \omega_i -$ $\theta_i (D_i/Y_i)(1 - \tau)/(1 - \tau_i)^2]$	$(1 + \theta_i)[(\tau - \tau_i)/(1 - \tau_i) -$ $\theta_i(D_i/Y_i)(1 - \tau)/(1 - \tau_i)^2] - \theta_i$
Excess credit parent	0	$(1 + \theta_i)\omega_i - \theta_i$

Note: These tax prices should be adjusted to take into consideration the ability of U.S. corporations to carry back and/or carry forward excess foreign tax credits. Dividend remittances that increase the amount by which a corporation is in excess limitation (i.e., with positive tax prices) may be used in the future to absorb excess credits if the corporation transits to an excess credit position within the next two years. Therefore, the tax price given will be an *overestimate* of the expected tax price. Dividend remittances that decrease the amount by which a corporation is in excess limitation have a negative current tax price that may *underestimate* the expected tax price if future periods are taken into consideration. Similarly, the current tax price of a repatriation that increases (decreases) the amount by which a parent is in excess credit may be an *underestimate* (*overestimate*) of the expected tax price if the corporation can absorb credits through carrybacks.

Split-rate Systems

Several major countries have split-rate corporate tax systems, including Germany[14] and Japan. Under these tax systems, distributed profits are taxed at a different, usually lower, rate than undistributed profits are. The derivation of the tax price of dividend remittances is much more complicated in this case because the average foreign tax rate, and hence the dividend gross-up and the foreign tax credit, vary with the level of dividend payments. We leave the derivations of the tax prices to appendix A and present only the results here.

Where the source country has a split-rate system, let τ_u and τ_d denote its tax rate on undistributed and distributed profits, respectively. If the U.S. parent is in excess credit, the U.S. tax price of an incremental dividend remittance is still zero, because excess credits offset any additional U.S. tax liability that would otherwise arise on remitted foreign-source income. If the U.S. parent is in excess limitation, then the U.S. tax price of an incremental dividend remittance is

$$dT_{US}/dD_i = (\tau - \tau_i)/(1 - \tau_i) - \omega_i + (D_i/Y_i)(\tau_u - \tau_d)(1 - \tau)/(1 - \tau_i)^2 .$$

Note that this is the same expression as derived for the classical system but with one additional term. The extra term will be positive if distributed profits

14. Germany's corporate tax system is actually a hybrid of a split-rate and an imputation system. However, because Germany provides no refunds of tax on distributions of profits to foreign direct investors, the imputation part of the system does not apply for our purposes.

are taxed at a lower rate than are undistributed profits. This increases the U.S. tax price of a dividend distribution, because increased dividend distributions lower foreign tax payments and thereby decrease the deemed-paid credit.

When the parent is in excess limitation, the global tax price of dividend payments is

$$dT_G/dD_i = (\tau - \tau_i)/(1 - \tau_i) + \tau_d - \tau_u +$$
$$(D_i/Y_i)(\tau_u - \tau_d)(1 - \tau)/(1 - \tau_i)^2 .$$

This expression has two additional terms. One of the terms has already been discussed above. The other, $\tau_d - \tau_u$, represents the net effect of the dividend payment on source-country corporate tax payments. For a parent in excess credit, the global tax price of a dividend payment is

$$dT_G/dD_i = \tau_d - \tau_u + \omega_i .$$

This price also includes the effect of the dividend payment on source-country corporate tax payments. The tax prices we have derived for subsidiaries in countries with split-rate corporate income tax systems are also summarized in table 3.1.

Imputation Systems

A number of countries partially or fully integrate the taxation of corporations and their shareholders through imputation systems. However, the tax credits generally provided to shareholders under these systems for the corporate income tax already paid on distributed profits are not usually extended to foreign direct investors. Only the United Kingdom, under the terms of its tax treaty with the United States, provides a partial credit to U.S. direct investors for its advanced corporation tax (ACT). In the other countries with imputation systems, such tax credits are not provided to U.S. direct investors, and the incentive effects of the tax system on dividend remittances to the U.S. are the same as they would be under a classical corporate tax system.[15]

As under split-rate systems, the tax price of a dividend remittance to a U.S. shareholder is complex because the average tax rate used to determine the dividend gross-up and the foreign tax credit varies with the level of the dividend. We leave the detailed derivation of this tax price to appendix A and present the results here.

Under the U.S.-U.K. tax treaty, the tax credit provided to U.S. shareholders for ACT on distributed profits is one-half of the credit given domestic shareholders. The United Kingdom applies its withholding tax to both the dividend payment and the ACT credit. The United States considers the tax credit paid to be part of the grossed-up dividend. In addition, for foreign tax credit purposes, the United States treats the reduction by one-half in the credit given to

---

15. As noted above, Germany has a split-rate system coupled with its imputation credit.

U.S. shareholders as an additional payment of U.K. corporate income tax by the U.S. subsidiary.

If we denote the tax credit given to U.S. shareholders for ACT as θ_i, then for U.S. parents in excess limitation the U.S. tax price to the parent of a dividend remittance from a U.S. subsidiary is

$$dT_{US}/dD_i = (1 + \theta_i)\{(\tau - \tau_i)/(1 - \tau_i) - \omega_i - \theta_i(D_i/Y_i)(1 - \tau)/(1 - \tau_i)^2\}.$$

If the U.S. parent is in excess credit, then the U.S. tax price to the parent is zero.

The global tax price for a parent in excess limitation is

$$dT_G/dD_i = (1 + \theta_i)\{(\tau - \tau_i)/(1 - \tau_i) - \theta_i(D_i/Y_i)(1 - \tau)/(1 - \tau_i)^2\} - \theta_i.$$

If the U.S. parent is in excess credit, then the global tax price is

$$dT_G/dD_i = (1 + \theta_i)\omega_i - \theta_i.$$

The third panel of table 3.1 summarizes the tax prices we have derived for subsidiaries in countries with imputation systems.

3.2.2   Tax Price for Tax-deductible Remittances

Rent, royalty, and interest payments from subsidiaries to their U.S. parent corporations are generally deductible against corporate income tax in the source country.[16] Each dollar remitted through one of these channels therefore saves τ_i dollars in source-country tax, although there is likely also to be a withholding tax on such payments. At the same time, there is no deemed-paid credit for such payments. This leads to the following net global tax prices: $\tau - \tau_i$ if the U.S. parent is in excess limitation, $\omega_i - \tau_i$ if the parent is in excess credit.

From subsidiaries facing high source-country tax rates, multinationals generally have an incentive to receive income remittances in one of the tax-deductible forms rather than in the form of dividends. A tax-deductible remittance decreases source-country tax payments directly, whereas dividend payments might only produce unusable excess credits. If withholding tax rates on the tax-deductible forms of payment are not substantially higher than they are on dividends, the incentive to make payments in these tax-deductible forms is especially strong when the parent is in excess credit. The excess credits can be used to offset any residual U.S. tax on these payments, and the dominant effect is the deductibility of the payments against source-country taxes.

---

16. There are exceptions. For example, Brazil does not allow the deductibility of royalty payments from Brazilian companies to related foreign parties.

3.3   The Data

To comply with the U.S. tax law, U.S. multinationals must file a number of tax and information forms. We created a data set from information obtained from three sets of these forms filed by U.S. taxpayers in 1986: corporate income tax returns filed by nonfinancial U.S. corporations,[17] called 1120 forms; forms filed in support of foreign tax credits claimed, called 1118 forms; and information returns, called 5471 forms, filed for each *controlled foreign corporation* (CFC) controlled by a U.S. taxpayer. A CFC is a foreign corporation that is at least 50 percent owned by a group of U.S. shareholders each of whom has at least a 10 percent interest in the company. Form 1120 contains firm-specific tax return data that includes U.S. taxable income, U.S. taxes paid, tax credits claimed, and balance sheet and income statement items. Information on foreign-source income, foreign taxes paid, and foreign tax credits claimed by foreign tax credit basket is reported on Form 1118. This form also provides us with data on foreign-source income and foreign taxes paid for the general limitation income basket which is the focus of this study. The CFC data from Form 5471 includes balance sheet and income statement variables along with detailed information on remittances to U.S. parent corporations.

Our full sample contains 617 U.S. parent corporations, 277 of which had nonpositive worldwide income in 1986.[18] Each parent in our sample controlled at least one CFC and filed a Form 1118 to claim a foreign tax credit in the general limitation income basket.[19] In relation to the entire universe of nonfinancial corporations, our sample contains only 31 percent of total assets. However, 92 percent of foreign tax credits in 1986 are claimed by parents in our sample, and this proportion increases to 95 percent if we consider only manufacturing parents. The majority of the parents in the sample were in the manufacturing industry (71.5 percent), followed by retail trade (11.2 percent), transportation (7.9 percent), services (5.0 percent), mining (2.6 percent), construction (1.5 percent), and agriculture (0.3 percent).[20]

17. Financial companies face some different tax rules, and they generally operate in other countries through branches rather than subsidiaries. For these reasons, financial companies were omitted from the analysis.

18. The firms in our sample were drawn from the sample collected by the Statistics of Income Division of the Internal Revenue Service. This sample was created by including all U.S. corporations with assets that exceeded $50 million and a subset of U.S. corporations with smaller asset size. A complete description of the sampling technique used by the Internal Revenue Service can be found in *Statistics of Income Corporation Income Tax Returns,* 1986 volume.

19. Because we are concerned primarily with CFC income repatriations, we eliminated from our sample parents that did not have general limitation income and parents that did not own any CFCs. The original sample contained 1,817 nonfinancial parent corporations. More than half of those eliminated from our study had no CFCs (1,101); the remainder either had not filed a foreign tax credit form (97) or had no general limitation basket foreign-source income (2). Removing multinationals that did not control any CFCs from our sample resulted in only a 7 percent reduction in general limitation basket foreign-source income.

20. These percentages are calculated for parents with positive worldwide income.

The CFC data set provides information detailing income remittances to U.S. parent corporations for the top 7,500 CFCs in terms of asset size in 1986. The U.S. parent corporations in our sample accounted for 6,121 of these large CFCs. Compared to the entire set of subsidiaries owned by our parents, these 6,121 CFCs accounted for 91.5 percent of assets and 93.0 percent of earnings and profits both before and after taxes.

Calculating CFC-specific tax prices for income remittances requires knowledge of both the appropriate foreign corporate tax rate and the withholding tax rate. We used the CFC's average foreign tax rate (foreign tax payments divided by before-tax earnings and profits both taken from Form 5471) to measure the rate τ_i at which dividends are grossed up and foreign tax credits created. Under some circumstances, calculating the average tax rate in this manner may lead to an unsatisfactory approximation of τ_i. In particular, problems arise when CFCs report negative earnings and profits, receive tax refunds from host countries, repatriate dividends in excess of current earnings and profits, and receive dividends from subsidiaries of their own. Appendix B describes how we handled CFCs in those situations.

Foreign withholding taxes on dividend remittances can affect the overall tax cost of repatriations and were therefore included in our tax price specification. We used Price Waterhouse guides and tax treaties to develop a list of country-specific withholding tax rates for 1986. The Price Waterhouse guides also provided the appropriate statutory tax rates for the countries in our sample with split-rate and imputation tax systems.

3.4 Results

3.4.1 Tax Payments and Income Remittance Patterns

Table 3.2 presents summary information on the income of the 340 U.S. parent corporations in our sample that had positive taxable income and on the taxes that they paid. The columns of the table present figures for the number of U.S. corporations in our sample and the book value of their assets, their U.S. total taxable income, the total U.S. taxes they paid after tax credits, their foreign-source income, the U.S. taxes they paid on foreign-source income, and the average U.S. tax rate on their foreign-source income. The rows of the table present industry totals, totals for firms in excess limitation and excess credit, and totals for all U.S. parent corporations in the sample, respectively.

Table 3.2 shows that U.S. tax collections on foreign-source income varied considerably by industry in our sample. Corporations in agriculture, transportation, and to a lesser extent service industries paid more U.S. taxes on their foreign-source income than did companies in the other industries we consider.[21] For example, the average U.S. tax paid on a dollar of income earned

21. This result is possibly of limited significance for agriculture, because there is only one corporation in that industry present in our sample. Confidentiality considerations required us to

Table 3.2   Tax Payments of U.S. Parent Corporations in the Sample ($ millions)

	Number of U.S. Parent Corporations	Assets	Total U.S. Taxable Income	Total U.S. Taxes Paid	Foreign-Source Income	U.S. Taxes Paid on Foreign-Source Income	Average U.S. Tax Rate on Foreign-Source Income
Total	340	$1,939,896	$80,147	$14,841	$47,286	$1,585	3.4%
By industry of parent							
Mining	9	10,482	1,121	105	934	2	0.2
Construction	5	15,009	163	9	148	0	0.0
Manufacturing	243	1,471,945	63,531	10,425	43,283	1,014	2.3
Transportation*	28	201,628	7,132	1,842	1,463	487	33.3
Retail trade	38	192,646	6,907	2,228	1,047	41	3.9
Services	17	48,186	1,294	232	412	41	10.0
By credit position							
Excess limitation	212	971,325	38,294	9,656	14,697	1,585	10.8
Excess credit	128	968,571	41,853	5,185	32,589	0	0.0

*The authors combined the agriculture and transportation industries to preserve the confidentiality of the tax return information. These two industries have similar average U.S. tax rates on their foreign-source income.

abroad was over 33 cents in the agricultural and transportation industries but less than 3 cents in manufacturing industries. The fact that corporations in the transportation and service industries pay lower foreign taxes on their foreign-source income and consequently have higher U.S. tax liabilities on that income is unsurprising. In many countries, income from the transportation and services activities of foreign companies is exempt from tax or is lightly taxed, either as a matter of domestic law or as a consequence of tax treaty provisions.

Table 3.2 also shows that, despite industry variation, most of the foreign-source income of the U.S. parent corporations in the sample bore little U.S. tax. For the sample as a whole, foreign-source income was a large percentage (59.0) of total U.S. taxable income, but the U.S. taxes paid on this income were small, both as a percentage of total U.S. taxes paid (10.7) and as a percentage of foreign-source income (3.4). Apparently, the U.S. corporations in the sample were able to offset most potential U.S. tax liability on their foreign-source income with credits for the foreign taxes they paid, or were deemed to have paid, on that income. This was definitely the case for those U.S. parents that were in excess credit, and although most (62 percent) of the U.S. parents in the sample were in excess limitation, most (69 percent) of the foreign-source income accrued to firms in excess credit. Even the U.S. parents in excess limitation paid relatively little U.S. tax on their foreign-source income, since the average U.S. tax rate on that income was less than 11 percent.

The fact that most of the foreign-source income of these firms bore little U.S. tax did not necessarily result from specific tax avoidance activities on their part. It could have arisen simply because tax rates were high in the jurisdictions in which most foreign income was earned and hence firms that received substantial foreign-source income were likely to be in excess credit. Table 3.3 presents some evidence bearing on this point.

Table 3.3 presents information for CFCs associated with parents that had positive worldwide income in 1986. CFCs are split into two groups: those with U.S. parents in excess limitation and those with U.S. parents in excess credit. Within each of these groups, the CFCs are classified by the average foreign tax rate they faced. The columns of table 3.3 present information on CFC assets, CFC after-foreign-tax earnings, and the different forms of U.S. taxable foreign-source income the parent corporations derived from the CFCs.[22] Although our original sample contained 6,121 CFCs, 1,646 were associated with parents that had tax losses in 1986. Of the remaining 4,475 CFCs, 3,410 had sufficient information to calculate average foreign tax rates

---

report the figures for that corporation grouped with the transportation industry, which faced a similar average U.S. tax rate on its foreign-source income.

22. The total foreign-source income in table 3.3 is smaller than in table 3.2 for at least two reasons. First, foreign sources of income other than CFCs, such as branch operations, are not included. Second, the sample of CFCs does not necessarily represent all the CFCs of the U.S. firms in the sample.

Table 3.3   Foreign Tax Rates and the Composition of U.S. Parent Corporation Income from CFCs in the Sample ($ millions)

	Number of CFCs	CFC Assets	CFC After-tax Earnings	Income from CFCs			
				Dividends	Interest, Rents, and Royalties	Subpart F Income	Total
U.S. parent in excess limitation							
Total	1,827	$122,683	$11,514	$2,658	$1,182	$1,093	$ 4,933
With foreign tax rate of							
≤ 20%	659	51,306	5,244	918	326	815	2,059
20–30%	170	13,326	1,385	345	152	69	565
30–40%	286	20,151	1,662	434	189	49	671
40–50%	443	22,125	2,233	688	295	95	1,078
50–60%	165	10,233	820	198	131	40	369
> 60%	104	5,542	171	76	89	26	191
U.S. parent in excess credit							
Total	1,583	221,454	19,780	9,650	3,843	1,499	14,993
With foreign tax rate of							
≤ 20%	593	72,433	7,689	2,721	539	1,050	4,311
20–30%	163	24,757	1,594	1,202	193	83	1,479
30–40%	275	36,036	3,875	1,232	895	98	2,225
40–50%	325	51,751	4,397	2,524	1,773	183	4,479
50–60%	142	20,005	1,568	1,190	384	30	1,605
> 60%	85	16,472	657	781	59	55	895

and are therefore included in table 3.3. As mentioned in section 3.3 and detailed in Appendix B, in some circumstances we did not have the appropriate information to calculate a CFC-specific tax rate.

The table shows that the assets and after-tax earnings of CFCs in the sample are distributed unevenly across foreign tax rates for both excess credit and excess limitation parents. There are concentrations of assets and earnings in the lowest (less than 20 percent) and middle (30–50 percent) tax rate ranges. This suggests that the parent corporations' low U.S. tax liabilities on foreign income may be due more to cross-crediting than to generally high foreign tax rates.

Table 3.3 shows that CFC dividend payments were distributed across foreign tax rates in much the same way as CFC earnings and assets were. This indicates that significant cross-crediting may be occurring, but whether it is by design or simply due to the distribution of tax rates on the earnings of these CFCs is not clear. The table does show some evidence of tax influences on dividend remittances. First, CFCs with parents in excess credit pay out relatively more as a percentage of assets or earnings than do other CFCs. One would expect this, since dividend payments from those CFCs incur no additional U.S. tax. Second, dividend remittances of high-tax CFCs of excess limitation parents generally bear a negative tax price, and those CFCs do pay out much more in relation to their earnings than do other CFCs of excess limitation parents. However, this last result does not hold when dividend payments are expressed as a percentage of CFC assets. Furthermore, one might expect high-tax CFCs of parents in excess limitation to have higher payout ratios than do CFCs with parents in excess credit—since in the former case the tax price of a dividend remittance is generally negative, while in the latter case it is at least zero—but the figures in table 3.3 suggest otherwise.

Table 3.3 does not provide any conclusive evidence for substantial tax influences on CFC dividend remittance patterns. But it should be remembered that we have ignored withholding taxes and variations in host country corporate tax systems here. As we show below, these turn out to be important.

Evidence that U.S. multinational corporations use different channels for income remittances in order to reduce their global tax liabilities is provided in table 3.3. Remitting income through the interest, rents, and royalties channels instead of the dividend channel takes advantage of the deductibility of such payments against the CFC's taxes. Therefore, we would expect to see relatively more of these forms of remittances from CFCs facing high source-country tax rates. Table 3.3 shows that pattern of remittances. Relatively more interest, rents, and royalties were paid from the CFCs with higher foreign tax rates than from those with lower foreign tax rates—although there is some concentration of payments in the lowest tax rate range. When these remittances are measured in relation to CFC assets or earnings, the concentration in the upper tax rate ranges appears particularly pronounced. CFCs with parents in excess credit also remitted substantially more income in these tax-deductible forms than did those with parents in excess limitation. This makes sense, because these firms are effectively averaging the excess credits created from other sources of foreign income to offset the additional U.S. tax liability generally created by interest, rent, and royalty payments.[23]

The distribution of subpart F income by CFC tax rate, as shown in table 3.3, illustrates the value of deferral to U.S. multinational corporations. The vast majority of this income was accounted for by CFCs facing low tax rates. Although there is no deferral for it, subpart F income may be earned on *passive* investments of retained *active* CFC income that *does* benefit from deferral. U.S. multinationals may choose to retain this active income in low-tax jurisdictions and earn subpart F income on it until such time as excess credits are available from elsewhere to offset the residual U.S. tax liability that would accrue if the active income were sent back immediately to the United States.

3.4.2   Cross-Crediting

Table 3.3 shows that the most important channel for income remittances from CFCs was through dividend payments. Dividend payments made up about 62 percent of the total foreign income derived by U.S. parents from the CFCs in the sample. And this understates the importance of dividends in the net receipts of the parent, because they are paid out of after-foreign-tax income and so get the deemed-paid credit, whereas interest, rents, and royalties are paid out of pre-foreign-tax income and do not get the deemed-paid credit. Therefore, much of the scope for tax minimization by U.S. parents may lie in coordinating CFC dividend payments properly. CFC dividend payment levels should also be easier to change in the short run than are the levels of interest, royalties, and rents. Thus dividends are particularly suitable for taking advantage of the ability to cross-credit provided by the overall limitation on the foreign tax credit. The question is how much U.S. corporations do use dividend payments in this way to reduce their tax liabilities, given that other factors may drive dividend remittance patterns as well.

Table 3.4 partitions the data in a way that may indicate the potential for cross-crediting through concurrent dividend payments from CFCs facing different levels of foreign taxation, and to some extent how much of that potential is realized. For this table, CFCs are classified as *high-tax* if their average foreign tax rate is greater than or equal to the U.S. statutory rate in 1986 (46 percent) and as *low-tax* otherwise. Dividends from a high-tax CFC would tend to create excess credits or offset U.S. tax on other foreign-source income, whereas dividends from a low-tax CFC would tend to create a U.S. tax liabil-

---

23. The analysis in Goodspeed and Frisch (1989) also suggests that parents average across income sources. The authors calculate average tax rates on all types of foreign-source income in the general limitation basket by country, using 1984 data. They find that the effective tax rate on dividends was high, while the effective tax rate on interest and other forms of deductible income repatriations was low. Comparing these effective tax rates with country-specific average tax rates suggests that parents cross-credit over foreign-source income types.

Table 3.4   **The Potential for and Extent of Cross-Crediting in CFC Dividend Remittances to U.S. Parent Corporations in the Sample**

	Number	Percentage of Total Number	Number Receiving Dividends	Percentage of Total Number Received Dividends	Dividends Received ($ millions)	Percentage of Total Dividends Received
Total U.S. parent corporations	290	100.0%	204	100.0%	$12,267	100.0%
U.S. parents with both high- and low-tax CFC	212	73.1	171	83.8	11,905	97.0
With dividends received from both high- and low-tax CFCs	111	38.3	111	54.4	11,488	93.7
With dividends received only from high-tax CFCs	34	11.7	34	16.7	196	1.6
With dividends received only from low-tax CFCs	26	9.0	26	12.7	220	1.8
Parent also has FTC carryforwards	11	3.8	11	5.4	146	1.2

Note: CFCs with average foreign tax rates greater than or equal to the U.S. statutory corporate rate in 1986 (46 percent) are classified as high-tax CFCs; all other CFCs for which an average foreign tax rate can be calculated are low-tax CFCs.

ity or absorb excess foreign tax credits.[24] As was the case with table 3.3, to construct this table we had to eliminate CFCs for which we did not have sufficient information to calculate average tax rates. Parents that did not control *any* CFCs for which we would compute an average tax rate were eliminated from the sample. As a result, our original sample of 340 parents with positive worldwide income was reduced to 290 parents. Of the 290 parent firms in the new sample, 212, or about 73 percent, had both high-tax and low-tax CFCs in our sample; these U.S. parents therefore had the potential to cross-credit through concurrent dividend payments from high- and low-tax CFCs. The table also shows that most (54.4 percent) of the parents receiving dividends received them from both high- and low-tax CFCs, and these parents accounted for the bulk (93.7 percent) of dividends received. Clearly, most of the parents with the potential to cross-credit did so, at least to some extent. About 17 percent of the parents receiving dividends from CFCs had both high- and low-tax CFCs but received dividend payments only from their high-tax CFCs. However, these dividends accounted for only 1.6 percent of total dividends received by U.S. parents in the sample. The bottom two rows of table 3.4 provide information on parents that had both high- and low-tax CFCs but received dividends only from their low-tax CFCs. These parents accounted for 12.7 percent of all parents but only 1.8 percent of total dividends received by parents from CFCs. In addition, the bottom row shows that about two-thirds of those dividends were received by parents with foreign tax credit carryovers that they could use to offset at least some of the additional U.S. tax liability that might otherwise arise on the dividend remittances.[25]

In addition to cross-crediting through concurrent remittances of foreign income from differently taxed sources, firms can use the ability to carry foreign tax credits back two years and forward five years to cross-credit over time. It appears that the use of these carryovers is not insignificant. The U.S. corporations in our sample carried over $4 billion worth of foreign tax credits into 1986 from previous years.[26] About 40 percent of these carryovers were used to offset U.S. tax on foreign-source income in 1986.

We cannot measure the full extent of cross-crediting over time because we do not have data on the amount of excess foreign tax credits created in 1986 which were carried back to offset tax liabilities in previous years or forward to offset tax in the future. (Note that a carryover created in 1986 would not have expired before 1991.) We do know, however, that foreign tax credit carryovers could only be of use to a firm in excess credit in 1986 if that firm was in excess

24. This will not always be true, because we are ignoring here the withholding tax rates and variations in foreign corporate tax systems that we account for below.

25. The figures presented in table 3.4 probably underestimate the potential for cross-crediting in concurrent dividend payments, and its actual use. Our sample does not include all the CFCs of each parent firm, for two reasons. First, as explained above, only the largest 7,500 CFCs were included in the sample. Second, as explained in the text and in appendix B, some CFCs were dropped from the sample because average tax rates could not be calculated for them.

26. The figures reported in this paragraph are not presented in a table.

limitation for at least one of the previous two years or moved into excess limitation before 1991. In general, the more frequently firms change their credit position, the more likely they are to be able to use these carryovers. In an effort to determine to what extent firms move between excess credit and excess limitation, we created a panel data set from tax return data for a sample of U.S. corporations. Unfortunately, data from foreign tax credit forms are compiled only in even years and were available to us only for the years 1980, 1982, 1984, and 1986. In addition, U.S. corporations generally file foreign tax credit forms only in years in which they claim a credit; as a result, the data are missing for parents with nonpositive worldwide income. In an effort to obtain the largest number of observations, we created three data sets that match tax returns over three-year periods. There were 449 U.S. corporations in the sample that linked the 1980 and 1982 tax returns, 388 in the sample that linked 1982 and 1984 returns, and 317 in the sample that linked returns from 1984 and 1986.

Table 3.5 presents our estimates of the percentage of firms that switched credit position over time. We divided the parents into four groups: those that were in excess limitation during the three-year time period under consideration, those that were always in excess credit, those that moved from excess credit to excess limitation during the time period, and those that transited from excess limitation to excess credit. To classify firms into these cells, we first determined their credit status in the two even years and then checked for the presence of foreign tax credit carryforwards in the most recent year of the sample under consideration. For example, a firm that was in excess limitation in 1984 and 1986 and that did not claim a foreign tax credit carryforward in 1986 was placed in the "always in excess limitation" cell. If the same firm claimed a foreign tax credit carryforward in 1986, it was placed in the "transit from excess credit to excess limitation" cell because the presence of the carryforward indicates that this firm was in excess credit in the previous year. Using this methodology, we developed what should be considered floor estimates of the extent to which firms switched credit position.[27] We present both unweighted estimates and figures that are weighted by assets and foreign-source income for the last even year of each sample.

Table 3.5 demonstrates that a significant number of firms transited both into

27. To divide the firms into the four cells that appear in table 3.5, we used the following methodology. For simplicity, we use the 1984–86 time period as an example. Firms that were in excess credit in 1984 and 1986 and that had foreign tax credit carryforwards in 1986 were placed in the "always in excess credit" cell. Firms that were in excess limitation in 1984 and 1986 and that did not have foreign tax credit carryforwards in 1986 were placed in the "always in excess limitation" cell. The set of firms that were in excess credit in 1984 and in excess limitation in 1986 were determined to have transited out of an excess credit state over the time period. We added to this group (the "transit from excess limitation to excess credit" cell) firms that were in excess limitation in both even years and that had foreign tax credit carryforwards in 1986. The final cell, "transit from excess limitation to excess credit," contains the following two groups of firms: those in excess limitation in 1984 and in excess credit in 1986, and those in excess credit in 1984 and 1986 that had no foreign tax credit carryforwards in 1986.

Table 3.5   Foreign Tax Credit State Transitions of U.S. Multinationals

Data Set	Totals	Percentage Transit from Excess Credit to Excess Limitation	Percentage Transit from Excess Limitation to Excess Credit	Percentage Always in Excess Limitation	Percentage Always in Excess Credit
Unweighted	Number of U.S. Corporations*				
1980–1982	449	14.3%	22.9%	53.2%	9.6%
1982–1984	338	18.3	20.1	46.9	14.7
1984–1986	317	24.3	21.8	42.3	11.7
Weighted by assets†	Assets ($ millions)				
1980–1982	$1,701,751	12.3	26.9	49.7	11.1
1982–1984	1,809,922	21.4	16.4	34.7	27.6
1984–1986	1,766,597	14.2	34.1	33.6	18.1
Weighted by Foreign-Source Income†	Foreign Source Income ($ millions)				
1980–1982	$20,931	13.2	34.4	38.4	14.0
1982–1984	43,671	20.2	21.7	18.0	40.1
1984–1986	40,563	10.2	42.5	11.9	35.4

*Firms must have positive taxable income in both even years to be in each sample.
†Figures are weighted by assets or foreign-source income in the last year of each sample period.

and out of excess credit during the 1980s. At least 37 percent of parents switched states in each of our three samples, and this figure increased over time to reach 46 percent in the 1984–86 time period. A similar story emerges when these numbers are weighted by assets or foreign-source income. In each of the sample periods under consideration, at least 37 percent of assets and 41 percent of foreign-source income were associated with parents that switched credit positions. During the 1984–86 time period, more than half of foreign-source income was generated by parents that changed credit position.[28] These results indicate that, as pointed out in section 3.2, it may not be correct to specify the tax price for dividend remittances as taking on one of two values depending on the credit position of the parent firm in that year. An *expected* tax price is the more appropriate concept when the credit position may change. We will return to this issue when we discuss the specification and estimation of our dividend equation.

3.4.3   Tax Consequences of Dividend Remittances

We now focus more closely on the tax implications of the dividend remittances of the CFCs in our sample. We ignore for the time being the use of foreign tax credit carryovers, so the tax price of a dividend payment to the parent corporation takes on the values derived in section 3.2. Even with this restriction, we find strong evidence that U.S. corporations in our sample were coordinating the level and source of dividend payments from their CFCs so as to reduce their U.S. and foreign tax liabilities.

We would expect the probability that a CFC pays a dividend to its parent, and the amount of any dividend paid, to depend on the effect the payment would have on the total tax liability of the CFC and the parent. For each CFC in the sample, we calculated the effect a dividend remittance from that CFC to its parent would have on tax payments by the CFC and its parent, given the parent's foreign tax credit position in the absence of any dividend remittance from that CFC. For CFCs that paid no dividend in 1986, this calculation was simple, because the tax price of the dividend payment would depend on the actual excess credit position of the parent. For CFCs that did pay a dividend, this calculation involved computing what the foreign tax credit position of the parent would have been if the dividend had not been paid.

Table 3.6 summarizes the impact of dividend remittances on tax payments

28. Because the passage of the Tax Reform Act of 1986 may have made 1986 an anomalous year, we also weighted the figures in table 3.5 for the 1984–86 time period by foreign-source income in 1984. In 1984, the total foreign-source income of corporations in the sample was $37.5 billion. The proportion of foreign-source income associated with parents remaining in the same credit position was 54.0 percent: 12.7 percent belonged to parents that remained in excess limitation, and 41.3 percent was associated with parents that remained in excess credit. The remaining proportion belonged to parents that switched credit positions: 24.1 percent transited to an excess credit position, and 21.9 percent transited to an excess limitation position. As table 3.5 shows, these percentages do differ from those weighted by foreign-source income in 1986. This may have been a result of anticipatory behavior on the part of U.S. corporations in response to the Tax Reform Act of 1986.

Table 3.6   **Tax Consequences of CFC Dividend Remittances to Their U.S. Parent Corporations**

CFC Group	Number of CFCs	CFCs Paying Dividends		CFC Dividend Payments		Ratio of CFC Dividends to:	
		Number	Percentage of Total	Dollars (millions)	Percentage of Total	Assets	After-tax Earnings
Parents with positive taxable income (by tax price of dividend)							
Increases U.S. taxes	1,014	193	19.0%	$ 992	8.1%	1.4%	13.9%
Does not change U.S. taxes	1,548	485	31.3	9,186	74.9	4.1	46.0
Decreases U.S. taxes	777	303	39.0	2,088	17.0	4.4	53.4
Increases global taxes	2,218	623	28.1	6,279	51.2	3.1	32.0
Does not change global taxes	252	79	31.3	1,624	13.2	3.9	50.2
Decreases global taxes	869	279	32.1	4,364	35.6	4.4	53.5
Total	3,339	981	29.4	12,267	100.0	3.6	39.6
Parents with tax losses							
Low-tax CFCs	761	107	14.1	712	71.7	1.6	16.2
High-tax CFCs	305	58	19.0	281	28.3	1.8	28.4
Total	1,066	165	15.5	992	100.0	1.7	26.4

for the CFCs in our sample for which we calculate an average tax rate.[29] We partition the data into two groups of CFCs: (1) those with parents that had positive U.S. taxable income and (2) those with parents that had U.S. tax losses. For each group, the table shows the number of CFCs, the number paying dividends, the percentage paying dividends, the total amount of CFC dividend payments, each group's percentage of total dividend payments, and the ratios of CFC dividend payments to assets and earnings, respectively.

In the first six rows of the table, those CFCs that had U.S. parents with taxable U.S. incomes are partitioned by whether a dividend payment from them to their parent would have increased, left unchanged, or decreased tax payments. The first three of these rows consider only the effect of a dividend payment on the U.S. tax liabilities of the parent company. Comparing the percentage of CFCs paying dividends and the average payout ratios across the different categories yields striking results. It appears that tax incentives strongly affected whether a multinational chose to receive dividend remittances from a CFC. About 29.4 percent of all CFCs paid a dividend, but only 19.0 percent of those CFCs from which dividend payments would have increased U.S. tax liabilities actually paid dividends, while 31.3 percent of those CFCs whose dividend payments would not have changed U.S. tax lia-

29. Because they appeared to be outliers, a small group of CFCs with extremely high (above 90 percent) calculated average tax rates were eliminated from the sample used to generate the results in tables 3.6 and 3.7.

bilities and 39.0 percent of those CFCs whose dividends would have decreased U.S. tax liabilities did pay dividends.[30] And tax incentives affected the amount of dividend payments as a percentage of CFC earnings or assets even more than they affected the number of CFCs paying dividends. In particular, the sixth column of the table shows that the ratio of dividend payments to assets for those CFCs whose dividend payments increased U.S. taxes was only 1.4 percent, while this ratio was 4.1 percent and 4.4 percent for CFCs whose dividend payments did not change or decreased U.S. taxes, respectively. The seventh column presents similar results for the ratio of dividend payments to CFC earnings. The fifth column shows that these CFC dividend payments generated little U.S. tax revenue; only 8.1 percent of the total dividend payments increased U.S. taxes at all, compared to 17.0 percent of the payments which actually decreased U.S. taxes.

The next three rows of table 3.6 partition CFCs by the effect of dividend payments on global—that is, both U.S. and source-country—tax liabilities. Taxes still appear to have had a strong influence on dividend remittance patterns, but the U.S. multinationals bore some taxes on 51.2 percent of these income flows. This occurs because remittances from CFCs with parents in excess credit often create a source-country withholding tax liability that is not offset by a reduction in U.S. taxes, because the withholding tax payment just creates more excess foreign tax credits.[31] However, comparing the proportions of CFCs paying dividends and CFC payout ratios yields a result similar to what occurs when only U.S. tax liabilities are considered: CFCs appear to have been far more likely to pay dividends and to pay larger dividends if those dividends bore a negative or zero tax price. Remarkably, 35.6 percent of CFC dividend payments appear to have decreased global tax liabilities for their U.S. parent corporations.

The last three rows of table 3.6 present results for CFCs with parents that had tax losses and therefore no U.S. taxes to pay. Our sample has 1,066 such CFCs, compared to 3,339 CFCs with parents having positive taxable income. Remittances from these CFCs do not incur any U.S. tax because the foreign taxable income they represent is offset by domestic (or foreign branch) tax losses. Because there is no current U.S. tax liability, any foreign tax credit on the remitted income cannot be taken currently, but it may be carried forward or back to other tax years.

We might expect large remittances of income from low-tax CFCs in this

30. A question arose as to how to classify those CFCs that paid a dividend large enough to change the foreign tax credit position of the parent. We opted to classify CFCs by the tax consequence of the first dollar of dividend payment made. Few enough CFCs in this position were in the sample that the results were not significantly changed by classifying CFCs by the tax consequence of the last dollar of dividend payment made.

31. Remittances from some CFCs incur a positive or zero U.S. tax liability but a *negative* global tax liability. This can occur because host country taxes are reduced by distributions of profits in countries with split-rate systems. The advance corporation tax (ACT) credit in the United Kingdom also decreases global tax when the firm is in excess credit.

situation, because the parent pays no additional U.S. tax currently, but the results in table 3.6 contradict this. Those CFCs paid out little in relation to their income and assets. For example, as a group these CFCs paid out only 26.4 percent of their earnings, compared to 39.6 percent for those CFCs that had parents with positive taxable income. Particularly puzzling is the result that low-tax CFCs paid out less than high-tax CFCs, because firms making losses save U.S. tax when they receive dividends from low-tax CFCs but not when they receive them from high-tax CFCs.

These results may not be as puzzling as they at first seemed to us, because a plausible tax motivation exists for CFCs to pay out less when their U.S. parents are making losses. When the parent receives a dividend from a CFC in this situation, it gives up a loss deduction that, according to U.S. tax rules, can be carried back to past years or forward to future years to offset taxable income and reduce taxes. In exchange for the forgone loss carryover, the parent saves the additional U.S. tax that would otherwise accrue immediately on the foreign income it repatriates. The parent also acquires excess foreign tax credits in the amount of the foreign tax paid or deemed paid on the remitted income. Together, the current savings in U.S. tax and the excess foreign tax credit are equal in dollar value to the loss carryover that the firm gives up. However, according to U.S. tax law, the loss deduction can be carried back up to three years and forward up to fifteen years, whereas the foreign tax credit can be carried back only two years and forward only five years. The foreign tax credit carryover is therefore much more likely to expire unused than is the loss carryover. U.S. multinationals may be reluctant to give up a loss carryover that they would probably be able to use at some point in the future in exchange for a smaller immediate tax gain and a foreign tax credit carryover that is more likely to expire unused. However, the result that low-tax CFCs pay out less than high-tax CFCs in this situation remains a puzzle.

3.4.4   Estimates of the Relationship between Dividend Remittances and Their Tax Price

The results reported in tables 3.3 through 3.6 suggest that taxation may have an important influence on dividend remittance patterns, but they do not allow us to gauge whether tax incentives are significant when other factors are taken into account. To do that, we estimated dividend equations of the following basic form:

$$(2) \qquad D_i = \alpha_0 + \alpha_1 TAX_i + \alpha_2 Y_i + \beta' X_i + \gamma' X_p + \varepsilon_i,$$

where D_i denotes the dividend payment of CFC i to its U.S. parent corporation; TAX_i denotes the tax price of dividend payments from the CFC to its parent; Y_i denotes CFC after-tax income; X_i is a vector of other CFC characteristics; X_p is a vector of the characteristics of the U.S. parent; and ε_i is a random error term.

Equation (2) is similar to the dividend equation estimated by Hines and Hubbard (1990), but our estimates differ in some important ways. As we have noted, our specification of the tax price variable includes withholding taxes and takes into account variations in source-country corporate income taxation systems. In addition, in some of our estimates we include an additional tax price variable designed to reflect *expected* tax price effects. We attempt to capture the possibility that the parent firm's excess credit position could change in the future and that the use of foreign tax credit carryovers could change the tax consequences of current dividend payments. We assume that the larger the parent firm's excess credit position (if it is in excess credit) or the greater its deficit of credits (if it is in excess limitation) relative to its total foreign-source income, the less likely it will be to change credit position during the period when carryovers could be used. This led us to the following dividend equation:

$$D_i = \alpha_0 + \alpha_1 TAX_i + \alpha_2 ETAX_i + \alpha_3 Y_i + \beta'X_i + \gamma'X_p + \varepsilon_i \, ,$$

where

(3) $$ETAX_i = (TAX_i - OTAX_i) \, e^{-(FTC_P/FSI_P)}$$

and $OTAX_i$ denotes the tax price of a dividend remittance if the parent which is currently in excess credit (excess limitation) were instead in excess limitation (excess credit); FTC_p denotes the current total excess credit or excess limitation of the parent; and FSI_p denotes the parent's total foreign-source income from all sources.

Although ad hoc, this specification has three attractive properties. To illustrate this, note that the probability of switching credit positions is P, so that the expected tax price is

$$(1 - P)TAX_i + P(OTAX_i) \, ;$$

then

$$P = \left(\frac{\alpha_2}{\alpha_1}\right) e^{-(FTC_P/FSI_P)}$$

Given this interpretation, the first attractive property of the specification is that α_1 represents the effect of the *expected* tax price no matter what value P takes on. The second attractive property is that as FTC_P/FSI_P gets large—that is, as the parent goes further into excess credit or excess limitation and is therefore less likely to move out of that state in the near future—$ETAX_i$, and hence P, gets small and eventually approaches zero. The third property is that as the foreign tax credit position, FTC_P, approaches zero, P approaches a fixed number, α_2/α_1.

Because over 70 percent of the CFCs in the sample pay no dividends at all, the dividend equations were estimated using a tobit model. The columns of table 3.7 report estimates of six different versions of the tobit model. Column

Table 3.7   Tobit Estimates of Tax Price Effects on CFC Dividend Remittances

Independent Variable	(1)	(2)	(3)	(4)	(5)	(6)
			Dependent Variable: Ratio of CFC Dividends to CFC Assets*			
Tax price	-0.058	-0.160	-0.135	-0.217	-0.218	-0.216
	(0.016)	(0.022)	(0.022)	(0.025)	(0.026)	(0.026)
Expected tax price variable†	—	-0.116	-0.100	-0.136	-0.137	-0.134
		(0.016)	(0.017)	(0.018)	(0.018)	(0.018)
Ratio of CFC earnings to CFC assets	1.039	1.056	0.944	1.053	1.054	1.046
	(0.024)	(0.025)	(0.024)	(0.026)	(0.026)	(0.026)
Years since CFC incorporation/10	0.035	0.032	0.028	0.039	0.038	0.037
	(0.004)	(0.004)	(0.004)	(0.004)	(0.004)	(0.004)
Ratio of parent dividends to parent assets	—	—	0.356	—	—	—
			(47.63)			
Ratio of CFC interest paid to CFC assets	—	—	—	—	-0.188	-0.170
					(0.166)	(0.167)
Excess credit dummy	—	—	—	—	0.023	0.022
					(0.011)	(0.012)
Parent dummies present	No	No	Yes	No	No	No
Country dummies present	No	No	No	Yes	Yes	Yes
CFC industry dummies present	No	No	No	No	No	Yes
Intercept	-0.339	-0.326	-0.410	-0.318	-0.324	-0.371
	(0.014)	(0.013)	(0.159)	(0.020)	(0.021)	(0.030)
Number of observations	3,116	3,116	3,116	3,116	3,116	3,116
Log likelihood	-1,086	-1,069	-741	-975	-975	-941
Parameter scale factor‡	0.2636	0.2618	0.2520	0.2470	0.2470	0.2413

*Standard errors are in parentheses.

†The expected tax price variable is as specified in text equation (3).

‡Multiply parameter estimates by the parameter scale factor to obtain slope coefficients.

(1) presents estimates of the basic dividend equation, including the tax price variable, CFC earnings, and CFC age measured by the number of years since incorporation. To control for variations in CFC size, CFC dividend remittances and earnings are divided by CFC assets. Column (2) shows estimates of the same equation with the addition of the variable to capture the expected tax price effect, *ETAX*. To capture parent-specific effects, we included the ratio of parent-company dividends to assets and a set of parent dummy variables in the estimates reported in column (3). Column (4) reports estimates of the equation including fifty-nine country dummy variables. For the estimates shown in column (5), we included CFC interest paid divided by CFC assets and a dummy variable for the U.S. parent corporation's excess credit position. Column (6) presents estimates of the dividend equation with CFC industry dummy variables in addition to the country dummy variables.

The estimated tax price effects on CFC dividend remittances are negative and significant in each model, suggesting that the larger the tax price of receiving dividends from a CFC, the lower the dividend payment from that CFC will be. Interestingly, adding the expected tax price variable improves the estimates overall and increases the estimated tax price coefficient substantially, from -0.058 in column (1) to -0.160 in column (2). The expected tax price effect appears to be larger and more significant than the estimated effect of the simple tax price specification used in the column (1) estimates.

The estimated parameters for the other variables present in these, and the other, specifications have unsurprising signs. Higher CFC earnings increase CFC distributions. CFC dividends increase with CFC age, a result predicted by some models of multinational behavior under taxation with a foreign tax credit and deferral (including Newlon 1987; Sinn 1990).

The estimates shown in column (3) are of interest in light of results reported in Hines and Hubbard (1990) and Hines (1991). Hines and Hubbard (1990) found a strong positive relationship between CFC dividend payments and parent company dividend payments. They suggest that this relationship may be due to cash flow constraints, because parent firms might need more internally generated funds when they are making distributions to their shareholders. Hines (1991) found a strong positive effect of foreign earnings in estimates of dividend payout equations for U.S. corporations. He is uncertain as to the reason for this relationship but suggests that it is consistent with a signaling view of dividends. In an earlier version of this paper, we presented estimates that were consistent with these findings: parent dividend payments had a large positive coefficient when added to our CFC dividend equations. However, the results reported in column (3) show that when separate parent effects are added to the equation, the relationship between parent and CFC dividend payments disappears. It appears that the parent dividend variable may simply have been capturing some omitted parent characteristics. In any case, the presence or absence of these and other parent variables does not affect the estimated coefficients on the other variables substantially.

Including country effects in column (4) increases the estimated tax effect from -0.160 to -0.217. Although not reported in the table, many of the estimated country effects are significantly different from the omitted country effect, Canada. For example, significant negative effects were estimated for the United Kingdom (-0.160), France (-0.073), and the Netherlands (-0.083). We found no evidence of a strong tax haven effect independent of the tax price effect. Whereas Hong Kong and the Cayman Islands have significant negative country effects of -0.097 and -0.158, respectively, the Netherlands Antilles have a significant positive effect (0.108), and other tax havens generally have significant country effects. Country risk factors may be evident in the positive country effects on dividend remittances found for Panama (0.089), South Africa (0.074), and the Philippines (0.145).

In order to control for differences in CFC capital structure, we included the ratio of CFC interest payments to CFC assets in the estimates reported in column (5).[32] The more debt financed a CFC, the greater its interest payments and the less funds may be available for dividend payments. The estimated coefficient on this variable has the expected negative sign, but it is not statistically significant. Including this variable does not change the estimated tax price effect.

A potential problem with our estimated tax effects is that they may measure no more than the fact that CFCs with parents in excess credit paid larger dividends. To test for this possibility, the estimates reported in column (5) also include a dummy variable equal to one if the parent is in excess credit and zero otherwise. While the estimated coefficient on this variable is positive and significant, the estimated tax price effect reported in column (5) remains highly significant and virtually unchanged from the column (4) estimate.

Our results are robust to the inclusion of other variables in the equation. For example, column (6) reports estimates of the dividend equation containing twenty-seven CFC industry dummy variables in addition to the country dummy variables.[33] The results are largely the same as in the other estimates.[34]

We have also estimated these equations including terms that interact the tax price variables with the CFC earnings variable. Such interactive terms are frequently included in empirical estimates of dividend equations. The results from those estimates are qualitatively the same as those presented in table 3.7, although the estimated tax price effects evaluated at the variable means are actually somewhat larger when the interactive terms are included. We present the results without the interactive terms because they are somewhat easier to evaluate visually.

A potential endogeneity problem associated with our tax price variable be-

32. Because CFC interest payments are an endogenous variable, it would be best to instrument them on some exogenous variable. However, we could not find suitable instrumental variables in our data.

33. These dummy variables were created using groupings of the IRS Statistics of Income (SOI) industry classifications, which correspond fairly closely to two-digit standard industrial classifications (SICs).

34. We have also estimated the same equation with parent industry effects, but the results were not significantly different from those reported in table 3.7.

comes apparent if one examines the formulas in table 3.1. Specifically, the value of the tax price variable depends on the size of the CFC's dividend payment when the host country has a split-rate or imputation tax system. We used instrumental variables estimates to evaluate whether this is an important problem. We instrumented the tax price variables on their values evaluated when dividend payments are zero. The instrumental variables estimates were very close to those reported in table 3.7, so it appears that this source of endogeneity in the tax variable is not important.

The results reported in table 3.7 show that the tax price of a dividend remittance has a significant negative impact on CFC dividend remittances. The estimates from columns (4) and (5) indicate that at the mean of the variables an increase in the tax price of 1 percentage point would decrease the dividend payout ratio by about 0.054 percentage points, which translates into approximately a 1.5 percent decrease in dividend payments. This effect may not seem large, but given that the tax price of remittances varied enormously across CFCs within the sample (from less than -300 percent to over 50 percent), the estimates indicate that tax incentives did have dramatic impacts on dividend remittance patterns.

As explained above, one can calculate implied values for the probability of switching credit position from our estimates. When the stock of excess credits equals zero, an estimate of this probability is given by the coefficient on the expected tax price variable. Using the parameter estimate from our preferred specifications in columns (4), (5), and (6), the implied probability of switching credit position is around 0.62. This probability may seem large, but considered in light of the substantial shifts in credit position shown in table 3.5 it appears to be more reasonable. In particular, note that table 3.5 shows that at least 46 percent of the parent corporations switched credit position during the period 1984–86. Over the seven-year period around 1986 during which excess credits could be carried back or forward, the percentage of firms switching credit position would probably be a lot higher.

Our results appear to suggest a greater and more significant tax price effect on dividend remittances than that found by Hines and Hubbard (1990) in their estimates of a similar equation. This may be due to our improved specification of the tax price variable or to differences in the data used.

Caution should be exercised in interpreting the estimated coefficients on our tax price variable. These estimates do not necessarily show the effect of tax policy changes on the aggregate level of dividend remittances from CFCs. What the figures show is that firms tend to structure their CFC dividend remittances so that they minimize taxes at the margin. If, given the income flows from other sources, the tax price of a dividend remittance from a particular CFC to its U.S. parent is low, our results suggest that the U.S. parent is more likely to receive a dividend payment from that CFC. But the tax price of a dividend remittance from one CFC will frequently depend on the foreign income its U.S. parent receives from other CFCs, foreign branches, and other sources. Because we have not estimated the parameters of a model that would simultaneously determine the levels of all of these income flows, our estimates will not capture all the effects of policy changes on aggregate dividend remittances.

3.5 Summary and Implications

Our results suggest that U.S. corporations are able to manipulate the flows of income from their CFCs in order to reduce the global tax on their foreign-source income. They are able to take advantage of deferral and the overall limitation on the foreign tax credit to avoid paying much U.S. tax on their foreign income.[35] The incentives for tax avoidance distort the timing and the source of remittances of income from abroad.

To the extent that it merely reflects high foreign taxes paid by U.S. corporations on their foreign-source income, the fact that U.S. multinational corporations avoid paying much U.S. tax on foreign-source income is not necessarily in conflict with U.S. policy goals. The foreign tax credit is, after all, meant to relieve double taxation. However, our results indicate that the low U.S. tax payments on this income are not merely the result of uniformly high foreign tax rates. Instead, they appear to arise to a significant extent from the ability of U.S. firms to cross-credit between different sources of income within the overall limitation on the foreign tax credit. In addition to lowering U.S. tax revenues, this may also affect the extent to which the tax system preserves capital-export neutrality. With cross-crediting, firms with excess credits have a tax incentive to invest in low-tax countries rather than in the United States or elsewhere, thereby violating capital-export neutrality. However, ignoring the effects of deferral, cross-crediting may tend to preserve capital-export neutrality for firms in excess limitation, because the tax consequences of earning income in high-tax countries and low-tax countries are the same. Whether this is, or should be, compatible with U.S. policy goals is an open question.

The current policy implications of our results should be qualified by the major changes in the tax law that have occurred since 1986. By increasing the number of separate limitation baskets, the Tax Reform Act of 1986 tightened up on the use of cross-crediting. Our results indicate that the concerns that led to these further restrictions on cross-crediting were justified, whatever the merits of the particular measures that were adopted. The 1986 act also lowered the U.S. corporate income tax rate substantially, which may have caused a much greater portion of the foreign-source income of U.S. multinationals to generate excess credits. Another possible limitation of this analysis is that 1986 may have been an anomalous year due to the anticipation of the tax law

---

35. The income does bear shareholder-level taxes when it is distributed to the U.S. parent corporation's own shareholders.

changes that took effect over the following two years. Slemrod (1990a) presents balance-of-payments data suggesting that there were such effects on multinational income flows in 1986. We plan to investigate the anticipatory impacts and subsequent effects of the 1986 tax legislation by linking our 1986 data to data from earlier and later years when the first multinational tax data from the period following 1986 become available.

Appendix A
Derivation of Tax Prices for Nonclassical Corporate Income Tax Systems

In this appendix, we present the derivations of the tax prices for dividend payments from CFCs in countries with split-rate and imputation corporate income tax systems.

Tax Prices under Split-Rate Systems

Under split-rate systems, there are different corporate tax rates for undistributed and distributed profits, denoted in the text as τ_u and τ_d, respectively. The total tax paid by CFC i to its country of residence before withholding taxes is

$$T_i = \tau_u(Y_i - D_i) + \tau_d D_i ,$$

where Y_i denotes the CFC's pretax income and D_i denotes its dividend payment to its U.S. parent corporation. Let τ_i represent the source-country average tax rate on the CFC's distributed and undistributed profits before withholding taxes, equal to T_i/Y_i, which is the tax rate used for the dividend gross-up and foreign tax credit calculation. If the parent is in excess credit, there is no additional U.S. tax to pay on dividends, and so the tax price of a dividend remittance must be zero. If the parent is in excess limitation, the U.S. tax payable on the dividend remittance is

$$T_{US} = D_i[(\tau - \tau_i)/(1 - \tau_i) - \omega_i] .$$

where ω_i represents the source-country withholding tax rate on dividend payments out of the country. Differentiating this with respect to D_i yields the U.S. tax price of dividend remittances when the parent is in excess limitation:

$$dT_{US}/dD_i = (\tau - \tau_i)/(1 - \tau_i) - \omega_i + (D_i/Y_i)(\tau_u - \tau_d)(1 - \tau)/(1 - \tau_i)^2 .$$

The global tax liability created by a dividend remittance is the sum of the U.S. and the foreign tax liabilities. If the parent is in excess limitation, that sum is equal to

$$T_G = (\tau_d - \tau_u)D_i + D_i(\tau - \tau_i)/(1 - \tau_i) \ .$$

The global tax price is then

$$dT_G/dD_i = \tau_d - \tau_u + (\tau - \tau_i)/(1 - \tau_i) + $$
$$(D_i/Y_i)(\tau_u - \tau_d)(1 - \tau)/(1 - \tau_i)^2 \ .$$

For a parent in excess credit, the global tax liability associated with the dividend payment is simply

$$T_G = (\tau_d - \tau_u + \omega_i)D_i \ ,$$

so the tax price is

$$dT_G/dD_i = \tau_d - \tau_u + \omega_i \ .$$

Tax Prices under the U.K. Imputation System

Under the U.S.-U.K. tax treaty, the tax credit provided to U.S. shareholders for advanced corporation tax (ACT) on distributed profits is one-half of the credit given domestic shareholders. The United Kingdom applies its withholding tax to both the dividend payment and the ACT credit. The United States considers the tax credit paid to be part of the grossed-up dividend. In addition, for foreign tax credit purposes, the United States treats the reduction by one-half in the credit given to U.S. shareholders as an additional payment of U.K. corporate income tax by the U.K. CFC.

Denoting the tax credit given to U.S. shareholders for ACT as θ_i, actual CFC tax payments to the United Kingdom are

$$T_i = c_iY_i - \theta_iD_i + \omega_i(1 + \theta_i)D_i \ ,$$

where c_i is the rate of tax on undistributed profits. Taxes deemed by the United States to have been paid by the CFC before withholding taxes are

$$T_{dp} = c_iY_i + \theta_iD_i \ .$$

The average U.K. tax rate used for the dividend gross-up and the foreign tax credit is

$$\tau_i = T_{dp}/Y_i \ .$$

Given these definitions, we can derive the U.S. tax liability on a dividend payment from a U.K. CFC after the foreign tax credit. If the U.S. parent corporation is in excess credit, the U.S. tax liability is zero. If the parent is in excess limitation, the U.S. tax liability is

$$T_{US} = (1 + \theta_i)D_i[(\tau - \tau_i)/(1 - \tau_i) - \omega_i] \ .$$

Differentiating this expression produces the tax price of dividend remittances when the parent is in excess limitation:

$$dT_{US}/dD_i = (1 + \theta_i)[(\tau - \tau_i)/(1 - \tau_i) - \omega_i - \theta_i(D_i/Y_i)(1 - \tau)/(1 - \tau_i)^2] .$$

The global tax liability created by the dividend payment for a parent in excess credit is

$$T_G = [(1 + \theta_i)\omega_i - \theta_i]D_i ,$$

and the corresponding tax price is

$$dT_G/dD_i = (1 + \theta_i)\omega_i - \theta_i .$$

The global tax liability for a parent in excess limitation is

$$T_G = (1 + \theta_i)D_i(\tau - \tau_i)/(1 - \tau_i) - \theta_i D_i ,$$

and the associated tax price is

$$dT_G/dD_i = (1 + \theta_i)[(\tau - \tau_i)/(1 - \tau_i) - \theta_i(D_i/Y_i)(1 - \tau)/(1 - \tau_i)^2] - \theta_i .$$

Appendix B
Data Issues

Problems in Imputing CFC-Specific Average Tax Rates from Tax Return Data

Calculating the tax price of dividend repatriations from the subsidiary information return (Form 5471) often requires more information than is reported. This is the case for CFCs that report negative earnings and profits, receive tax refunds from host countries, repatriate dividends in excess of current earnings and profits, or receive remittances from their own subsidiaries. As described below, to reduce measurement errors we eliminated CFCs in some of these situations from our analysis. In other instances, we opted to include observations after careful analysis.

We eliminated two groups of CFCs that are apt to have true gross-up rates that differ from average foreign tax rates. The first group were CFCs with negative earnings and profits. For these CFCs, the rate used to gross up dividends for the purpose of the foreign tax credit is the rate that applied when the earnings from which dividends are distributed were generated. No information on this rate is available because it is a function of past tax rates.

Another problem arose due to the existence of negative CFC foreign income tax payments. CFCs may receive tax refunds from host countries that reduce tax payments on current earnings and profits. This causes no problem for the imputation of average tax rates for CFCs that paid positive foreign taxes but leaves us with an indeterminate gross-up rate for CFCs with negative foreign income tax payments. Because there is insufficient information to impute a tax rate, we also eliminated CFCs in this situation.

There are two nuances in the tax law that complicate the calculation of the gross-up rate for CFCs. First, prior to 1987, if a CFC's dividend payment exceeded its current-year after-tax profits, then the excess was considered to have been distributed from the accumulated profits of previous years, starting with the next previous year and moving backward. The gross-up rate on the excess remittance is therefore calculated based on the foreign taxes that were paid on those prior-year profits. Second, if a CFC itself receives dividend payments from a subsidiary of its own—termed a *lower-tier CFC*—then any dividend payment from the first-tier CFC to its U.S. parent is considered to be paid proportionately out of its own profits and the profits of the lower-tier CFC. Therefore, the gross-up rate is based on a weighted average of the average tax rates of the first-tier CFC and the lower-tier CFC, with the weights determined by the fraction of the first-tier CFC's profits accounted for by the dividend from the lower-tier CFC. After careful analysis, we chose to have our sample include CFCs in both of these situations. Imputed average tax rates were calculated by dividing current-year tax payments by current-year earnings and profits. A description of the procedures we used to determine if the inclusion of these two groups of CFCs caused any bias in our results appears in the next section of this appendix.

In summary, we included in our sample those CFCs that received dividend payments from lower-tier CFCs and CFCs that paid out dividends in excess of current-year earnings and profits. Excluded from our sample are CFCs that made negative foreign income tax payments and CFCs that reported negative earnings and profits. Our sample consisted of 340 parents with positive worldwide income. These corporations owned 4,475 CFCs with assets large enough to be included in the top 7,500 CFCs. Of this group of CFCs, 884 had negative earnings and profits and 159 received tax refunds from host countries. Eliminating these CFCs resulted in a decrease of $601 million of dividend remittances. These omissions accounted for less than 5 percent of the almost $13 billion of dividend payments from CFCs to parents included in the sample. Our sample was made up of the remaining 3,410 CFCs, of which 333 paid out dividends in excess of current earnings and profits and 420 received dividends from lower-tier CFCs. Dividend remittances total $12.3 billion; $2.8 million of dividends were remitted from CFCs that paid out dividends above current earnings and profits, and $6.2 million of dividends were remitted from CFCs receiving dividend payments from lower-tier CFCs.

Potential Sources of Bias

CFCs that Received Dividends from Lower-Tier Subsidiaries

CFCs receiving dividends from lower-tier CFCs may or may not remit dividends to U.S. parent corporations. To determine whether dividend remittance patterns differed between CFCs with lower-tier remittances and those without, we separated from the sample those CFCs for which lower-tier dividend payments constituted more than 10 percent of earnings and profits. We then generated tables 3.3–3.6 for both samples and compared the results. Although CFCs that received substantial amounts of dividends from lower-tier CFCs were more likely to make dividend payments to U.S. parents and paid out more dividends, we found that the relationship between tax prices and dividend payments did not differ across the two samples. As a result, we included in our tabulation and econometric work all CFCs that derived income from lower-tier dividend payments.

CFCs That Paid Out Dividends in Excess of Current-Year After-tax Profits

CFCs that paid out dividends in excess of current earnings and profits are also a potential source of measurement error. We compared tabulations for this group of CFCs with all other CFCs paying dividends and determined that including this set of CFCs did not systematically bias our results.

References

Alworth, Julian. 1988. *The financial, investment, and taxation decisions of multinationals.* Oxford, U.K.: Basil Blackwell.
Boskin, Michael, and William Gale. 1987. New results on the effects of tax policy on the international location of investment. In *The effects of taxation on capital accumulation,* ed. M. S. Feldstein, 201–19. Chicago: University of Chicago Press.
Goodspeed, Timothy, and Daniel J. Frisch. 1989. U.S. tax policy and the overseas activities of U.S. multinational corporations: A quantitative assessment. Washington, D.C.: U.S. Department of the Treasury. Mimeograph.
Hartman, David. 1981. Domestic tax policy and foreign investment: Some evidence. NBER Working Paper no. 784. Cambridge, Mass.: National Bureau of Economic Research, October.
———. 1985. Tax policy and foreign direct investment. *Journal of Public Economics* 26:107–21.
Hines, James R. 1989. Credit and deferral as international investment incentives. Princeton, N.J.: Princeton University, August. Mimeograph.
———. 1991. Dividends and profits: Some unsubtle foreign influences. NBER Working Paper no. 3730. Cambridge, Mass.: National Bureau of Economic Research.
Hines, James R., and R. Glenn Hubbard. 1990. Coming home to America: Dividend repatriations by U.S. multinationals. In *Taxation in the global economy,* ed. A. Razin and J. Slemrod, 161–207. Chicago: University of Chicago Press.
Jun, Joosung. 1990. U.S. tax policy and direct investment abroad. In *Taxation in the global economy,* ed. A. Razin and J. Slemrod, 55–78. Chicago: University of Chicago Press.
Kopits, George F. 1972. Dividend remittance behavior within the international firm: A cross-country analysis. *Review of Economics and Statistics* 54:339–42.
———. 1976. Intra-firm royalties crossing frontiers and transfer-price behavior. *Economic Journal* 86:791–805.
Leechor, Chad, and Jack Mintz. 1990. On the taxation of multinational corporate investment when the deferral method is used by the capital exporting country. Toronto: University of Toronto. Mimeograph.

Mutti, John. 1981. Tax incentives and repatriation decisions of U.S. multinational corporations. *National Tax Journal* 34:241–48.

Newlon, Timothy Scott. 1987. Tax policy and the multinational firm's financial policy and investment decisions. Ph.D. dissertation, Princeton University.

Price Waterhouse. 1986. *Corporate taxes: A worldwide summary.* New York.

———. 1991. *U.S. international tax policy for a global economy.* Prepared for the National Chamber Foundation, April 15.

Redmiles, Lissa. 1990. Corporate foreign tax credit 1986: An industry focus. *SOI Bulletin* 10(2).

Sinn, Hans-Werner. 1990. Taxation and the birth of foreign subsidiaries. NBER Working Paper no. 3519. Cambridge, Mass.: National Bureau of Economic Research.

Slemrod, Joel. 1990a. The impact of the Tax Reform Act of 1986 on foreign direct investment to and from the United States. In *Do taxes matter? The impact of the Tax Reform Act of 1986,* ed. J. Slemrod, 168–202. Cambridge, Mass.: MIT Press.

———. 1990b. Tax effects on foreign direct investment in the U.S.: Evidence from a cross-country comparison. In *Taxation in the global economy,* ed. A. Razin and J. Slemrod, 79–122. Chicago: University of Chicago Press.

Tillinghast, David R. 1990. International tax simplification. *American Journal of Tax Policy* 8:187–258.

U.S. Department of the Treasury. 1984. *Tax reform for fairness, simplicity, and economic growth.* Washington, D.C.: U.S. Government Printing Office.

———. 1985. *The president's tax proposals to the Congress for fairness, growth, and simplicity.* Washington, D.C.: U.S. Government Printing Office.

II Investment

4 Taxation and Foreign Direct Investment in the United States: A Reconsideration of the Evidence

Alan J. Auerbach and Kevin Hassett

In recent years, a large body of research, dating back to Hartman (1984, 1985), has focused on the effects of taxation on foreign direct investment (FDI) into and from the United States. For the most part, this literature has related capital flows to some measure of an effective tax rate on capital income. The empirical results relating to inward FDI, on which we shall concentrate in this paper, have been mixed. Although there is some evidence that tax rates affect investment, there has been little robustness to such findings.

We argue below that this lack of satisfactory results may be due, in part, to the fact that past efforts have typically studied financial flows rather than investment itself and have failed to account adequately for the different methods foreign multinationals can use to invest in the United States, each of which carries its own particular tax implications. By lumping together all forms of investment and relating this aggregate value to some measure of the U.S. tax rate, previous researchers have obscured the possible impact of taxation on foreign investment.

A foreign multinational seeking to undertake real investment in the United States can do so in three different ways: it can acquire an existing U.S. company, establish a new U.S. branch or subsidiary, or invest through an affiliate branch or subsidiary already operating in U.S. markets. The relevant tax factors affecting the decision of the multinational depend not only upon the

Alan J. Auerbach is professor of economics and law at the University of Pennsylvania and a research associate of the National Bureau of Economic Research. Kevin Hassett is assistant professor of economics and finance at the Graduate School of Business, Columbia University.

This paper has been prepared for an NBER conference on international taxation. The authors are grateful to participants in the NBER Summer Institute, participants in the international taxation conference, George Mundstock, James M. Poterba, Bill Gale, Joel Slemrod, and Deborah Swenson for comments and suggestions, the Bureau of Economic Analysis for providing unpublished data, Jason Cummins for superlative research assistance, and the National Science Foundation for financial support.

source of funds and the home country's tax rules, two factors which previous authors have emphasized, but also critically upon the chosen method of undertaking the investment. Although most authors have modeled the taxation of FDI as if it proceeded through the acquisition of new capital goods, the predominant channel of FDI actually has been through mergers and acquisitions. This distinction is of particular importance for the interpretation of recent FDI behavior.

In a provocative work, Scholes and Wolfson (1991) argue that the Tax Reform Act of 1986 (TRA86) provided a strong incentive for foreign multinationals to increase their investment activity in the United States. The authors' argument rests upon the observation that foreign companies whose home countries credit U.S. taxes (those with so-called worldwide tax systems) are relatively unaffected by increases in U.S. taxes because any payments made are credited at home upon repatriation. Because TRA86 raised effective tax rates on certain corporate assets, the relative (to domestic U.S. investors) tax position of these selected foreign investors may have improved. Scholes and Wolfson offer stylized evidence that the boom in investment predicted by these tax effects has actually occurred, and Swenson (1989) provides some supporting evidence with respect to the recent pattern of FDI across industries and countries. We reevaluate the Scholes-Wolfson hypothesis in this paper because we view it as a litmus test for the importance of taxes in determining FDI into the United States and because we feel that econometric analysis in the spirit of earlier studies would be difficult to interpret given the limited sample sizes and clear nonstationarity in the variables we feel are important.

As we shall discuss below, a significant part of the FDI boom of the late 1980s came through takeovers rather than through the purchase of new assets. Yet, given the distinct tax treatment of takeovers (as opposed to new investment) and the additional provisions of TRA86 regarding takeovers, it is questionable whether the boom in FDI is really consistent with the 1986 tax changes. In particular, it is not clear that tax factors would predict an increase in FDI generally or a relative increase in FDI from home countries following a worldwide tax system. We demonstrate this point using a model of FDI developed in Section 4.4. In light of the model's implications, we consider the recent patterns of FDI and argue that the evidence of a tax-induced boom after 1986 is not as strong as others have suggested it to be.

4.1   Foreign Direct Investment in the United States

Foreign direct investment into the United States has been the subject of a burgeoning empirical literature. Table 4.1 suggests why. The last column of the table presents annual flows of FDI, the data series studied by most of the previous empirical efforts examining inbound FDI.[1] This series grew at an

---

1. In addition to the papers already mentioned, the literature attempting to explain inward FDI includes Boskin and Gale (1987), Froot and Stein (1989), and Newlon (1987). For an excellent and comprehensive review of the literature, see Slemrod (1990b).

Table 4.1   **FDI Investment in the U.S., by Year ($ millions)**

Year	Affiliate	Acquisition	Establishment	Total	Capital Flow
		Investment Type			
80	$16,891	$ 8,974	$ 3,198	$ 29,063	$16,918
81	26,716	18,151	5,067	49,934	25,195
82	28,068	6,563	4,254	38,885	13,792
83	23,179	4,848	3,244	31,271	11,946
84	25,225	11,836	3,361	40,422	25,359
85	28,919	20,083	3,023	52,025	19,022
86	28,516	31,450	7,728	67,694	34,091
87	33,035	33,933	6,377	73,345	46,894
88	44,322	64,855	7,837	117,014	58,435
89	52,258	59,708	11,455	123,421	72,244
90	NA	56,773	7,651	NA	25,709

Source: Survey of Current Business, various issues.
Note: NA = Not available.

average annual rate of 18 percent between 1980 and 1989 before dropping sharply in 1990.

One drawback of the use of capital flow data is that they are not directly related to the actual physical investment of interest to the researcher and on which are based the theoretical models used to form effective tax rates. For example, if a foreign company borrows in the United States in order to purchase a machine, the transaction will not appear in the capital flow data. Quijano (1990, 33, tab. 4) reports that roughly 81 percent of debt financing of U.S. affiliates occurs through U.S. sources of funds, suggesting that this omission may be quite important. Although payments to cover the borrowing by the foreign parent will appear in the flow data, the timing of the investment will be obscured, and any relationship between the tax treatment of investment in a particular year and the observed flow series may be spurious.[2]

Alternative measures of FDI that are in some respects closer to the desired measure are given in the first three columns of table 4.1. The first is total investment in plant and equipment undertaken by foreign affiliates, the second is the total value of U.S. firms acquired by foreign companies, and the third is the value of foreign branches and subsidiaries newly established by foreign companies.[3]

2. There are other possible shortcomings of the flow data. Firms from territorial countries (those not receiving credits for U.S. taxes at home) might have a higher incentive to borrow in the United States to avoid U.S. taxes, so we might expect the flow data to systematically understate their investment relative to that from worldwide countries.

3. For a useful discussion of the differences in coverage of the different measures, see Quijano (1990). The balance-of-payments flow data and affiliate financial and operating data track the behavior of existing U.S. affiliates of foreign corporations. The acquisition and establishment data survey existing U.S. companies acquired by foreign investors, and new companies established by foreign investors. The reported affiliate investment here is affiliate investment in new plant and

Each of these alternative measures also shows a striking increase in the 1980s. Affiliate investment grew approximately 13 percent a year from 1980 to 1989, while establishment investment grew at a rate of 15 percent. FDI through acquisition of existing U.S. assets grew approximately 23 percent a year over the same period, suggesting that the U.S. merger boom of the eighties was not confined to domestic parents. In our view, it is the plant and equipment investment by affiliates plus the establishment of new operations that correspond most closely to the theory on which past studies have been based, since these studies have generally ignored the special tax provisions affecting the acquisition of existing companies or their assets. Yet, by 1988, these two categories combined accounted for less foreign direct investment than did acquisitions.

4.2   Tax Treatment of FDI

The tax treatment of foreign-source income can be very complicated, making empirical study difficult. Countries generally treat foreign-source income in one of two ways. A "territorial," or source-based, approach involves taxing only home-source income, essentially exempting from domestic tax the income a domestic multinational earns on its operations abroad. For companies based in territorial countries, the relevant corporate tax provisions directly relating to investment are clearly those imposed by the host country.

At the other extreme is the "worldwide" approach that adopts the residence principle of taxation, whereby the home country attempts to tax the worldwide income of its companies, normally offering a credit for income taxes already paid on such income abroad. In principle, the income of companies based in worldwide countries faces a tax burden determined by the home country's tax provisions, since foreign taxes are simply offset by credits against the home country's taxes. This is the essence of the Scholes-Wolfson argument.

In practice, of course, there are many additional provisions that attenuate this sterilization of a worldwide multinational's foreign tax burden. First, if the foreign tax rate exceeds that of the home country, there will typically be excess foreign tax credits, making the marginal tax burden dependent on the foreign tax provisions, as with territorial home countries. Second, in practice the residence principle is commonly applied only upon the repatriation of income. As with the taxation of a corporation's dividends upon their payment,

---

equipment only. If an affiliate purchases an existing U.S. firm, this shows up in the acquisition data. (Appendix A discusses further the sources of the data presented in the tables.)

The total of the three investment series, given in the fourth column of table 4.1, is roughly double the flow series given in the last column. This reflects both the absence of domestically financed capital from the flow series and the fact that some of the domestic affiliates are only partially owned by foreign investors. Moreover, the flow data net out sales of domestic firms back to domestic parents. Still, we view the affiliate, acquisition, and establishment data as more closely related to business fixed investment activity.

the additional taxes paid upon repatriation may have no effect on investment financed by retained earnings, a point first made in the foreign context by Hartman (1985).

Beginning with Hartman's work, much of the empirical literature on FDI into the United States has focused on the distinction between retained earnings and transfers. The theory suggests that U.S. tax provisions should matter least for the investment from worldwide countries that is financed by transfers, but the empirical evidence offers, at best, weak support. Indeed, Slemrod (1990b) finds that the transfer of funds is described well by tax and return variables but that retention of earnings is not.

A possible problem with this literature is the dependence on flow data which, as discussed above, do not necessarily correspond to investment itself. One study, by Swenson (1989), used the acquisition and establishment data (given in the second and third columns of table 4.1) and did find some evidence that average U.S. tax rates are positively correlated with inbound FDI, as the Scholes-Wolfson hypothesis would suggest. However, Swenson also found a negative impact of the effective marginal tax rate, a result difficult to reconcile with the apparent theory. We believe part of this puzzle may be traced to the lack of attention to the alternative modes of foreign direct investment. That is, the effective tax rates used by Swenson should not be expected to describe acquisition activity well.

As indicated above, the theoretical discussion and empirical analysis of the impact of taxation on FDI has treated the problem as one of acquiring new capital, even though this is only one of the possible modes. The other important mode is the acquisition of an existing U.S. company. The mode of investment chosen affects tax liability differently because the choice to acquire a U.S. company will depend on the U.S. merger laws governing, for example, step-up in basis and transfer of tax benefits, whereas investment in new capital will depend on the statutory tax rate, the investment tax credit, and depreciation schedules. Because the tax burden incurred depends upon the method chosen and the investor doing the choosing, it makes little sense to group these forms of investment together and relate them to a single tax variable, as has frequently been done in the past.

A firm can choose to acquire another in the United States in a number of ways. The first choice is whether to acquire with cash or in exchange for the shares of the acquirer, and the second choice is whether to acquire the shares or assets of the target. If an exchange of shares is chosen, the deal may completely avoid immediate tax consequences, with the depreciable basis of the acquired corporation being absorbed into the acquirer and, in general, the U.S. shareholder that sells the stock deferring tax liability until such time as the shares received in exchange are sold. The tax basis of the new stock is the same as that of the relinquished stock, and tax is paid upon realization of any gains.[4]

---

4. This is generally the case if the acquisition qualified as a "B" or "C" reorganization, so designated because the relevant code is section 268(a)(1) (B) or (C) of the Internal Revenue Code.

In a sample we have constructed, virtually all foreign acquisitions were financed with cash throughout the 1980s. If the acquirer chooses to pay cash or a combination of stock and cash for the stock of the target, there will generally be no deferral of shareholder capital gains tax. However, there is still the choice of whether to acquire the company as a going concern or a collection of assets. If the acquirer chooses to perform a corporate stock acquisition, the U.S. tax attributes of the acquired company will be inherited by the corporation, without any immediate corporate-level taxation.[5] Alternatively, the parent company can acquire the assets of the target, either explicitly or by electing to treat a stock acquisition as an asset acquisition via section 338 of the Internal Revenue Code. In this case, the acquirer can step up the basis of the depreciable assets of the target, but in order to do so the liquidating corporation must pay some corporate tax on the basis step-up, and no transfer of net operating losses is allowed.

To the extent that an acquiring foreign corporation is influenced only by U.S. taxes at the margin (the territorial case), the incentives it faces in deciding how to structure a deal are similar to those facing a U.S. parent. In the other extreme (worldwide) case, in which U.S. taxes are absorbed by tax credits at home, there seems less reason to opt for the basis step-up, because this provides no ultimate tax relief but does require the payment of taxes by the liquidating corporation.

4.3   Tax Reform Act of 1986

The passage of the Tax Reform Act of 1986 brought several changes in the taxation of U.S. corporate investment. The literature on FDI has focused primarily on the reduced investment incentives and the apparent advantages this offers worldwide countries (see, for example, Scholes and Wolfson 1991; Slemrod 1990a; and Swenson 1989). However, TRA86 also introduced important changes in the tax treatment of mergers and acquisitions.

Prior to 1986, the General Utilities doctrine allowed firms electing to acquire the assets of the target to step up the basis of the acquired assets while

---

Since 1986, the tax losses of the acquired firm will be available only for restricted use, subject to the annual limitation that the losses claimed not exceed the value of the target multiplied by the federal long-term tax-exempt rate, provided that the acquirer can show that the acquired firm is an "ongoing" enterprise. If the acquired firm is liquidated within two years of the acquisition, the net operating losses cannot be used. This limitation on the use of losses applies to stock acquisitions generally, regardless of whether they qualify for treatment as a tax-free reorganization.

5. Scholes and Wolfson (1991) argue that these transactions might also provide a way for foreign corporations to avoid taxes on an eventual basis step-up by transferring from the subsidiary to a foreign parent the assets initially acquired by a U.S. subsidiary in a stock transaction. However, this type of transaction is taxable under section 367(e)(2) of the Internal Revenue Code. There was some uncertainty as to whether the IRS could enforce this section. Notice 87-5, issued at the end of 1986, argued that this treatment violates some tax treaties, but eventually the IRS withdrew this notice (Notice 87-66), making clear its commitment to impede such tax avoidance strategies.

paying tax only on the recaptured depreciable basis for those assets subject to recapture. For example, if the target had purchased a machine for $50 and depreciated it to $10, then the acquirer, upon purchasing the machine for $100, was allowed to claim depreciation allowances on the full $100 after paying tax on the $40 of recaptured basis. Some believed this to have provided a strong tax incentive for mergers, although aggregate evidence in support of this claim is lacking (Auerbach and Reishus 1988). The repeal of this provision may have played a role in the enormous surge in acquisition activity in the final two quarters of 1986. The removal of the tax gain from basis step-up should provide a powerful disincentive for FDI in the form of acquiring U.S. firms, at least to the extent that such acquisitions take the form of assets purchases.[6]

In addition to these provisions directly affecting mergers and acquisitions, the 1986 act altered the structure of taxation in a way that may indirectly have influenced takeovers. In reducing investment incentives (most importantly through the elimination of the investment tax credit) and at the same time reducing the corporate rate, TRA86 sharply narrowed the distinction in the treatment of new and existing assets, providing apparently large windfalls to the value of existing firms. In theory, this represents a large tax-induced increase in the price of firms and should have influenced the incentives to purchase such firms—particularly for the worldwide company, which by assumption cannot obtain the offsetting benefits of reduced domestic taxation of the existing capital it purchases.

In summary, there are three sets of U.S. tax provisions relevant to FDI: those that apply to new capital, those that apply to mergers and acquisitions, and those affecting existing assets. Quantifying the relative importance of these effects requires an explicit model of the FDI process.

4.4   A Model of Foreign Investment

In this section, drawing heavily on Auerbach (1989), we introduce a model which allows us to derive effective tax rates for foreign firms interested in acquiring U.S. assets. In this model, there are three types of firms: domestic, foreign territorial (which are subject only to U.S. taxes), and foreign worldwide (which, at the margin, are not affected by U.S. taxes they pay).

The model proceeds in two stages. In the first stage, the representative domestic firm acts much like the firm in Auerbach (1989), maximizing value subject to a constant-returns-to-scale production function with quadratic adjustment costs of investment and potentially changing taxes. Given the constant-returns technology, the determinacy of equilibrium is provided by an endogenous price of output, which varies inversely with the level of aggregate

---

6. Good information on the fraction of transactions by foreign parents taking this form is not available.

production. The domestic firm's optimization problem leads to a system of first-order differential equations in the capital stock K and the shadow value of new capital, q, which we linearize in order to solve. The solution for the path of K and q also provides a path for the output price, p. The combination of q and U.S. tax provisions determine the price of existing capital, q^K.

In the model's second stage, the foreign firm observes the equilibrium path of q, p, and q^K determined by the domestic firm and decides, in light of the tax provisions that it faces, how much capital to acquire at each instant. In order to make the problem tractable, we assume that the foreign firm's decision to acquire domestic capital has no effect on domestic output or price and that the foreign firm distributes its new purchases between existing and new capital subject to an exogenously given proportion, β.[7] This approach incorporates the idea that, in order to grow within the United States, foreign firms may need to grow extensively as well as intensively, thereby establishing a toehold in new markets.[8]

We model behavior as if a steady state existed in 1986 and consider change in the rate of investment after the passage of TRA86, which change we treat as unanticipated and permanent. To obtain relatively simple expressions for the level of FDI, we make a variety of additional simplifying assumptions (discussed in detail in Appendix B), where the following expressions are derived for FDI by worldwide and territorial companies, respectively (with "*" representing a steady-state value around which the linearization takes place):

$$(1) \qquad \frac{\dot{K}_0^F}{K^{*F}} = -\frac{1}{\phi^F}\left(\left[\frac{a\lambda_1\phi}{\eta}\right]\left\{-\frac{\lambda_1}{\rho} + \beta\left[\frac{1 - k - \Gamma}{1 - k^* - \Gamma^*[1 - \hat{\delta}/(\delta' + \pi)]}\right]\right\} + \beta B\right)$$

and

$$(2) \qquad \frac{\dot{K}_0^F}{K^{*F}} = -\frac{1}{\phi^F}\left(\frac{a\lambda_1\phi}{\eta}\right)(\beta - 1),$$

where λ_1 (< 0) is the stable root of the domestic corporation's capital accumulation problem; ϕ is the domestic firm's adjustment cost parameter (ϕ^F being the corresponding value for the foreign firm); η is the elasticity of demand for output; ρ is the firm's real discount rate; $\hat{\delta} = [\delta(1 - \delta\phi/2)]$ is an adjusted rate of economic depreciation; π is the rate of inflation; and β is the

---

7. When a foreign firm purchases old capital (i.e., an existing U.S. firm), the transaction is simply a change in ownership and should obey our assumptions. When a foreign firm purchases new capital, however, this could, in principle, change domestic output and price unless the foreign investment is quite small relative to domestic investment.

8. While β may range between zero and one in the model, it does not vary over time. Thus, we have not incorporated the possibility that β may depend upon a foreign corporation's domestic experience, with relative newcomers perhaps more likely to weigh takeovers heavily at first. We return to this issue below (see footnote 13).

fraction of FDI done in the form of acquisition (as opposed to new capital purchases).

The remaining terms in these two equations all relate to changes in U.S. taxation, with k the investment tax credit, Γ the present value of depreciation allowances, and δ' the rate at which assets are written off for tax purposes. The term a is the proportional change in the domestic effective tax rate associated with TRA86, while B is the proportional change in the relative value of old to new capital. In general, $B > 0$ because the act raised the relative valuation of existing assets. If the cost of capital increased, then $a > 0$ as well. Note that B appears only in the first expression, since territorial firms are assumed to get the benefits of the reduced taxation of existing assets that the price reflects. Worldwide firms, on the other hand, must pay for these benefits but do not, by assumption, receive them: the reduced U.S. tax burden simply leads to increased taxes at home.

The other major difference between the two expressions is in the sign of the term multiplying the expression $(a\lambda_1\phi/\eta)$, which relates to the decline in domestic capital accumulation. For worldwide firms, there are two effects, both of which increase investment (for $a > 0$). The first, $(-\lambda_1/\rho)$, is associated with the rise in prices coming from the reduction in the scale of domestic operations. The second comes from the decline in q and reflects the benefits of a reduction in the price of capital goods acquired through existing companies, holding the relative valuation of new and existing goods constant.

For the territorial firm, the overall effect is negative unless $\beta = 1$, since the increase in p results from the reduced domestic incentive to invest, to which territorial firms are also subject. Indeed, when $\beta = 0$, the territorial firm's problem is essentially the same as that of the domestic firm. However, as $\beta \to 1$, the impact of the U.S. tax increase is muted by the offsetting benefit of the decline in q.

In summary, the impact of TRA86 on the FDI of territorial firms should go in the same direction as domestic investment, although these firms will face no disincentive to the extent that FDI occurs through the acquisition of firms rather than new capital. Hence, for assets facing a higher cost of capital, FDI should be discouraged in general but should shift toward acquisitions. The impact on the FDI of worldwide firms is of a more ambiguous nature for those assets for which investers face an increased cost of capital, as the reduction in domestic investment activity should encourage entry but the higher valuation of existing capital should discourage it. As long as the net effect of the tax reform is to increase the value of domestic firms (i.e., the terms multiplying β have a positive sum), worldwide firms will have an incentive to shift their activity away from acquisitions.[9]

9. We note, however, that this conclusion regarding the relative shift toward acquisitions by territorial companies ignores the possibility that worldwide and territorial companies' acquisitions may also have been affected by the repeal of the General Utilities doctrine, the effects of which our model does not include.

The sign of the impact of TRA86 on investment by worldwide companies is an empirical question, which can be elucidated by considering several examples motivated by the tax treatment of different assets and the actual distributions of FDI among the alternative modes of investment. Table 4.2 reports the results of simulations of the effect of the tax reform on FDI for various assumptions about the relevant parameters. The numbers given in the table are the initial change in the investment-capital ratio associated with the 1986 tax change, multiplied by the foreign adjustment cost parameter ϕ_F. That is, one should divide the given number by one's estimate of ϕ_F to obtain an estimated first-year change in the investment-capital ratio.

The top panel displays the results for hypothetical worldwide firms; the bottom panel gives comparable results for territorial firms. For our simulations, we considered four types of asset: equipment, structures, land, and intangibles. Equipment, which depreciates relatively rapidly and received the investment tax credit before 1986, typifies the investment that should have been discouraged by TRA86 and perhaps been made more attractive to worldwide investors. Structures, at least those in the corporate sector, were treated relatively favorably by the 1986 act.[10] Land is not depreciable for tax purposes, whereas the creation of intangibles (as, for example, through advertising) may generally be expensed.

For each asset and country type, we consider a range of potential values for the fraction of FDI taking the form of mergers and acquisitions (β) and for the quadratic adjustment cost term facing domestic investors (ϕ). For β, we consider values of 0 (all direct purchases of new capital), 1 (all takeovers), and 0.5 (a reasonable value, given the relative importance of the two methods indicated in table 4.1). For ϕ, we consider values of 5 and 15, meant to represent reasonably low and high levels of adjustment costs.

Let us consider first the results for territorial firms. Recall that, since the value of existing capital reflects its future productivity, the net effect of any of the tax changes is zero if $\beta = 1$. For the intermediate value of β, 0.5, we can see that the tax reform provided a disincentive for equipment investment and increased incentives for investment in structures and land (since $a > 0$ for these assets). For intangibles, there is no effect because our assumption of immediate expensing makes the cost of capital impervious to the corporate tax rate. When $\beta = 0$, the effects of the reform are even stronger but in the same direction. In general, territorial firms' investment in equipment should shift toward acquisition and away from new investment after 1986.

The results for worldwide firms reflect the offsetting effects described above. The results are generally opposite those of the territorial firms, as only investment in equipment may have been encouraged by the 1986 act. Invest-

---

10. The effect of lengthened depreciation lifetimes was more than offset by the reduction in the corporate tax rate. We have not attempted to quantify the impact of other provisions, such as the strengthened corporate minimum tax.

Table 4.2   **Effects of Changes in the Incentives for Foreign Direct Investment**

	$\phi = 5; \beta =$			$\phi = 15; \beta =$		
	0	.5	1	0	.5	1
			Worldwide Countries			
Equipment	.214	.136	.058	.034	−.103	−.240
Structures	−.171	−.222	−.273	−.121	−.190	−.258
Land	−.116	−.149	−.182	−.085	−.134	−.182
Intangibles	0	−.111	−.222	0	−.111	−.222
			Territorial Countries			
	0	.5	1	0	.5	1
Equipment	−.060	−.030	0	−.042	−.021	0
Structures	.068	.034	0	.099	.050	0
Land	.065	.033	0	.096	.048	0
Intangibles	0	0	0	0	0	0

Note: Table 4.2 records values of textequation (1). For equipment, the parameters assumed are $\pi = .04$, $\rho = .04$, $\delta' = 2$, $\eta = 1$, and $\phi_F = 1$. For structures, we assume the same, except that $\delta = .033$ and $\delta' = .05$. For land, $\delta = \delta' = 0$. For intangibles, $\delta = .09$, $\delta' = \infty$. The values of δ for equipment and structures are taken from Auerbach and Hines (1987).

ment in land and structures was doubly discouraged, because these assets received both windfalls to the value of existing capital and reductions in the effective tax rate on new investment. Hence, these assets would have cost more (to the extent acquired via takeover) and returned less, as domestic investors were encouraged to invest. Investment in intangibles was discouraged because of the windfall to existing capital, with no offsetting effect coming from changes in the tax treatment of new investment. Only for equipment could the higher price of existing capital have been offset by higher returns in the future, and the table indicates that for this to occur would have required a combination of low adjustment costs (so that domestic investment would drop and before-tax returns to capital rise quickly) and a high fraction of capital purchased directly rather than through mergers and acquisitions. Indeed, for the high-adjustment-cost case with half of all capital acquired through takeover, all types of investment by worldwide investors are discouraged, and even equipment investment is discouraged more than for territorial investors.

Hence, the notion of worldwide investors rushing in to own domestic capital requires a very particular alignment of assumptions about the type of capital being acquired, the mode in which it is acquired, and the speed with which domestic investors leave the market to make foreign entry attractive. In all of the cases, however, worldwide companies should have been encouraged to shift their mode of investment from acquisitions of companies to direct purchases of new assets.

In summary, we can conclude the following from the simulations in table 4.2: Relative to territorial firms, worldwide firms should have shifted their investment toward equipment and utilized the takeover route less often. The overall impact on investment by territorial firms should have been negative, but unless a preponderant share of FDI by worldwide companies took the form of purchases of new equipment, these firms' overall incentive for investment should also have decreased. We can evaluate these predictions using a variety of data on the composition and level of FDI before and after TRA86.

4.5 Recent FDI Experience

Tables 4.3 through 4.5 record the FDI data by country and type of investment from 1980 to 1989. All three tables report investment both for the major worldwide countries, the United Kingdom and Japan, and for the major territorial countries, Canada, France, West Germany, and the Netherlands.[11] Clearly, the sharp increase observed in table 4.1 is also evident in table 4.3, with virtually every country experiencing growth in affiliate FDI both before and after TRA86. The growth rates from 1986 to 1989 were large for all countries. Japanese affiliate FDI grew 98 percent over this period; U.K. affiliate FDI grew 62 percent. The territorial countries experienced a smaller boom, with growth rates over the period ranging from 17 percent for the Netherlands to 46 percent for West Germany.

Table 4.4 reports acquisition FDI for the same countries. These series also show an increase throughout the sample, but the increases by the worldwide countries, the United Kingdom and Japan, after TRA86 are truly striking. From 1986 to 1988, Japanese acquisition activity increased by nearly a factor of ten, and British acquisitions increased by a factor of nearly three. The most notable event in the territorial data is the large temporary increase in acquisitions in 1986, something consistent with the view that the suspension of the favorable tax treatment of acquisitions induced these firms to get their acquisitions in under the wire. Table 4.5 reports establishment FDI, which shows a solid increase for worldwide countries but nothing striking for territorial ones.[12]

Figures 4.1 through 4.4 record the composition of worldwide and territorial

11. These characterizations are taken from Slemrod (1990b). We note, however, that the distinction is not so clear in reality. Territorial countries do not necessarily exempt all types of foreign-source income. On the other hand, investors in worldwide countries may face no effective tax rate on foreign-source income, because of either excess foreign tax credits or the use of retained earnings as the marginal source of finance (see section 4.2 above).

12. It might be argued that the general increase in FDI during the late 1980s simply reflects exchange rate movements. To control for this effect, we recalculated the figures in tables 4.3 through 4.5 in units of the home currency. Indeed, this did reduce the measured growth rate in FDI from 1986 to 1988. The explosion in acquisitions by worldwide countries stands out even more. Denominated in yen, Japanese acquisitions grew by a factor of 7.5 from 1986 to 1988, while U.K. acquisitions, stated in pounds, grew by a factor of 2.5.

Table 4.3   **FDI Affiliate Investment by Country of Origin, by Year (U.S. $ millions)**

| | Territorial | | | | Worldwide | |
Year	Canada	France	West Germany	Netherlands	Japan	United Kingdom
80	$3,868	$1,423	$2,317	$2,719	$ 1,237	$2,363
81	8,116	1,704	2,658	3,650	1,254	4,108
82	7,771	1,489	2,317	3,350	1,795	5,055
83	5,451	1,191	1,950	2,482	1,675	4,834
84	5,810	1,285	2,183	2,856	2,339	4,765
85	6,437	1,318	2,715	3,467	3,072	5,392
86	5,842	1,332	2,920	3,095	3,925	4,788
87	6,445	1,236	3,186	3,324	6,075	5,727
88	8,345	1,894	4,251	3,823	7,757	7,767
89	9,920	2,573	4,734	3,897	11,132	7,105

Table 4.4   **FDI Acquisition Investment by Country of Origin, by Year (U.S. $ millions)**

| | Territorial | | | | Worldwide | |
Year	Canada	France	West Germany	Netherlands	Japan	United Kingdom
80	$1,743	$ 516	$1,186	$ 783	$ 521	$2,793
81	5,100	801	800	408	469	5,309
82	914	359	315	139	137	2,002
83	718	167	378	360	199	1,448
84	2,185	145	476	460	1,352	2,964
85	2,494	593	2,142	579	463	6,023
86	6,091	2,403	1,167	4,406	1,250	7,699
87	1,169	1,949	4,318	204	3,340	14,648
88	11,162	3,691	1,849	2,067	12,233	22,237
89	3,786	2,979	2,300	3,041	10,184	20,357

FDI over the same period. Figure 4.1 indicates that the proportion of total acquisitions of U.S. companies accounted for by worldwide countries leapt dramatically after 1986; by 1988, roughly 55 percent of all acquisitions by foreign firms were accounted for by those based in the United Kingdom and Japan. Figure 4.2 shows that the gap in affiliate investment between territorial and worldwide countries has been narrowing, and figure 4.3 indicates that worldwide countries account for roughly 60 percent of all establishment investment by 1988.

How do these trends mesh with the Scholes-Wolfson hypothesis and the predictions of our model? Recall that the model predicts that if there is a boom

| Table 4.5 | | FDI Establishment Investment by Country of Origin, by Year (U.S. $ millions) | | | | |

		Territorial			Worldwide	
Year	Canada	France	West Germany	Netherlands	Japan	United Kingdom
80	$213	$ 83	$238	$867	$ 75	$ 273
81	984	104	349	163	147	869
82	282	124	285	191	450	1,126
83	354	128	206	132	193	918
84	402	186	210	102	454	751
85	420	161	127	192	689	708
86	412	88	184	295	4,166	872
87	107	96	347	188	3,666	494
88	198	508	241	147	3,956	321
89	141	146	253	237	4,712	1,611

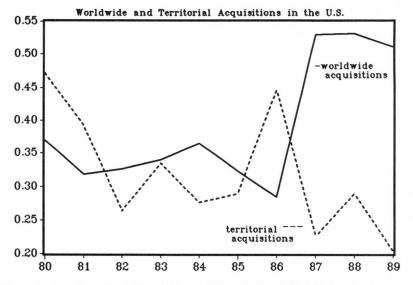

Fig. 4.1   Fraction of total foreign acquisitions in the United States

in investment by worldwide firms, then it should occur in the form of direct purchases of capital, not in acquisitions. Although investment in new capital has increased, as reflected in the increased affiliate and establishment investment, acquisition activity has increased even more, something inconsistent with tax factors.[13] In fact, as figure 4.4 shows, the proportion of worldwide

13. The merger boom might be less damaging if it reflected a choice by new foreign parents to acquire existing U.S. firms in order to gain a foothold in the U.S. market and facilitate further

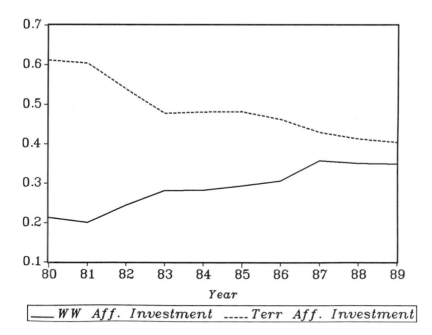

Fig. 4.2   Fraction of total U.S. affiliate investment

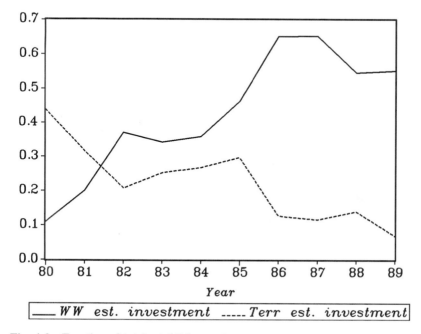

Fig. 4.3   Fraction of total establishment investment

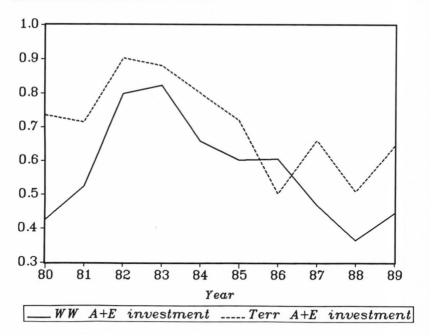

Fig. 4.4   Affiliate and establishment FDI relative to total

investment accounted for by affiliate and establishment investment dropped precipitously after the 1986 reform, going from roughly 60 percent in 1986 to only 35 percent in 1988.

More consistent with the model is the shift of territorial investment toward acquisitions, although the trend is not as clear-cut. The 1987 proportion of new investment is slightly less than that in 1985, and a large decline followed in 1988.

Figure 4.5 plots the share that U.S.-bound FDI has in total overflows from the territorial and worldwide countries.[14] Quite striking is the fact that the share of U.S. investment in total FDI from worldwide countries is roughly constant after 1986, suggesting that the boom in investment experienced in

---

expansions through the purchase of new equipment. In terms of our model, this would reflect a shift over time from a very high to a very low value of β. If this effect were powerful, then the boom in foreign merger activity could have been a signal of intended further expansion through purchases of new equipment.

To examine this hypothesis, we calculated the percentage of acquisitions by new acquirers, for each year in a sample described below, of U.S. firms acquired by foreign parents. The ratio of new entrant to total acquisitions is uniformly high throughout the eighties and increases from roughly 0.7 in 1985 to 0.99 in 1986 and 0.93 in 1987. Thus, the jump appears a year too early to be consistent with this view.

14. Unfortunately, data on the breakdown of these flows among the various modes of investment (acquisition, establishment, and direct capital purchase) are not available.

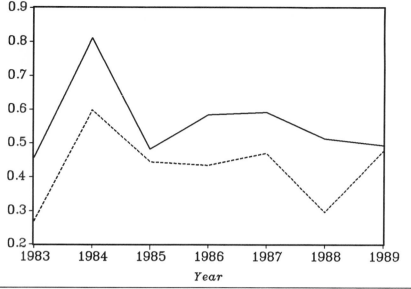

Fig. 4.5   U.S. inflow as fraction of foreign outflows

the United States is just part of a broader increase in foreign investment activity by these countries. The U.S. share in total investment by territorial countries shows a slight increase in 1987, followed by a decline in 1988 and an increase in 1989. For the period 1987–89, there is no clear trend in either investment share. The results do not offer much support for the Scholes-Wolfson predictions of a surge in U.S.-bound tax-driven FDI.

Additional evidence comes from the industrial composition of FDI. Our model suggests that firms from worldwide countries should have faced potential tax incentives to invest in the United States only in equipment. While we do not have detailed investment data on types of assets purchased, we do know the industrial composition of FDI and the asset mix of different industries. In particular, manufacturing is the major equipment-intensive sector in which FDI occurs.

Table 4.6 presents the proportion of total FDI inflow accounted for by investment in the manufacturing sector for the major foreign investors into the United States. Consistent with the theory, the proportion of FDI in manufacturing for worldwide companies has increased dramatically since 1986, going from 0.430 in 1986 to 0.780 in 1989 for the United Kingdom and from 0.129 to 0.292 in the same years for Japan. Contrary to the theory, the same upward trend generally occurs for territorial FDI in manufacturing as well. It is difficult, considering the two together, to judge whether the switch to manufactur-

Table 4.6   **Proportion of FDI Flow in Manufacturing**

| | Territorial | | | | Worldwide | |
Year	Canada	France	West Germany	Netherlands	Japan	United Kingdom
81	.306	1*	.159	.315	.097	.307
82	1*	1*	.062	.209	.155	.218
83	1*	1*	.299	.494	.005	.194
84	.225	0*	0*	.290	.138	.099
85	.852	1*	.628	.193	.087	.395
86	.486	1*	.541	0*	.129	.430
87	.682	.617	.641	.430	.233	.452
88	.498	1*	1*	.435	.380	.526
89	.748	.752	.448	.556	.292	.780

Source: Unpublished Bureau of Economic Analysis data.

*Items for which the value is outside the range of 0–1. This can occur because the flow data are based on inbound FDI net of transfers out of the United States.

ing by worldwide firms was caused by TRA86 or if the swing toward manufacturing is just part of a general trend toward increased manufacturing investment by foreign countries.

An alternative source of information about the mix of assets acquired is the balance sheets of U.S. companies themselves. For the period 1980:1 to 1990:4, we compiled a sample of 243 companies acquired by foreign parents. As a control, we also compiled a sample of 4,485 companies acquired by domestic parents. For each company with available data, we calculated the fraction of equipment and structures in their overall fixed capital stock in the year before the acquisition. In table 4.7, these fractions are aggregated into the pre- and post-1986 periods for the sample of firms acquired by foreign worldwide and territorial parents, for the Compustat universe of firms, and for domestic acquisitions.

As the table clearly shows, the fraction of structures rose and that of equipment fell for two of the three target groups, while the fraction for all firms changed little.[15] While the results for the different target groups are similar, we note that it was among territorial, not worldwide, firms that the share of equipment rose. The similarity across worldwide and territorial targets is consistent with our model of the effects of the 1986 act, but it offers no support for the view that the post-1986 surge in acquisitions by worldwide firms was driven by tax-induced bargains in equipment investment. For example, under the high-adjustment-cost scenario, assuming an adjustment cost parameter of fifteen and allowing the fraction of acquisitions in total FDI to be one, world-

15. When weighted averages were used, the ratios were not significantly different from the full sample means, because of the huge influence of a small number of very large targets.

Table 4.7   **Structures and Equipment as a Share of Capital Stock, by Type of Acquisition pre- and post-TRA86 (unweighted, by all files)**

	Before TRA86			After TRA86			
		t-statistic			t-statistic		
	Proportion	(1)*	(2)†	Proportion	(1)*	(2)†	t-Statistic‡
Structures							
Territorial	.262	.126	− 1.64	.309	1.41	− 1.25	1.00
Worldwide	.330	3.08	1.19	.346	2.17	− .358	.219
Compustat firms	.259			.254			
Domestic							
acquisitions	.305			.362			
Equipment							
Territorial	.521	− .633	.077	.553	.092	1.34	.579
Worldwide	.527	− .768	.048	.512	− .809	.472	− .161
Compustat firms	.543			.549			
Domestic							
acquisitions	.519			.488			

*Testing the difference from the full sample means.
†Testing the difference from the domestic acquisition means.
‡Testing the difference between the two periods.

wide firms investment in equipment and in structures is deterred to roughly the same degree.

4.6 Conclusion

This paper presents a model of FDI that takes into account the different tax treatments of acquisition of old and new capital in order to isolate more precisely the effects of taxation on FDI into the United States. Our simulation results suggest that the Tax Reform Act of 1986 generally decreased investment incentives for worldwide countries in all assets other than equipment and that the sign of the effect on equipment depends upon assumptions about adjustment costs and the proportion of investment accounted for by acquisitions.

The model also suggests that TRA86 provided an incentive for territorial firms to invest relatively less in equipment and relatively more in structures and land. Also, acquisitions by companies from worldwide countries were generally discouraged by the tax reform.

Examination of recent trends suggests that many of the changes in the composition of FDI predicted by either Scholes and Wolfson (1992) or our model have not occurred, casting doubt on the position that the recent boom in foreign direct investment is due to the changes in tax incentives brought about by TRA86. Other factors, such as exchange rate movements and the liberalization of capital markets (see, e.g., Froot and Stein 1989) may have played a role in the process. In future work using panel data, we hope to examine in more detail the characteristics of U.S. firms acquired by foreign multinationals in order to understand more fully the impact of taxation on FDI.

Appendix A
Data Sources

The FDI data are taken from various issues of the *Survey of Current Business* and from floppy diskettes provided by the Bureau of Economic Analysis.

The means-of-payment data for foreign acquisitions were constructed as follows. A list of foreign acquisitions was constructed from MLR Publishing's *Mergers and Acquisitions: The Journal of Corporate Venture.* The means of payment for each acquisition was then taken from Commerce Clearing House's *Capital Changes Reporter.*

The means-of-payment data for domestic acquisitions were purchased from MLR Publishing.

The investment outflow data were taken from the *International Financial Statistics Yearbook, 1990.*

The numbers reported in table 4.7 are the ratios of Compustat data items 156 (machinery and equipment—net) and 155 (buildings—net) to data item 8 (property plant and equipment—total net). Data from the industrial, research, and full coverage files were used to construct the full sample means.

Appendix B
A Model of FDI

This appendix presents a model in which the various effects of taxation on foreign direct investment may be measured and compared. The analysis closely follows that in Auerbach (1989), Where possible, we will use the same notation and omit steps in the derivation that follow from this earlier treatment.

We assume that U.S. firms are price takers and that they invest subject to a constant-returns-to-scale production function in capital alone, subject to quadratic adjustment costs. Foreign firms invest in the United States only via takeover (an assumption we will relax later), with these acquisitions also subject to adjustment costs. This means that one may separate the questions of investment and ownership, with the former being determined by U.S. firms and the latter by foreign firms.

Domestic Firms

The assumption of the model give rise to a system of differential equations in the capital stock, K, and the shadow value of new capital, q. Linearizing the model and substituting for q yields

(A1) $$\dot{K}_t - \rho \dot{K}_t \doteq \frac{\rho + \hat{\delta}}{\phi} K^* \tilde{a}_t \, ,$$

where ρ is the firm's real discount rate, ϕ is the quadratic adjustment cost term, $\hat{\delta} = \delta(1 - \frac{1}{2}\delta\phi)$ is an adjusted measure of the depreciation rate δ, K^* is the steady-state capital stock, and

(A2) $$\tilde{a}_t = \frac{(k^* + \Gamma^*) - (k_t + \Gamma_t)}{1 - k^* - \Gamma^*} - \frac{\tau^* - \tau_t}{1 - \tau^*} +$$
$$\left(\frac{1}{\rho + \hat{\delta}} \cdot \frac{k_t + \Gamma_t}{1 - k^* - \Gamma^*} \right) - \frac{p_t - p^*}{p^*} = a_t - \frac{p_t - p^*}{p^*} \, ,$$

where k is the investment tax credit, Γ is the present value of tax savings from depreciation, τ is the corporate tax rate, p is the relative output price, and the superscript asterisk indicates a steady-state value.

If we assume a constant elasticity demand specification for output,

(A3) $$\frac{p - p^*}{p^*} = -\eta \left(\frac{K - K^*}{K^*} \right) ,$$

then (A1) may be rewritten:

(A4) $$\dot{K}_t - \rho \dot{K}_t - \frac{\eta(\rho + \hat{\delta})}{\phi} K_t = \frac{-\eta(\rho + \hat{\delta})}{\phi} K^* \left(1 - \frac{1}{\eta} a_t \right) .$$

Assuming that the economy is initially in a steady state at date zero (say 1986) and that the tax parameters shift immediately and permanently at that date ($a_t = a$), the solutions for K_t and q_t ($t \geq 0$) are

(A5.a) $$K_t = K^* \left[1 - \frac{1}{\eta}(1 - e^{\lambda_1 t})a \right]$$

and

(A5.b) $$q_t = 1 + \frac{\lambda_1 \phi}{\eta} a e^{\lambda_1 t} ,$$

where λ_1 is the stable (< 0) root of equation (A4). Equations (A5) provide the typical saddle-path behavior of K and q, with (for $a > 0$) K steadily falling to its new level as q rises steadily back to its long-run value of 1 after jumping initially at $t = 0$.

Foreign Firms

The foreign firm's problem differs in two ways from that of the domestic firm. First, its acquisition policy has no impact on domestic output in the output price, p. Second, it must acquire capital in the form of firms. Specifically, we assume that increases in foreign-owned capital (as opposed to simple replacement investment) require the purchase of existing firms and their capital. Hence, the price a foreign firm faces for capital (net of adjustment costs) is not the new capital goods price, 1, but the value of the firm, say σ (the determination of which will be discussed below). Thus, if we define ρ^F and ϕ^F in a way comparable to ρ and ϕ, the foreign firm's behavior will be characterized by (compare to A1 and A2)

$$(A6) \qquad \dot{K}_t^F - \rho^F \dot{K}_t \doteq \frac{\rho^F + \hat{\delta}}{\phi^F} K^{*F} \hat{a}_t^F ,$$

where

$$(A7) \qquad \hat{a}_t^F = \tilde{a}_t^F + \left(\frac{\rho^F}{\rho^F + \hat{\delta}} \cdot \frac{\sigma_t - \sigma^*}{\sigma^*} \right) - \left(\frac{1}{\rho^F + \hat{\delta}} \cdot \frac{\dot{\sigma}_t}{\sigma^*} \right)$$

and $\tilde{a}^F$ is defined in parallel fashion to $\tilde{a}$ in (A2), $= a_t^F - \eta[(p_t - p^*)/p^*]$. The cost of capital term in (A7) includes an additional component due to the changing price of existing capital, σ.

Because the output price change included in $\tilde{a}^F$ does not depend on the size of the foreign-owned capital stock, K^F, expression (A6) is a first-order equation in K, yielding the solution at $t = 0$:

$$(A8) \qquad \frac{\dot{K}_0^F}{K^{*F}} = - \frac{\rho^F + \hat{\delta}}{\phi^F} \cdot \int_0^\infty e^{-\rho_i^F} \hat{a}_t^F dt ,$$

which may be broken up into three pieces, using the definition of $\hat{a}^F$ in (A7), due to changes in taxation (a^F), changes in output prices (p), and changes in the cost of acquiring firms ($\sigma, \dot{\sigma}$). Only the first two effects are present for domestic firms in this model.

From (A3) and (A5.a), we have

$$(A9) \qquad \frac{p_t - p^*}{p^*} = -(1 - e^{\lambda_1 t})a ,$$

which put into (A8) provides the initial change in the rate of FDI due to price changes:

$$(A10) \qquad \frac{-a\lambda_1(\rho^F + \hat{\delta})}{\phi^F \rho^F (\rho^F - \lambda_1)} ,$$

which has the same sign as a. Hence, a rise in domestic taxes, through a restriction of domestic output and a rise in domestic prices, in itself encourages FDI. However, we must also consider the impact of taxation and the cost of acquisitions. Even firms that do not face any direct tax increase at all may still face a change in the cost of acquiring capital goods.

Before proceeding with a full analysis, let us note some additional properties of the solution (A8). If we ignore changes in σ, we obtain

(A11)
$$\frac{\dot{K}_0^F}{K^{*F}} = -\left[\frac{a^F(\rho^F + \hat{\delta})}{\phi^F \rho^F} + \frac{a\lambda_1(\rho^F + \hat{\delta})}{\phi^F \rho^F(\rho^F - \lambda_1)}\right],$$

which adds to (A10) a term reflecting the direct effect of taxation on investment (negative if $a^F > 0$). If $a^F = a$, this entire term is negative (because $\lambda_1 < 0$) and may be shown to equal the investment rate for the domestic firm if, in addition, $\rho^F = \rho$ and $\phi^F = \phi$: for common tax and economic parameters, only the behavior of the price term σ causes the foreign firm to behave differently, adding an additional term to (A11).

What will existing domestic firms cost? Absent taxes, the capital of existing firms will have a value of q per unit. If foreign firms actually paid this price, the expression for the rate of foreign investment at date zero would be the term in (A11) plus

(A12)
$$-\frac{a\lambda_1\phi}{\phi^F\eta}.$$

In this case, assuming that $(\rho^F, a^F) = (\rho, a)$ yields a solution $K^F_0 = 0$, the changes in q just offset changes in taxes and prices. This is not really surprising, because q reflects the present value of after-tax cash flows from new capital.

Even if we assume for simplicity that $\rho^F = \rho$ and $\phi^F = \phi$, differences in tax rules ($a^F \neq a$) and the wedge between the costs of firms and new capital ($\sigma \neq q$) will cause $K^F_0 \neq 0$.

Costs of Acquisition

The effective price of capital to foreign firms, σ, as well as the effective tax rate on that capital, which determines a^F, depends on the nature of the acquisition itself. If we assume a competitive market for existing firms, then the owners of a firm must receive payment equal to the market value of the existing capital, which is the firm's only asset. If assets are written off at rate δ' on an historical cost basis, then the value of existing capital at date t (assuming it was acquired in a steady state) is

(A13)
$$q_t^K = q_t(1 - k - \Gamma) + \frac{\hat{\delta}}{\delta' + \pi}\Gamma,$$

where π is the rate of inflation. Combined with (A5.b), (A13) yields

$$(A14) \quad q_t^K = \left[(1 - k - \Gamma)\left(1 - \frac{\hat{\delta}}{\delta' + \pi}\right)\right] + \lambda_1 \frac{\phi}{\eta}(1 - k - \Gamma)ae^{\lambda_1 t}.$$

Normally, $q^K < q$, reflecting the relatively favorable treatment of new capital. An important change in 1986 was to lessen the relative burden on existing capital, leading to an increase in q^K, given q.

A remaining element of the cost of acquisition involves capital gains and recapture taxes. As nearly all FDI acquisitions use cash as a means of payment and do not qualify as reorganizations, selling shareholders are liable for individual capital gains taxes. If the acquisition is treated as an asset purchase, with a step-up in the basis of assets, the acquired corporation is liable for recapture taxes and, since the 1986 repeal of the General Utilities doctrine, for capital gains taxes as well. This change, along with the increase in individual capital gains tax rates, should have discouraged acquisitions in general, but especially asset acquisitions, for all acquiring parties.

Because we are interested primarily in the *relative* incentives for acquirers from different countries and in whether some foreign parents may have an *increased* incentive to acquire U.S. firms, we shall concentrate on the most favorable assumptions for foreign acquisitions in general, supposing that shareholder capital gains taxes are unimportant and that deals were structured as acquisitions of stock to avoid corporate-level taxes.

These assumptions imply that existing capital costs foreign acquirers q^K per unit and that the tax attributes of the acquired firms carry over. For simplicity, we shall consider two polar cases: worldwide firms for which direct tax effects were not affected by the 1986 act ($a_F = 0$) and territorial firms for which only U.S. tax parameters matter.

Worldwide Firms

Letting $\sigma_t = q_t^K$ and $\sigma^* = [1 - k - \Gamma^*(1 - \hat{\delta}/(\delta' + \pi))]$ (see A14) yields the solution (for $a_F = 0$):

$$\frac{\dot{K}_0^F}{K^{*F}} = -\frac{1}{\phi^F}\left\{\frac{a\lambda_1(\rho^F + \hat{\delta})}{\rho^F(\rho^F - \lambda_1)} + \right.$$

$$\left. \frac{a\lambda_1\phi}{\eta}\left[\frac{1 - k - \Gamma}{(1 - k^* - \Gamma^*)(1 - \hat{\delta}/(\delta' + \pi))}\right] + B\right\},$$

where

$$B = \frac{-(k - k^*) - (\Gamma - \Gamma^*)\left[1 - \hat{\delta}/(\delta' + \pi)\right]}{1 - k^* - \Gamma^*\left[1 - \hat{\delta}/(\delta' + \pi)\right]}.$$

The first two terms, representing the effects of increased output prices and reduced capital goods prices (for $a > 0$), encourage investment. The last term, B, represents the increased cost of existing capital and discourages investment.

Territorial Firms

Instead of computing a_F for existing capital, it is easier to note that the difference between q^K and q reflects the difference between the tax treatment of existing and new capital. Hence, buying existing capital for q^K or new capital for q results (for the *territorial* firm) in the same present value, with the difference in future taxes just offsetting the initial difference in price. This means that we may replace q^K with q and let $a^F = a$ to obtain the solution for the territorial firm. Combining (A11) and (A12), we obtain

$$\frac{\dot{K}_0^F}{K^{*F}} = -\frac{1}{\phi^F}\left[\frac{a(\rho^F + \hat{\delta})}{\rho^F} + \frac{a\lambda_1(\rho^F + \hat{\delta})}{\rho^F(\rho^F - \lambda_1)} + \frac{a\lambda_1\phi}{\eta}\right]$$

$$= -\frac{a}{\phi^F}\left(\frac{\rho^F + \hat{\delta}}{\rho^F - \lambda_1} + \frac{\lambda_1\phi}{\eta}\right) = -\frac{a}{\phi^F}\left(\frac{\rho^F + \hat{\delta}}{\rho^F - \lambda_1} - \frac{\rho + \hat{\delta}}{\rho - \lambda_1}\right),$$

where the last step uses the fact that $\lambda_1(\rho - \lambda_1) = \dfrac{(\rho + \hat{\delta})\eta}{\phi}$. As suggested above, if $\rho^F = \rho$, then the entire expression equals zero.

Extensions

If, more generally, we wish to assume that firms obtain a fraction $(1 - \beta)$ of their new capital through the direct purchase of assets, paying a price 1 per unit (net of adjustment costs) rather than q^K, we obtain the more general expressions for investment by worldwide and territorial firms:

(A15)

$$\text{Worldwide: } \frac{\dot{K}_0^F}{K^{*F}} = -\frac{1}{\phi^F}\left\{\frac{a\lambda_1(\rho^F + \hat{\delta})}{\rho^F(\rho^F - \lambda_1)} + \beta\frac{a\lambda_1\phi}{\eta}\left[\frac{1 - k - \Gamma}{(1 - k^* - \Gamma^*)(1 - \hat{\delta}/(\delta' + \pi))}\right] + \beta B\right\}$$

$$\text{Territorial: } \frac{\dot{K}_0^F}{K^{*F}} = -\frac{1}{\phi^F}\left[\frac{a(\rho^F + \hat{\delta})}{\rho^F - \lambda_1} + \beta\frac{a\lambda_1\phi}{\eta}\right]$$

If $\beta = 0$, investment by worldwide firms is positive if $a > 0$ (because $\lambda_1 < 0$), while investment by territorial firms is negative. As $\beta \to 1$, investment by territorial firms rises to zero while that of worldwide firms falls, as long as q^K actually rises. The overall sign of investment by worldwide firms cannot be unambiguously determined without additional assumptions. In our numerical calculations, we assume that $\rho^F = \rho$, which allows us to simplify (A15):

Worldwide: $\dfrac{\dot{K}_0^F}{K^{*F}} = -\dfrac{1}{\phi^F}\left(\left[\dfrac{a\lambda_1\phi}{\eta}\right]\left[\dfrac{\lambda_1}{\rho} + \beta\left[\dfrac{1 - k - \Gamma}{1 - k^* - \Gamma^* (1 - \hat{\delta}/\delta' + \pi)}\right]\right] + \beta B\right)$

Territorial: $\dfrac{\dot{K}_0^F}{K^{*F}} = -\dfrac{1}{\phi^F}\left(\dfrac{a\lambda_1\phi}{\eta}\right)(\beta - 1)$.

References

Auerbach, Alan J. 1989. Tax reform and adjustment costs: The impact on investment and market value. *International Economic Review* 30:933–62.

Auerbach, Alan J., and James R. Hines. 1987. Anticipated tax changes and the timing of investment. In *The effects of taxation on capital accumulation*, ed. M. Feldstein. Chicago: University of Chicago Press.

Auerbach, Alan J., and David Reishus. 1988. The effects of taxation on the merger decision. In *Corporate takeovers*, ed. A. Auerbach. Chicago: University of Chicago Press.

Boskin, Michael J., and William G. Gale. 1987. New results on the effects of tax polices on the international location of investment. In *The effects of taxation on capital accumulation*, ed. M. Feldstein. Chicago: University of Chicago Press.

Froot, Kenneth A., and Jeremy C. Stein. 1989. Exchange rates and foreign direct investment: An imperfect capital markets approach. NBER Working Paper no. 2914. National Bureau of Economic Research, March.

Hartman, David G. 1984. Tax policy and foreign direct investment in the United States. *National Tax Journal*.

———. 1985. Tax policy and foreign direct investment. *Journal of Public Economics* 26:107–21.

Newlon, Timothy. 1987. Tax policy and the multinational firm's financial policy and investment decisions. Ph.D. dissertation. Princeton University.

Quijano, Alicia M. 1990. A guide to BEA statistics on foreign direct investment in the United States. *Survey of Current Business*, January.

Scholes, Myron S., and Mark A. Wolfson. 1991. Multinational tax planning. In *Taxes and business strategy*. Englewood Cliffs, N.J.: Prentice Hall.

Slemrod, Joel. 1990a. The impact of the Tax Reform Act of 1986 on foreign direct investment to and from the United States. In *Do taxes matter?* ed. J. Slemrod. Cambridge, Mass.: MIT Press.

———. 1990b. Tax effects on foreign direct investment in the United States: Evidence from a cross-country comparison. In *Taxation in the global economy*, ed. A. Razin and J. Slemrod. Chicago: University of Chicago Press.

Swenson, Deborah L. 1989. The impact of U.S. tax reform on foreign direct investment in the United States. MIT. Mimeograph.

Comment   James M. Poterba

The rapid growth in foreign direct investment (FDI) in the United States during the past decade, and particularly since 1985, has energized both academic economists and policymakers to search for the underlying cause of this development. One particularly simple and ingenious explanation, developed by Myron Scholes and Mark Wolfson, points to tax policy as a central factor in the rise of FDI. Scholes and Wolfson focused on the Tax Reform Act of 1986, which raised the effective tax rate on corporate capital in the United States. They recognized that such a reform should, in the long run, reduce capital intensity and raise the pretax marginal product of capital. Although the resulting after-tax return to U.S. firms would be less than or equal to their return prior to the tax change, foreign firms that could credit U.S. taxes against their home-country tax liability would actually earn *higher* after-tax returns. These firms would have a substantial incentive to invest in the United States, and this could explain the rise in FDI. Previous empirical studies by Joel Slemrod and Deborah Swenson support the Scholes-Wolfson analysis and suggest that tax changes may have been an important contributor to the increase in FDI.

In this important paper, Alan Auerbach and Kevin Hassett argue that the evidence is actually less convincing than it appears. The authors make two significant contributions to our understanding of how tax policy affects foreign direct investment. First, they demonstrate marked differences between the incentives for foreign firms to undertake greenfield investments and their incentives to acquire assets in takeovers. Although the Scholes-Wolfson hypothesis applies to greenfield investment, most of the increase in FDI during the late 1980s involved foreign purchases of existing assets and firms. Second, they argue that the incentives for foreign investment differ substantially across different types of assets, for example, between structures and equipment, and that it is difficult to make broad generalizations about the net effect of the Tax Reform Act even on the incentives for foreign greenfield investment. The Scholes-Wolfson hypothesis is most applicable to investments in equipment. For other assets, the authors argue, the Tax Reform Act had much smaller, or in some cases opposite-signed, effects on the incentives for foreign investment.

This paper advances our understanding of tax incentives for foreign direct investment in much the same way that research on tax loss carryforwards, interasset distortions, and expected tax changes has advanced our understanding of domestic investment incentives. It demonstrates that firms' actual incentives are difficult to describe with simple stylizations of the tax system and that once we recognize the details it is difficult to draw broad conclusions.

James M. Poterba is professor of economics at the Massachusetts Institute of Technology and program director in public economics at the National Bureau of Economic Research.

The authors also advance the empirical debate on taxes and FDI in a novel way, by comparing FDI in the United States by firms from several nations with the FDI *in other nations* by these firms. Whereas the first generation of studies on taxation and FDI asked whether inbound FDI from nations with worldwide tax systems rose after the Tax Reform Act of 1986, this paper tests whether the FDI by firms in these countries was redirected toward the United States. The findings suggest that outbound FDI from these nations increased in the United States as well as in other nations during the late 1980s. This empirical regularity undermines previous conclusions about the central role of U.S. tax policy in the rise of FDI.

The results in this paper, however, are not conclusive. Because the United States was not the only developed nation to reform its tax system during the mid-1980s, a definitive analysis of the tax policy and FDI would need to investigate whether investment incentives in other nations changed at roughly the same time as the changes in U.S. policy. One should also remember that conclusions based on very short time series—in this case, only two years of data for the period since 1986—are likely to be fragile. This is not a criticism of the present analysis, since it applies with equal (or greater) force to previous studies with strong conclusions about the explanation of rising FDI.

The findings in this study leave unanswered a basic question. If tax policy changes do not explain the rapid increase in FDI during the 1980s, what does? There are many explanations of why firms undertake FDI, but relatively few of them can account for sharp changes in the flow of such investment during short time periods. One possibility is that the worsening U.S. trade deficit in the early 1980s brought new pressures for protectionist policies and that foreign firms from countries with large bilateral trade surpluses, such as Japan, viewed FDI as a way to ensure a continued share of the U.S. market. This may be correct, but it is not clear why such firms would undertake acquisitions of U.S. capacity rather than new construction. A given set of capital assets could exhibit differential productivity under the control of different managers, but demonstrating this requires case study investigations of changes in operations at foreign-acquired plants.

A second possible explanation of the rise in FDI focuses on exchange rate fluctuations. Foreign direct investment rose when the dollar fell, suggesting a possible link. It is difficult to understand why foreign firms should find acquisitions of U.S. firms attractive just because the dollar is low. Under standard "random walk" models of exchange rate evolution, a low current exchange rate should portend similar rates in the future. Ignoring possible effects of the exchange rate on the cash flows of projects within the United States, the rate of return on an investment in U.S. assets should be roughly independent of the exchange rate.

A more ingenious link between exchange rates and FDI, suggested by Kenneth Froot and Jeremy Stein, builds on recent cash flow models of corporate investment. Froot and Stein argue that because foreign firms with a fixed amount of foreign currency to spend on acquiring U.S. assets can purchase more when the dollar is low than when it is high, FDI will rise when the dollar falls. This model implies that both U.S. and foreign corporate tax policies may have important effects on FDI. In particular, changes in average tax rates in the home countries of firms undertaking FDI should affect their cash flow and hence their FDI. Shocks to corporate profitability in the home country for these firms should have similar effects.

The current paper underscores the need for additional study of the determinants of foreign direct investment and, in particular, for further evidence on how public policies affect FDI. New data on these questions are accumulating at a rapid rate. In the last half-decade, there have been sharp changes in exchange rates, stock market values, and other factors that might affect investment incentives of firms in different nations. As data on the patterns of FDI become available, it should be possible to provide much more detailed answers to the questions that motivate this paper.

5 On the Sensitivity of R&D to Delicate Tax Changes: The Behavior of U.S. Multinationals in the 1980s

James R. Hines, Jr.

The U.S. government has a long-standing interest in encouraging research and development (R&D) by American companies. Congress feels that the common-property nature of the know-how produced by R&D, and the competitive advantage that greater R&D affords U.S. firms in global markets, means that too little R&D is likely to be undertaken by private firms in the absence of strong government support.[1] Concern over the sluggish rate of U.S. productivity growth in the 1970s, combined with alarm over rising foreign competition, led Congress to enact two tax changes in 1981 designed to stimulate R&D.[2] The first, the research and experimentation tax credit, established a 25 percent credit for new research expenditures by U.S. firms. The second change, a suspension of Treasury regulation §1.861-8, offered very generous tax treatment of R&D performed in the United States by certain multinational corporations.

In this paper, I examine the incentives introduced by this second change—the suspension of §1.861-8—and the way that American multinationals re-

James R. Hines, Jr., is associate professor of public policy at the John F. Kennedy School of Government, Harvard University, and a faculty research fellow of the National Bureau of Economic Research.

The author is grateful to James Laity for superb research assistance, to him and to Martin Feldstein, Therese Flaherty, Daniel Frisch, Zvi Griliches, Harry Grubert, Adam Jaffe, Robert Lawrence, James Poterba, Joel Slemrod, Martin Sullivan, and especially Bronwyn Hall for many helpful comments on an earlier draft of this paper. Financial support was provided by NBER and by Princeton University's John M. Olin Program for the Study of Economic Organization and Public Policy.

1. In theory, the welfare consequences of subsidizing R&D are ambiguous, because some industries might attract too much competitive R&D and the presence of foreign competitors raises the possibility that foreigners could benefit from domestic subsidies (or in other ways influence the domestic market). See Dixit (1988) and Reinganum (1989) for surveys of the theory. The position of the U.S. Congress is that R&D generates significant positive externalities, a view that is consistent with the empirical literature surveyed in Griliches (1991).

2. Congressional sentiment is described in U.S. Congress (1981).

sponded to those incentives. The §1.861-8 rules were modified several times between 1986 and 1990 in a manner that affected only certain firms, so it is possible to infer the effect of the law by observing the responses of different companies to the changes. Based on these results, it appears that American multinationals significantly changed their R&D expenditures in response to tax policy in the 1980s. Nevertheless, the 1981 change may not have had the intended effect of greatly increasing R&D activity in the United States. In part, this may be due to some misunderstandings about the incentives that were embodied in the law prior to 1981 (and in its modifications after 1986).

The U.S. government has yet to settle on a permanent tax policy toward the R&D activities of multinational corporations. Congress enacted temporary changes in the R&D rules in 1984, 1985, 1986, 1988, 1989, and 1990; currently, the political process is at an impasse in which all sides agree that a long-range policy is needed but in which there is no agreement on the policy to pursue. This indecisiveness is due in part to the general complexity of taxing multinational corporations and in part to the difficulty of forging a coherent approach to R&D performed by multinationals. The government would like to encourage R&D, but there is a feeling that some of the benefits of R&D undertaken by U.S. multinationals accrue not to Americans but to foreigners who buy products produced by the R&D (and to foreign governments who tax the proceeds of those sales). These issues are important in designing national R&D policy, since U.S. multinationals perform most of the privately financed R&D in the United States.

There are two reasons why it is instructive to explore the reactions of U.S. multinationals to the tax changes. The first is that these firms reveal the price sensitivity of their demand for R&D by their reactions to the tax changes. There is considerable interest in learning the impact of the cost of R&D on the level of R&D performed, both for its own sake and to identify the effect of other, nonprice, factors such as scientific opportunities on the rate and direction of R&D. The second reason is that, in designing laws to tax their resident multinational corporations, governments must decide on the extent to which to permit firms to deduct general expenses against their own tax bases. R&D is one important category of such expenses, but there are others, such as interest charges and administrative overhead. Greater deductions may encourage more business activity but could do so at the cost of lost tax revenue. By estimating the price responsiveness of R&D, it is possible to learn what trade-offs are involved in designing policy.

In this paper, I analyze the behavior of a panel of manufacturing firms for which comprehensive data are available on R&D histories and foreign business operations. Due to the peculiarities of the tax code, firms differed in the degrees to which they were affected by the legislative changes after 1986. These differences are based largely on the tax rates they face in foreign countries. As a result, the legislative changes introduced in the 1980s offer a not quite natural experiment by changing the after-tax prices of R&D for a subset of firms that is close to randomly selected. The results suggest that the 1986 and subsequent changes had the predicted effect of discouraging R&D, though not dramatically.

Section 5.1 of the paper reviews some of the history of R&D undertaken by U.S. multinational firms. Section 5.2 summarizes elements of the tax system that are relevant to R&D by U.S. multinationals. Section 5.3 then explores the incentives introduced by U.S. law, and section 5.4 estimates the responsiveness of U.S. firms to those incentives over the period 1984–89. Section 5.5 compares the consequences of current U.S. law to some major alternative tax treatments of R&D. Section 5.6 is the conclusion.

5.1   R&D by U.S. Multinational Firms

The U.S. government's 1981 decision to increase the tax subsidy for R&D performed in the United States is best understood in the context of the relatively weak American R&D performance in the 1970s. Table 5.1 contains data on annual movements in R&D/GNP for the United States, France, West Germany, Japan, and the United Kingdom over the period 1961–87. For the United States, this ratio steadily declined, starting at a value of 2.9 percent in 1965 and finding its nadir at 2.1 percent in 1977–78. Over the same period, France and the United Kingdom were holding steady at their somewhat lower levels of R&D relative to GNP, while West Germany and Japan exhibited growing R&D intensity. Because Congress feels that an erosion in technological leadership is not in the interest of the United States, it is understandable that it was eager to prevent further relative decline in U.S. R&D activity.

Another concern that appears to have motivated Congress is the possibility that U.S. firms would move their R&D operations to offshore locations that offered more attractive tax or regulatory environments. Of course, few low-tax foreign locations offer the scientific infrastructure and proximity to important markets available in the United States. Nevertheless, U.S. firms perform some of their R&D offshore, and it was feared that the foreign share of R&D performed by American companies would rise in the 1980s along with the general trend to globalize U.S. business.

The prediction proved false. The foreign share of R&D performed by U.S. companies, which has never been very large, remained small throughout the 1980s despite the rapid growth of foreign sales by U.S. firms. Figure 5.1 illustrates this pattern.[3] In 1974, R&D performed abroad by foreign affiliates equaled 8.1 percent of the total foreign and domestic R&D expenditures of

3. The data on which fig. 5.1 is based come from a National Science Foundation (1991) survey of virtually all firms in the United States with annual R&D expenditures of $1 million or more. The survey is directed at R&D performed in the United States and, partly for that reason, has a somewhat disappointing response rate to its questions about R&D performed by foreign affiliates. There are other omissions as well. Cohen and Levin (1989) note that R&D reported in Compustat files is 12 percent higher than R&D reported in the NSF survey, and there is a view that the Compustat figures are the more reliable ones. Nevertheless, the NSF surveys cover the foreign R&D undertaken by the largest firms and appear to capture the important aggregate trends in R&D activity.

Table 5.1   **R&D Expenditure as a Percentage of GNP: 1961–1987**

	France	West Germany	Japan	United Kingdom	United States
1961	1.4%	—	1.4%	2.5%	2.7%
1962	1.5	1.2%	1.5	—	2.7
1963	1.6	1.4	1.5	—	2.8
1964	1.8	1.6	1.5	2.3	2.9
1965	2.0	1.7	1.6	—	2.8
1966	2.1	1.8	1.5	2.3	2.8
1967	2.2	2.0	1.6	2.3	2.8
1968	2.1	2.0	1.7	2.2	2.8
1969	2.0	1.8	1.7	2.3	2.7
1970	1.9	2.1	1.9	—	2.6
1971	1.9	2.2	1.9	—	2.4
1972	1.9	2.2	1.9	2.1	2.3
1973	1.8	2.1	2.0	—	2.3
1974	1.8	2.1	2.0	—	2.2
1975	1.8	2.2	2.0	2.1	2.2
1976	1.8	2.1	2.0	—	2.2
1977	1.8	2.1	2.0	—	2.1
1978	1.8	2.2	2.0	2.2	2.1
1979	1.8	2.4	2.1	—	2.2
1980	1.8	2.4	2.2	—	2.3
1981	2.0	2.5	2.3	2.4	2.4
1982	2.1	2.6	2.4	—	2.5
1983	2.1	2.6	2.6	2.2	2.6
1984	2.2	2.6	2.6	—	2.6
1985	2.3	2.8	2.8	2.3	2.7
1986	2.3	2.7	2.8	2.4	2.7
1987	2.3	2.8	2.9	—	2.6

Source: National Science Board (1989).

Note: French data are based on gross domestic product (GNP); consequently, percentages may be slightly overstated, compared to GNP. Omissions (—) indicate that R&D data are unavilable.

U.S. firms. This ratio grew to 9.7 percent by 1979 but fell steadily to 7.2 percent in 1982 and 6.0 percent in 1985. After 1985, the foreign share of R&D rose somewhat but was only 8.5 percent by 1989. U.S. firms chose not to move their R&D operations out of the country *en masse* in the 1980s.

It would be possible to infer from figure 5.1 that tax policy was partly responsible for the movement in the foreign share of R&D undertaken by U.S. companies. The foreign share fell at about the same time that Congress made R&D in the United States more attractive from a tax standpoint, and it rose again after 1986, when some of the tax benefits for R&D in the United States were removed. But foreign exchange rate movements may represent a more compelling explanation of much of the pattern visible in figure 5.1. Using a trade-weighted foreign exchange rate index to measure all foreign and domestic expenditures in 1974 dollars, figure 5.2 presents the ratio of real (using

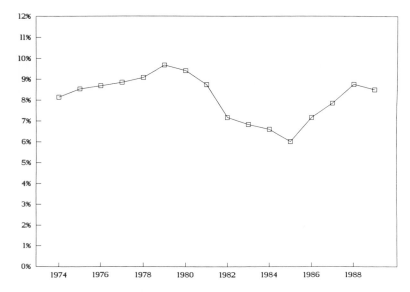

Fig. 5.1   Foreign affiliate R&D share, based on nominal exchange rate

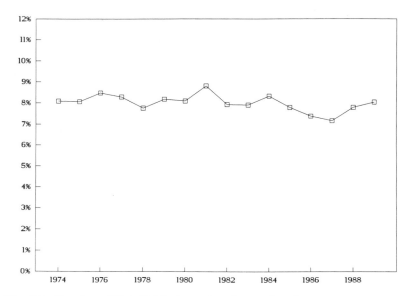

Fig. 5.2   Foreign affiliate R&D share, based on real exchange rate

1974 as the numeraire) foreign to total R&D expenditures. Over the period 1974–89, there is very little movement in this ratio from the 8.1 percent value it took in 1974.

U.S. tax policy may very well have influenced the foreign R&D activities of U.S. firms over the 1974–89 time period but could have done so in ways that were just offset by foreign market conditions (or, for that matter, foreign tax changes). Nevertheless, it is clear from the relative magnitudes involved that U.S. government policy reforms such as those enacted in 1981 and 1986 are likely to induce greater changes in R&D performed by U.S. firms in the United States than in their R&D performed abroad. In order to understand how the incentives U.S. firms face have changed over time, it is helpful to consider the U.S. system of taxing multinational corporations.

5.2   R&D and the Law

This section reviews the tax treatment of R&D by U.S. corporations, with particular emphasis on the tax treatment of firms with international income.

5.2.1   General Treatment of R&D

Expenditures on research and development by firms in the United States are deductible for income tax purposes.[4] Because a firm's stock of R&D usually has the character of a capital good, in that it generates revenues both currently and over a number of future years, immediate expensing of R&D is an attractive tax feature.[5] By contrast, physical capital such as plant and equipment is depreciated for tax purposes and, despite occasional inducements such as the investment tax credit, has always been tax-disfavored relative to R&D.[6] Generally speaking, the effective rate of tax on R&D is zero, because firms will choose R&D expenditures that equate the (after-tax) marginal product of R&D to the (after-tax) cost of R&D. Because the same tax rate applies to both the marginal product of R&D and the marginal cost, the tax rate should not influence the level of R&D.

The research and experimentation (R&E) credit was introduced in 1981 to

4. An exception is that expenditures for the acquisition or improvement of depreciable property, or land, used in conjunction with research are not deductible. Assets other than land can be depreciated for tax purposes at rapid rates. For example, the Tax Reform Act of 1986 classifies equipment used for research as five-year recovery property. Special rules apply to certain industries.

5. Ravenscraft and Scherer (1982) find that the profitability of the firms in their sample appeared to be influenced by R&D expenditures lagged four to six years. Griliches and Mairesse (1984) estimate firm productivity to be a function of the stock of accumulated R&D capital, which they take to depreciate at a rate of 15 percent per year. In their study of patent renewals, Pakes and Schankerman (1984b) find evidence of a somewhat higher depreciation rate for R&D capital, 25 percent per year, but one that is much below the 100 percent rate that is implied in the tax law.

6. See Auerbach (1983) for a historical survey of the effective tax rates on investments in plant and equipment. The relative attractiveness of the immediate expensing of R&D expenditures is the basis of Fullerton and Lyon's (1988) estimates of the efficiency cost of "excessive" R&D (relative to investments in tangible capital) in the United States.

stimulate additional R&D activity in the United States.[7] The R&E credit initially offered a 25 percent tax credit for R&D expenditures above a base level determined by the average of a firm's previous three years' worth of R&D expenditures. The idea behind the design of the credit was to offer an incentive for marginal research activities, but one that did not subsidize inframarginal research. Of course, in practice, matters are not so simple, and the R&E credit can often have the perverse effect of discouraging research and development or of providing only trivial incentives to undertake marginal R&D, because by undertaking additional R&D activities today a firm may reduce the credit it would otherwise receive in future years. Furthermore, various limits built into the credit reduce the incentive it provides in certain cases.[8]

The R&E credit came under fire from various arguments that implied that it was not a cost-effective way of stimulating R&D.[9] Partly in response, the Tax Reform Act of 1986 reduced the R&E credit to 20 percent and tightened some of the definitions of R&D eligible for the credit. The 1988 tax act further reduced the subsidy afforded by the R&E credit by making half of the credit amount taxable income, and the 1989 tax act made the credit amount 100 percent taxable. In addition, the 1989 act changed the way that the base was calculated, so that, starting in 1990, additional R&D expenditure in one year does not reduce a firm's tax credit in subsequent years. The R&E tax credit limped through the 1980s on the basis of temporary extensions (in 1986, 1988, 1989, and 1990) that may have strengthened its impact by introducing uncertainty about whether any credit at all would be available in the future, but the credit seems unlikely to have had an important effect on overall R&D activities. More important for the present study, the R&E credit was available to all firms without regard to their foreign activities (indeed, offshore R&D was ineligible for the credit). In order to analyze those tax changes in the 1980s that did influence firms on the basis of their foreign activities, it is necessary to consider some of the international features of the U.S. tax system.[10]

---

7. There are some small distinctions between activities that qualify for the R&E credit and R&D that is deductible but must be allocated according to §1.861-8. The Tax Reform Act of 1986 tightened the definition of R&D that is eligible for the tax credit.

8. For example, R&D expenditures in excess of 200 percent of the base amount are eligible for only half the credit rate, even though they raise the base for future years. Furthermore, firms must have taxable profits (or the potential to carry credits forward or back against taxable profits) to benefit from the credit. See Eisner, Albert, and Sullivan (1984) and Altshuler (1988) for analyses of the effective rates of subsidy provided by the R&E credit. Eisner, Albert, and Sullivan estimate the average effective credit rate for 1981 to be zero and for 1982 to be 4 percent. Altshuler, using a slightly different methodology, finds the effective credit rate for 1981 to be between 1 percent and 2 percent.

9. See, for example, Mansfield (1986), who argues that the R&E credit had only a very small effect on R&D in the United States and that it reduced tax collections by an amount equal to three times the additional R&D it generated. Wozny (1989) and the U.S. General Accounting Office (1989) report similar findings for a GAO-conducted study of the R&E credit.

10. Parts of the following brief description of the tax system are excerpted from Hines (1990).

5.2.2 U.S. Taxation of Foreign Income

The United States taxes income on a "residence" basis, meaning that U.S. corporations and individuals owe taxes to the U.S. government on all of their worldwide income, whether earned in the United States or not. Because foreign profits are usually taxed in host countries, U.S. law provides a foreign tax credit for income taxes (and related taxes) paid to foreign governments, in order not to subject U.S. multinationals to double taxation. With the foreign tax credit, a U.S. corporation that earns $100 in a foreign country with a 12 percent tax rate (and a foreign tax obligation of $12) pays only $22 to the U.S. government, because its U.S. corporate tax liability of $34 (34 percent of $100) is reduced to $22 by the foreign tax credit of $12. The foreign tax credit is, however, limited to U.S. tax liability on foreign income. If, in the example, the foreign tax rate were 50 percent, then the firm pays $50 to the foreign government, but its U.S. foreign tax credit is limited to $34. Hence, a U.S. firm receives full tax credits for its foreign taxes paid only when it is in a "deficit credit" position—that is, when its average foreign tax rate is less than its tax rate on domestic operations. A firm has "excess credits" if its available foreign tax credits exceed U.S. tax liability on its foreign income.[11] Firms average together their taxable incomes and taxes paid in all of their foreign operations in calculating their foreign tax credits and the foreign tax credit limit.

Deferral of U.S. taxation of certain foreign earnings is another important feature of the U.S. international tax system. A U.S. parent firm is taxed on its subsidiaries' foreign income only when that income is returned ("repatriated") to the parent corporation. This type of deferral is available only to foreign operations that are separately incorporated in foreign countries ("subsidiaries" of the parent) and not to consolidated ("branch") operations. The U.S. government taxes branch profits as they are earned, just as it would profits earned within the United States.

The deferral of U.S. taxation may create incentives for firms with lightly taxed foreign earnings to delay repatriating dividends from their foreign subsidiaries.[12] This incentive arises in those cases in which firms expect never to repatriate their foreign earnings or anticipate that future years will be more

---

11. Furthermore, income is broken into different functional "baskets" in the calculation of applicable credits and limits. In order to qualify for the foreign tax credit, firms must own at least 10 percent of a foreign affiliate, and only those taxes that qualify as income taxes are creditable.

12. The incentive to defer repatriation of lightly taxed subsidiary earnings is attenuated by the Subpart F provisions, introduced in U.S. law in 1962, that treat a subsidiary's passive income, and income invested in U.S. property, as if it were distributed to its U.S. owners, thereby subjecting it to immediate U.S. taxation. The Subpart F rules apply to controlled foreign corporations, which are foreign corporations owned at least 50 percent by U.S. persons holding stakes of at least 10 percent each. Controlled foreign corporations that reinvest their foreign earnings in active businesses can continue to defer their U.S. tax liability on these earnings. See Hines and Rice (1990) and Scholes and Wolfson (1991) for the behavioral implications of these rules.

attractive for repatriation (either because domestic tax rates will be lower or because future sources of foreign income will generate excess foreign tax credits that can be used to offset U.S. tax liability on the dividends).[13] It appears that, in practice, U.S. multinationals choose their dividend repatriations selectively, and they generally pay dividends out of their more heavily taxed foreign earnings first.[14] Consequently, the average tax rate that firms face on their foreign income need not exactly equal the average foreign tax rate faced by their branches and subsidiaries abroad.

Branch earnings and dividends from subsidiaries represent only two forms of foreign income for U.S. income tax purposes. Interest received from foreign sources also represents foreign income, although foreign interest receipts are often classified within their own basket and hence are not averaged with other income in calculating the foreign tax credit. Royalty income received from foreigners, including foreign affiliates of U.S. firms, is also foreign-source income. Foreign governments often impose moderate taxes on dividend, interest, and royalty payments from foreign affiliates to their U.S. parent companies; these withholding taxes are fully creditable against a U.S. taxpayer's U.S. tax liability on foreign income.

5.2.3   Interaction of R&D and Foreign Income Rules

U.S. firms with foreign income are generally not permitted to deduct all of their R&D expenditures in the United States against their domestic taxable incomes. Instead, the law provides for various methods of allocating R&D expenses between domestic and foreign income. The intention of the law is to retain the relatively generous treatment of R&D, but only for that part of a firm's R&D expenditures that is devoted to production for domestic markets. R&D-performing firms with foreign sales and foreign income are presumed to be doing at least some of their R&D to enhance their foreign profitability.

From the standpoint of taxpaying firms, the U.S. tax law's distinction between domestic and foreign R&D deductions is potentially quite important. If an R&D expense is deemed to be domestic, then it is deductible against the taxpayer's U.S. taxable income. Alternatively, if it is deemed to be foreign, then the R&D expense reduces foreign taxable income *for the purposes of U.S. income taxation only*. Foreign governments do not use U.S. methods of calculating R&D deductions and generally do not permit U.S. firms to reduce their taxable incomes in foreign countries on the basis of R&D undertaken in the United States. Consequently, an R&D expense deduction allocated against foreign income is valuable to a U.S. firm only if it has deficit foreign tax credits. If it does have deficit credits, then some of the firm's foreign income is subject to U.S. tax, and any additional dollar of R&D deduction allocated

---

13. The deferral of U.S. tax liability does not itself create an incentive to delay paying dividends from foreign subsidiaries, because the U.S. tax must be paid eventually. See Hartman (1985).

14. See the evidence presented in Hines and Hubbard (1990).

against foreign income reduces the firm's U.S. taxable income by a dollar.[15] With deficit credits, firms are indifferent between allocating R&D expenses against foreign income and allocating it against domestic income.[16] If, on the other hand, firms have excess foreign tax credits, then R&D expense allocated against foreign income does them no good, since foreign income generates no U.S. tax liability anyway.

The tax law governing the allocation of R&D expenses was for years rather vague but was codified by U.S. Treasury regulation §1.861-8 in 1977. The 1977 rules provide for several stages in allocating R&D expenditures for tax purposes. R&D in the U.S. that is undertaken to meet certain legal requirements (such as R&D devoted to meeting pollution standards) can be 100 percent allocated against domestic income. Firms that perform more than half of their (other than legally required) R&D in the United States are permitted to allocate 30 percent of that R&D against U.S. income. The remaining 70 percent is then to be allocated between domestic and foreign sources on the basis of sales (including the sales of controlled foreign corporations). R&D is generally allocated according to activities within product lines (defined similarly to two-digit SIC codes), so that a corporation need not allocate part of its chemical R&D against foreign income simply because the electronics part of its business has foreign sales.

There are several options available to taxpayers who are unsatisfied with the outcome of the R&D allocation method just described. Firms are permitted to apportion more than 30 percent of their domestic R&D against U.S. income if they can establish that it is reasonable to expect the R&D so apportioned to have very limited application outside of the country; the remaining portion of the R&D expenses are then allocated on the basis of sales. Alternatively, firms are permitted to allocate their R&D on the basis of total foreign and domestic income (though without the 30 percent initial allocation to U.S. source) so that firms with foreign operations that generate sales but not income (relative to domestic operations) might prefer the income allocation method. There is, however, a limit to the income allocation method: firms are not permitted to reduce their R&D allocation to foreign source to less than 50 percent of the allocation that would have been produced by the sales method (including the 30 percent initial apportionment).

The Economic Recovery Act in 1981 changed these rules by permitting U.S. firms to allocate 100 percent of their R&D performed in the United States against U.S. income. This change was intended to be temporary (two years) in order to offer strong R&D incentives while affording Congress the

15. Curiously, the law is written so that the additional dollar of R&D deduction reduces taxable income without reducing the foreign tax credits available for foreign income taxes paid.

16. This statement, along with much of the analysis described in the paper, abstracts from the ability of firms to carry excess foreign tax credits backward two years and forward five years. Firms that can exploit carryforwards or carrybacks may (depending on specific circumstances) face incentives that are intermediate between those of deficit credit and excess credit firms.

opportunity to rethink its R&D policy. At the end of that time, the U.S. Department of the Treasury (1983) produced a study concluding that the tax change offered a small R&D incentive to U.S. firms and was desirable on that basis.[17] In 1984 and 1985, Congress extended the temporary change permitting 100 percent deductibility of U.S. R&D expenses against U.S. income, so these rules remained in place until the end of the 1986 tax year.

The Tax Reform Act of 1986 removed the 100 percent deductibility of U.S. R&D expenses, replacing it with a new, and again temporary, system of R&D expense allocation.[18] Under the act, 50 percent of U.S. R&D expenses (other than for R&D to meet regulations, which were 100 percent allocated to domestic source) were allocated to domestic source, with the remaining 50 percent allocated on the basis of sales or of income, at the taxpayer's choice. There was no limit imposed on the degree to which allocation on the basis of gross income could reduce foreign allocation relative to the sales method. These rules, it turned out, were in effect only for 1987.

The Technical and Miscellaneous Revenue Act of 1988 greatly complicates the analyst's task of understanding the incentives to undertake R&D in 1988. For the first four months of the year, firms were permitted to allocate 64 percent of U.S. R&D expenses against U.S. domestic income, with the remaining 36 percent allocated between foreign and domestic sources on the basis of either sales or income (at the taxpayer's choice). The 1988 act further provides that if the 36 percent were allocated on the basis of income, then the R&D allocation against foreign income must equal at least 30 percent of the foreign allocation that would have been produced by the sales method. For the remaining eight months of the year, taxpayers were required to use the allocation method set forth in §1.861-8 as of 1977 (and described above).

The Omnibus Budget Reconciliation Act of 1989 again changed the R&D allocation rules, this time reintroducing the same rules that applied for the first four months of 1988. A temporary extension in 1990 extended this treatment of R&D through 1991. Consequently, 64 percent of domestically performed R&D in 1989–91 can be allocated against domestic income, with the remaining 36 percent allocated on the basis either of sales or of income (though income allocation to foreign source must not be less than 30 percent of what the sales allocation would have been).

It would be difficult not to conclude from this brief history of the R&D

17. The Treasury study based its conclusions on a range of assumed elasticities of R&D with respect to price changes; there was no attempt made to ascertain how firms responded to the changes introduced in 1981. The study is a very careful analysis of firm-level tax return data and the significant issues involved in the §1.861-8 change. On the other hand, the study uses the average price reduction introduced by the 1981 tax law change, rather than the changes in marginal prices of R&D and other inputs, to estimate the effects of the law.

18. The Tax Reform Act of 1986 also introduced a number of other changes relevant to R&D investment decisions, including reducing the statutory corporate tax rate from 46 percent (the rate from 1979 to 1986) to 40 percent in 1987 and 34 percent for 1988 and subsequent years. The 1986 act also removed a number of investment incentives such as accelerated depreciation of capital assets and the investment tax credit for new equipment purchases.

expense allocation rules that they are intricate, confusing, and subject to frequent changes. For the purpose of analyzing the effects of legislative changes, however, we can discern a clear pattern. All U.S. firms could deduct their R&D expenses against domestic income from 1981 to 1986. Starting in 1987, multinational firms with excess foreign tax credits have been able to use only some of their R&D deductions, because part is allocated against foreign income (and thereby does not reduce their overall tax liabilities). For firms with deficit foreign tax credits, however, the period since 1987 is just as attractive as 1981–86; even though some of their R&D expenses are allocated against foreign income, this foreign allocation reduces their U.S. tax liabilities by just as much as would an allocation against domestic income.

5.3   Some Curious Incentives

The incentives built into current and proposed tax treatments of R&D are rather complicated and require some elaboration. In this section, in order to simplify matters, I focus on the allocation rules governing R&D (§1.861-8 and its temporary modifications) and not on the R&E credit.

It is helpful to separate the research activities of multinationals into three types in order to isolate the incentives for each. The first type is R&D performed in the U.S. that generates only domestic sales and income. The second type is R&D undertaken in the U.S. that generates only foreign sales and income. The third type is the offshore R&D activities of U.S. multinationals. There is no doubt that this separation is somewhat artificial in that the same R&D project often generates both foreign and domestic income; for that matter, firms frequently undertake R&D without complete knowledge of what kind of output will result, much less whether the ensuing sales will occur in the United States or abroad. Nevertheless, the incentives for each type of R&D can differ significantly, and it clarifies the analysis to divide projects this way.

5.3.1   Domestic R&D for Domestic Markets

The first type of R&D is a major source of concern among critics of the §1.861-8 system of allocation. The fear is that by allocating a fraction of new R&D expenditures against foreign income, the law may discourage domestic R&D intended for domestic markets.

To evaluate this argument, consider the behavior of a profit-maximizing firm with domestic sales that are a function of its variable inputs (I) and its R&D expenditures devoted to products sold domestically (R). For the time being, consider the case in which this domestic R&D does not influence the firm's foreign profitability and in which domestic sales are unaffected by foreign R&D. Let R_f denote the domestic R&D that the firm undertakes to generate foreign sales and $\underline{R}$ the firm's total domestic R&D (so that

$R + R_f = \underline{R}$). The domestic sales function is $S(R, I)$. The firm's after-tax profits from its domestic operations equal [19]

$$(1) \qquad [S(R, I) - I - R - \pi R \tau/(1 - \tau)] (1 - \tau) ,$$

in which τ is the domestic tax rate facing the firm and π represents the fraction of the firm's domestic R&D expenditures that is not deductible against domestic taxes. If the firm has deficit foreign tax credits, then $\pi = 0$ under the tax systems in effect during the 1980s. Suppose instead that the firm has excess foreign tax credits, and let $(1 - \alpha)$ denote the fraction of a firm's R&D that is immediately allocated against domestic income, with the remaining α allocated on the basis of domestic and foreign sales. Denote foreign sales by S^*. Then $\pi = \alpha S^*/(S + S^*)$. The firm's first-order condition that corresponds to maximizing equation (1) over the choice of R is

$$(2) \qquad \partial S/\partial R - 1 - \pi \tau/(1 - \tau) - (\partial \pi/\partial R) \underline{R} \tau/(1 - \tau) = 0 .$$

The corresponding first-order condition for the choice of I is

$$(3) \qquad \partial S/\partial I - 1 - (\partial \pi/\partial I) \underline{R} \tau/(1 - \tau) = 0 .$$

And the derivatives of the allocation function (π) are

$$(4) \qquad \partial \pi/\partial R = - \alpha(\partial S/\partial R) S^*/(S + S^*)^2$$

and

$$(5) \qquad \partial \pi/\partial I = - \alpha(\partial S/\partial I) S^*/(S + S^*)^2 .$$

Combining (2) and (4) yields

$$(6) \qquad \frac{\partial S}{\partial R} = \frac{1 - \tau \left[1 - \dfrac{\alpha S^*}{(S + S^*)} \right]}{1 - \tau \left[1 - \dfrac{\alpha \underline{R} S^*}{(S + S^*)^2} \right]} \equiv PR ,$$

in which PR is the after-tax cost of domestic R&D. Equations (3) and (5) together yield

19. The distinction between the domestic and foreign source of profits is somewhat arbitrary, because the output of an R&D project may contribute to domestic and foreign profits and even the firms undertaking the R&D project might not know in advance whether domestic or foreign markets will be more suitable for the product ultimately produced. Nevertheless, the tax incentives for the two types of projects differ significantly, and if firms are able to estimate the likely location of the future sales generated by their R&D, then R&D should be sensitive to this difference. As a more minor matter, it is not quite correct to describe the profit-maximizing choice of R by differentiating (1), since R also affects (through its impact on S) the allocation (π) of deductions for R_f (because the same π applies to both R and R_f). This complication is the reason that $\underline{R}$, rather than R, appears in (2), (3), (6), (7), (9), (10), (13), and (14).

(7)
$$\frac{\partial S}{\partial I} = \frac{1 - \tau}{1 - \tau\left[1 - \dfrac{\alpha \underline{R} S^*}{(S + S^*)^2}\right]} \equiv PI.$$

There are two notable features of the first-order conditions (6) and (7). The first is that the marginal product of R&D, which equals the right side of (6), exceeds one as long as the ratio $\underline{R}/(S + S^*)$ is less than one. This value reflects the direct effect of the allocation rule in discouraging domestic R&D by permitting only a fraction of it to be deducted against domestic taxable income. As a consequence, the required return on a dollar of marginal R&D is higher than it would be in the absence of taxation.

The second feature of equations (6) and (7) is that the marginal product of variable inputs other than R&D—PI in equation (7)—is always less than one. The reason is that the R&D allocation rule encourages the use of ordinary domestic inputs to generate domestic sales, since greater domestic sales permit a higher fraction of the firm's inframarginal R&D to be allocated against domestic income. This effect is greater, the larger is $\underline{R}/(S + S^*)$. In practice, $\underline{R}/(S + S^*)$ takes a value of something like 4 percent.

It is likely that this second effect—the subsidy to ordinary domestic inputs—encourages domestic R&D and has such an impact that it partly undoes the first, more direct, effect on the level of R&D. The reason is that ordinary inputs and R&D are likely to be complementary in the firm's production function, so that a subsidy to one indirectly encourages the use of the other. The subsidy to ordinary inputs operates through the level of inframarginal R&D, while the direct tax on R&D operates through its effect on the marginal product of R&D. The more R&D-intensive a firm's operations are, the more of an incentive the firm faces to expand its domestic operations in order to allocate a high fraction of that R&D against domestic taxable income. If the firms with greater R&D intensity are also those firms with the most total R&D, then the tax rules might have the effect of not discouraging R&D to the degree that a simple calculation based on the fraction deductible might suggest.[20]

5.3.2 Domestic R&D for Foreign Markets

The analysis so far has addressed the incentives to undertake domestic R&D intended to stimulate sales in domestic markets. Of course, part of the premise of §1.861-8 and other legislation is that multinational firms doing R&D in the United States are able to use the fruits of that R&D to stimulate the profitability of their foreign business operations. This section considers the incentives created by the allocation rules in such a case.

---

20. A third feature of (6) and (7) is that the marginal products of R&D and of other inputs are endogenously determined, since $\underline{R}$ and S are elements of (6) and (7). As a consequence, it is not correct to treat PR and PI as exogenous tax prices of R&D and other inputs unless instruments are available for $\underline{R}$ and S. The difficulty is that an hypothesized linear relationship between $\underline{R}$ and PR becomes nonlinear once it is acknowledged that PR is a function of $\underline{R}$. The small magnitude of $\underline{R}/(S + S^*)$ may, however, make linearization with an instrument acceptable in practice.

Let $S^*(R_f, I^*)$ denote the firm's foreign sales function, in which R_f represents domestic R&D performed to stimulate foreign sales and I^* represents ordinary foreign inputs. Suppose that the firm operates its foreign sales through foreign subsidiaries that are required to remit to their U.S. parent firms royalties equal to the value of the R&D that generates their sales. If the royalties are calculated on the basis of arm's-length prices, as U.S. and almost all foreign laws provide,[21] then the subsidiary should retain, after royalties, just enough of its sales revenue to cover the cost of its expenditures on I^*. All of the profits on foreign sales are returned as royalties and are subject to withholding taxes imposed at rate w^* by the foreign country. If the U.S. firm has excess foreign tax credits, then this withholding tax is the only tax it pays on the profits generated by its foreign sales. If, instead, the firm has deficit foreign tax credits, then the royalties generate a tax liability to the U.S. government (and the withholding taxes generate a foreign tax credit), so foreign profits are effectively taxed at the domestic tax rate. In the case of a firm with excess foreign tax credits, its objective is to maximize[22]

$$(8) \qquad \{[S^*(R_f, I^*) - I^*](1 - w^*)\} - (1 - \tau)R_f - \pi R_f \tau .$$

The firm's first-order condition over the choice of R_f is

$$(9) \qquad (1 - w^*)\partial S^*/\partial R_f - (1 - \tau + \pi\tau) - (\partial\pi/\partial R_f)\underline{R}\tau = 0 ,$$

and the corresponding first-order condition over the choice of I^* is

$$(10) \qquad (1 - w^*)(\partial S^*/\partial I^* - 1) - (\partial\pi/\partial I^*)\underline{R}\tau = 0 .$$

R&D deductions are allocated in the same way for R_f as they are for R, so $\pi = \alpha S^*/(S + S^*)$, and the derivatives of the allocation function are

$$(11) \qquad \partial\pi/\partial R_f = \alpha(\partial S^*/\partial R_f)S/(S + S^*)^2$$

and

$$(12) \qquad \partial\pi/\partial I^* = \alpha(\partial S^*/\partial I^*)S/(S + S^*)^2 .$$

Combining (9) and (11) yields

$$(13) \qquad \frac{\partial S^*}{\partial R_f} = \frac{1 - \tau\left[1 - \dfrac{\alpha S^*}{(S + S^*)}\right]}{1 - w^* - \dfrac{\tau\alpha\underline{R}S}{(S + S^*)^2}} \equiv PR^* ,$$

---

21. Of the twenty-five industrialized countries surveyed by Lawlor (1985), twenty-four applied to the arm's length principle to the taxation of related-party transactions; Hong Kong was the exception.

22. If, instead, the firm has deficit foreign tax credits, then expression (8) must be modified by setting $\pi = 0$ and $w^* = \tau$. It is then straightforward to show that, with deficit foreign tax credits, the tax prices PR^* and PI^* both equal one.

in which PR is the after-tax cost of domestic R&D. Equations (10) and (12) together imply

(14)
$$\frac{\partial S^*}{\partial I^*} = \frac{1 - w^*}{1 - w^* - \frac{\tau \alpha \underline{R} S}{(S + S^*)^2}} \equiv PI^* .$$

There are several differences between the tax-induced incentives to undertake domestic R&D generating foreign sales—as revealed by (13) and (14)—and those for domestic R&D directed at domestic sales. The term w^* in the denominator of (13) reflects the extremely generous treatment of royalty exports by U.S. firms with excess foreign tax credits. Royalty income is considered to have foreign source under U.S. law. Hence, if a U.S. firm has excess foreign tax credits, it can use the credits to eliminate its U.S. tax liability on the royalty income. As a result, the firm is subject only to whatever withholding taxes are imposed by foreign governments on royalties paid to the United States. At the same time, the firm can deduct a considerable fraction of its U.S. R&D expenditures against its taxable U.S. income.

In practice, the withholding tax rates applied to royalties remitted to U.S. firms are, on average, very low. Table 5.2 lists the withholding rates charged by twenty-one other major countries on royalty payments to the U.S. in 1990. Many of these countries do not impose any withholding tax at all, and the average withholding tax rate, calculated using weights based on 1984 royalties, is 4.9 percent.

Domestic R&D directed at foreign markets is therefore very lightly taxed but is not favorably treated by the R&D expense allocation rules after 1986. The allocation rules are responsible for the third term in the numerator of (13), which increases the numerator, and the third term in the denominator of (13), which decreases the denominator, relative to a system of 100 percent domestic deductibility. Consequently, the required marginal product of domestic R&D for foreign markets is higher than it would be under 100 percent domestic allocation. Similarly, the system of less than 100 percent domestic deductibility reduces the denominator of (14), raising the required before-tax marginal product of ordinary foreign inputs for the same output.[23] As a result, for firms with excess foreign tax credits, the tax law after 1986 can be expected to discourage R&D directed at foreign markets, relative to the incentives those firms enjoyed prior to 1986. It is interesting to note, however, that after 1986 domestic R&D directed at foreign markets may still be subsidized by the U.S.

23. Equation (14) indicates that foreign inputs have required marginal products that exceed one, since the foreign sales they generate raise π and thereby reduce domestic R&D tax deductions. The firm forgoes some foreign profits in order to keep π down. The specification of (8) assumes that in losing foreign profits the firm also reduces the royalty it must pay; if, instead, the royalty is set by the amount that an unaffiliated firm (with the same production function) would pay to exploit R_f, then the firm's maximand will change slightly, and (14) will appear with τ^* in place of w^* in both the numerator and the denominator.

Table 5.2   **Withholding Tax Rates on Royalties Paid to the United States**

Country	1990 Tax Rate	1984 Royalties ($ millions)
Argentina	36%	$ 68.3
Australia	10	297.6
Austria	0	48.1
Belgium	0	170.9
Brazil	0	56.6
Canada	10	818.1
Finland	5	50.0
France	5	642.0
Germany	0	722.2
Hong Kong	0	42.5
Ireland	0	46.1
Italy	10	372.5
Japan	10	1,213.8
Korea	15	48.4
Netherlands	0	326.4
New Zealand	10	42.3
Norway	0	1,236.4
Singapore	31	49.9
Spain	10	108.9
Switzerland	0	138.0
United Kingdom	0	1,022.6

Sources: Price Waterhouse (1991); Mose (1989/1990).

tax system even for excess credit firms, since (13) is likely to take a value well below one (though [14] will exceed one).

Foreign R&D by U.S. Firms

There remains the issue of R&D performed by U.S. firms in foreign countries. R&D preformed abroad is generally subject to foreign tax rules (as well as U.S. rules for purposes of U.S. income taxation). Because foreign tax rates and tax rules pertaining to R&D were changing at the same time that U.S. law changed, it is difficult to summarize even the direction taken by the incentives for U.S. firms to do R&D offshore. To make matters worse, firm-level data on R&D performed abroad are not available. Consequently, the remainder of this study avoids specific consideration of the incentives U.S. firms have to undertake R&D abroad, noting that aggregate offshore R&D is small relative to domestic R&D and taking as a working assumption that foreign R&D grows at a steady rate that is unaffected by events in the United States.

5.4   Behavior of U.S. Firms

This section evaluates the responses of U.S. firms to changes in the R&D allocation rules over the period 1984–89, using the framework sketched in section 5.3.

5.4.1 Incentives

In order to determine how firms responded to the tax changes after 1986, it is helpful to outline a simple structure for their production relationships. Consider a firm i with a production function that generates sales as a Cobb-Douglas function of its R&D and ordinary inputs (including labor and capital). Such a function looks thus:

$$(15) \qquad S_{it}(R_{it}, I_{it}) = R_{it}^{\gamma} I_{it}^{\mu} \exp(\phi_t + \psi_i + u_{it}) ,$$

in which ϕ_t is a parameter common to all firms in period t, ψ_i is a fixed effect for firm i, and u_{it} is a normally distributed error term. Differentiating (15) with respect to R and I and imposing (6) and (7) yields

$$(16) \qquad \ln(R_{it}) = (1 - \mu - \gamma)^{-1} [\phi_t + \psi_i + (1 - \mu)\ln(\gamma) + \\ \mu\ln(\mu) - (1 - \mu)\ln(PR) - \mu\ln(PI) + u_{it}] .$$

Equation (16) indicates that the level of R&D a firm will choose is a negative function of the tax price of R&D and a negative function of the tax price of other inputs.[24] The relative magnitude of the effects of these two prices depends on the size of μ, which reflects the contribution of inputs other than R&D to firm sales. Griliches (1986) estimates a cross-sectional relationship for the years 1967, 1972, and 1977 in which firm value added is a Cobb-Douglas function of inputs including R&D, finding the share of other inputs, μ in (16), to range between 0.8 and 0.9. Jaffe (1988) obtains similar results with sales on the left side and using within-firm changes in inputs from 1972 to 1977 to estimate production parameters (including technological spillovers from other firms as an input). Given that the relationship in (15) is specified in terms of sales and not value added, one might expect the relative difference between the coefficients on PR and PI to be on the high side of this range, around 1:9.[25]

---

24. As written, equation (16) expresses the demand for R&D as a function of tax prices (PR and PI) only. It is also true that movements in the real market prices of inputs and outputs should be expected to influence a firm's desired R&D. Relative prices of R&D inputs are notoriously difficult to measure (for an important attempt, see Mansfield, Romeo, and Switzer 1983), as are output prices. If relative price movements are similar for all multinational firms, however, then this effect is likely to be captured by the year constant ϕ_t.

25. In separate cross-sectional production function regressions (not elsewhere reported) on the subset of firms in my sample reporting total labor expenses (amounting to fifty-two firms in the 1986 sample), the 1986 results were

$$\ln(S + S^*) = \underset{(0.13)}{1.39} + \underset{(0.04)}{0.28} \ln(CG) +$$

$$\underset{(0.06)}{0.35} \ln(L) + \underset{(0.05)}{0.28} \ln(PPE) +$$

$$\underset{(0.04)}{0.07} \ln(RD) \quad R^2 = 0.983 ,$$

in which L is labor expense; PPE is book property, plant, and equipment; RD is the firm's R&D stock in 1986; and CG represents the accounting entry "cost of goods sold," minus the other inputs

Suppose that the same firm i also generates its foreign sales by a Cobb-Douglas function of R&D devoted to foreign products and other foreign inputs. Such a function looks like:

(17) $S^*_{it}(R_{fit}, I^*_{it}) = R_{fit}^{\gamma*} I_{it}^{\mu*} \exp(\phi^*_t + \psi^*_i + u^*_{it})$,

and when differentiated and combined with (13) and (14) it yields

(18) $\ln(R_{fit}) = (1 - \mu^* - \gamma^*)^{-1}[\phi^*_t + \psi^*_i + (1 - \mu^*)\ln(\gamma^*) +$
$\mu^*\ln(\mu^*) - (1 - \mu^*)\ln(PR^*) - \mu^*\ln(PI^*) + u^*_{it}]$.

Unfortunately, (16) and (18) cannot be estimated directly, because even though $\underline{R}$ is observable it is not possible to observe its components R_{it} and R_{fit} separately. Taking antilogs of (16) and (18) and adding them does produce an equation specified in terms of observable variables but, in doing so, removes some of the attractive linearity of the system. An alternative approximation is available that maintains the linearity of the system for those cases in which R_f is not too large relative to R. Assume that this is the case. Then, from the definition of $\underline{R}$,

(19) $\underline{R}_{it} = R_{it} + R_{fit} = R_{it}(1 + R_{fit}/R_{it})$.

Taking logs and using a first-order Taylor approximation,

(20) $\ln(\underline{R}_{it}) \approx \ln(R_{it}) + R_{fit}/R_{it}$

Taking period zero to be the base period in a short panel, the ratio on the right side of (20) can be written

(21) $R_{fit}/R_{it} = \{R_{fi0}[1 + (R_{fit} - R_{fi0})/R_{fi0}]\}/\{R_{i0}[1 + (R_{it} - R_{i0})/R_{i0}]\}$,

and for small differences over time it becomes

(22) $R_{fit}/R_{it} \approx (R_{fi0}/R_{i0})(1 + (R_{fit} - R_{fi0})/R_{fi0} - (R_{it} - R_{i0})/R_{i0})$.

Then, using the approximation that $(R_{it} - R_{i0})/R_{i0} \approx \ln(R_{it}) - \ln(R_{i0})$, (22) becomes

(23) $R_{fit}/R_{it} \approx (R_{fi0}/R_{i0})[1 + \ln(R_{fit}) - \ln(R_{fi0}) - \ln(R_{it}) + \ln(R_{i0})]$.

Combining (23) and (20),

(24) $\ln(\underline{R}_{it}) \approx 1 - (R_{fi0}/R_{i0}) \ln(R_{it}) + (\underline{R}_{fi0}/R_{i0}) \ln(R_{fit}) + \theta_i$,

in which θ_i is a firm-specific constant equal to $(R_{fi0}/R_{i0}) [1 + \ln(R_{i0}) - \ln(R_{fi0})]$. Combining (24), (16), and (18) then yields

---

included in the regression. Similar regressions on other years and with different specifications produced similar results. Although cross-sectional results based on accounting data should be viewed skeptically (because firm-specific factors are obscured and the regression is subject to the problem noted by Schankerman [1981], that many of the R&D inputs are included among other right-side variables and consequently double counted), they suggest that it is not unreasonable to expect μ to take a value around 0.9.

(25) $\ln(\underline{R}_{it}) = \lambda_t + \eta_i + \xi_t \nu_i + \beta_1(1 - \nu_i)\ln(PR) +$
$\beta_2(1 - \nu_i)\ln(PI) + \beta_3 \nu_i \ln(PR^*) + \beta_4 \nu_i \ln(PI^*) + \varepsilon_{it}$,

in which $\nu_i \equiv R_{fi0}/R_{i0}$ is the ratio of foreign to domestic application of R&D in the base period, and additional information about production parameters implies further restrictions among the coefficients $\beta_1 - \beta_4$. The prices PR, PI, PR^*, and PI^* differ among firms and over years for the same firm; the values of the domestic prices PR and PI are equal to one over the 1981–86 period and for firms with deficit tax credits equal to one after 1986. The parameters λ_t and η_i are new combined year and individual effects, while the term ξ_t premultiplying ν_i reflects year-specific shocks that affect foreign and domestic markets differently. The equation (25) is then in a form that permits linear estimation of the responses of firms to the four (potentially) changing prices on its right side.

The only remaining difficulty in estimating (25) is that the term $\nu_i = R_{fi0}/R_{i0}$ is unobservable, since firms do not report (and indeed might not be able to report if they wanted to) the fraction of their R&D devoted to foreign markets. On the other hand, each firm's ratio of foreign to domestic sales is observable, and over the period 1981–86 should be unaffected by the R&D allocation rules, since the rules were the same for all firms. Suppose that

(26) $$R_{fi0}/R_{i0} = \rho(S^*_{i0}/S_{i0}) \ \forall \ i \ .$$

Then it is possible to use values of (S^*_{i0}/S_{i0}) from the 1981–86 period for ν_i on the right side of (25) and to estimate the equation while simultaneously estimating the value of ρ. One additional assumption is necessary in order to linearize this estimation. If the foreign and domestic production functions have the same production shares for R&D and other inputs, so that $\gamma = \gamma^*$ and $\mu = \mu^*$, then from (16) and (18) it should be the case that $\beta_1 = \beta_3$ and $\beta_2 = \beta_4$ in (25). Imposing this restriction, using (26), and defining $\sigma_i \equiv (S^*_{i0}/S_{i0})$, equation (25) becomes

(27) $\ln(\underline{R}_{it}) = \lambda_t + \eta_i + \xi_t \sigma_i + \beta_1 \ln(PR) + \beta_2 \ln(PI) +$
$\beta_3 \sigma_i [\ln(PR^*) - \ln(PR)] + \beta_4 \sigma_i [\ln(PI^*) - \ln(PI)] + \varepsilon_{it}$.

In this form of the estimating equation, the ratios β_3/β_1 and β_4/β_2 are estimates of ρ.

5.4.2 The Data

The analysis in this section uses a panel of firm-level data reported in Compustat over the period 1984–89. As a special project initiated in 1984, Compustat culls from a subset of its firms' information on their foreign pretax earnings and foreign income taxes paid. Firms are not required to report the countries in which they earned their profits, nor are they required to indicate if profits were repatriated or reinvested abroad. In a sample of 2,800 firms, foreign earnings and tax data are available for approximately 500 firms for each of the reporting years.

Unfortunately, the main Compustat file does not include data on firms' foreign sales. In order to obtain foreign sales information, it was necessary to use the Compustat Geographic Segment File, which reports separate business segments for certain firms with major foreign operations. This file contains data on foreign sales of U.S. firms, though it offers little other detail on foreign operations.[26] In order to identify those firms that are likely to have excess foreign tax credits, it is necessary to construct estimates of the foreign tax rates they face; this is possible only if firms report their foreign tax liabilities along with their (positive) foreign incomes. Firms were excluded from the sample if they did not report their domestic and (positive) foreign income and sales, along with their R&D expenditures, continuously from 1984–89. Firms involved in major mergers—those in which firm sales rose by 50 percent or more—were also omitted. These exclusions left a sample of 116 firms.

These 116 firms were at least three times the size of average firms in Compustat, with U.S. federal tax liabilities in 1989 averaging $91.9 million (versus $30.4 million for the Compustat average). In addition, the sample firms had average foreign tax liabilities of $121.9 million. Column 1 of table 5.3 is a list of some of the sample's characteristics.

In order to construct the tax prices firms face, it is necessary to establish whether or not they have excess foreign tax credits.[27] Unfortunately, the only way to do so precisely is to examine their U.S. federal income tax returns, which are confidential.[28] Given the data at hand, it is necessary instead to treat each firm as though all of its foreign income were taxed at the same, average, rate, so that firms with average foreign tax rates above the U.S. statutory rate are considered to have excess foreign tax credits. This ignores the endogeneity of a firm's dividend repatriation decision and, perhaps more important, ignores the separation of some of its foreign income into separate baskets for the purposes of the foreign tax credit calculation.[29] Column 2 of table 5.3

26. In particular, the Geographic Segment File does not indicate the magnitude of a firm's foreign R&D. Information about sales and profits in individual foreign countries is available only sporadically.

27. It is also necessary to construct tax prices for firms that would prefer to use one of the alternatives to the sales allocation method. These prices were constructed and applied for those firms that would do better to use one of the alternative methods.

28. Even with access to a firm's income tax records, it is still difficult to identify its foreign tax credit status for purposes of estimation, because the magnitude of creditable foreign taxes claimed by the firm in part depends on its dividend repatriations and other discretionary choices that may be endogenous to the policies under study. By contrast, the average foreign tax rate the firm faces may be much closer to an exogenous variable for some firms.

29. One way to correct for this problem would be to adjust a firm's observed foreign tax rate downward in determining its excess credit status. A number of the regressions reported in tables 5.5–5.12 were run with foreign tax rates adjusted downward by 0.02 and 0.04, with virtually identical results to those in the tables. An alternative correction would be to adjust the foreign tax rates *upward,* because firms can choose the pattern of their dividend repatriations from foreign subsidiaries and, all other things equal, are more likely to repatriate dividends from locations with higher tax rates (as Hines and Hubbard [1990] find to be the case for dividend repatriations by U.S. multinationals in 1984). Even the post-1986 tightening of the basket definitions could justify

Table 5.3   Characteristics of Subsamples in 1989 ($ millions)

Sample Characteristic	Whole Sample	Deficit FTC*	Nonmerging Firms†
Mean sales in 1989	$6,280.6	$5,694.5	$6,036.8
Percent foreign-source sales	35.4%	37.5%	37.8%
Mean income in 1989	$569.5	$591.7	$598.0
Percent foreign-source income	57.2%	50.9%	67.3%
Mean R&D expenditure in 1989	$259.3	$278.2	$310.0
Number of firms	116	21	40

*Firms having deficit foreign tax credits every year from 1987 to 1989.
†Firms exhibiting no merger activity over the 1984–89 period.

presents summary statistics of those firms that have deficit foreign tax credits continuously over the 1987–89 period. They look quite similar to the 116 firms in the main sample.

Merger and acquisition activity represents another potential difficulty facing the estimation of (27). The model is specified under the assumption that a firm's characteristics are reasonably stable over a short time span. Firms that acquire other firms presumably absorb not only the acquired firm's accumulated R&D stock and tax characteristics but also its firm-specific production function characteristics. The changes induced by mergers may introduce noise, if not bias, into the estimation of (27),[30] so a separate sample of 40 firms with no merger activity at all over the 1984–89 period was created. Column 3 of table 5.3 describes the properties of the nonmerger sample, which is slightly more R&D-intensive than the sample of 116 firms but is otherwise similar.

One final specification issue in estimating (27) is the choice of left-side variable. Plausible cases could be made for including either R&D stock or R&D flow on the left side of this equation. The argument for estimating (27) on the stock of R&D rests on the appropriateness of R&D stock as an argu-

---

an upward adjustment in the sample's foreign tax rate, because certain low-tax foreign-income sources are segregated into their own basket. But, on net, important high-tax items with their own baskets—such as oil income and high withholding tax interest income—make a downward adjustment more likely to capture the incentives firms face.

30. The direction of potential bias is not clear. As a general matter, Hall (1988) finds no difference between the mean growth rates of R&D intensity of firms involved in mergers and those not involved. Griliches and Mairesse (1984) find that firms with mergers produce significantly different panel estimates of productivity growth equations than do nonmerger firms; they argue on that basis that merger firms should not be excluded from productivity regressions. A successful merger increases the size of the acquiring firm, which might be expected to influence R&D intensity, though the evidence (Cohen, Levin, and Mowery 1987) suggests that size alone has very little effect.

ment of the sales function in (15). The difficulty with estimating (27) with the stock variable on the left side is that stock adjustment costs are implicitly assumed to be equal to zero, so that desired equals actual stock in every year. Although the price changes—and consequently the induced changes in desired stocks—are small over this time period, it may be unreasonable to expect immediate adjustment. Unfortunately, the time dimension in the panel does not permit reliable estimation of adjustment costs. An alternative is to use *current* R&D expenditures as the argument of the sales function (15) and on the left side of the factor demand equation (27); this specification is somewhat less compelling from the standpoint of the underlying production function but is less subject to the problem of slow adjustment. Consequently, each specification of (27) was estimated twice, first with R&D stock as a dependent variable and second with R&D flow; the results were not greatly affected by the choice of dependent variable.[31]

Table 5.4 describes characteristics of the tax prices faced by subsets of firms in the sample over the 1987–89 period. The data suggest that there is considerable variation both within and between industrial classifications (the first thirteen lines in the table present summaries by the most populated two-digit standard industrial classifications) in the tax prices firms face. The last six lines of the table exhibit average prices faced by the whole sample of 116 firms and the restricted sample of 38 nonmerging firms that is used in much of the estimation. For the average firm in the sample, the own-price of R&D [ln(PR)] increased approximately 5 percent in response to the 1986 tax change. For the 38 nonmerging firms, the average price rise was slightly higher (5.5 percent). These changes in own-prices of R&D were offset by reductions in cross-prices of R&D [ln(PI)] that were on average 3–4 percent of the magnitude of the own-price changes. While these cross-price movements are small, examination of (27) reveals that small changes on these prices have considerable impact on R&D levels and partly attenuate the effects of the own-price changes during 1987–89.

5.4.3   Their Behavior

Table 5.5 presents estimates of (27) for the sample of forty firms that did not exhibit merger activity over the 1984–89 period. The first two columns report the coefficients from the model in which R&D stock is the dependent variable, while columns 3 and 4 report results from regressions on R&D flow. Columns 1 and 3 present ordinary least squares (OLS) estimates of (27). As predicted, both domestic prices exert negative and significant effects on R&D activity, and the coefficient on the PI term is substantially larger (in absolute value) than the coefficient on the PR term (though this coefficient is impre-

---

31. R&D capital stocks were constructed using a perpetual inventory method, starting with R&D expenditures in 1975 (in constant 1984 dollars) and—following Griliches and Mairesse (1984) and Jaffe (1986)—applying a 15 percent rate of geometric decay to old stocks.

Table 5.4   **Characteristics of Tax Prices, 1987–1989**

Industry	Number of Firms	Price	Mean	Standard Deviation	Minimum	Maximum
Food and tobacco	3	ln(*PR*)	0.0181	0.0337	0	0.1024
Paper products	5	ln(*PR*)	0.0372	0.0430	0	0.1184
Chemicals	27	ln(*PR*)	0.0512	0.0541	0	0.1977
Petroleum	5	ln(*PR*)	0.0536	0.0486	0	0.1651
Rubber products	5	ln(*PR*)	0.0548	0.0475	0	0.1230
Stone and glass	3	ln(*PR*)	0.0325	0.0202	0	0.0548
Primary metals	2	ln(*PR*)	0.0079	0.0193	0	0.0474
Fabricated metals	7	ln(*PR*)	0.0318	0.0328	0	0.0857
Machinery	26	ln(*PR*)	0.0644	0.0587	0	0.2208
Electrical equipment	8	ln(*PR*)	0.0350	0.0550	0	0.1566
Transportation equipment	8	ln(*PR*)	0.0409	0.0315	0	0.0967
Scientific instruments	13	ln(*PR*)	0.0769	0.0722	0	0.2303
Other manufacturing	2	ln(*PR*)	0.0313	0.0485	0	0.0963
All firms	116	ln(*PI*)	0.0507	0.0544	0	0.2303
All firms	116	ln(*PI*)	−0.0015	0.0030	−0.0159	0
All firms	116	ln(*PR**)	−0.1615	0.1286	−0.3517	0
Nonmerging firms	38	ln(*PR*)	0.0550	0.0575	0	0.2194
Nonmerging firms	38	ln(*PI*)	−0.0023	0.0039	−0.0159	0
Nonmerging firms	38	ln(*PR**)	−0.1659	0.1271	−0.3517	0

cisely measured in the R&D stock regression). Domestic R&D appears to respond much more strongly to domestic price terms than it does to foreign price terms, suggesting a value of ρ that is imprecisely measured but in the neighborhood of 0.2–0.3. The estimated own-price elasticity of domestic R&D for domestic purposes is −1.3 in the R&D stock regression and −1.7 in the flow regression.

There is an important difficulty that arises in interpreting the OLS results, in that the tax prices (for firms with excess foreign tax credits) are endogenous to R&D expenditure levels. In order to reduce the bias that accompanies this endogeneity, columns 2 and 4 present instrumental variables (*IV*) estimates of (27), with instruments constructed by using values of $R/(S + S^*)$ and $S^*/(S + S^*)$ for the 1984–86 period for each firm in place of their yearly values in constructing price instruments. The *IV* estimates yield results that are quite similar to their OLS counterparts, though the cross-price effects fall in magnitude and the estimated effect of the price of R&D directed at foreign markets is now significant in the R&D stock regression. The estimated own-price elasticity of domestic R&D for domestic markets is −1.3 in the stock regression and −1.8 in the flow regression.

Table 5.6 presents results of the same regressions run on the whole sample of 116 firms. The *IV* estimates suggest an own-price elasticity of domestic R&D for domestic purposes that is somewhat smaller in magnitude, around

Table 5.5   **R&D Price Responsiveness in Nonmerging Firms, 1984–1989**

	Dependent Variable: ln (R&D stock)		Dependent Variable: ln (R&D flow)	
	OLS	IV	OLS	IV
ln(PR)	− 1.2947	− 1.2670	− 1.6874	− 1.7954
	(0.3982)	(0.4167)	(0.5595)	(0.5845)
ln(PI)	− 22.3221	− 12.8442	− 63.2821	− 59.0972
	(11.4838)	(12.3754)	(16.1359)	(17.3570)
ln(PR*)	− 0.2881	− 0.3166	− 0.4250	− 0.4605
	(0.1501)	(0.1511)	(0.2110)	(0.2119)
ln(PI*)	− 10.1741	− 6.5294	− 37.1077	− 35.5633
	(6.8583)	(7.0852)	(9.6367)	(9.9373)
Y85(S*/S)	− 0.0666	− 0.0665	− 0.0452	− 0.0503
	(0.1215)	(0.1218)	(0.1707)	(0.1709)
Y86(S*/S)	− 0.0732	− 0.0705	0.0452	0.0473
	(0.1211)	(0.1214)	(0.1701)	(0.1703)
Y87(S*/S)	− 0.0641	− 0.0373	0.2410	0.2601
	(0.1313)	(0.1322)	(0.1845)	(0.1854)
Y88(S*/S)	− 0.0591	− 0.0249	0.3367	0.3608
	(0.1334)	(0.1346)	(0.1874)	(0.1887)
Y89(S*/S)	− 0.0192	− 0.0025	0.4644	0.4770
	(0.1259)	(0.1264)	(0.1769)	(0.1773)
Firm dummies	Yes	Yes	Yes	Yes
Year dummies	Yes	Yes	Yes	Yes
Number of firms	40	40	40	40
$\hat{\sigma}$	0.1359	0.1362	0.1909	0.1911

Note: Values in parentheses are standard errors. *PR* and *PI* are the two domestic tax prices relevant to R&D, while *PR** and *PI** are their foreign counterparts (and are premultiplied by [S^*/S]). See text for description.

− 0.6 for the R&D stock and − 0.8 for R&D flow. In the stock regression, the other price coefficients have estimated standard errors that make them insignificant, and (except for the coefficient on *PI*) they are roughly half the size of the estimates in table 5.5. In the R&D flow regression, the coefficients on other prices are somewhat smaller than in the regression reported in table 5.5, although (except for the coefficient on *PR**) they remain significant. The sample of 116 firms would appear to exhibit less well defined responsiveness of R&D to changes in the tax prices of R&D, which may in part reflect the randomness introduced by the characteristics of their acquired assets and lines of business.

One of the difficulties that arise in estimating (27) is that the price terms on the right side are likely to exhibit considerable multicollinearity. The firms that experience substantial movements in one price term are likely to show simultaneous movements in others. One way to tighten the precision of the estimates is to restrict the coefficients still further. An attractive restriction to

Table 5.6   **R&D Price Responsiveness in 116 Firms, 1984–1989**

	Dependent Variable: ln (R&D stock)		Dependent Variable: ln (R&D flow)	
	OLS	IV	OLS	IV
ln(PR)	−0.6645	−0.6425	−0.8566	−0.8082
	(0.2242)	(0.2727)	(0.3754)	(0.4567)
ln(PI)	−17.3433	−13.3606	−46.5677	−41.9770
	(6.5991)	(10.1127)	(14.3947)	(16.9387)
ln(PR*)	−0.1155	−0.1587	−0.2611	−0.3734
	(0.0828)	(0.1196)	(0.1386)	(0.2003)
ln(PI*)	−9.5135	−9.0595	−28.0481	−29.6616
	(4.9956)	(5.6233)	(8.3625)	(9.4189)
Y85(S*/S)	−0.0608	−0.0661	−0.1334	−0.1480
	(0.0611)	(0.0624)	(0.1022)	(0.1045)
Y86(S*/S)	−0.0600	−0.0595	−0.0464	−0.0454
	(0.0593)	(0.0593)	(0.0993)	(0.0994)
Y87(S*/S)	−0.0503	−0.0409	0.0170	0.0385
	(0.0611)	(0.0612)	(0.1022)	(0.1025)
Y88(S*/S)	−0.0204	−0.0150	0.1207	0.1343
	(0.0626)	(0.0627)	(0.1047)	(0.1050)
Y89(S*/S)	−0.0177	−0.0138	0.1705	0.1805
	(0.0607)	(0.0608)	(0.1015)	(0.1019)
Firm dummies	Yes	Yes	Yes	Yes
Year dummies	Yes	Yes	Yes	Yes
Number of firms	116	116	116	116
σ̂	0.1331	0.1332	0.2228	0.2231

Note: Values in parentheses are standard errors. *PR* and *PI* are the two domestic tax prices relevant to R&D, while *PR** and *PI** are their foreign counterparts (and are premultiplied by [*S*/S*]). See text for description.

impose is to force $\mu = \mu^*$ and set their value equal to 0.9. Then (27) can be reestimated with both domestic price terms combined into a new term, $P \equiv (1 - \mu)\ln(PR) + \mu\ln(PI)$, and similarly for the foreign price terms $P^* \equiv (1 - \mu^*)[\ln(PR^*) - \ln(PR)] + \mu^*[\ln(PI^*) - \ln(PI)]$.[32]

Table 5.7 presents estimates of the restricted regression on a sample of thirty-eight of the firms without mergers.[33] The *IV* coefficient estimates are quite similar to their values in table 5.5 (recalling that the price terms are premultiplied by new coefficients), suggesting an own-price elasticity of do-

32. Some specification testing suggested that $\mu = 0.9$ fit the R&D stock specification quite well. Judging from the results reported in tables 5.5–5.12, it may be that an appropriate choice of μ for the R&D flow equation would be somewhat larger than 0.9.

33. Two firms were removed from the sample because there were no others in their two-digit SIC industries (in the nonmerging sample) and they had to be dropped for the regressions (table 5.11) that include industry dummy variables. In order to put the regressions reported in tables 5.7, 5.9, and 5.11 on a comparable basis, these firms were not included in the earlier regressions either. When the two additional firms were included, the results in tables 5.7 and 5.9 were virtually unchanged.

Table 5.7   **Response to Domestic and Foreign Tax Prices by 38 Nonmerging Firms, 1984–1989**

	Dependent Variable: ln (R&D stock)		Dependent Variable: ln (R&D flow)	
	OLS	IV	OLS	IV
ln(P)	−11.2955	−11.6830	−15.1322	−16.3360
	(3.1643)	(3.2860)	(5.5772)	(5.7931)
ln(P*)	−2.4655	−2.6773	−4.4408	−5.2222
	(1.1912)	(1.1973)	(2.0996)	(2.1110)
Y85(S*/S)	−0.0332	−0.0369	−0.0218	−0.0353
	(0.0983)	(0.0983)	(0.1732)	(0.1733)
Y86(S*/S)	−0.0212	−0.0209	0.0884	0.0896
	(0.0981)	(0.0982)	(0.1730)	(0.1731)
Y87(S*/S)	−0.0109	−0.0103	0.2528	0.2557
	(0.0986)	(0.0986)	(0.1737)	(0.1738)
Y88(S*/S)	0.0168	0.0169	0.3853	0.3861
	(0.0982)	(0.0982)	(0.1731)	(0.1732)
Y89(S*/S)	0.0653	0.0660	0.4840	0.4866
	(0.0984)	(0.0984)	(0.1734)	(0.1735)
Firm dummies	Yes	Yes	Yes	Yes
Year dummies	Yes	Yes	Yes	Yes
Number of firms	38	38	38	38
σ̂	0.1081	0.1081	0.1905	0.1906

Note: Values in parentheses are standard errors. P is the domestic tax price relevant to R&D, while $P*$ is its foreign counterpart (and is premultiplied by [$S*/S$]). See text for description.

mestic R&D for domestic markets of −1.2 in the stock regression and −1.6 in the flow regression. The price sensitivity of domestic R&D directed at foreign markets is considerably lower, again implying a value of ρ between 0.2 and 0.33.

Table 5.8 repeats the estimation of this system for the whole sample of 116 firms. The combined domestic price term in the stock regression is significant and slightly smaller in magnitude than its estimated counterparts in earlier regressions, implying an own-price elasticity of domestic R&D for domestic markets of −0.6. The foreign price effect in the stock regression is estimated to be much smaller, again between 0.2 and .25 of the domestic price effect, and is not significantly different from zero. The domestic price term in the R&D flow equation is considerably smaller than in the estimates reported in table 5.6, implying an estimated elasticity of −0.5 that is not significantly different from zero. The foreign price term in this regression is again smaller than the domestic price term but is also insignificant.

One of the difficulties that confronts this analysis is the problem of measuring the tax price faced by firms in the sample. The tax prices that underlie the results reported in tables 5.4 through 5.8 were constructed under the assumption that firms use the foreign and domestic income figures reported in their

Table 5.8   **Response to Domestic and Foreign Tax Prices by 116 Firms, 1984–1989**

	Dependent Variable: ln (R&D stock)		Dependent Variable: ln (R&D flow)	
	OLS	IV	OLS	IV
ln(P)	− 5.9925	− 5.6212	− 6.3367	− 4.9683
	(2.1829)	(2.5556)	(3.6761)	(4.3043)
ln(P*)	− 0.9737	− 1.3783	− 2.1102	− 2.7268
	(0.8212)	(1.1900)	(1.3831)	(2.0043)
Y85(S*/S)	− 0.0578	− 0.0637	− 0.1237	− 0.1328
	(0.0611)	(0.0623)	(0.1029)	(0.1050)
Y86(S*/S)	− 0.0599	− 0.0598	− 0.0452	− 0.0452
	(0.0594)	(0.0594)	(0.1000)	(0.1000)
Y87(S*/S)	− 0.0650	− 0.0650	− 0.0098	− 0.0099
	(0.0594)	(0.0594)	(0.1000)	(0.1000)
Y88(S*/S)	− 0.0457	− 0.0501	0.0626	0.0532
	(0.0599)	(0.0600)	(0.1008)	(0.1011)
Y89 (S*/S)	− 0.0339	− 0.0359	0.1337	0.1305
	(0.0595)	(0.0596)	(0.1002)	(0.1005)
Firm dummies	Yes	Yes	Yes	Yes
Year dummies	Yes	Yes	Yes	Yes
Number of firms	116	116	116	116
$\hat{\sigma}$	0.1332	0.1333	0.2244	0.2245

Note: Values in parentheses are standard errors. P is the domestic tax price relevant to R&D, while P* is its foreign counterpart (and is premultiplied by [S*/S]). See text for description.

10-Ks for R&D allocation on their tax returns. Unfortunately, the definitions differ, and they do so in ways that cannot be identified from publicly available information. A firm's tax situation depends on a number of rather subtle choices by the firm, and legal distinctions between observationally similar activities of the firm, that make it very difficult to identify their incentives.[34]

In order to check the robustness of the results presented in tables 5.5 through 5.8 to changes in the specification of tax prices, tables 5.9 and 5.10 report the results of reestimating (27) under the assumption that all firms use the income allocation method to reduce their tax obligations to the point that the fractional sales constraint binds. The estimated price elasticities for the nonmerging sample of thirty-eight firms, reported in table 5.9, are about half

34. The U.S. Department of the Treasury (1983) found that for the small number (twenty-four) of firms for which enough data were available on tax returns and in 10-K filings to observe their R&D allocation procedures, it appeared that those firms took more R&D deductions against their U.S. taxable income than even the most generous treatment (full use of the income method) would have indicated. This does not mean that these firms necessarily took excessive R&D deductions, because there are several circumstances in which firms are permitted to allocate more R&D against their domestic income than is provided by the allocation rule, if the deductions can be justified. All of this points to the difficulty of using available data—even confidential tax return data—to measure tax prices exactly. But at the same time, observable tax prices can offer useful approximations to the prices firms face.

Table 5.9   **Response to (Constrained) Tax Prices by Nonmerging Firms, 1984–1989**

	Dependent Variable: ln (R&D stock)		Dependent Variable: ln (R&D flow)	
	OLS	IV	OLS	IV
ln(P)	− 7.9749	− 7.8978	− 8.7179	− 8.5307
	(1.6931)	(1.6549)	(2.9895)	(2.9928)
ln(P*)	− 3.0145	− 3.0766	− 3.7677	− 3.8940
	(1.1788)	(1.1791)	(2.1318)	(2.1324)
Y85(S*/S)	− 0.0419	− 0.0430	− 0.0096	− 0.0120
	(0.0963)	(0.0963)	(0.1742)	(0.1742)
Y86(S*/S)	− 0.0199	− 0.0199	0.0876	0.0877
	(0.0959)	(0.0959)	(0.1735)	(0.1735)
Y87(S*/S)	− 0.0566	− 0.0564	0.1954	0.1960
	(0.0965)	(0.0965)	(0.1746)	(0.1746)
Y88(S*/S)	− 0.0057	− 0.0061	0.3554	0.3546
	(0.0964)	(0.0964)	(0.1743)	(0.1743)
Y89(S*/S)	0.0264	0.0265	0.4342	0.4346
	(0.0963)	(0.0963)	(0.1741)	(0.1741)
Firm dummies	Yes	Yes	Yes	Yes
Year dummies	Yes	Yes	Yes	Yes
Number of firms	38	38	38	38
$\hat{\sigma}$	0.1057	0.1057	0.1911	0.1911

Note: Values in parentheses are standard errors. Tax prices used in the regressions reported in this table were constructed under the assumption that all firms can reduce their tax liabilities using the income allocation method, up to the point that the sales allocation method constraint binds. P is the domestic tax price relevant to R&D, while $P*$ is its foreign counterpart (and is premultiplied by $[S*/S]$). See text for description.

the magnitude of the corresponding elasticity estimates in table 5.7: the domestic price elasticities are − 0.5 in the stock regression and − 0.9 in the flow regression. The foreign price elasticities are, as in table 5.7, considerably smaller than their domestic counterparts; and in the R&D flow regression, the estimated foreign price elasticity is not significantly different from zero. The estimated price elasticities reported in table 5.10 are similar to the estimates in table 5.8, with the difference that the magnitudes are slightly smaller and the domestic price elasticities are both significantly different from zero (− 0.4 in the stock regression and − 0.5 in the flow regression) in table 5.10.

Another difficulty in interpreting (27) is the omission of industry-specific effects. Firms in some industries are more likely than those in others to have operations in high-tax foreign locations and to have high $\underline{R}/(S + S*)$ ratios. If those industries also are the ones that are shrinking relative to other manufacturing industries over the 1987–89 period (for ordinary business reasons unrelated to §1.861–8), then one might mistakenly interpret negative coefficients on the price terms to imply an important price effect on R&D when no effect is present. One way to avoid such a misinterpretation would be to run (27) with industry dummy variables, interacted with time trends, on the right

Table 5.10	Response to (Constrained) Tax Prices by 116 Firms, 1984–1989			
	Dependent Variable: ln (R&D stock)		Dependent Variable: ln (R&D flow)	
	OLS	IV	OLS	IV
ln(P)	−4.1080	−4.0382	−4.9362	−4.7330
	(1.1683)	(1.1697)	(1.9713)	(1.9737)
ln(P*)	−1.1207	−1.1768	−2.1105	−2.2168
	(0.8152)	(0.8154)	(1.3755)	(1.3759)
Y85(S*/S)	−0.0595	−0.0604	−0.1232	−0.1249
	(0.0609)	(0.0609)	(0.1027)	(0.1027)
Y86(S*/S)	−0.0596	−0.0596	−0.0450	−0.0450
	(0.0591)	(0.0591)	(0.0997)	(0.0997)
Y87(S*/S)	−0.0817	−0.0818	−0.0331	−0.0330
	(0.0594)	(0.0594)	(0.1002)	(0.1002)
Y88(S*/S)	−0.0707	−0.0714	0.0334	0.0320
	(0.0600)	(0.0600)	(0.1012)	(0.1012)
Y89(S*/S)	−0.0507	−0.0510	0.1109	0.1104
	(0.0599)	(0.0599)	(0.1010)	(0.1010)
Firm dummies	Yes	Yes	Yes	Yes
Year dummies	Yes	Yes	Yes	Yes
Number of firms	116	116	116	116
$\hat{\sigma}$	0.1327	0.1327	0.2239	0.2239

Note: Values in parentheses are standard errors. Tax prices used in the regressions reported in this table were constructed under the assumption that all firms can reduce their tax liabilities using the income allocation method, up to the point that the sales allocation method constraint binds. P is the domestic tax price relevant to R&D, while $P*$ is its foreign counterpart (and is premultiplied by $[S*/S]$). See text for description.

side, thereby removing average industry effects on R&D growth. The disadvantage of this approach is that it also removes the average industry price variation, leaving only within-industry variation with which to identify the effect of tax prices on R&D. The remaining variation may not always be adequate to identify price effects precisely.

Tables 5.11 and 5.12 present estimates of (27) that include on the right side time trends interacted with industry dummy variables for each of the two-digit SIC manufacturing industries listed in table 5.4.[35] Because these regressions are intended to probe the robustness of the specification of (27), the tax prices used in these regressions were constructed under the assumption that all firms use the income method (up to the sales method constraint) to allocate their R&D deductions.[36] The estimated coefficients on tax price variables in tables

35. To be specific, the industry growth dummy variables take values of zero for firms outside the (two-digit SIC) industry, while for firms in the industry the values are one in 1985, two in 1986, and so on. For a more subtle treatment of interindustry differences in R&D growth rates, see Pakes and Schankerman (1984a).

36. Very similar results were obtained in specifications with industry growth variables included on the right side but tax prices calculated in the standard manner (as in tables 5.7 and 5.8).

Table 5.11   **Response to (Constrained) Tax Prices, Industry Effects Removed, by Nonmerging Firms, 1984–1989**

	Dependent Variable: ln (R&D stock)		Dependent Variable: ln (R&D flow)	
	OLS	IV	OLS	IV
ln(P)	−5.3825	−5.2497	−4.7604	−4.4716
	(1.4439)	(1.4456)	(2.7846)	(2.7878)
ln(P*)	−2.6111	−2.6551	−2.7488	−2.8342
	(0.9919)	(0.9922)	(1.9129)	(1.9134)
Y85(S*/S)	0.0241	−0.0249	0.0268	0.0252
	(0.0809)	(0.0809)	(0.1559)	(0.1559)
Y86(S*/S)	0.0344	0.0343	0.1811	0.1809
	(0.0814)	(0.0814)	(0.1571)	(0.1571)
Y87(S*/S)	0.0468	0.0472	0.3723	0.3732
	(0.0839)	(0.0839)	(0.1617)	(0.1617)
Y88(S*/S)	0.1205	0.1200	0.5757	0.5748
	(0.0865)	(0.0865)	(0.1668)	(0.1669)
Y89(S*/S)	0.1922	0.1923	0.7197	0.7200
	(0.0896)	(0.0896)	(0.1728)	(0.1729)
Industry growth dummies	Yes	Yes	Yes	Yes
Firm dummies	Yes	Yes	Yes	Yes
Year dummies	Yes	Yes	Yes	Yes
Number of firms	38	38	38	38
$\hat{\sigma}$	0.0881	0.0881	0.1699	0.1699

Note: Values in parentheses are standard errors. Tax prices used in the regressions reported in this table were constructed under the assumption that all firms can reduce their tax liabilities using the income allocation method, up to the point that the sales allocation method constraint binds. Industry growth dummies are industry-specific constant time trends. P is the domestic tax price relevant to R&D, while $P*$ is its foreign counterpart (and is premultiplied by $[S*/S]$). See text for description.

5.11 and 5.12 remain negative but are generally only half of the magnitude of the corresponding coefficients in tables 5.9 and 5.10; also, although they are significant in the R&D stock regressions (except for the foreign price coefficient in the large sample regression reported in table 5.12), estimated price effects become insignificant in the R&D flow regressions. It appears that removing the variation in prices between industries simply leaves too little variation to identify the price effects very precisely. An alternative interpretation would be that the price effects that appear in tables 5.5 through 5.10 are simply spurious correlations, but this interpretation would not square with the results from the R&D stock regressions.

The results described in tables 5.5 through 5.12 present a consistent picture of R&D activity that is sensitive to the tax changes introduced after 1986. The evidence in the tables suggests, however, that tax changes that affected the after-tax profitability of R&D performed in the United States and directed at foreign markets had significantly less impact than the tax changes that affected

Table 5.12   **Response to (Constrained) Tax Prices, Industry Effects Removed, by 116 Firms, 1984–1989**

	Dependent Variable: ln (R&D stock)		Dependent Variable: ln (R&D flow)	
	OLS	IV	OLS	IV
ln(P)	−3.1211	−2.9981	−3.7319	−3.4691
	(1.0802)	(1.0815)	(1.9552)	(1.9575)
ln(P*)	−0.5232	−0.5655	−1.0773	−1.1698
	(0.7502)	(0.7504)	(1.3579)	(1.3582)
Y85(S*/S)	−0.0501	−0.0508	−0.1196	−0.1212
	(0.0550)	(0.0550)	(0.0995)	(0.0995)
Y86(S*/S)	−0.0466	−0.0468	−0.0552	−0.0555
	(0.0538)	(0.0538)	(0.0973)	(0.0974)
Y87(S*/S)	−0.0549	−0.0550	−0.0386	−0.0387
	(0.0549)	(0.0549)	(0.0994)	(0.0994)
Y88(S*/S)	−0.0333	−0.0341	0.0299	0.0281
	(0.0568)	(0.0568)	(0.1027)	(0.1027)
Y89(S*/S)	−0.0039	−0.0043	0.1045	0.1035
	(0.0581)	(0.0581)	(0.1051)	(0.1051)
Industry growth dummies	Yes	Yes	Yes	Yes
Firm dummies	Yes	Yes	Yes	Yes
Year dummies	Yes	Yes	Yes	Yes
Number of firms	116	116	116	116
$\hat{\sigma}$	0.1193	0.1193	0.2159	0.2159

Note: Values in parentheses are standard errors. Tax prices used in the regressions reported in this table were constructed under the assumption that all firms can reduce their tax liabilities using the income allocation method, up to the point that the sales allocation method constraint binds. Industry growth dummies are industry-specific constant time trends. P is the domestic tax price relevant to R&D, while P^* is its foreign counterpart (and is premultiplied by $[S^*/S]$). See text for description.

the after-tax profitability of R&D performed in the United States and directed at the American market. The foreign market effect is smaller than that for the domestic market, even when corrected for firms' relative sales in the two markets.

Why the foreign market effect should be so much smaller is unclear. One possibility is that measurement error reduces the estimated magnitude of what is truly a substantial effect. There is no doubt that the heterogeneity of foreign markets, and foreign tax rates, makes the average foreign price measures PR^* and PI^* only approximations to the true tax prices of performing R&D for foreign markets. Another possibility is that the analysis might fail to find the true effect because it is not possible to identify separately the changes in offshore R&D performed by subsidiaries of U.S. firms.[37] But the third, and per-

---

37. For an exploratory study of the determinants of offshore R&D by U.S. firms, see Mansfield, Teece, and Romeo (1979).

Table 5.13   **Royalties Paid versus R&D Devoted to Foreign Sources, based on Relative Sales (current $ millions)**

Year	Affiliate Sales	Parent Sales	Affiliate Sales Share	U.S. R&D	Affiliate R&D Share	Royalties
1982	$271,099	$1,017,591	21.0%	$40,105	$ 8,437	$3,308
1983	270,363	1,080,267	20.0	44,588	8,925	3,597
1984	285,970	1,207,297	19.2	51,404	9,844	3,921
1985	293,989	1,246,401	19.1	57,043	10,887	4,096
1986	335,700	1,264,513	21.0	59,932	12,573	5,518
1987	388,424	1,338,593	22.5	62,806	14,126	7,039
1988	464,112	1,429,967	24.5	66,463	16,286	8,455

Source: U.S. Department of Commerce (various years); National Science Foundation (1991).
Note: Data are limited to manufacturing industries only.

haps most likely, possibility is that firms do not concentrate on foreign tax factors when undertaking R&D in the United States. This is likely to be the case if, in fact, domestic R&D does not greatly promote foreign profitability relative to its effect on domestic profitability.[38]

It is difficult to assess this third possibility, because some R&D performed in the United States clearly is directed primarily at foreign markets, whereas other R&D activities are directed at the U.S. market. Table 5.13 offers some aggregate evidence on the relationship between the foreign sales share of U.S. affiliates (multiplied by U.S. domestic R&D), and their use of domestic U.S. technology, as reflected in royalty payments to the United States. It appears that royalty payments equal only about half of the foreign share based on a simple sales formula. There are, of course, several possible explanations for the pattern displayed in table 5.13. The aggregate R&D figures represent the sum of firms with and without foreign affiliates. There might be long delays between expenditures on R&D and the production of know-how that would merit the payment of a royalty. Firms may not pay the royalties that they should according to arm's-length pricing principles.[39] But another possibility is that R&D in the United States is directed primarily at domestic markets.

38. Or if its effects on foreign profitability appears only after considerable time has elapsed. Mansfield and Romeo (1980) find that new technologies developed in the United States are transferred to industrialized foreign countries six years, on average, after they are first used in U.S. production. It would undoubtedly be a mistake to conclude that domestic R&D has no influence on foreign profitability; for example, Flaherty (1984) documents the importance of technological leadership for market shares of foreign affiliates of U.S. firms. Furthermore, manufacturing executives undertake R&D projects anticipating that a substantial fraction (though less than half) of the returns will come in foreign markets, according to the survey results presented in Mansfield, Romeo, and Wagner (1979).

39. Kopits (1976) offers evidence that multinationals systematically adjust their royalty payments to pursue global tax-minimizing strategies. Given the tax-favored status of royalty receipts in the United States, this argument implies that the royalty might be overstated rather than understated.

5.5   Alternative Tax Structures

The price responsiveness of R&D as estimated in tables 5.7 and 5.8 suggests that proposed changes in the tax treatment of R&D might have observable, if small, effects on the R&D efforts of U.S. multinationals. In this section, I examine the likely consequences of two reforms. One alternative to the current tax system is to restore the system that existed from 1981 to 1986, in which U.S. multinationals effectively could deduct 100 percent of their R&D for tax purposes. The second proposal, advocated by McIntyre (1989) and others, is to allocate U.S. R&D expenses on the basis of foreign and domestic sales without an initial fractional apportionment against U.S. income and without optional income apportionment.

Table 5.14 presents both proposals' estimated effects on revenue and R&D levels, based on data from a somewhat expanded set of 189 firms for 1989. (Firms were included if enough data were available to construct their responses to the proposed tax changes in 1989.) Collectively, these 189 firms had $41 billion of R&D expenditures in 1989, representing half of the total R&D expenditure reported for all 2,800 Compustat firms in 1989. The revenue consequences of the proposed reforms were calculated on the assumption that any tax-induced changes in levels of R&D represent flows of resources between equally taxed activities and hence do not affect tax revenues. In order to convert changes in R&D stocks into yearly flows for presentation in table 5.14, the 1989 ratio of aggregate R&D expenditure to aggregate R&D stock (20.8 percent) was multiplied by the implied changes in R&D stocks from the reforms.

Using reported foreign and domestic incomes and foreign tax rates to calculate tax liabilities, a reform that permitted firms to deduct 100 percent of their R&D expenses against U.S. income would have cost the U.S. Treasury $1.2 billion from these 189 firms in 1989. In return, U.S. firms would have increased their domestic R&D expenditures by somewhere between $1.4 billion and $2.2 billion, in which the $2.2 billion figure is constructed from the estimated elasticity of R&D flow, while the $1.4 billion figure represents the change in long-run flow corresponding to the stock change constructed from stock demand estimates.[40]

The alternative of apportioning R&D expenses 100 percent on the basis of foreign and domestic sales would have even more dramatic consequences. Again taking observed foreign tax rates to be reliable, sales apportionment would yield an additional $2.5 billion in tax revenue from these 189 firms. As a consequence of sales apportionment, these firms would be expected to re-

---

40. R&D responses reported in table 5.14 are based on coefficients estimated using the non-merging sample; they are reported in table 5.7, columns 2 and 4. The estimated change in R&D stock from moving to 100 percent domestic deductibility is $7.0 billion. If there are no adjustment costs, then the first-year change in R&D expenditure might be of this magnitude, with the (smaller) figure in the text indicating the annual flow to which this corresponds.

Table 5.14   **Estimated Effects of Two Policy Reforms on R&D and Tax Revenue (current $ millions)**

		Change in R&D	
Contemplated Reform	Change in Tax Revenue	Flow Estimates	Stock Estimates
100 percent domestic deductibility	$ − 1,166	$2,230	$1,444
Pure sales apportionment	2,542	− 2,590	− 1,783

Note: Figures are based on 189 multinational firms with $41 billion of R&D expenditures in 1989. Firms are assumed to use the sales apportionment method to allocate their R&D deductions. The flow estimates of R&D change are constructed from the estimated price responsiveness of the nonmerging sample (table 5.7, col. 4). The stock estimates of R&D change are also constructed from the estimated price responsiveness of the nonmerging sample (table 5.7, col. 2), with the estimated stock adjustment converted into an annual flow equivalent by applying the 1989 ratio of R&D flow to R&D stock.

duce their domestic R&D by between $1.8 billion (constructed from stock demand estimates) and $2.6 billion (constructed from flow demand estimates).[41]

These results suggest that R&D undertaken by U.S. multinationals is not likely to change dramatically in response to either of the contemplated tax reforms, largely because the changes themselves are rather minor when framed in the broader context of R&D policy. Nevertheless, the changes in R&D that would accompany the reforms slightly exceed the tax revenue changes they would induce. The U.S. Department of the Treasury (1983) study offers similar findings, though it does so from different premises.[42] In particular, the estimates of R&D price elasticities that can be found in the literature are so small that they would not typically support the kind of conclusions presented in this paper or assumed in the Treasury study.[43] The reason may have to do with the difficulty of finding exogenous price changes. Researchers typically use time-series variation in prices, making it impossible to

41. The stock estimates correspond to a change in R&D stock demand of $8.6 billion.

42. The Treasury study uses the rather low range of elasticities available in the literature but applies them to the *average*, rather than *marginal*, prices firms face; these two differences from the present study roughly equal each other, so the final results are similar (though they can differ by a factor of two).

43. See, for example, Bernstein and Nadiri (1989), who estimate R&D price elasticities to be between − 0.4 and − 0.5 for a sample of manufacturing firms, while Nadiri and Prucha (1989) find the R&D price elasticity to be much closer to zero for the U.S. Bell System. In a study of Canadian firms, Bernstein (1985) reports estimated R&D price elasticities of between − 0.1 and − 0.4. Mansfield (1986) and the GAO study (U.S. General Accounting Office 1989) summarize the literature with the conclusion that the consensus range of price elasticities is − 0.2 to − 0.5. The price elasticity one expects may be a matter of judgment, but many observers find the − 0.2 to − 0.5 range to be unreasonably close to zero. Certainly firms *claim* to be influenced by after-tax prices; Brown (1984) reports that two-thirds of the executives included in a 1984 Conference Board survey anticipated that tax incentives would influence their R&D expenditures over the next one to three years.

exploit firm-specific variations and raising a number of problems related to omitted variables and the endogeneity of prices.

It is important to interpret the policy simulations with caution. The 189 firms on which the calculations are based do not represent all of the firms that would be affected by the envisioned changes, though these firms perform half of the country's R&D and, because these are the firms with (on average) the highest foreign sales concentrations, they are likely to represent by far the majority of the impact of §1.861–8 changes. There are, however, some limitations in the way that the revenue implications are calculated[44] and also some restrictive assumptions built into the estimated R&D responses to the tax changes.[45]

5.6   Conclusion

The ability of U.S. multinationals to deduct their U.S. R&D expenses against U.S. income for tax purposes has changed many times over the past fifteen years. It appears that U.S. multinationals have changed their R&D spending behavior, albeit mildly, in response. The estimates presented in this paper imply that domestic R&D spending responds to changes in the after-tax price of R&D with an elasticity between -1.2 and -1.6. This elasticity is considerably higher than estimates found in the literature.

44. Some of the firms in the sample may have (in 1989) used the income allocation method to a greater degree than it appears from their financial data. Under the assumption that all of the 189 firms were able to exploit the income allocation method to the limit in 1989, replacing the existing system with 100 percent domestic deductibility was estimated to reduce tax revenues by $368 million a year, while moving to pure sales allocation would raise revenues by $3.341 billion. A second adjustment to estimated tax revenues might come in response to induced changes in R&D. The revenue estimates are constructed to show the first-order revenue effect of changing the deductibility of current levels of R&D; any induced changes are assumed to be financed by reducing the level of other similarly taxed activities. If, instead, greater R&D in the economy generates greater tax revenue, either by drawing resources out of untaxed activities or by stimulating greater aggregate productivity through spillovers into other firms and industries, then tax cuts that stimulate R&D do not reduce tax revenues by as much as first-order calculations suggest.

45. The contemplated policy reforms would influence aggregate R&D, and the endogeneity of the prices of products produced by R&D attenuate the effects of the tax changes on R&D. The model is estimated on the basis of firms' reported R&D; if firms have some flexibility in what they call R&D, then some part of the estimated responsiveness of R&D may reflect reporting choices rather than resource allocations. The estimation of the elasticity parameters ignores the role of the R&D tax credit, which may (or may not) serve to accentuate the incentives created by changes in §1.861-8; consequently, the estimated elasticities could be too great. On the other hand, the estimates also ignore the role of foreign tax credit carryforwards and carrybacks, which probably biases the estimates toward zero. A number of tax changes introduced in 1986 discouraged investment in plant and equipment and may thereby have influenced R&D spending; for an analysis of the interaction between R&D and other capital, see Lach and Schankerman (1989) and Hall and Hayashi (1989). The data are unable to distinguish domestic from foreign R&D, so a firm might reduce its domestic R&D in response to the tax changes and nevertheless appear to be unaffected. The role of aggregate R&D incentives in changing the strategic environments in which firms operate (see, for example, Meron and Caves 1990) is ignored, as are effects of direct government funding of private R&D (for analyses, see Levy and Terleckyj 1983; Scott 1984; and Lichtenberg 1987). It appears that the weight of these limitations is to bias the estimated R&D price elasticities toward zero, but it is difficult to know for sure.

These estimates imply that some proposed changes in the tax treatment of R&D are unlikely to have an enormous impact on the level of research and development in the United States. Nevertheless, by making R&D performed in the United States 100 percent deductible against U.S. taxes, Congress would stimulate between $1.4 billion and $2.2 billion in additional annual R&D spending. This change would reduce U.S. government tax revenues by $1.2 billion annually. An alternative policy of requiring multinationals to allocate their R&D deductions purely on the basis of foreign and domestic sales would reduce their annual R&D by between $1.8 billion and $2.6 billion but would raise $2.5 billion in yearly tax revenues. Whether either of these reform plans represent likely future alternatives may well depend on whether Congress feels that increased R&D or increased tax revenue is a more important national goal.

References

Altshuler, Rosanne. 1988. A dynamic analysis of the research and experimentation credit. *National Tax Journal* 41:453–66.

Auerbach, Alan J. 1983. Corporate taxation in the United States. *Brookings Papers on Economic Activity* 2:451–505.

Bernstein, Jeffrey I. 1985. Research and development, patents, and grant and tax policies in Canada. In *Technological change in Canadian industry,* ed. D. G. McFetridge. Toronto: University of Toronto Press.

Bernstein, Jeffrey I., and M. Ishaq Nadiri. 1989. Rates of return on physical and R&D capital and structure of production process: Cross section and time series evidence. In *Advances in econometrics and modeling,* ed. B. Raj. Dordrecht: Kluwer.

Brown, James K. 1984. *The impact of technological change on corporate and R&D management.* Research Bulletin 170. New York: Conference Board.

Cohen, Wesley M., and Richard C. Levin. 1989. Empirical studies of innovation and market structure. In *Handbook of industrial organization,* ed. R. Schmalensee and R. D. Willig. vol. 2. Amsterdam: North-Holland.

Cohen, Wesley M., Richard C. Levin, and David C. Mowery. 1987. Firm size and R&D intensity: A re-examination. *Journal of Industrial Economics* 35:543–65.

Dixit, Avinash. 1988. International R&D competition and policy. In *International competitiveness,* ed. A. M. Spence and H. A. Hazard. Cambridge, Mass.: Ballinger.

Eisner, Robert, Steven H. Albert, and Martin A. Sullivan. 1984. The new incremental tax credit for R&D: Incentive or disincentive? *National Tax Journal* 37:171–83.

Flaherty, M. Therese. 1984. Market share determination in international semiconductor markets. Working Paper 1-782-004. Cambridge, Mass.: Harvard Business School.

Fullerton, Don, and Andrew B. Lyon. 1988. Tax neutrality and intangible capital. In *Tax policy and the economy,* ed. L. H. Summers. Vol. 2. Cambridge, Mass.: MIT Press.

Griliches, Zvi. 1986. Productivity, R&D, and basic research at the firm level in the 1970s. *American Economic Review* 76:141–54.

———. 1991. The search for R&D spillovers. NBER Working Paper no. 3768. Cambridge, Mass.: National Bureau of Economic Research.

Griliches, Zvi, and Jacques Mairesse. 1984. Productivity and R&D at the firm level. In *R&D, patents, and productivity,* ed. Z. Griliches. Chicago: University of Chicago Press.

Hall, Bronwyn H. 1988. The effect of takeover activity on corporate research and development. In *Corporate takeovers: Causes and consequences,* ed. A. J. Auerbach. Chicago: University of Chicago Press.

Hall, Bronwyn H., and Fumio Hayashi. 1989. Research and development as an investment. NBER Working Paper no. 2973. Cambridge, Mass.: National Bureau of Economic Research.

Hartman, David G. 1985. Tax policy and foreign direct investment. *Journal of Public Economics* 26:107–21.

Hines, James R., Jr. 1990. The flight paths of migratory corporations. Olin Discussion Paper no. 65. Princeton, N.J.: Princeton University.

Hines, James R., Jr., and R. Glenn Hubbard. 1990. Coming home to America: Dividend repatriations by U.S. multinationals. In *Taxation in the global economy,* ed. A. Razin and J. Slemrod. Chicago: University of Chicago Press.

Hines, James R., Jr., and Eric M. Rice. 1990. Fiscal paradise: Foreign tax havens and American business. NBER Working Paper no. 3477. Cambridge, Mass.: National Bureau of Economic Research.

Jaffe, Adam B. 1986. Technological opportunity and spillovers of R&D: Evidence from firms' patents, profits, and market value. *American Economic Review* 76:984–1001.

———. 1988. Demand and supply influences in R&D intensity and productivity growth. *Review of Economics and Statistics* 70:431–37.

Kopits, George F. 1976. Intra-firm royalties crossing frontiers and transfer-pricing behaviour. *Economic Journal* 86:791–805.

Lach, Saul, and Mark Schankerman. 1989. Dynamics of R&D and investment in the scientific sector. *Journal of Political Economy* 97:880–904.

Lawlor, William R., ed. 1985. *Cross-border transactions between related companies: A summary of tax rules.* Deventer: Kluwer.

Levy, David M., and Nestor E. Terleckyj. 1983. Effects of government R&D on private R&D investment and productivity: A macroeconomic analysis. *Bell Journal of Economics* 14:551–61.

Lichtenberg, Frank R. 1987. The effect of government funding on private industrial research and development: A re-assessment. *Journal of Industrial Economics* 36:97–104.

Mansfield, Edwin. 1986. The R&D tax credit and other technology policy issues. *American Economic Review* 76:190–94.

Mansfield, Edwin and Anthony Romeo. 1980. Technology transfer to overseas subsidiaries by U.S.-based firms. *Quarterly Journal of Economics* 94:737–50.

Mansfield, Edwin, Anthony Romeo, and Lorne Switzer. 1983. R&D price indexes and real R&D expenditures in the United States. *Research Policy* 12:105–12.

Mansfield, Edwin, Anthony Romeo, and Samuel Wagner. 1979. Foreign trade and U.S. research and development. *Review of Economics and Statistics* 61:49–57.

Mansfield, Edwin, David Teece, and Anthony Romeo. 1979. Overseas research and development by U.S.-based firms. *Economica* 46:187–96.

McIntyre, Robert S. 1989. Tax Americana. *New Republic* 200 (March 27) 18–20.

Meron, Amos, and Richard E. Caves. 1990. Rivalry among firms in research and development outlays. Harvard University. Mimeograph.

Mose, Vergie. 1989/1990. Corporate foreign tax credit, by industry, 1984. *S.O.I. Bulletin* 9:57–90.

Nadiri, M. Ishaq, and Ingmar R. Prucha. 1989. Dynamic factor demand models, productivity measurement, and rates of return: Theory and an empirical application to the U.S. Bell System. NBER Working Paper no. 3041. Cambridge, Mass.: National Bureau of Economic Research.

National Science Board. 1989. *Science and engineering indicators—1989.* Washington, D.C.: U.S. Government Printing Office.

National Science Foundation. 1991. *Selected data on research and development in industry: 1989.* Washington, D.C.: NSF.

Pakes, Ariel, and Mark Schankerman. 1984a. An exploration into the determinants of research intensity. In *R&D, patents, and productivity,* ed. Z. Griliches. Chicago: University of Chicago Press.

———. 1984b. The rate of obsolescence of patents, research gestation lags, and the private rate of return to research resources. In *R&D, patents, and productivity,* ed. Z. Griliches. Chicago: University of Chicago Press.

Price Waterhouse. 1991. *Corporate taxes: A worldwide summary* and various individual country guides. New York: Price Waterhouse.

Ravenscraft, D., and F. M. Scherer. 1982. The lag structure of returns to research and development. *Applied Economics* 14:603–20.

Reinganum, Jennifer F. 1989. The timing of innovation: Research, development, and diffusion. In *Handbook of industrial organization,* ed. R. Schmalensee and R. D. Willig. Vol. 1. Amsterdam: North-Holland.

Schankerman, Mark. 1981. The effects of double-counting and expensing on the measured returns to R&D. *Review of Economics and Statistics* 63:454–58.

Scholes, Myron S., and Mark A. Wolfson. 1991. *Taxes and business strategy: A planning approach.* Englewood Cliffs, N.J.: Prentice Hall.

Scott, John T. 1984. Firm versus industry variability in R&D intensity. In *R&D, patents, and productivity,* ed. Z. Griliches. Chicago: University of Chicago Press.

U.S. Congress, Joint Committee on Taxation. 1981. *General explanation of the Economic Recovery Tax Act of 1981.* Washington, D.C.: U.S. Government Printing Office.

U.S. Department of Commerce, Bureau of Economic Analysis. *Survey of current business.* various issues.

U.S. Department of the Treasury. 1983. *The impact of the section 861–8 regulation on U.S. research and development.* Washington, D.C.: U.S. Government Printing Office.

U.S. General Accounting Office. 1989. *The research tax credit has stimulated some additional research spending.* Report GAO/GGD-89-114. Washington, D.C.

Wozny, James A. 1989. The research tax credit: New evidence on its effect. *Proceedings of the National Tax Association* 82:223–28.

Comment   Bronwyn H. Hall

James Hines's paper addresses the question of whether the complex and frequent changes to the tax treatment of R&D performed by multinational corporations in the United States during the 1980s had any incentive effects on the actual level and direction of such R&D. Interest in this topic is motivated by a general interest in the optimal tax treatment of R&D and by specific interest in the effects of the many changes incorporated into the tax legislation of the Reagan era. Hines summarizes the features of the tax code that apply to

Bronwyn H. Hall is assistant professor of economics at the University of California at Berkeley and a faculty research fellow of the National Bureau of Economic Research.

R&D and uses them to construct tax prices for R&D directed toward domestic and foreign sales. He then estimates the factor demand equation for R&D as a function of these changing tax prices and uses the estimates to perform a series of policy simulations. His conclusions are twofold: first, the tax price elasticity of R&D expenditure is actually fairly high (approximately unit); second, the overall effects of the changes were not that large when benefits (in terms of increased R&D spending) and costs (reduced tax revenue) are canceled out.

The paper consists of two parts: a careful description of the changes in the tax treatment of R&D during the 1980s, with an emphasis on the implications of these changes for multinationals, and an empirical evaluation of the responsiveness of R&D to these changes for 116 multinational firms. The first part performs a real service to the economics research community, because these tax changes are complex and difficult to summarize in a concise way. Hines does an excellent job of presenting them and analyzing their likely impact. I do not have much to add to this presentation, except to emphasize that the most important subsidy to R&D that arises from the combined effects of the tax system facing multinationals is due to a part of the system not under control of the U.S. government: the low tax rates imposed on the income that is repatriated to the United States as royalty income (see table 5.2 of the paper). To the extent that corporations are in an excess foreign tax credit situation, as most of them are (see table 5.3 of the paper), this subsidy is substantial.

Most of my comments will be directed toward the second part of the paper, which presents empirical evidence on the effects of these tax changes. I want to emphasize at the outset that, in spite of my reservations about what can and cannot be learned from these data, I found reading and thinking about the research described in this paper extremely helpful, and I compliment Hines both on his clear presentation of complex tax laws and on the careful empirical work with which he measures their effects. My remarks begin with a general discussion of the characteristics of R&D investment and their implications for interpretation of the results here; this is followed by some discussion of the interpretation of the tax price formulas presented in the paper. Finally, I make more specific comments on the model and empirical results.

The first important fact about R&D is that its output is largely nonrivalrous, which implies that a large fraction of the results of R&D can be used in many markets simultaneously. This is in fact a major cause of the movement of corporations across borders: a desire to reap the fruits of a unique rent-producing factor (a new innovation) in a broader market. Only a small fraction of R&D will be performed specifically to satisfy the requirements of a particular market. This limits the extent to which R&D can be directed toward sales in a single foreign market and implies that one does not expect a strong tax price response of R&D expenditures to changes in allocation rules. This does not mean, however, that an overall response to changes in tax prices (which may be induced by changes in allocation rules) would not be observed, and this is exactly what Hines documents in this paper. Later in this discussion, I will come back to this issue of what Hines can and cannot measure with the data he has available.

From a policy perspective, other implications of the nonrivalrous nature of R&D spending are twofold: first, if much of the output of R&D spending is shared across domestic and foreign sales, worries about subsidizing foreign consumption as well as domestic while subsidizing R&D spending do not seem that important because the cost is small. Second, the fact that R&D has positive externalities suggests that too little R&D will be performed if the performance is left entirely to a private sector facing full prices for R&D. As Hines says, this is the view taken by Congress quite frequently when writing tax legislation. If you believe the positive externality argument, you would not choose the tax treatment of R&D as an instrument for raising tax revenue. To put it another way, the benefits due to increased R&D spending by corporations, properly measured, may exceed the cost of the tax subsidy by amounts greater than that which are measured by Hines when he simply adds up the additional R&D thus induced.

A second, frequently documented, characteristic of R&D is its relative lack of volatility compared to ordinary investment (see, among others, Bernstein and Nadiri 1989; Hall and Hayashi 1989; Lach and Schankerman 1989; Himmelberg and Petersen 1990; Hall 1992), a fact that most of these researchers interpret as implying fairly high adjustment costs for R&D spending. This view is supported by the fact that about half of R&D spending is the salaries of highly trained technical personnel, who are not easily hired and fired without losing the part of the firm's R&D capital that is embodied in their human capital. This has two implications for the Hines paper: first, the relatively large price elasticity he observes for R&D spending is somewhat surprising and worth further investigation in order to reconcile it with the results of others who have estimated factor demand equations for R&D; second, the omission of adjustment costs from his model of production could be an obstacle to interpretation of his results relative to those of others.

The centerpiece of Hines's theoretical and empirical analysis of the R&D behavior of multinationals is the derivation of the tax prices faced by these firms, which are treated as the primary predetermined instruments which shift the demand for R&D investment. These prices are derived by positing a profit-maximizing firm with a profit function which is additively separable in the foreign and domestic operations. For all the reasons I suggested earlier, the weakest part of the model is that R&D must be specifically directed toward foreign or domestic markets in this framework and that these markets are not allowed to interact. In fact, in the estimation, Hines allows the responsiveness of R&D to the foreign sales tax price to differ from that for the domestic, and the resulting estimated coefficient ($\rho \cong 0.2$) suggests that R&D directed specifically toward foreign sales is "piggybacking" on domestic R&D by a fairly wide margin (since ρ would be unity if the two markets were completely separate).

To analyze somewhat more clearly the tax prices Hines derives and the incentives for investment they provide, I make a slight change in notation. In so doing, I also subscript the variables explicitly by i (firm) and t (year) in order to highlight the sources of variation in these prices. Define the share of sales which is foreign as

$$f_{it} = S^*/(S + S^*)$$

and the worldwide R&D intensity as

$$r_{it} = \bar{R}/(S + S^*).$$

Both of these variables are observable in the data. With these definitions, text equations (6) and (7) can be written

(C1)
$$PR = \frac{1 - \tau_{it} + \tau_{it}\alpha_t f_{it}}{1 - \tau_{it}(1 - \alpha_t f_{it} r_{it})}$$

and

$$PI = \frac{1 - \tau_{it}}{1 - \tau_{it}(1 - \alpha_t f_{it} r_{it})}.$$

These equations imply that, for multinationals, R&D directed only toward domestic sales is *more* expensive than other ordinary (nondepreciable) expenses to the extent that the allocation rules do not allow such R&D to be completely allocated to domestic income ($\alpha_t > 0$).[1] However, the reverse is true for R&D directed toward foreign sales. Using the same notation, text equations (13) and (14) for the foreign tax prices become

(C2)
$$PR^* = \frac{1 - \tau_{it} + \tau_{it}\alpha_t f_{it}}{1 - w^* - \tau_{it}\alpha_t f_{it} r_{it}}$$

and

$$PI^* = \frac{1 - w^*}{1 - w^* - \tau_{it}\alpha_t f_{it} r_{it}},$$

where I have suppressed the firm and year subscripts for w^* because that reflects Hines's construction of this variable. These equations imply that the relative price of foreign R&D differs from that of ordinary inputs by two terms:

$$\frac{PR^*}{PI^*} = 1 - \frac{\tau_{it} - w^*}{1 - w^*} + \frac{\tau_{it}\alpha_t f_{it}}{1 - w^*}.$$

---

1. Such R&D will still be cheaper than ordinary investment, however, to the extent that ordinary investment must be depreciated over several years rather than expensed.

Thus, the relative price of this type of R&D is reduced by a factor proportional to the difference in tax rates in the two localities and increased by a term similar to that for domestic R&D; the latter term arises because of the allocation rules. For plausible values of the parameters, the first term dominates and R&D is subsidized relative to other inputs to the extent that it is a cost of foreign sales. Table 5A.1 emphasizes the point that the dominant difference in these tax prices is the light taxation of foreign royalty income for firms with excess foreign tax credits. To first order, the relative subsidy to foreign-directed R&D is equal to the difference in tax rates on domestic and foreign income for these firms and does not depend on the allocation rules or share of foreign sales. It is all the more unfortunate, then, that Hines does not have good measures of w^* available and must use a single value, 5 percent, for all firms.

Turning to a discussion of the measurement of the impact the tax law changes during the 1980s had on R&D spending, which is the main focus of the paper, I first point out that estimating the effects of these tax changes on R&D is a challenge, using the data that are available. From Compustat, one has relatively good data on the behavior of the multinational firm as a whole: sales, R&D spending, profit and loss statement, and so forth. However, the only data available that separate foreign and domestic activities are for sales and profits, from the Geographic Segment File. There are no public data available[2] on R&D directed toward foreign sales (or R&D performed in foreign countries), if indeed such a concept makes any sense. The implication is that ultimately the estimated response of R&D spending to two *different* tax prices, one for R&D directed toward domestic sales and one for R&D directed toward foreign sales, is identified only through strong functional form assumptions. This forces Hines to use a rather peculiar hybrid model, one that describes the investment response to R&D tax prices by deriving it from a traditional profit or production function which does not contain any costs of adjustment for R&D (or ordinary) capital and which assumes additively separable profit functions across domestic and foreign operations. For all the reasons I mentioned earlier, this latter assumption seems highly questionable in the case of R&D spending. The former leads to confusion in the estimation, since it is not clear whether the appropriate variable is the stock of R&D, which is what would enter the production or profit function, or the flow of R&D, which is what would respond to the tax price. If adjustment costs were zero, this would not matter, but most researchers have estimated very substantial adjustment costs for R&D (references cited earlier).

In spite of these reservations, I think the derivation of the actual estimating

---

2. The Bureau of the Census collects data at the firm level for the National Science Foundation, but such data are confidential and not released to the public except as aggregate statistics. See National Science Board (1991).

Table 5A.1   Illustrative Tax Prices for Multinational Corporations*

Years†	alpha	r(R/S)	PR	PI	PR/PI	PR*	PI*	PR*/PI*
1982–86	0.0%	0.0%	1.00	1.00	1.00	0.63	1.00	0.63
	0.0	5.0	1.00	1.00	1.00	0.63	1.00	0.63
	0.0	10.0	1.00	1.00	1.00	0.63	1.00	0.63
1988–89	36.0	0.0	1.08	1.00	1.08	0.68	1.00	0.68
	36.0	5.0	1.08	1.00	1.08	0.69	1.00	0.68
	36.0	10.0	1.07	0.99	1.08	0.69	1.01	0.68
1987	50.0	0.0	1.12	1.00	1.12	0.71	1.00	0.71
	50.0	5.0	1.11	0.99	1.12	0.71	1.00	0.71
	50.0	10.0	1.10	0.99	1.12	0.71	1.01	0.71
1977–81	70.0	0.0	1.16	1.00	1.16	0.73	1.00	0.73
	70.0	5.0	1.15	0.99	1.16	0.74	1.01	0.73
	70.0	10.0	1.14	0.98	1.16	0.74	1.01	0.73

Note: Foreign sales = 35%; Corporate tax rate = 40%; Foreign tax rate = 5%.
*Tax prices are for a firm with excess foreign tax credits.
†Shows the period for which the allocation rule was approximately equal to alpha.

equation is a tour de force, given the lack of the variables needed for the original two-region model. Hines begins with profit functions for domestic and foreign sales separately as functions of domestic and foreign R&D and other inputs, respectively, and derives a kind of factor demand equation for total R&D as a function of tax prices for the two different types of R&D. This factor demand equation is in the dual form, where total R&D spending is a function of all four tax prices (because of substitution effects in inputs). Equation (25) of the paper makes it clear that if the production functions for the two regions, foreign and domestic, are the same, so that $\beta_1 = \beta_3$ and $\beta_2 = \beta_4$, there is in effect a single price for each input which is the weighted sum of foreign and domestic prices with weights equal to the respective shares of R&D in the total R&D expenditure. The fact that the estimated responses differ by a factor of four or so implies that the production function does not have the simple additively separable form assumed by Hines or that the measurement error in the foreign tax price of R&D is very large. I incline more toward the first explanation, although the second must also be playing a role.

Hines uses equation (27) of the paper to estimate the price responsiveness of R&D investment in several different ways; all of them involve using firm and year dummies, so that the only variability which is being used is that within firm. The key experiment is to relate movements of real R&D expenditures over time to changes in the prices of R&D, which are given by equations (C1) and (C2) (in this comment). These equations show that the key sources of variability across firms are changes in the fraction of sales that are foreign, changes in their marginal tax rates, and *changes in R&D intensity.* The tax prices are inversely proportional to this last variable; because R&D itself is the dependent variable, this means that *negative* simultaneity bias is likely to be present in the ordinary least squares estimates. For this reason, I prefer the instrumental variable estimates reported in the paper, although I think the choice of instrument (average firm R&D intensity for 1984–86) is not likely to be completely free of this bias. It is possible that the relatively large price elasticities that Hines obtains (-1.0 rather than the -0.2 to -0.5 range reported in the literature; see the paper for references) are due to this simultaneity bias.

In summary, although I have doubts about the exact methodology used and numbers reported in this paper, I think Hines has shown us the way to do a far more careful evaluation of the effects of tax policy on R&D. I would hope that future work that examines the impact of the R&D tax credit on the R&D behavior of corporations would take advantage of the tax price variability available when one studies multinational corporations, which are an increasingly large share of the firms involved in R&D. It is quite possible that changes in R&D allocation rules have a far greater impact than playing with the R&D tax credit.

References

Bernstein, J. I., and M. I. Nadiri. 1989. Rates of return on physical and R&D capital and structure of production process: Cross section and time series evidence. In *Advances in econometrics and modeling,* ed. B. Raj. Dordrecht: Kluwer.

Hall, Bronwyn H. 1992. Investment and R&D at the firm level: Does the source of financing matter? University of California at Berkeley and National Bureau of Economic Research. Photocopy.

Hall, Bronwyn H., and Fumio Hayashi. 1989. Research and development as an investment. Working Paper no. 2973. Cambridge, Mass.: National Bureau of Economic Research.

Himmelberg, Charles P., and Bruce C. Petersen. 1990. R&D and internal finance: A panel study of small firms in high-tech industries. Federal Reserve Bank of Chicago. Photocopy.

Lach, S., and M. Schankerman. 1989. Dynamics of R&D and investment in the scientific sector. *Journal of Political Economy* 97:880–904.

National Science Board. (1991). *Science and engineering indicators 1991.* Washington, D.C.: Government Printing Office.

6   The Role of Taxes in Location and Sourcing Decisions

G. Peter Wilson

This descriptive study examines how nine firms integrate tax planning into other business planning.[1] More specifically, it considers how taxes influence companies' decisions on capacity expansion (the location decision) and on the use of existing capacity (the sourcing decision). The study will identify important tax and nontax factors that firms consider when making location and sourcing decisions and will assess the relative importance of different factors on these decisions. The findings are based on interviews with chief financial officers and high-level manufacturing, treasury, tax, and strategy managers. These conversations centered on sixty-eight location decisions that were made during the past twenty-five years.

The subsequent analysis argues that the relative importance of taxes in explaining location and sourcing decisions varies considerably across industries and business activities (e.g., R&D, manufacturing, marketing). A conceptual framework, based largely on theory discussed in Porter (1990) and Scholes and Wolfson (1991), is proposed to identify salient industry and business ac-

G. Peter Wilson is associate professor of business administration at the Harvard Business School.

The author gratefully acknowledges the countless hours and valuable insights contributed by participating managers, as well as the generous financial support of the Harvard Business School. Jane Palley Katz, research associate at the Harvard Business School, contributed significantly to this research; her enthusiasm and numerous suggestions are greatly appreciated. The author also wishes to thank R. Glenn Hubbard, Bob Kaplan, Krishna Palepu, and Joel Slemrod for their helpful comments.

1. As will be discussed in section 6.2, the sample firms were selected because they were known to have operations in low-tax countries. All of the firms are in an excess foreign tax credit limitation, though most of them claim to be close to an excess credit position. Thus, the usual caveat about drawing inferences from small biased samples is amplified here. To facilitate the exposition, however, I have not qualified the text to account for this bias. Wherever possible, I integrate my findings into the conceptual framework developed in section 6.1. This should help readers assess whether these findings extend to other firms.

tivity characteristics that determine the role of taxes in location decisions.[2] The framework builds on the Scholes and Wolfson theme that efficient tax planning differs from tax minimization. In the Scholes and Wolfson framework, tax planning is subordinate (as a managerial objective) to maximizing firm value. Therefore, tax planners must sometimes sacrifice tax benefits because of nontax considerations. Scholes and Wolfson refer to these nontax considerations as restrictions and frictions that impede tax minimization. Restrictions are government rules. Frictions are all other impediments to tax minimization, including costs associated with meeting other business purposes. Frictions and restrictions are related.[3] By identifying frictions, or equivalently nontax considerations, associated with location and sourcing decisions and by understanding how they evolve over time, we can better understand the role that taxes play in these decisions.[4]

The framework proposes three categories of frictions that are based on Porter's global strategy theory: coupling frictions, which tend to fuse activities together in a firm's value chain; country frictions, which are the opportunity cost of locating a specific activity, or collection of activities, in a particular country; and coordination frictions, which are associated with incentive and communication mechanisms that impede tax minimization. Firms assign activities in their product value chains to countries where the maximum value is added at a minimum after-tax cost. To this end, they must first identify spots in their value chains where coupling frictions are small, and then locate these separate activities, taking account of country and coordination frictions and local taxes.

The interviews with the sample firms' managers suggest a number of conclusions:

- Tax considerations largely dictate location decisions for business activities where these frictions are small, such as administrative and distribution centers
- Nontax considerations are very important in all *manufacturing* location de-

---

2. In developing their frameworks, both Porter (1990) and Scholes and Wolfson (1991) acknowledge other authors' contributions. Rather than conduct an extensive literature review, I cite these two works repeatedly because they summarize and/or develop the requisite strategy and tax background for this paper.

3. Scholes and Wolfson develop the relationship between frictions and restrictions. In particular, frictions curb both favorable and unfavorable economic activity. When they curb unfavorable activity, they preclude the necessity for government restrictions (e.g., tax rules). When they curb desired activity, policymakers must offer tax benefits to compensate for the cost associated with the frictions.

4. Admittedly, referring to marketing, manufacturing, and other business considerations as frictions is a rather egocentric view of taxes. An alternative expositional approach would have been to describe taxes as but one of several costs that managers must consider to maximize firm value when making location and sourcing decisions. The Scholes and Wolfson framework is used here because my primary objective is to study how nontax factors affect tax planning.

cisions, including those where the final decision is to locate in a low-tax country

- Flexibility in setting transfer prices is related to gross margins and the ability to decouple activities in the value chain
- Threats of significant penalties and extensive audits in many countries have recently curbed managers' ability to transfer price aggressively[5]
- Tax transfer prices do not affect performance evaluations for the sample firms, either because they use separate transfer prices for managerial and tax purposes or because they use pretax evaluation measures that do not depend on transfer prices
- Larger decentralized firms use location team contests to coordinate more efficient local and corporate tax planning
- The role that taxes play in location and sourcing decisions and, more generally, the relative importance of various nontax considerations in these decisions have changed dramatically during the past twenty years
- Tax compliance costs have also increased considerably

Furthermore, public goods that are subsidized by taxes, such as education and transportation, weigh heavily in many location decisions.[6] Thus, because tax rates can reflect infrastructure differences, resource allocations are not necessarily inefficient when location decisions are tax motivated.

Section 6.1 presents an informal conceptual framework for analyzing the role of taxes in location and sourcing decisions. Section 6.2 describes the sample firms and the interview procedures. Section 6.3 shows how the sample firms' location decisions are related to this framework. Several examples are used to demonstrate the role of tax and nontax considerations in location decisions. In Section 6.4, the emphasis shifts to sourcing decisions, transfer prices, and performance measures. Section 6.5 summarizes the major findings.

6.1 Conceptual Framework for Analysis

Two research areas motivate the analysis: (1) strategy research, where taxes are acknowledged in passing as important but tax features central to international tax planning and location decisions are usually absent; (2) tax research, where the consequences of nontax considerations are recognized but not ex-

---

5. The sample firms were selected because they have facilities in low-tax countries and the conventional wisdom is that tax-haven firms set transfer prices aggressively. While some of the sample firms' managers admit to transfer pricing aggressively (particularly in the past), they emphasize that they mean aggressively relative to other firms and that their transfer prices are within acceptable bounds. In this paper, I use the modifier "aggressively" in this relative sense.
6. Labor and capital, the central factors in location decision models proposed by many economists, are also very important considerations, but, like taxes, they do not tell the whole story.

plored sufficiently to fully explain location and sourcing decisions. Although this study embraces both research areas, the primary objective is to extend the tax literature. Specifically, the objective is to identify the frictions, or equivalently nontax issues, associated with location and sourcing decisions and show how they affect tax planning. The strategy literature discusses many of these nontax issues.

In Porter's global strategy theory, firms gain competitive advantage in two ways: by determining where their facilities are located and by coordinating their dispersed activities. These activities include all the elements in firms' value chains: research and development, various manufacturing stages, marketing, distribution, and certain administrative activities. Porter argues that in configuring worldwide activities, firms must first decide whether to concentrate activities in a few nations or to disperse them to many nations. Second, firms must decide where to locate these activities. Porter argues that the concentration versus dispersion decision differs across value-chain activities. In addition to choosing whether or not to concentrate and where to locate, firms must also decide where to decouple their value chains. For example, presuming a firm elects to concentrate development and manufacturing, it must still decide whether to couple these value-chain activities—locate them together. I refer to the nontax considerations that fuse different types of value-chain activities (such as marketing and manufacturing) or that concentrate a specific activity (such as manufacturing) in a few locations as *coupling frictions* and *coupling restrictions*. Coupling frictions include, but are not limited to, technology constraints, transportation costs, company culture, the need to be close to customers, and the need to concentrate manufacturing in a few world-scale plants to compete on cost. For example, in developing drugs, certain intermediate chemicals are not stable enough to transport or can only be transported after costly environmental testing. If an intermediate chemical could be produced efficiently in a low-tax country but the entire compound were too costly to produce there (relative to alternative sites), then the coupling frictions that make it too costly would preclude locating any manufacturing in the low-tax country. Coupling restrictions are government rules that make it costly or impossible for firms to decouple value-chain activities. Such rules include duties, import restrictions, local content requirements, and (in some industries) product and price regulatory authority. For example, high duties can, de facto, force companies to manufacture close to their markets.

Even if a firm can completely decouple its value chain at low cost, it will not locate activities in low-tax countries if the nontax costs of doing so exceed the tax benefits. *Country frictions* (or country-specific factors) are the opportunity cost of locating a value-chain activity, or collection of activities, in a particular country relative to the next best alternative location (ignoring differences in tax benefits in the two locations). Thus, just as coupling frictions and restrictions are related to concentration and dispersing strategies, country frictions are related to location strategies. Depending on the value-chain activity, country frictions include the differences across countries in factors such as the labor force, infrastructure, political stability, proximity to markets, and financial systems. Typically, a country will have a relative advantage in one or more of the requisite resources for a facility but a comparative disadvantage (high friction) in others.

Coordination mechanisms, such as transfer prices and performance measures, are used to motivate divisional managers and to align corporate and local planning. Just as companies sometimes sacrifice operating conditions to locate in tax havens, they will also use inferior coordination mechanisms (that is, mechanisms that are inferior before tax considerations) to facilitate tax planning when the benefits from doing so exceed the costs. *Coordination frictions* are the opportunity cost of using a coordination mechanism relative to the next-best alternative (ignoring differences in tax benefits). For example, the opportunity cost of using transfer prices that are based on tax considerations rather than those that are based on nontax considerations include forgone operating efficiencies. Like the other frictions, coordination frictions arise when there are conflicts between tax and nontax considerations. Of particular interest in this study, firms must coordinate sourcing decisions in such a way as to maximize corporate after-tax income. These sourcing decisions frequently involve trading off higher operating costs for lower taxes.

Countries also play their own strategies. They want to attract high-value facilities and benefit from these facilities as much as possible, either through high wages, taxes, or other means. Countries with large developed markets, such as Japan, or potentially large markets, such as China or India, use duties, import restrictions, price regulations, or local-content restrictions to induce companies to manufacture locally. Essentially, they exert their market leverage to prevent companies from locating facilities in lower-cost countries. In the process, they can extract an additional return on a resource, their market, either by taxing these manufacturing facilities or through wages, et cetera. In contrast, countries that do not have large markets or do not have unique manufacturing capability frequently compete for companies by offering tax or other incentives.

6.2   Sample Selection

This section briefly explains the sample selection and interview procedures and describes some characteristics of the sample firms. The research strategy was to identify firms with manufacturing facilities in both low- and high-tax countries and to study their location and sourcing decisions. Fourteen firms with manufacturing facilities in Ireland, Singapore, or Puerto Rico were contacted; nine agreed to participate, including three pharmaceuticals, three semiconductor companies, and one company each from chemicals, specialty materials, and software. The emphasis on semiconductors and pharmaceuticals is intentional. These industries have significant presence in low-tax countries and are known to have sophisticated tax departments. Firms from other industries, although interesting in their own right, were included primarily as benchmarks. Thus, the sample is biased toward firms that traditionally have been regarded as aggressive tax planners. As indicated earlier, this bias is reflected in the fact that all of the firms are in excess foreign tax limitation, although most claim to be close to an excess credit position. Because these firms are in excess foreign tax limitation, their tax planning is probably different from that of other firms. However, foreign tax credit issues per se did not appear to affect most of the decisions studied. Many of these decisions were made prior to the Tax Reform Act of 1986, when there was less concern about being in an excess credit position. Also, when managers were questioned about how their foreign tax credit position affected recent decisions, they downplayed its importance.

Three of the sample firms' 1990 sales exceeded $5 billion, six had sales greater than $750 million, and one had sales of less than $100 million. Research and development as a percentage of sales exceeded 9 percent for most of the sample; the exceptions were the chemical and materials companies.

Two visits were made to most of the firms. The primary objective of the first trip was to identify the most important tax and nontax factors that firms consider when making location and sourcing decisions. Managers from several functional areas were interviewed, usually including the chief financial officer and high-level managers from manufacturing, treasury, and strategy. For each firm, I began by asking managers to identify the important issues in location and sourcing decisions. Follow-up questions queried whether managers had made sacrifices when their company elected to locate a facility in, or source from, a low-tax country. I soon discovered that I learned more when I asked managers to discuss recent decisions. Invariably, these discussions revealed important issues that had not surfaced earlier and were not covered in my preplanned questions. Seven of the firms were revisited to resolve open issues.

For the nine sample firms, sixty-eight location decisions were considered in some detail, and approximately thirty of these were discussed extensively. Although the years in which these decisions were made were not recorded in all cases, at least seven decisions were made during the 1960s, seven during the 1970s, four from 1980 through 1985, and twenty after 1985. Forty-seven decisions concerned manufacturing facilities, fourteen administrative, financial, or distribution centers, one R&D facility, and six marketing centers. These facilities are spread throughout the world, including the United States, Puerto Rico, and twenty-four other countries. Thus, while the sample firms were initially chosen because they have some facilities in low-tax countries, this geographic dispersion indicates that taxes do not dictate all of their location decisions.

6.3   Location Decisions

This section uses examples to demonstrate how the sample firms make location decisions within the framework discussed in section 6.1. Section 6.3.1 is a lengthy examination of manufacturing location decisions, the issue that dominated most of the interviews. Section 6.3.2 and 6.3.3 briefly consider marketing and administrative centers. Research and development (R&D) is not examined separately because these decisions were discussed infrequently during the interviews.

6.3.1   Manufacturing

The examples in this subsection demonstrate how coupling frictions, gross margins, and country frictions, restrictions, and tax and financial incentives affect manufacturing location decisions.[7] In the first part, I consider location decisions in the pharmaceutical industry. In this industry, gross margins are extremely high because operating risks are high, because the harvest period is short—patents expire shortly after products are launched—and because most costs have been incurred and expensed before manufacturing commences. For the pharmaceutical industry, manufacturing coupling frictions are relatively minor, while government restrictions profoundly influence location and sourcing decisions. Next I consider decisions in the semiconductor industry. In this industry, gross margins (for microprocessors) are higher than in most industries but lower than the pharmaceutical industry, harvest periods are short because of technological obsolescence, and government coupling restrictions are important but typically not binding. Manufacturing costs are higher for semiconductor than for pharmaceutical companies, primarily because wafer fabrication facilities (fabs) are so expensive to build and operate. But, as in pharmaceuticals, the bulk of the expenses are incurred prior to the start of manufacturing. Also, manufacturing facilities require a more sophisticated infrastructure. Thus, in the semiconductor industry, country frictions play an important role in fab location decisions. I consider a single location in the chemical industry, where gross margins are relatively low compared to pharmaceuticals and semiconductors. Thus, tax considerations are less important in location decisions. Then I examine a software company where coupling, coordination, and country frictions and foreign government restrictions are essentially nonexistent. Here, taxes are the driver for location decisions and U.S. tax restrictions are a counterbalancing force. The other extreme—a materials company where coupling frictions force manufacturing facilities to locate in close proximity to customers and taxes are relatively unimportant consideration—is discussed last.

---

7. Section 6.4.1 contains an explanation for why firms with larger gross margins typically have more flexibility in setting transfer prices.

Pharmaceuticals

Success in the pharmaceutical industry depends on a company's ability to discover effective new drugs, get them through the regulatory approval processes in various countries, and market them quickly to harvest profits before their patents expire. Although manufacturing costs have been increasing recently, they are small for most drugs, compared to the estimated $200 million to $350 million required to get a drug through R&D and regulatory approval. Likewise, manufacturing costs pale in comparison to the forgone revenues when patents expire. For blockbuster drugs, with peak sales approaching a billion dollars a year, the lost revenues from delaying a product launch can be staggering. As one sourcing manager noted, "Manufacturing can never afford to be the bottleneck, because the relative costs of manufacturing are too low." Notwithstanding these relatively low manufacturing costs, the location of manufacturing facilities is still important for regulatory, duty, and tax reasons. Regulatory considerations are broadly defined in this paper. They include product approvals, government price approvals, and, increasingly, environmental and safety issues.[8]

Price approval is a particularly important consideration in location decisions because, unlike the United States, most governments regulate drug prices. Industry sources indicate that companies frequently negotiate price increases in exchange for local manufacturing. In this regard, price increases substitute, albeit imperfectly, for tax benefits as incentives to lure manufacturing sites. Similarly, lower prices substitute for higher taxes and duties as the admission price that some countries command for access to attractive markets. Perhaps countries prefer prices to taxes as a policy instrument because it is easier to target preferential treatment for specific drugs by using product prices. Alternatively, tax breaks may not be as valuable to multinationals, such as the sample firms, that are in excess foreign tax limitation.

Timing the grants of regulatory approvals across different countries is also important. Ultimately, pharmaceuticals must secure price and product approvals in all of their markets, but the approval processes differ dramatically across countries. Countries that approve a drug quickly, for example, might offer a lower price in exchange for a longer harvest period.[9] However, it is not always advantageous to push for quick approval in those countries. Because other countries peg prices to those set elsewhere, it can be costly to get a drug

---

8. In the pharmaceutical industry, environmental and safety considerations are becoming more important in explaining location and sourcing decisions. Some countries, especially in Europe, do not allow intermediate chemicals to be transported in large quantities unless they pass stringent, time-consuming, and costly safety tests. This creates a coupling restriction (manufacturing is fused to markets) and helps explain why pharmaceutical companies are consolidating their European manufacturing operations.

9. Strictly speaking, countries do not explicitly trade off quicker product approvals for lower prices. Product and price approvals are negotiated separately with different authorities in each country. However, the outcomes from these negotiations are consistent with such a trade-off.

through product approval quickly in a low-price country. Accordingly, companies strategically select the countries where they get early approvals.

Approval in the United States by the Food and Drug Administration (FDA) is usually the most difficult and time consuming to secure of all countries.[10] Also, until recently, a drug could not be exported from the United States until it was approved here, even if it was approved elsewhere. This meant that, historically, American companies had a strong incentive to manufacture abroad. Recent legislation that allows an American company to export to one of twenty developed countries where the drug is approved has partially mitigated this incentive. Now, pharmaceuticals have an incentive to quickly get approval in at least one of these twenty countries, either to start manufacturing in the United States for the U.S. market before they get U.S. approval or to manufacture abroad for approved countries.

During the regulatory approval process, pharmaceutical companies decide where they are going to produce the drug.[11] They can readily split production into distinct steps because coupling frictions within the manufacturing stages are relatively small. For dry products, such as the drug exemplified in figure 6.1 (discussed shortly), the manufacturing stages include bulk chemical production (developing standard inorganic compounds), active ingredient production (further developing the chemical compound specific to a drug), dispersion (diluting the active ingredient by granulation and mixing), tablet production (forming and coating the tablets), and fill/finishing (bottling, labeling, boxing, and palletizing). Except for the chemical stages, country frictions associated with manufacturing are also relatively small; once the active ingredient is produced, the remaining manufacturing stages do not require a sophisticated infrastructure.[12]

Figure 6.1 shows a representative sourcing pattern for a successful drug distributed by one of the sample firms. The subsequent discussion illustrates

10. In the United States, the three-phased process starts when a new molecule, referred to as a new chemical entity (NCE), is discovered and patented. Phase I generally takes about three years and emphasizes safety tests on lower species such as mice. Phase II, which can be done simultaneously with Phase I, focuses on whether the product works. After these phases are complete, extensive documentation is submitted to the FDA as part of an investigative new drug application (IND) to get permission to try the drug on humans. Extensive clinical tests on humans, carefully monitored by the FDA, are conducted in Phase III. At the end of Phase III, a new drug application (NDA) is submitted to the FDA along with a "truckload" of supporting data. The entire approval process typically takes eight to thirteen years.

11. Traditionally, these location and sourcing decisions were made toward the end of the product approval process. However, because of recent changes in the U.S. product approval process, these decisions must now be made considerably earlier. Currently, manufacturing sites must be operating and pass strict regulatory hurdles before a product is approved.

12. Although the sample firms have made numerous location decisions during recent years, they have not established new chemical sites. Nevertheless, they did indicate that the decision process for bulk chemical facilities was considerably more thorough than for new drugs and that taxes and financial incentives play a larger role in these decisions. From what I learned in casual discussions, these bulk chemical decisions resemble those discussed later for the bulk chemical and semiconductor wafer fabrication manufacturing facilities. Accordingly, the remainder of this section considers the nonchemical manufacturing stages only.

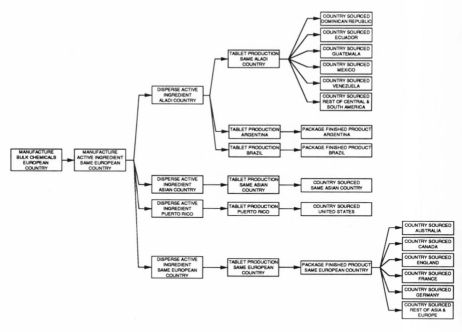

Fig. 6.1   A representative sourcing pattern for a successful drug

how regulatory, duty, and tax considerations influenced where the company located various manufacturing stages. Manufacturing starts in a major European country, where a bulk chemical facility that supports several other drugs produces the initial compound. This is subsequently converted to the active ingredient in a new facility that cost over $40 million. The new facility has an annual output of 150 to 200 kilos which, when diluted in a stabilizer for transporting, yields twelve to fifteen metric tons. Because the output from the existing bulk chemical plant is potentially unstable and could cause environmental or safety problems if transported and because the required infrastructure to support the new and existing plant are similar, the new facility was located adjacent to the bulk chemical plant. More generally, coupling frictions in the production of the active ingredient are typically too large to justify multiple locations. However, the company could have located the new facility adjacent to a bulk chemical facility in the United States. They chose the European site for regulatory approval reasons. By producing outside of the United States, they were able to extend the harvest period on non-U.S. sales by one year. As noted earlier, the marginal revenues from a longer harvest period can dwarf all other considerations. The original decision to locate the bulk chemical facility in this particular European country was, however, influenced by both tax benefits and country frictions.

By the time the drug is in pill form, the twelve to fifteen metric tons of stabilized active ingredient will be further diluted by a factor of one thousand. As indicated in figure 6.1, dispersing, tablet production, and fill/finishing have been decoupled, and multiple facilitates are used for each stage. As we shall see, the benefits from this arrangement exceed the related coupling frictions, including transportation costs and forgone economies of scale. Moreover, this company has reduced the transportation costs by locating the dispersing facilities close to the tablet production facilities. Taxes, duties, and a desire to service particular markets from a single location explain the remaining manufacturing sites in figure 6.1.

The top box in the third column of the figure represents a dispersion facility in a major ALADI country. The ALADI is a trade agreement among several Latin American countries that reduces duties on trades among members. There is, for example, a 102 percent import duty on tablets entering Brazil from the United States but only a 10 percent duty if the product is partly manufactured in an ALADI country.[13] The ALADI agreement largely explains why tablets for Latin America are manufactured and subsequently distributed as indicated in figure 6.1. Again, country restrictions rather than frictions or taxes are dictating a site location.

The "Asian country" dispersion, tablet, and packaging facilities that start in column 3 and the Argentinian facilities that start in column 4 were largely tax motivated. However, the sourcing manager for this company cautioned that the company had paid dearly for these tax benefits and, given the same opportunities, would probably not repeat these decisions. Duties are high in the Asian country so, absent tax benefits, the company had an incentive to locate facilities there. Nonetheless, they now regret the decision to locate in a tax-favored zone. "The location is physically beautiful but it is located in the middle of nowhere." The labor pool is "totally inadequate," and the company cannot get executives to live there even though they have built homes at the site. The $7 million facility, which produces other drugs besides the one in figure 6.1, runs at only 20 percent capacity. Similarly, the sourcing manager said that the company recently had sold the Argentinian facility because it was too inefficient. "When I finally arrived at the plant, I thought that I had reached the edge of civilization." When queried as to why these manufacturing inefficiencies were not identified earlier by a location team, the sourcing manager indicated that historically the decision process was very informal for these relatively minor manufacturing facilities. "Local management in both Argentina and the Asian country heard about tax breaks, and corporate management trusted their judgment." He also indicated that the company had learned some valuable lessons from these experiences, noting that in the future they will scrutinize country frictions more carefully before they jump at tax breaks. This example demonstrates that even though country frictions are minor for these facilities, they are important and must be identified prior to

13. Thus, the duty savings is on the value added in Mexico.

the location decision. Other sample firms also reported that they have learned to identify and carefully scrutinize country-specific factors (frictions) before they jump at tax breaks.

The Puerto Rican facilities that start in the third column were also largely tax motivated, but the country frictions in the Asian-country and Argentinian tax-favored zones are not present.[14] More generally, the sample pharmaceutical companies agree that the country frictions (opportunity costs) of manufacturing in Puerto Rico are relatively low. Although, they would probably not "put any new roofs" in Puerto Rico absent the tax breaks, the incremental costs of producing there (rather than in the next-best location) are small. In particular, during the past twenty years, the Puerto Rican infrastructure has improved significantly. Modern four-lane highways have replaced two-lane roads clogged with farm machinery; the labor force is more sophisticated because the educational system has improved dramatically; and the managers, who are now Puerto Ricans rather than expatriates, have twenty years of experience managing people and operations.

Because there are no duties on imports from Puerto Rico to the United States and there are generous tax breaks for producing there, it is not surprising that most prescription drugs sold in the United States are at least partially produced in Puerto Rico. Indeed, some drugs are completely produced in Puerto Rico, including the active ingredients. However, as indicated in figure 6.1, U.S. pharmaceutical companies also have significant manufacturing presence outside of Puerto Rico. Why? Because other countries, with large or potentially large markets, impose coupling restrictions, including duties and the threat of lower selling prices. These restrictions, not taxes, frequently explain why manufacturing facilities are located outside the United States and Puerto Rico.[15] Taxes are still considered when U.S. pharmaceutical firms must decide where to manufacture. Their short list of site alternatives usually includes a low-tax country such as Puerto Rico or Ireland, and they have significant manufacturing capacity in both of these countries. But frequently the tax benefits are not sufficient to compensate for the costs associated with the

---

14. The Tax Reform Act of 1976 included §936, which has two major provisions. First, it grants U.S. corporations a 100 percent credit equal to (and therefore fully offsetting) the U.S. tax both on income earned in the active conduct of a trade or business in a possession and on qualified possession source investment income (which is nonbusiness income earned and invested within the possession). Second, §936 exempts the corporation from U.S. tax on any dividends remitted to the U.S. parent. Before 1982, there were no explicit statutory guidelines on the proper allocation of costs and profits between a U.S. parent and its possession subsidiaries. Under the Tax Equity and Fiscal Responsibility Act of 1982, Congress provided two alternative methods for allocating profits from intangibles. In the example in this paper, the pharmaceutical company uses the profit-split method that allocates 50 percent of the profit to both the parent and subsidiary. Apparently, this method is popular because it reduces the risk of litigation.

15. For expositional convenience, lower prices are considered restrictions that countries use to promote local manufacturing. The intent here is not to argue that these prices are lower than those that would obtain in a competitive market. Rather, they are lower than those that would obtain if the company had a local manufacturing facility.

coupling restrictions. The ALADI duties provides an example of these government coupling restrictions. The price approval process considered next is another coupling restriction that has a major impact on location decisions.

Several factors explain the fill/finishing facilities in figure 6.1. To gain price and regulatory approval, some countries require that fill/finishing activities be done locally, and independent of this restriction, foreign sales offices prefer this local presence for marketing purposes. In addition, sample firms indicated that many of their tablet and fill/finish facilities are obtained when they acquire foreign companies to gain access to local markets.

Note that for the drug in figure 6.1 all manufacturing stages for the European market take place in a single European country. Recent regulatory emphasis on manufacturing and safety and increased pressure on profit margins from competitive forces in Europe have encouraged firms to consolidate operations to capture economies of scale. Ten years ago, the European sourcing pattern would have looked quite different. In particular, there might have been multiple dispersion and tablet facilities and multiple fill/finishing facilities spread throughout Europe for this one drug. At that time, companies completed the final stages of production for several drugs in each European country. The number of stages located in each country was largely determined by the country's negotiating position.

What has caused this change in manufacturing strategy? With the establishment of a common European market, coupling restrictions, in the form of duties and import restrictions, have been removed. Relaxing these restrictions allows pharmaceuticals to consolidate operations to capture economies of scale. Recall, however, that there is another coupling restriction that fuses manufacturing and markets; countries can threaten lower drug prices to lure manufacturing. Historically, companies responded by locating minor manufacturing stages for each drug in several European countries. Now, some countries offer price increases for several products in exchange for an agreement to establish a single-drug facility that will serve all of Europe. This compensates for lower prices a pharmaceutical might receive in other countries. Furthermore, as European markets expand and pharmaceuticals assume a global perspective, American companies want to have a local presence. In addition, regulatory authorities both in the United States and abroad are imposing strict manufacturing requirements that can be met more efficiently in single-purpose facilities.

In summary, both tax and nontax factors influence most pharmaceutical manufacturing location decisions. Government restrictions, including duties, local-content rules, and regulatory approval, are the most important nontax factors. To a lesser extent, coupling frictions, such as transportation costs and environmental and safety considerations, and country frictions, such as infrastructure quality, also matter. Likewise, tax benefits influence these decisions, particularly in Puerto Rico, where coupling restrictions are minor (there are no duties or price approvals for U.S. sales) and country frictions are relatively low. Pharmaceuticals also locate facilities in Ireland, although to a lesser extent than in Puerto Rico, to get both tax benefits and a stronger European presence. However, as illustrated in the example, nontax factors also explain many site selections. Furthermore, during the past twenty years, the relative importance of various nontax factors has changed, and nontax factors overall have assumed greater importance in decisions. As one manager noted,

> In the past, taxes were the primary driver, but as we become more global we are paying more attention to three other factors: (1) our desire to have a manufacturing presence in our key markets, (2) price breaks that we get in exchange for locating facilities in specific countries, and (3) economies of scale that can be gained either in a tax haven or in another country but not in both. Nevertheless, there are big bucks in tax, and these other considerations must be quite large to offset the tax benefits.

Semiconductors

Semiconductor products include both high-volume commodity chips, where the competitive emphasis is on minimizing production costs, and microprocessors, were the emphasis is on product innovation.[16] Successful microprocessors have relatively high gross margins. Like pharmaceuticals, the business is risky and the harvest periods are short. The short harvest periods, however, are due to product obsolescence rather than patents expiring. Still, semiconductor companies have lower gross margins than pharmaceuticals, partly because they sell more low-margin products such as memory chips but also because their sales and marketing expenses, which do not affect gross margin calculations, are lower and their cost of goods sold, which does affect gross margin calculations, is higher.[17] Nevertheless, there are important differences between semiconductor and pharmaceutical firms: the semiconductor industry experiences more extreme fluctuations in demand; success depends more on manufacturing innovation and expertise; the manufacturing learning curve is steeper; and the transfer of this learning from high-volume to proprietary products is more important.[18]

---

16. This description of the semiconductor industry is highly simplified. For additional details, an excellent reference is Yoffie (1987).

17. Semiconductor innovation depends on costly advancements in manufacturing equipment that must be upgraded frequently. This translates into high depreciation charges and, thus, high cost of goods sold. In contrast, while bulk chemical facilities for pharmaceuticals are costly, the upgrade costs are considerably less.

18. Yoffie (1987, 6) discusses the importance of learning in semiconductor manufacturing: "One of the reasons that learning produced such dividends was that semiconductor manufacturing routinely yielded more defects than sound products. For new products, yields as low as 10 percent for inexperienced manufacturers, and 25 percent for experienced manufacturers were quite common. For more mature products, however, yields could be as high as 90 percent. The need to raise yields led firms to manufacture high-volume products that could act as 'technology drivers.' It was generally believed that skills learned in manufacturing large volumes of a simple product could be transferred to lower-volume and higher-value-added devices and help 'drive' the firm down a very steep learning curve."

Semiconductor manufacturing has three stages: wafer fabrication (fab), where millions of electronic building blocks are embedded in a small silicon wafer using highly advanced technology; assembly, where the wafers are "diced" into chips and mounted onto a frame; and testing, where the chips are checked for accuracy (Carolin et al. 1984). The coupling frictions across these manufacturing stages are minimal. For example, at all stages, the output is very light and can be easily transported. "Our products have a lot of mileage on them," stated one manager, explaining that wafers are produced in the United States, shipped to one Asian country where they are converted to chips, sent to a more developed Asian country for testing, returned to the United States for packaging, and finally distributed worldwide.[19]

Until very recently, assembly and test location decisions have been largely determined by labor costs and taxes. Assembly required relatively low skilled labor and basic materials that were both available in many countries. Asian sites were chosen because they offered the best labor at the lowest price and very attractive tax incentives. Similarly, test facilities were located in Asia but in more developed countries such as Singapore because testing requires medium-skilled labor. Taxes were very important in these decisions, but generally they were not pivotal. Commonly, a firm might negotiate for and receive very generous tax benefits including an eight-year tax holiday that would start when production reached a specified level; an agreement that preholiday losses could be offset against postholiday gains; a reduction of the postholiday tax rate in exchange for locating in a specified zone; an accelerated depreciation schedule and generous investment credits that would also offset postholiday gains; and permanent exemption for all other taxes. Some of the sample firms stated that they plan to extend these tax holidays in the future by adding additional facilities. In addition to these tax benefits, the company often received training allowances, exemptions from duties, flexibility in setting their legal and financial structures, capital allowances, and a generous financing package. Notwithstanding all of these tax and financial incentives, the company's choice was largely based on nontax considerations, essentially because comparable tax benefits were available in competing countries. Also, semiconductor managers emphasize that the most important considerations for their test and assembly decisions have been the technical knowledge of the local work force; available local raw materials, especially chemicals and indirect materials, political stability; and, more generally, low operating costs. Recently, automation has become more important for test and assembly, and firms are beginning to consider single locations for all three manufacturing stages. If this becomes a trend, fab location choices will dictate where companies locate manufacturing.

Fabs, in contrast to assembly and test, require resources found in relatively few countries. These resources include a highly educated and stable work

19. Recently, the sample semiconductor firms began combining assembly and test facilities.

force to achieve and maintain high yields, political stability to ensure that the large capital outlays are not expropriated, a strong legal system to defend against technology transfers, local support from vendors to maintain the sophisticated equipment, large quantities of pure water, and consistent electricity. Countries with the requisite resources typically have relatively high statutory tax rates. For most manufacturers, these taxes can be viewed as the rental rates they pay for the sophisticated infrastructure. Yet, many countries compete aggressively, using tax benefits and other financial incentives to lure fabs.

The decision process for locating a fab is similar for all of the sample semiconductor firms. More generally, these fab decisions illustrate the way most of the sample firms make location decisions requiring large capital expenditures. Each of the sample semiconductor firms has built at least one fab in the United States during the past ten years after giving serious consideration to foreign sites. As one manager said, "We prefer to keep fabs close to home because they require a lot of nurturing." Nevertheless, all three have either recently built or have plans to build fabs abroad. The following is a representative composite discussion about how these decisions are made.

The location decision is generally sparked by capacity requirements rather than marketing considerations. In this example, a European division informed the international semiconductor group during the 1980s that it needed additional capacity and suggested building a fab in Europe to avoid a 17 percent duty. Because the company is highly decentralized, the European division, under the guidance of the International Group, began the search process for a European site. After considerable deliberation, to be discussed shortly, the European division recommended a specific European country to the International Group. Shortly after the International Group recommended this site to the sector level, a U.S. semiconductor division began lobbying vigorously for an American site. At this point, a contest ensued between the U.S. and international groups.[20]

When the European division started their site search for this $250 million facility (estimated replacement cost in 1990 was $500 million), they quickly narrowed their short list to West Germany, France, Scotland, and Ireland. Each site had tax and nontax benefits, and country officials aggressively sold their advantages. Ireland offered generous tax and financial benefits,[21] but management was concerned at that time that Northern Ireland might be too unstable politically and that Southern Ireland might lack the requisite infrastructure, including equipment vendors. Like Ireland, Scotland had a lower tax rate than West Germany or France and offered other tax and financial ben-

---

20. In many respects, this example is representative of how large capital outlay decisions are made. However, the smaller centralized firms do not conduct these contests. Rather, corporate managers serve on the location teams and are actively involved at all stages of the decision process.

21. Management did not specify whether these benefits were offered by Northern or Southern Ireland, or both.

efits. More important, both Ireland and Scotland were deemed to have a flexible labor force and lower wage rate. A manager commented: "We wanted to feel comfortable, and governments are easy to work with in the United Kingdom. The semiconductor business is cyclical, and when business turns down it is easier to adjust in Scotland and Ireland than in other European countries." These advantages for Scotland and Ireland had to be weighed against higher productivity in West Germany and France. At this point, the European group made its recommendation.

The contest between the U.S. and European sites centered on differences in technology bases, proximity to customers, and financial considerations including duties, grants, and taxes. The financial considerations weighed heavily in favor of Europe. The European country offered generous incentives, including a large cash rebate on fixed asset expenditures, a training grant, and a discretionary grant that was added as a sweetener. As indicated earlier, the 17 percent duty rate (on European sales) also put the U.S. site at a major disadvantage. Aside from these financial advantages, the European site was favored because management felt that European customers would be more comfortable buying from a local supplier. The U.S. site had one major advantage. Its technology base and local infrastructure were superior to the European site. As a result, management felt that it would achieve higher yields more quickly.

How were these considerations weighed? Like most of the sample firms, this company uses a blend of science and art in such a process. They begin with a sophisticated quantitative analysis—actually several spreadsheets. Given estimated demands for several products, the spreadsheets account for equipment requirements and related expenditures, a time series of yield projections, local labor requirements and costs, local duties, local utilities, transportation costs to get the product to market, taxes, and grants.[22] The output, an internal rate of return (IRR) for each site, reflects the firm's transfer pricing policy and the duration of the tax benefits.[23] Although the quantitative analy-

22. Some of the sample firms were asked whether they preferred grants, investment tax credits, or lower tax rates at all levels of income. A semiconductor firm responded that they prefer lower tax rates because, "If you use investment incentives, then your marginal tax rate depends on how much you continue to invest." In contrast, the chemical company prefers grants and tax incentives. "Grants in the form of cash from the government or investment tax credits are perhaps more important in making location decisions because, on a net present value basis, the grants may lower the cost of the plant sufficiently to offset a lower tax rate. In determining which is more important, the cost of the plant and profitability of the product are significant factors. If the product is more capital intensive, grants generally are more important. If the product is a high value added product because of technology, tax rates would be more important." Finally, a pharmaceutical company stated, "Because our foreign plants are not capital intensive, we prefer low rates to capital incentives. We are also very concerned about the duration of the low tax rates."

23. A tax manager emphasized that the transfer prices do not depend on the location. "We use uniform transfer prices for all location decisions." Also, even though this firm has been very successful at extending tax holidays, they do not include possible extensions in their IRR calculations.

sis plays a role in the decision process, it is best viewed as a vehicle for anchoring the discussion. Qualitative considerations, including concerns about political stability, potential to penetrate a market, availability of vendors, and other infrastructure issues mentioned earlier, often dominate the quantitative analysis.

What was the role of taxes in this decision? One manager emphasized that even though taxes are an important consideration, tax benefits are short lived: "In the long run, tax incentives and government grants go away, but your factory stays in place. We prefer to base our location decisions on our long-term business objectives in a country. We try to consciously look at a decision to make a major investment in a country, especially a high-tech investment such as a fab, without considering tax incentives." Nevertheless, taxes and duties were the critical advantages favoring the particular European site chosen. More generally, once the list of alternative sites is narrowed to locations with comparable country frictions, taxes and duties frequently become tie-breakers. Thus, taxes and duties are important in fab location decisions, even though managers claim that they are not as important as nontax considerations. A corporate vice president made a typical comment: "First we decided to go to Europe to avoid duties (more recently, local-content requirements), and then, given the decision to go to Europe, we located in the lowest-cost country (including taxes) where business requirements were satisfied."

The contest between the location teams facilitates planning in general, but tax planning in particular. For example, consider the role of the corporate tax office in the decision. A manager at the International Group said that, while they kept the corporate tax office informed of their plans and occasionally received corporate advice, they relied largely on their own tax staff and their European counterparts. The European managers, including tax, did the early negotiations with various countries and the International Group managers did the final negotiations with government officials in the European country. Although the corporate tax office participated little in the decision (relative to more centralized firms), the corporate vice president for tax indicated that his office spends considerable effort communicating the corporate tax position (e.g., their foreign tax credit position and their tax profile in various countries) and the corporate tax strategy to foreign and sector-level tax managers. Also, because location teams compete for sites, each team is motivated to negotiate aggressively with local authorities for tax and other benefits and to demonstrate how their site benefits overall corporate tax planning. Nevertheless, the corporate vice president of tax indicated that the company might get more generous tax benefits if he, like his counterparts in more centralized firms, were involved in country negotiations.

In summary, until recently, location decisions in the semiconductor industry have been strongly influenced by country frictions and tax considerations, while coupling frictions have been much less important. Prior to the early 1980s, most fabs (for U.S. firms) were in the United States, and most test and assembly operations were in Asia. More recently, foreign governments have imposed local-content restrictions that have encouraged U.S. companies to build fabs closer to their major markets. Coupling frictions are also becoming more important as customers press for local manufacturing. Finally, this section demonstrates that larger decentralized firms use location team contests to coordinate more efficient planning.

Chemicals

The sample chemical company has significantly lower gross margins than the pharmaceutical and semiconductor firms do. Historically, it has concentrated production in world-scale plants that each cost approximately $400 million to $500 million (in 1991 dollars) and has competed in commodity markets as a low-cost producer. More recently, it is also seeking to gain competitive advantage by specializing in more advanced chemicals tailored to customers' needs. As a result, some of their new plants are smaller, with costs in the $100 million range. In this industry, unlike pharmaceuticals and semiconductors, transportation costs are large. Thus, although companies must consolidate operations into a few world-scale plants to be competitive, they must locate these plants close to their major markets and suppliers to minimize transportation costs. Thus, coupling frictions are a major consideration for chemical companies.

Taxes are less important for chemical company location decisions than they are for pharmaceutical and semiconductor firms. Although chemical facilities, like fabs, require large capital outlays, they are not as attractive to host countries. Generally, chemical facilities demand large quantities of water and electricity, are considered an environmental risk, and have relatively small medium-skilled work forces. As a consequence, although some countries offer limited tax incentives in the form of rapid depreciation and favorable financing, these benefits are thought to be considerably smaller than the ones countries offer to lure fabs. Collectively, these modest financial and tax benefits, the earlier arguments that tax benefits increase as gross margins increase, and the large coupling frictions related to transportation costs and economies of scale explain why nontax considerations frequently dictate location decisions for major chemical facilities. Nevertheless, as the following example illustrates, even when taxes do not dictate the outcome they are still an important consideration in the decision process. This example also underscores the advantages of expanding an existing location versus starting a new greenfield site. This greenfield disadvantage was a factor in many of the location decisions studied.

Recently, the sample chemical firm began a search for a site to produce an existing product using a new and cheaper process to serve the North American market. Transportation costs quickly focused attention on a Canadian and U.S. site. The U.S. site had an advantage because it was an expansion, whereas the Canadian site was a greenfield. Existing sites often have excess infrastructure capacity (sewage, parking lots); their local management has a working relationship with local government, contractors, and suppliers; and they have an experienced work force. Furthermore, expansions can be completed more quickly than greenfield sites: the infrastructure is in place, building permits are easier to acquire, and building contracts can be completed sooner. The higher costs of a greenfield site are typically too large for any single division to absorb.[24] When existing sites are not in low-tax countries, these costs effectively increase the opportunity cost of locating in low-tax countries and, thus, increase tax-haven country frictions. In addition to these greenfield disadvantages, the Canadian site could not capitalize on a manufacturing synergy available at the U.S. site.[25] The Canadian site offered financial and tax benefits that were modest compared to those used to lure a fab but significant enough to make the decision close.[26]

Several rounds of meetings were conducted that included representatives from the competing location teams and corporate managers. During each round, according to the vice president of tax, the location teams upgraded their information and renegotiated with local authorities for more benefits. As a result, they continually changed the assumptions underlying their net present value calculations (which were based on detailed procedures documented in a company manual). At these meetings, the vice president of tax served as a referee who attested to the soundness of the tax assumptions underlying these calculations. He did not meet with local tax authorities, but tax managers at both locations, who report functionally to him, operated on his behalf. Also, as indicated earlier, the competitive spirit of the geographic teams partly compensated for his not participating directly in local tax planning.

The net present value calculations were comparable for the two sites. In these situations, "the tiebreaker is to go to the country where operations are most efficient," said the chief strategist. "The tax benefits are generally short run, while the operating benefits continue," he stated, suggesting, once again, that the net present value calculations are not precise enough to capture qualitatively the differences between the locations. The decision to locate in the

24. In some companies, successful greenfield sites must be promoted by the corporate office in conjunction with a corporate strategic initiative. Also, divisions with considerable autonomy over location decisions will not usually choose a greenfield site unless the corporate office absorbs part of the start-up costs associated with the infrastructure. For example, the corporate office could charge a fee based on the ratio of the division's requirement to the planned capacity for the entire site. Although I did not pursue this issue as part of my interview protocol, the chemical sample firm is just now considering this type of fee arrangement. The reason why these fee schedules may not be common and, thus, why there is such a first-mover disadvantage to greenfield sites is that many firms probably do not or cannot anticipate future expansions. Rather, they expand in a piecemeal fashion over an extended period of time.

25. The new production process uses the heat released in the manufacturing process to produce steam that can produce electricity or be used to heat facilities. At the U.S. site, the new facility would produce enough of these utilities to service existing operations (that have a net utility demand). Because there were no immediate plans to add operations that would benefit from these utilities at the Canadian site, the U.S. site had an advantage.

26. The company did not provide the details of these financial and tax benefits.

United States resulted in tax benefits being left on the table because the opportunity costs of operating in Canada (country frictions) were too large relative to the United States. More generally, because many U.S. firms are just beginning to expand globally and have excess infrastructure at existing U.S. sites, this greenfield friction (associated with foreign sites) probably encourages U.S. firms to expand at home.

Software

The sample software company, the smallest firm in the study, is a recent start-up with annual sales approaching $100 million.[27] Because manufacturing costs are very small compared to R&D and marketing costs and because software is a risky business, the company's gross margins are very large. All of their software is developed in the United States. The Puerto Rican facility transcribes the code to floppy disks and packages the disks for sale. The manufacturing process is straightforward, so there are virtually no coupling, country, or coordination frictions associated with these Puerto Rican operations. Not surprisingly, the chief financial officer (CFO) stated that taxes are the primary driver in location decisions. In fact, when the firm decided to expand operations, it chose a short list of sites by requesting a list of low-tax countries from an outside tax advisor. The CFO stated that "we decided to go to Puerto Rico to get the product with the highest gross margin in the country with the lowest tax rates."

Scholes and Wolfson predict that, absent frictions, restrictions will be imposed to curb overly aggressive tax planning. But what is considered overly aggressive? The company uses strict statutory rules to split profit between Puerto Rico and the United States, so their transfer prices per se are acceptable to the U.S. taxing authorities. However, the U.S. Treasury argues that many Puerto Rican software operations do not constitute legitimate manufacturing.[28] This is a grey area, but although managers at the sample company agree that software firms have taken an aggressive tax position, they also believe that Puerto Rican operations do constitute manufacturing. A current court case is considering the validity of this claim. If the courts rule in favor of the taxing authority, transfer prices will have to be set using a cost-plus formula, regardless of where the facilities are located outside the United States. Considering the low manufacturing costs, this will greatly reduce the benefits of locating in a low-tax country.

Materials

The materials company competes by specializing in niche markets. Its competitive advantage is that its engineers spend so much time at their customers'

---

27. Although the focus here is on software, the company also sells related hardware that is produced in Asia by third parties. These hardware sales are part of the $100 million figure.

28. Income that is not derived from manufacturing is deemed subpart F and taxed immediately in the United States. Regulation § 1.954-3(a)(4) provides general guidelines as to what constitutes manufacturing.

facilities that they know the material engineering aspects of their customers' businesses better than the customers do. When customers' processing changes, because of slight variances in operating conditions or materials, the sample company must quickly modify its products as needed. Of all the sample firms, the materials firm had the largest coupling friction between marketing and manufacturing. In fact, it feels compelled to locate manufacturing facilities as close as possible to its customers. Thus, taxes are a relatively minor consideration in location decisions.

The chief financial officer stated that they are more inclined to minimize tax barriers among a list of countries that satisfy business conditions than they are to go for the tax benefits. For example, the company went to Singapore because it wanted to be near customers that were locating facilities in Malaysia and Singapore. Once there, it applied for pioneer status for its manufacturing operations.[29]

6.3.2   Marketing and Distribution Centers

This subsection briefly describes two examples of marketing and distribution centers that were largely motivated by tax or duty considerations. In the first, a sample firm recently established a marketing center in Belgium to shift income from high-tax-rate European countries to the United States without changing the income's foreign-source character. The Belgian operation was set up as a branch of the U.S. parent. The European manufacturing sites pay the U.S. parent for marketing services that are rendered in Belgium, and the branch pays a small Belgian tax that is based on their administrative expenses. The company tries to set the marketing fees as high as the European taxing authorities will tolerate.

In the second example, another sample firm recently established a European distribution center in the Netherlands, primarily to minimize duties. As with the above marketing center, nontax considerations were minimal.[30] Figure 6.2 illustrates how goods were invoiced both before and after the new center was set up. Previously, the American parent (AP) invoiced Italy directly. Duties were based on the transfer price and the relatively high Italian duty rate for American imports. The company established a new American subsidiary, AP-International, that in turn established a branch in the Netherlands (NB). After the distribution center was set up in the Netherlands, goods were invoiced from AP-International to the Netherlands and then to Italy. Under the new structure, duties were based on the transfer price between AP and AP-International (not the transfer price between AP-International and

29. Pioneer status refers to special tax treatment for firms starting operations in Singapore. This firm recently abandoned pioneer status because its manufacturing operations were not profitable and because it wanted to average these losses with other Singaporean operations (which do not have pioneer status) and carry forward their losses (not allowed under pioneer status).

30. Logistical concerns were the most important nontax requirements, and they were easily satisfied.

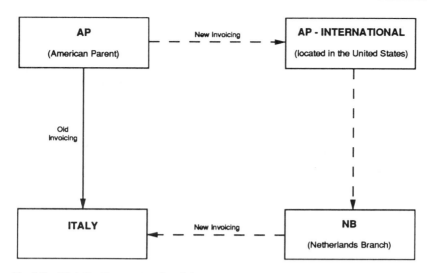

Fig 6.2   Distribution center invoicing patterns

NB) and the relatively low Dutch duty rate for U.S. imports. Importantly, after the change, AP's European corporate-support expenses were moved from AP to AP-International, justifying a lower transfer price and thus lower duties from AP to AP-International.

6.3.3   Administrative Centers

With the recent removal of exchange controls and intra-European duties and withholding taxes, firms are starting to consolidate European administrative activities, largely for tax reasons. Apparently, Belgian coordination Centers (BCCs) are a particularly attractive way to shift income and related economic activities from high-tax European countries to Belgium. The income shifted may be taxed immediately in the United States but retains its foreign-source character for the purpose of determining foreign tax credit limitations.[31] Also, because less taxes are paid in high-tax countries, companies reduce the likelihood of being in an excess foreign tax credit position. A small Belgian tax is incurred, based on the administrative costs of running the center.

A sample company recently selected Belgium over the Netherlands, another popular site for an administrative center. The Belgian facility purchases receivables at a discount (the shifted profit) from other European sites and centralizes hedging activities that were previously conducted separately by each country manager. All countries involved have agreed on a discount-rate

---

31. Under section §954(d), this income is deemed subpart F and is taxed immediately in the United States.

formula based on the economic activity in Belgium. The formula has two components representing the normal interest rate and a hedging charge. In principle, country and coupling frictions affect the amount of activity that is centralized. For example, the sample firm elected not to centralize credit functions, because the local managers have superior information. This coupling friction fuses sales and distribution to the credit function. Also, in this case, the foreign tax credit benefit of shifting credit risk is smaller because credit risk income would be assigned to the related party–factor income basket, whereas the hedging and normal interest fall in the general basket. When queried about how aggressive they were in negotiating the discount rate, the CFO responded, "There is some room here, but you can't be overly aggressive. Eventually, you have to deal with the European tax authorities when you are audited. Bears and bulls can both make money, but pigs never do."

This firm also considered embedding the BCC in a legal structure involving its Dutch and Swiss operations but eventually abandoned this idea in favor of establishing the BCC as a subsidiary of a U.S. operation. However, the proposed legal structure has features common to those established by other sample firms. Currently, the Swiss operation is a branch of a Dutch parent, and the plan was to establish the BCC as another Dutch branch. The resulting structure would have had several advantages. First, it would have allowed the Swiss operation to serve as a banking center for all of Europe, a common practice for the sample firms. Second, it would have allowed access to the Dutch treaty network. Third, it would have also taken advantage of the low Swiss-Dutch combined tax rate on interest income generated from investing the Belgian profits. The sample firm ultimately abandoned the plan because it divested a manufacturing operation in Holland and, as a result, no longer qualified for the favorable tax rates on interest income.

6.4   Sourcing Decisions: Transfer Pricing and Performance Evaluation

Sourcing decisions, like location decisions, are affected by both tax and nontax considerations that frequently conflict. Location decisions involve trading off coupling and country frictions (and restrictions) for tax benefits. Several mechanisms, including evaluation and control systems and transfer prices, are used to coordinate sourcing decisions. As we have seen, nontax considerations (e.g., factor availability) can be viewed as frictions that frequently impede tax planning related to location decisions. Similarly, the design of transfer prices and evaluation systems to coordinate dispersed activities can result in coordination frictions that impede tax planning related to ongoing operations. Management's challenge is to identify situations where conflicts between tax and nontax considerations are prominent and either to make a trade-off or to mitigate the frictions by creating alternative coordination mechanisms.

Firms can shift profit from high- to low-tax countries by sourcing more product from the low-tax country (while keeping transfer prices constant), by changing transfer prices (while holding sourcing decisions constant), or by combining these alternatives. Thus, the tax benefits associated with sourcing derive from two activities: (1) setting tax transfer prices and (2) setting the quantities that will be sourced from various locations. For the sample firms, setting tax transfer prices is a corporate responsibility that typically requires less coordination with noncorporate managers (including sector, group, and divisional managers) than does setting quantities. Less coordination is required partly because the sample firms' tax transfer prices do not affect operating decisions or performance evaluations.[32] In contrast, sourcing quantities do affect, and are affected by, performance measures and, unlike transfer prices, can be easily adjusted to account for changes in economic circumstances during a tax year. Also, for the sample firms, there frequently are sourcing (quantity) situations where managers' performance measures are in conflict with the corporate objective of maximizing after-tax worldwide income.[33] The extent of these conflicts varies depending on whether the firm uses a pretax or after-tax performance measure. In this section, I consider separately how tax transfer prices and performance measures affect sourcing decisions. In contrast to the previous section, where the primary focus was on location *decisions,* the discussion here centers more on the mechanisms (tax transfer prices and performance measures) that influence sourcing decisions than on the decisions per se.

In subsection 6.4.1, I examine the role of transfer prices in sourcing decisions. First I consider differences in firms' abilities to transfer price aggressively when there are no frictions or restrictions to impede this behavior. I then discuss a coordination friction that involves the conflict between setting transfer prices to reduce taxes and setting them to motivate managers. Specifically, the coordination friction associated with setting transfer prices for tax reasons is the forgone operating efficiencies (from not using the optimal transfer prices for managerial purposes). The discussion then turns to the two ways that the sample firms cope with this friction. Some use separate transfer prices for tax and managerial purposes, while others use performance measures that are not affected by tax transfer prices. Presumably, the choice of whether to explicitly use two sets of transfer prices depends on whether the cost of explicitly maintaining a separate set of managerial transfer prices exceeds the

---

32. Nevertheless, some coordination is required when setting tax transfer prices, because foreign managers must defend these prices when they are audited locally.

33. In principle, a performance measure could be designed to ensure the correct distribution of quantities to maximize after-tax worldwide income. For such an ideal performance measure, there would be no situations where managers' actions would conflict with corporate objectives. Whether such an ideal performance measure exists and can be cost-effectively implemented is beyond the scope of this research.

forgone coordination benefits (or friction) of using an evaluation system that does not depend on tax transfer prices. The discussion then proffers a reason why these coordination frictions might be particularly small for some of the sample firms. Interestingly, the argument concludes that the firms that have the most flexibility in setting transfer prices also face the smallest coordination friction. This absence of frictions, it is further argued, explains recent transfer pricing restrictions including more extensive audits and more stringent enforcement penalties.[34] The transfer pricing discussion closes by illustrating how these restrictions have curbed aggressive transfer pricing. In fact, tax managers now say that they are on the defensive and there is some evidence presented later to back this claim.

Subsection 6.4.2 illustrates how sourcing decisions are coordinated differently by firms that use pretax and after-tax performance systems. Because tax transfer prices do not influence these performance measures, the relevant managers must communicate regularly to ensure better sourcing decisions. This communication travels in both directions. Local managers are encouraged to pursue local tax planning opportunities and to communicate these opportunities to the corporate tax office. The corporate office communicates the corporate tax profile and corporate tax strategy to the local managers and motivates them to use this information appropriately. Importantly, this communication is less critical for firms that use after-tax performance measures, suggesting that there must be reasons why firms use before-tax performance measures. One explanation is that after-tax measures are costly to develop and implement. Determining the "correct" tax rate for these after-tax performance measures is a complex, if not impossible, problem that requires considerable coordination between corporate and foreign tax planners.[35] Section 6.4.2 contains a brief discussion of how firms that use pretax performance measures

---

34. In the United States, §6662 sets the penalty for §482 adjustments in excess of $20 million at 40 percent of the contested amount. However, §6664 provides an exception. Specifically, no penalty is imposed if the taxpayer can show reasonable cause and demonstrate that it acted in good faith. One of the sample firms views the "defensive" transfer pricing strategies discussed in subsection 6.4.1 as evidence of reasonable cause and good faith. Japanese tax officials are also scrutinizing transfer prices more carefully recently. On March 31, 1986, the Japanese taxing authority received statutory authority to enforce transfer prices on foreign transactions.

35. It requires knowledge about the company's repatriation strategy, its forecasts of future profitability at various locations, and a host of other tax planning considerations. When foreign managers are evaluated after-tax, using such a rate, they will essentially share tax benefits with other facilities. Corporate tax rates on worldwide income are reduced because foreign tax credits of various foreign subsidiaries and gains and losses (within the same country) are averaged when corporate taxes are determined. More generally, corporate tax rates are reduced because corporate tax managers coordinate the separate activities of foreign tax managers. The reduction in corporate taxes due to synergies resulting from this coordination, like the benefits of foreign tax credit averaging, cannot be attributed to a specific foreign location. Viewing tax as another cost, the challenge is to determine the correct marginal cost of an action that is affected by and affects others' past, current, and future actions. From the cost accounting literature, we know that this is a tough challenge, both theoretically and practically.

manage tax versus nontax conflicts related to sourcing decisions. Another subsection illustrates, in general, how a large multinational firm coordinates worldwide tax planning and, in particular, how the budgeting process and after-tax performance measures influence sourcing patterns.

6.4.1 Transfer Pricing

Flexibility

Subject to restrictions imposed by tax authorities throughout the world, tax transfer prices can be set so that profits are shifted from high- to low-tax locations. Why do opportunities to transfer price aggressively differ across firms? The magnitude of the tax transfer price benefit depends on the firm's repatriation policy, the dispersion of its tax rates across different countries, the size of its gross margin, its ability to decouple activities in its value chain and locate them in low-tax countries, and the extent of government restrictions. If profits are repatriated immediately from all worldwide locations, then the tax transfer price benefit is reduced. There is still an incentive to shift profits to avoid high foreign taxes and to manage foreign tax credits. But, without deferral, the lowest tax rate possible on worldwide income is the American rate. Several of the sample firms' managers claim that firms with high gross margins are in the best position to transfer price aggressively. This may be true, because gross margins are typically high for products that have no comparable unrelated-party prices (cups). Gross margins are high, for example, when there are barriers to entry, when operating risks are high, and when firms have large investments in intangibles such as R&D and marketing. Products with these traits have fewer comparable products, and as one manager indicated, "their correct transfer prices are almost impossible to determine." Gross margins alone, however, do not provide the opportunity to transfer price aggressively. Firms must also be able to decouple their business activities and disperse them to low-tax countries. As we shall see in section 6.4.2, aggressive transfer pricing has been curbed recently. However, in some industries, transfer pricing is still an important tax planning consideration.

In addition to managerial and tax considerations, duties and (in the pharmaceutical industry) price approvals reduce the flexibility in setting transfer prices. In the pharmaceutical industry, price approvals are frequently based on cost-plus formulas, so companies have a strong incentive to increase transfer prices on intermediate products. Because most sales are in high-tax countries, the tax and regulatory incentives are concordant. Specifically, firms want to transfer goods into high-tax countries at higher transfer prices. However, if there is pressure to lower transfer prices because of duties, the prices of goods sold are also lowered. This duty-price trade-off probably explains, at least partially, why duties are so high for pharmaceuticals; countries can use duties to help regulate prices. It also explains why pharmaceutical firms' transfer pricing committees have members from more functional areas than the other sample firms do. Nevertheless, both tax and nontax managers at the sample firms generally agreed that tax "has the loudest voice" when it comes to transfer pricing.[36]

Coordination Frictions

Transfer prices can also be used for nontax reasons, including motivating foreign tax managers to source more efficiently. When firms use the same transfer prices for tax and managerial purposes, they will be less inclined to let tax considerations dictate how these prices are set if the nontax benefits are large. The nontax benefits associated with transfer prices (coordination frictions) differ across firms. Smaller centralized firms rely less on mechanisms such as transfer prices to coordinate activities. For example, a manager at one of the more centralized sample firms stated, "We do not view ourselves as a company with several independent businesses around the world, just plants and sales offices. Thus, transfer prices, as devices to motivate efficient decision making, are not important." In contrast, the potential benefits from designing transfer prices and evaluation systems to meet nontax objectives are substantial for the decentralized sample firms that have multiple strategic business units (SBUs). One of the sample firms uses transfer prices to facilitate long-run strategic initiatives. In particular, it transfers additional profit (on its managerial books only) to compensate for large start-up losses in countries where it envisions tremendous growth potential in the next century. The objective is to motivate local managers.

In addition to firm size and the extent of decentralization, companies that have unique intermediate products benefit less from the nontax advantages associated with transfer prices. Specifically, a major nontax benefit of transfer prices is that they can motivate managers to source intermediates from the lowest-cost supplier. Thus, when intermediates are not available from outside vendors, the forgone coordination benefits associated with using transfer prices are relatively small. Interestingly, firms that sell blockbuster products that are very unique at all stages of manufacturing have both the most flexibility in setting tax transfer prices and the smallest coordination frictions.

How Firms Cope with Coordination Frictions

When the coordination frictions associated with transfer pricing become large, firms have an incentive to develop alternative mechanisms to motivate managers. To this end, they can establish separate transfer prices for tax and managerial purposes or use performance measures that do not depend on transfer prices. All of the sample firms use one of these alternatives.

---

36. This does not necessarily mean, however, that tax has the most clout because they can shift profits and increase after-tax cash flow. Tax managers must defend their transfer prices to taxing officials around the world, and some tax managers indicated that, left on their own, nontax managers would set transfer prices that would not pass a tax audit.

A common view is that taxing authorities will challenge two sets of transfer prices. Presumably, the argument is that tax transfer prices must pass a business purpose test and that they cannot possibly do so if the business is using alternative prices. The fallacy with this argument is that transfer prices can serve multiple business purposes. Taxing authorities expect tax transfer prices to assign an "appropriate" amount of profit to each location, and there clearly are situations where tax transfer prices will also meet firms' nontax incentive objectives. But firms with both cost and profit centers have no managerial reason to assign profit to the cost centers. Indeed, some of the sample firms assign all profit to the managers who set customer sales prices, presumably to protect gross margins. Also, some take losses on their corporate office managerial books to motivate subsidiary managers. In these situations, the total profit assigned to subsidiaries exceeds the company profits. For example, as indicated earlier, one sample firm's managerial transfer prices are used to facilitate the long-term corporate strategy. Additional profit is assigned to foreign managers, to compensate for start-up losses, in a location where the firm is trying to "get in early," and an offsetting loss is recorded at the corporate office.

Besides using different transfer prices for tax and performance evaluation purposes, firms reduce coordination frictions that impede tax planning by designing performance evaluation measures that do not depend on transfer prices. The resulting performance systems may not be optimal from a nontax perspective, but they allow the firm to base transfer prices on tax considerations. For example, some of the sample firms evaluate manufacturing facilities as cost centers but only include costs related to transactions outside the firm. Thus, transfer prices do not affect these performance measures. By excluding transfer prices, as mentioned earlier, the company might be sacrificing an opportunity to increase foreign managers' incentive to control costs. Implicitly, these firms are using different transfer prices for tax and managerial purposes. These implicit managerial transfer prices assign zero profit to the manufacturing facilities and all of the profits to the distribution centers.

Current Strategies: Offensive or Defensive?

The pressure on tax transfer prices from authorities throughout the world has significantly checked aggressive transfer pricing. This subsection examines more closely why managers' ability to set transfer prices to reduce taxes has been curbed. It closes with an example that illustrates reinvoicing, a common way to assign profit. This example demonstrates how the collective pressures from taxing authorities are causing transfer prices to converge closer to economic reality—to assign profit commensurate with the economic value added.

How aggressively do sample firms set transfer prices? Tax managers uniformly agreed that even if there are "correct" transfer prices, they are virtually impossible to estimate (for products that have no comparable unrelated-party prices). As a result, managers have tremendous discretion in setting them. They also agree that the taxing authorities, especially those in the United States, are making it very difficult for firms to exercise this discretion as freely as they once did. Some firms are more aggressive than others, but most concur that the grey area for setting transfer prices has narrowed and that firms need to develop a comprehensive transfer pricing policy and apply it consistently. A vice president of tax emphasized the trend toward a defensive transfer pricing strategy:[37]

> There are two strategies—offensive or defensive. An offensive strategy is simply shifting income to the lowest tax jurisdiction under the darkness of night approach—essentially hoping the taxing authorities will not find it. A defensive strategy views a corporate taxpayer more like a stakeholder; that is, the company is going to pay taxes somewhere in the world, thus what the company wants to do is avoid costly and time-consuming price disputes by putting into place a pricing policy that will withstand scrutiny by all taxing authorities. These are not necessarily either/or strategies and can be used selectively in tandem. In the past, my personal view was that most taxpayers were offensive. However, a number of things are changing, such as better and tougher audits both here and overseas and substantial penalties for being overly aggressive. As a result, I think that most multinationals are shifting to a defensive mode.

The following example illustrates how a sample firm modified its transfer pricing policy to reflect their more defensive posture. This example also illustrates that transfer pricing can be somewhat more complicated than just setting the price between two locations to reduce worldwide taxes. The firm uses reinvoicing (explained below) to get the "right" profit into two countries. The company assembles in a low-tax Asian country a product that is sold in numerous locations, including Australia. Although the product is physically shipped from the low-tax Asian country directly to an Australian sales and distribution center, the invoices follow one of two triangular routes: either from the low-tax Asian country to Hong Kong and then to Australia or from the low-tax Asian country to the United States and then to Australia. Hong Kong is also a low-tax location for this firm, and the Australian and American operations are taxed at approximately the same higher rate.

The product in this example is very profitable. The reinvoicing objective is to put profit in the low-tax Asian country, Australia, and the United States in such a way as to satisfy all of the taxing authorities and, presumably, still reduce worldwide taxes. Without reinvoicing, the company believes that too much profit, relative to the value added, would be split between the low-tax Asian country and Australia. One tax manager suggested that the collective profit was too large because historically royalty payments back to the United

---

37. On reading this quote, tax managers at one of the sample firms emphasized that the offensive strategy described is "too strong." They agreed that many firms had been more offensive in the past but emphasized that none would have dared use this "darkness of night" strategy.

States were probably too small. The vice president of tax was particularly interested in having the Australian profit be consistent with the economic value of the distribution center because of concerns about future tax audits. Although the Australian taxing authority would not object to having too much Australian profit now, it might object to large losses later if the market experiences a downturn. According to the tax manager, "It is better to get the right amount of profit there in the first place and to be consistent." Also, the tax managers were concerned that the Australian authorities might mistakenly interpret the reinvoicing as an effort to shift profit from Australia to a low-tax country (and to the United States because the income is subpart F):

> We used Hong Kong rather than a low-tax country such as the Cayman Islands because our Hong Kong operation deserved the profits (on their local-legal books) and because we were concerned about Australian audit exposure. In the event the Australian authorities challenge the transfer prices, we want to be in a position to argue business purpose; the Hong Kong operation is the heart of our regional operations, and sales between the low-tax Asian country and Australia are facilitated by the Hong Kong office. Also, the Hong Kong operation was already paying royalties on other products, so they could conveniently start royalty payments on the new product.

Under the reinvoicing arrangement, a cost-plus transfer price is used for product leaving the low-tax Asian country, a common pricing approach for manufacturing facilities, and a resale-minus transfer price is used for product entering Australia, also a standard approach for sales and distribution centers. Consistent "plus" and "minus" percentages are used throughout the world for comparable products, even if costs and sales prices differ. Regardless, of whether the reinvoicing goes through Hong Kong or the United States, the residual profit is taxed immediately in the United States and is characterized as foreign-sourced for the purpose of determining the foreign tax credit limitation.

6.4.2 Performance Measures

Pretax Performance Measures

Many of the sample firms evaluate managers below the rank of the vice president using pretax measures that are not influenced by transfer prices.[38] In some, manufacturing centers are evaluated as cost centers, and sales offices are evaluated based on companywide profit, defined as sales price less total costs at all locations. Thus, although transfer prices are influenced by duties,

---

38. Although I did not systematically ask managers why they did not use an after-tax performance measure, a few offered reasons. One claimed that foreign managers did not control transfer prices, and their impact on foreign taxes swamped other planning considerations. Another emphasized the difficulty of allocating the benefits of foreign tax credits and other items to various divisions. They speak from experience; they make these allocations at the SBU level.

taxes, and regulatory issues, they are not designed to coordinate activities or align effort.

How do corporate managers ensure *after-tax* profit maximization when sourcing managers are evaluated *pretax?* A potential conflict occurs, for example, when the tax savings from producing in a lower-tax country exceed the operating cost savings from producing in a higher-tax country. When there is a downturn in worldwide sales, corporate managers would prefer that production be reduced in the higher-tax country. However, their choice conflicts with that of the sourcing manager—presuming the sourcing manager is motivated strictly by pretax profits. How is this situation managed? Typically, the sourcing managers communicate their concerns about not making their production targets to the corporate managers. In some of the sample companies, corporate managers convey this concern to their bonus committees, and informal adjustments are made. In others, an explicit adjustment is made on the managerial books to protect the sourcing manager's profits. The corporate office absorbs a loss equal to the marginal operating costs of producing in the lower-tax country.[39]

After-tax Performance Measures

Two of the firms are very decentralized and use after-tax evaluation systems. Tax transfer prices do not affect evaluations for reasons discussed earlier. The following example illustrates how one firm coordinates worldwide tax planning, how its after-tax performance measure is determined, and how sourcing targets are established as part of the budget process.

The company is organized both by strategic business units (SBUs) and by geographic regions. As in the other sample firms, the vice president of tax reports directly to the CFO, as do the vice presidents of treasury, control, and international finance. A domestic tax manager and international tax manager each report directly to the vice president of tax, along with several other managers not relevant to this example. The international tax manager coordinates international operations with geographic tax managers located throughout the world, who report indirectly to the vice president of international finance. None of the above managers are in the SBU organizations. The SBU general managers report directly to the chief executive officer (CEO), as does the CFO. Each SBU organization has a finance staff at its sector offices in the United States and financial managers spread throughout the world. The SBU country financial managers control the local operating entities and convey important information that is used for annual tax planning.

---

39. Some would argue that taxes distort real economic activity in this situation; production is shifted to the higher-cost location. A fallacy in this argument is that it ignores operating benefits related to public goods that are priced in tax rates. For example, the higher-operating-cost country might have toll roads (which are reflected in the operating costs), while the lower-operating-cost country might recoup these costs through taxes.

Each year, an annual worldwide tax plan is developed following a procedure similar to the one used to develop nontax budgets. Besides establishing guidelines, this process facilitates worldwide communication. The local offices convey the specific information needed to develop the worldwide tax plan, and the corporate office in turn communicates the company's tax profile to local managers to encourage them to keep a companywide perspective when executing the plan.

To see how the process works, consider the United Kingdom, where the company has several SBU offices. The U.K. financial manager is responsible for tax, treasury, and statutory accounting and is part of the geographic organization managed by the vice president of international finance. He or she coordinates finance, recruiting, and training for the SBUs and files a consolidated U.K. tax form. Tax planning starts during the second fiscal quarter, immediately after the tax office completes compliance for the prior year. The U.K. financial manager collects profitability projections and other vital tax planning information from the SBUs. This information is incorporated into the first draft of the U.K. tax plan that is submitted to the European tax manager, along with similar plans from all of Europe. Next, the first stage of sourcing coordination starts, with the European tax manager serving as a liaison between the international tax manager at the corporate office and the country financial managers. For example, after a negotiation with the country managers, a decision might be made to source more of a specific intermediate product from France and less from the United Kingdom. These country sourcing targets are the basis for the SBU budgets that are subsequently used to establish the after-tax performance measures discussed later.

Throughout the next year, when the plan is executed, the international and geographic tax managers communicate regularly to adjust for unexpected events and to exchange information required for setting tax policies. The international tax manager—who, along with the general tax attorney, the vice president of tax, and the vice president of international finance, is part of the transfer pricing committee—ensures that transfer price policy is applied consistently and collects information that is used to amend it. Country financial managers, for example, voice concerns about local audit pressures. Also, the international tax manager helps regional and country managers interpret transfer price policy and coordinates sourcing adjustments similar to the one in the reinvoicing example given above.

Evaluations for all managers responsible for outside sales, including those that manage a single product line, are largely based on return on net assets, with most business units using after-tax return on net assets.[40] The denominator of this measure, net assets, is assets less liabilities for the unit being evaluated. The numerator depends on market profit and loss statements that have

---

40. The exceptions are business units that do not influence taxes, and situations where corporate tax allocations would be too arbitrary.

several incentive features and are based on managerial, rather than tax, transfer prices. These transfer prices change over time as the corporate office changes managerial emphasis.[41] As was the case for the example in the previous section, when the profit at a specific site differs from the legal-entity profit (reported for local tax, financial reporting, and duty considerations), a corporate account picks up the difference. Note that return on net assets does not provide individual managers with a direct incentive to coordinate activities such as sourcing. Thus, the tax planning and ongoing communication considerations, discussed earlier, work in tandem with return on net assets to facilitate planning.

6.5   Summary and Conclusions

This field study examines how taxes influence nine firms' location and sourcing decisions. A conceptual framework is introduced to help organize salient industry and business activity characteristics that determine the role of taxes in location decisions. It proposes three categories of nontax considerations (or frictions): coupling frictions, which tend to fuse activities together in a firm's value chain; country frictions, which are the opportunity cost of locating a specific activity, or collection of activities, in a particular country; and coordination frictions, which are associated with incentive and communication mechanisms that impede tax minimizations. Firms assign facilities in their product value chains to countries where the maximum value is added at a minimum after-tax cost. To this end, they must first identify spots in their value chains where coupling frictions are small and then locate these separate facilities, taking account of country and coordination frictions and local taxes. Given existing facilities, firms must also utilize existing capacity in response to unexpected changes in demand, operating conditions, and tax circumstances. Several mechanisms, including evaluation and control systems and transfer prices, are used to coordinate these sourcing decisions. The design of these mechanisms can result in coordination frictions that impede tax planning related to these ongoing operations. A field study is a particularly useful way to identify both nontax and tax factors that managers consider when making these location and sourcing decisions.

The results are based on interviews with chief financial officers and high-level managers from manufacturing, treasury, tax, and strategy, about sixty-eight location decisions that were made during the past twenty-five years.

---

41. This is the sample firm that uses managerial transfer prices as a mechanism to achieve strategic objectives. For example, the company is an Asian country for long-term strategic reasons, especially for marketing reasons (to get a foothold) and for technology exchange considerations. Although it eventually expects to realize profits, it is currently operating at a loss (in the sense that current-period revenues do not cover the current-period "true" economic costs). Because no one enjoys working for an unprofitable firm, the firm sets transfer prices that make the Asian operation appear profitable when reasonable operating targets are met.

These interviews suggest several conclusions related to location decisions. First, tax considerations largely dictate location decisions for business activities where these frictions are small, such as administrative and distribution centers. The examples in sections 6.3.2 and 6.3.3 illustrate how taxes frequently dominate the decision to locate administrative and distribution centers in countries where these activities are tax favored. Second, nontax considerations are very important for all manufacturing location decisions, including those where the final decision is to locate in a low-tax country. Moreover, while taxes are an important consideration in locating manufacturing facilities, they rarely dominate the decision process. Even when taxes prevail, the decisions are typically close. Depending on the industry, these decisions are also influenced by operating requirements, marketing issues, or, more generally, global strategic considerations. The examples in section 6.3.1 underscore the importance of nontax considerations, even for basic manufacturing such as assembly operations in the semiconductor industry and dispersion and fill/finish manufacturing in the pharmaceutical industries.

Transfer prices affect both sourcing and location decisions and the sample firms' managers claim that firms with high gross margins are in the best position to transfer price aggressively. This follows because firms with high gross margins usually have no comparable unrelated-party prices (cups) that can be used as transfer price benchmarks. The Scholes and Wolfson framework suggests that nontax frictions should prevent these firms from transfer pricing too aggressively (relative to taxing authorities' assessments) or, absent these frictions, that government restrictions should be forthcoming. The findings suggest that the coordination frictions commonly thought to curb aggressive transfer pricing do not affect the sample firms. The standard argument is that transfer prices can facilitate efficient local decisions, effort alignment, and communication, and firms thus will be reluctant to distort transfer prices for tax reasons. Central to this argument is the presumption that the same transfer prices are being used for tax and managerial purposes. For the sample firms, this assumption is not valid; either they use separate transfer prices for tax and managerial purposes, or transfer prices do not affect performance measures. Instead, the interviews suggest that managers' ability to transfer price aggressively has been considerably curbed recently by the threats of hefty penalties and extensive audits in many countries including the United States, Germany, and Japan. These restrictions seem to have been very effective. While some of the interviewed managers claim to push transfer prices toward the boundaries of the gray area that defines acceptable practice, most of them agree that the gray area has shrunk dramatically. Indeed, some now employ a defensive transfer pricing strategy; they have developed comprehensive transfer pricing policies that they use consistently throughout the world. Thus, while the sample firms' tax managers are very sophisticated and prefer not to "leave tax benefits on the table," they are also sensitive to government restrictions.

The findings also indicate two reasons why common concerns about inefficient resource allocations related to overly aggressive tax planning may be exaggerated. First, the amount of real economic activity in low-tax countries seems to be commonly understated. The argument that drug companies simply put pills in bottles in Puerto Rico grossly underestimates both the sophistication and amount of manufacturing activity in Puerto Rico. Moreover, while Puerto Rico continues to offer attractive tax benefits to pharmaceuticals, the amount of these benefits is not influenced by transfer prices for many firms (because they currently use the profit-split method discussed in footnote 14). This demonstrates that taxes can influence location and sourcing decisions in situations where managers are not aggressively setting transfer prices. Second, even when large tax benefits are required to compensate for nontax considerations and firms locate in low-tax countries, it does not necessarily follow that taxes are distorting efficient resource allocations. In making location decisions, managers consider differences across country infrastructures that (among other things) are partially reflected in tax rates. For example, they consider the quality of education systems, communication systems, transportation systems, and other public goods that are generally subsidized by taxes. Thus, because tax rates reflect infrastructure differences and infrastructure demands vary across industries and activities, *efficient* resource allocations can, at least in principle, depend on taxes.

The results also suggest that the role of taxes and the relative importance of various nontax considerations in location and sourcing decisions have changed dramatically during the sample period. First, twenty years ago, firms were primarily looking for low-cost labor in low-tax countries to manufacture for the U.S. market. These location decisions were, in part, a response to foreign competition in U.S. markets. Today, many U.S. companies' markets are global, and their location decisions are motivated by regional marketing considerations. They want a manufacturing operation in Europe or Asia because their marketing departments believe that sales will increase if they are perceived as a local company or because they need to meet local-content requirements. Having made the decision to locate a manufacturing facility in one of these economic zones, they then minimize after-tax costs. Second, automation in manufacturing has resulted in a dramatic decline in direct labor costs as a proportion of total manufacturing costs, especially for low-cost unskilled labor. As a consequence, firms are less inclined to locate offshore to reduce labor costs than they were previously. Third, with the opening of global financial markets and the removal of exchange controls, financial operating costs have declined. As a result, firms are beginning to locate financial centers in low-tax countries. Fourth, tax benefits are not as plentiful in Asia as they were ten years ago. Japanese firms have made large investments throughout Asia recently. This has caused countries to decrease tax concessions. Fifth, and more of a conjecture, if tax rates in Europe harmonize more slowly than drug prices, pharmaceuticals will begin to locate major facilities in Ireland and other low-tax European countries. Currently, price approvals, not taxes, determine pharmaceuticals' site choices in Europe; but if prices are harmonized, these choices will more closely resemble those in the semiconductor industry.

A sequel to this paper will examine how firms coordinate tax and treasury planning. In particular, it will examine how the sample firms used in this study move cash and finance new foreign facilities.

References

Carolin, R., H. Diener, C. McConnell, and R. Jaikumar. 1984. *Note on integrated circuit manufacturing.* Harvard Business School Case number 9-684-071.
Porter, M. E. 1990. *The competitive advantage of nations.* New York: Free Press.
Scholes, M., and M. Wolfson. 1991. *Taxes and business strategy: A global planning approach.* Englewood Cliffs, N.J.: Prentice Hall.
Yoffie, D. 1987. *The global semiconductor industry,* Harvard Business School Case number 9-388-052.

Comment   R. Glenn Hubbard

Peter Wilson's paper differs from the standard offering in the literature on international aspects of taxation. It offers descriptive evidence from careful case studies, as opposed to econometric analysis of existing firm-level data or aggregate time-series data. The goal of the research agenda begun in this paper is to identify and characterize *nontax* benefits and costs in order to formulate better economic models of location, investment, transfer pricing, and financial policy decisions.

An analogy to studies of corporate debt by specialists in public finance or corporate finance is instructive. We know a great deal about tax incentives for alternative financial structures. We know much less about nontax benefits and cost of leverage. Understanding the latter is nonetheless important for understanding connections between tax factors and capital structure. Financial economists can use case studies to improve modeling of nontax benefits and costs of corporate debt.

Wilson's paper is offered in this spirit. There is an immediate problem confronting such an approach, however. If tax factors in international decisions are often complicated and confusing, nontax factors can be even more so. It is certainly possible to list nontax considerations. Field studies such as Wilson's

R. Glenn Hubbard is professor of economics and finance at the Graduate School of Business, Columbia University, former deputy assistant secretary (tax analysis), U.S. Department of the Treasury, and a research associate of the National Bureau of Economic Research.

are definitely useful for identifying tax and nontax considerations in various corporate decisions. The more difficult and interesting task is to organize these considerations in such a way as to guide the development of economic models. It is this more ambitious agenda that he has in mind.

Building on the approach in Scholes and Wolfson (1991), he categorizes nontax factors as "restrictions" (government rules) or "frictions" (costs associated with meeting other business purposes). I think it is simplest to think of these as "institutional factors" or "nontax benefits and costs." Straightforward industrial organization considerations suggest that plausible subcategories include product- or industry-specific characteristics (e.g., production process, importance of distance to market, economies of scale or entry strategies), country-specific characteristics (e.g., regulation or presence of particular infrastructure), and firm-specific characteristics (e.g., intrafirm coordination issues and information and incentive problems).

The usefulness of field interviews depends in part, of course, on the sample. Wilson conducted detailed on-site interviews with chief financial officers and their staffs in nine U.S. multinational corporations. The industrial mix is three pharmaceutical firms, three semiconductor firms, one chemical firm, one materials firm, and one software firm. The overrepresentation of pharmaceuticals and semiconductors reflects the perceived importance of international tax planning in those industries.

The interviews gathered information on sixty-eight location decisions in twenty-five countries; the decisions spanned the decades of the 1960s, 1970s, and 1980s. Wilson was also able to obtain some information on transfer pricing and compensation policy. The primary focus of the study is an examination of tax and nontax factors in location (capacity expansion) and sourcing (capacity utilization) decisions.

Wilson's conclusions are intuitive but nonetheless important, given the paucity of information about the role of tax planning in multinationals' decisions. First, for manufacturing location decisions, nontax considerations are very important. In particular, part of the apparent insensitivity to tax considerations could reflect the link between taxes paid and the provision of important infrastructure (e.g., in education and transportation support). Second, where nontax considerations are not particularly important (e.g., for administrative or distribution centers), tax considerations are paramount. Third, the effectiveness of transfer pricing in reducing multinationals' worldwide tax burdens is limited by nontax factors. Interestingly, government restrictions dominate problems in intrafirm coordination in this respect. In principle, firms' use of transfer pricing for tax planning could be reduced by the need to evaluate managers for compensation or other purposes. Wilson finds that firms can effectively use information from multiple accounts to guide tax planning on the one hand and managerial evaluation and compensation on the other.

Perhaps the most useful information in this stage of the research is the analysis of differences across industries and stages of production within an industry in the importance of nontax considerations. Again, one can straight-forwardly think of these as product- or industry-specific, country-specific, or firm-specific.

One would expect country-specific considerations (e.g., the availability of skilled workers) to be important in stages of production in which there are high fixed costs for research and development or regulatory approval. These fixed costs figure prominently in the pharmaceutical and semiconductor industries. For those industries, tax considerations are not as important as location-specific nontax benefits and costs in the early stages of product development. On the other hand, in the production stage, both pharmaceutical and semiconductor products have low marginal costs of production and can be manufactured in many places. Country-specific nontax factors are much less important, and tax considerations are correspondingly more important.

Where infrastructure and product regulation concerns are not significant, one would expect tax planning to be important in high-margin lines of business. Software manufacturing is a good example in which high margins reflect the value of intangible assets and the manufacturing process is simple. Aggressive use of transfer pricing should be important in the software business, subject to limitations arising from firm-specific concerns (e.g., intrafirm coordination problems) or government restrictions. Wilson finds that the latter, government restrictions, provide the principal discipline against aggressive transfer pricing. That is, firm-specific considerations do not appear to limit tax incentives to the same extent that country-specific considerations do.

In the case of the chemical industry, for which margins and the value of research and development intangibles are low, distance to market (a country-specific factor) is the principal consideration in location and sourcing decisions. Because chemical manufacturing facilities arguably generate fewer nontax benefits and more nontax costs for host countries than would, say, pharmaceutical or semiconductor facilities, fewer tax incentives are offered. As a result, tax considerations are more likely to be important in expansion decisions than in greenfield investment decisions.

Similarly, industry- and country-specific nontax factors are most important for firms in the materials industry. Product characteristics and individual customer needs place geographic limits on location. As a result, tax considerations are significant only among geographically close jurisdictions that offer the desired nontax benefits for the business.

Wilson's analysis of possible tensions between tax-motivated transfer pricing and firm-specific requirements for evaluation and control is very interesting. From a tax planning perspective, the principal factors governing the usefulness of transfer pricing include the dispersion of tax rates across countries in which the parent has operations, gross margins and the importance of intangibles, and government restrictions. Tax-motivated transfer pricing is most beneficial for firms with high gross margins as a result of intangible assets with few comparable unrelated-party prices (e.g., pharmaceutical manufacturers), as long as government restrictions are not too severe. Tax considerations are not the only motivation, however. Noting "multiple business purposes," Wilson's interviews document firm-specific plans to shift profits for nontax reasons to motivate managers.

A priori, one might imagine that the need to evaluate and motivate managers would reduce a corporate parent's willingness to "relocate" profits across its foreign subsidiaries to minimize its worldwide tax burden. According to Wilson, firms are generally able to reduce nontax costs that impede tax planning by designing measures for performance evaluation that do not depend on transfer prices. How do corporate managers ensure *after-tax* profit maximization when managers are evaluated on a *pretax* basis? Wilson notes that "informal adjustments are made." Interviews and case studies are useful for describing these adjustments. Much more detail here would be instructive.

I have a related concern with the paper's analysis of effects of tax planning on real resource allocation—a question critically important to economists. Wilson argues that "the amount and sophistication of real economic activity in low-tax countries seems to be commonly understated." Much more specific discussion would be useful. Returning to the discussion of country-specific factors, for example, to the extent that cross-country heterogeneity in tax rates reflects differences in infrastructure or other benefits, there may be little distortion of real resource allocation.

Finally, three avenues for further research seem particularly promising. First, for the current sample, an analysis of shifts in firms' decisions before and after the Tax Reform Act of 1986 would be instructive. Second, multinationals' *financial policy* decisions (e.g., repatriation or capital structure decisions) offer a good laboratory for analysis. In contrast to the decisions studied in the present paper, country-specific and product- or industry-specific factors should be less important, and firm-specific factors should be more important. As a result, one could study trade-offs between tax factors and firm-related nontax factors. Finally, at the "extensive margin," detailed interviews and case studies for non-U.S. parents would facilitate our discrimination among alternative tax and nontax factors in affecting multinational firms' decisions.

These suggestions are more easily offered than executed. Wilson's paper is a difficult and important first step in our using case study evidence to shape economic models of multinational firm decisions.

III   Income Shifting

7 Explaining the Low Taxable Income of Foreign-Controlled Companies in the United States

Harry Grubert, Timothy Goodspeed, and
Deborah Swenson

The low taxable income reported by foreign-controlled companies in the United States has recently attracted a great deal of attention. For instance, the abnormally low rate of return of foreign-controlled companies has fueled concern in Congress over U.S. taxation of these companies and, more specifically, concern that foreign firms operating in the United States are able to escape U.S. taxation.

A glance at the aggregate data shows the reason for congressional concern over this issue. Table 7.1 shows that the ratio of taxable income to assets was only .58 for foreign-controlled companies, as compared with 2.14 for domestically controlled companies in 1987. Moreover, this differential persists when the data are separately presented for nonfinancial, manufacturing, and wholesale industries and when the ratios are recomputed using sales rather than assets as the scaling factor in the denominator.

The low earnings and tax payments of foreign-controlled firms can result from many factors, including transfer price manipulation, greater debt costs than their U.S. counterparts, various effects of mergers and acquisitions, start-up costs, fluctuations in exchange rates, and differences in the cost of capital. Before proceeding, we briefly examine how each of these factors might lower the rate of return of foreign-controlled corporations.

Transfer pricing may be used to price goods, intangibles, and management services such that taxable income is shifted to a low-tax jurisdiction. The in-

Harry Grubert is an international economist in the Office of Tax Analysis, U.S. Treasury Department. Timothy Goodspeed is assistant professor of economics at Florida International University. Deborah Swenson is assistant professor at the Fuqua School of Business, Duke University.

The authors are indebted to Paul Dobbins for constructing the basic data files and providing them in a form that greatly simplified the statistical work. He also did much of the initial programming and made many helpful suggestions. Donald Rousslang, Joel Slemrod, and Gordon Wilson also offered many helpful suggestions. Nothing in this paper should be construed as a Treasury Department position.

centive for shifting income out of the United States depends in part on the tax system of the home country. For example, a clear incentive exists to shift income to a home country that has both a low statutory tax rate and a tax exemption on foreign dividends.[1] However, the bilateral comparison between U.S. and home-country tax rates should not be overemphasized, because income can easily be shifted to some tax haven interposed between the two. Most industrialized countries do not have the strict antiabuse rules that are contained in U.S. law limiting the routing of sales or services income through a tax haven.[2]

With the data that are available, it is difficult to identify transfer price distortions directly. Part of the strategy of this paper is to evaluate the extent to which the foreign-domestic differential is attributable to other explanations. By controlling for other factors that contribute to the differential, we can set an upper bound on the significance of transfer price manipulation. It is also possible to look at indirect evidence of earnings management, such as the distribution of foreign-controlled companies' profitability ratios. That is, do foreign returns concentrate around zero, or are the aggregate foreign results attributable to extreme losses by a limited number of companies?

Higher debt costs are a second means by which foreign-controlled companies might achieve relatively low U.S. taxable income. This may reflect more debt from unrelated lenders. Large debt costs may also result from "earnings stripping," in which large interest payments are made to related offshore companies. In either case, high debt costs will lead to low taxable income, because interest expenses are deductible.

Foreign direct investment in the United States in the form of acquisitions can have a number of accounting and tax consequences, which in turn affect the measured foreign rate of return. This may be particularly relevant because the major source of new direct investment in the United States since at least the late 1970s has been acquisitions rather than greenfield start-ups.[3] One consequence is the straightforward increase in the book value of assets, which lowers the measured ratio of taxable income to assets. A second consequence of asset revaluation is that a firm that maintains a given ratio of debt to assets will experience an increase in interest expenses, which in turn erodes the firm's taxable income. Finally, an acquisition would often, particularly before 1987, lead to a step-up in basis and higher depreciation deductions, again leading to lower taxable income.

---

1. The significance of the exemption is that foreign taxes paid are of no value as a credit against home-country taxes. There may be other aspects of home-country tax systems that are relevant. For example, countries with some form of corporate tax integration usually do not pass foreign tax credits through to the personal level.

2. The recent Price Waterhouse (1991) study on U.S. International Tax Policy outlines these differences between U.S. and foreign practice.

3. See the annual articles in the *Survey of Current Business* on U.S. business enterprises acquired or established by foreign investors. In 1989, for example, acquisitions accounted for 86 percent of investment outlays.

Foreign acquirers may also tend to buy relatively unprofitable U.S. companies with the intention of making better use of the assets. This possibility is suggested by the annual Department of Commerce data on U.S. businesses acquired by foreign investors, which give the income of the company in the year preceding the acquisition (presumably as reported by the buyer). Eventually, the assets acquired would be expected to become more productive. But the current average profitability of foreign-controlled companies may be temporarily reduced due to the significance of recent acquisitions.

A fourth possible cause for the low observed return of foreign-controlled companies is start-up costs. These refer to the temporary up-front losses or low accounting profits arising from diseconomies of small scale, learning-by-doing activities in the firm's early stages, investment in marketing and R&D, and so forth. As the previous discussion suggests, a similar unprofitable phase may take place in the case of acquisitions as well. These costs may be particularly high for foreign firms that must get to know a market different from its home base. Because these are presumably temporary costs, one would expect them to diminish over time as a firm matures.

A fifth possibility is that an unexpected fall in the dollar after 1984 raised costs and thereby lowered the rate of return of foreign-controlled companies. Although exchange rate changes could not be used to explain rates of return that are permanently below domestic rates of return, they may have significant temporary effects. Because foreign-controlled companies, in particular those in wholesaling, rely on imports more heavily than domestic companies do, an unexpected drop in the U.S. dollar will increase relative costs more for foreign-controlled companies (see Graham and Krugman 1989, tab. 3.1). Irrespective of whether the foreign-controlled companies absorb the cost increase to maintain market share, as is sometimes alleged, or simply raise their prices with a resulting loss in sales, their rates of return would be expected to fall as a result.

Finally, some claim that foreign companies have a lower cost of capital than U.S. companies. A lower cost of capital may cause foreign firms to accept a permanently lower rate of return. It may also lead them to prefer profit profiles in which initial returns are relatively low and grow over time.

Many allegations have been made, but very little systematic evidence has been presented to evaluate the causes of the low rate of return of foreign-controlled corporations. This paper uses several firm-level data files to investigate the issue.

As we indicate in later sections, the results present a mixed picture. First, the profits of foreign manufacturing companies increase over time relative to U.S. companies, suggesting some type of maturation process. Second, exchange rates have a significant effect on the profits of foreign-controlled wholesaling companies. Third, the ratio of taxable income to assets is understated for foreign companies because of the asset revaluation in recently acquired companies. Similarly, the comparison of companies' ratio of income to sales is distorted by differences in the role of outside purchases and of investment income. These effects explain about half of the differential between the rates of return of foreign- and domestically controlled companies. This still leaves us with a significant difference that we are unable to explain by forces other than transfer pricing. Moreover, we find, even after accounting for these other factors, that foreign-controlled firms were more likely to maintain a rate of return close to zero over the 1980–87 period.

We can also reject some other explanations of foreign companies' low taxable income. First, debt and earnings stripping do not seem to be important in explaining the low taxable income of foreign-controlled companies. Second, U.S. companies acquired by foreigners seem to be similar in profitability to the average U.S. company prior to acquisition. Furthermore, cost-of-capital advantages do not seem to be important. For one thing, the parents of foreign-controlled companies are more profitable than comparable U.S. companies.

The remainder of the paper is organized as follows. Section 7.1 provides a brief discussion of our data sources and other issues that relate the data. Based on data from a cross section of firms in 1987, section 7.2 presents evidence on revaluation effects, debt and earnings stripping, and cross-country differences. In section 7.3, we turn to the 1980–87 panel of firms to shed light on the importance of exchange rate and maturation effects. Section 7.4 contains a look at the distribution of foreign companies' returns to determine whether it is consistent with income shifting. Again using the 1980–87 panel, we gauge the propensity of foreign and domestic firms to persist in particular rate-of-return categories. Section 7.5 is an exploration of the relationship between foreign parent characteristics and their U.S. subsidiaries' profitability, while in section 7.6 we compare the profitability of foreign targets before acquisition with the profitability of the average U.S. nonfinancial company. Finally, we summarize and conclude in section 7.7.

7.1   Data Issues

7.1.1   Description of Data

As noted above, we use several firm-level data files to cast more light on the issue. The basis of these data is information collected from IRS Form 1120, the basic corporate tax form. Information from these forms is collected and edited by the Statistics of Income Division (SOI) of the Internal Revenue Service and is then provided to the Treasury Department. SOI uses a stratified sampling procedure. The data include all companies reporting assets of $50 million or more, although a company with fewer assets may also be chosen with certainty if its "proceeds," a measure of cash flow, are large enough. In addition, there is a sample of smaller firms.

Form 1120 contains various useful variables, including a company's year of incorporation, gross income, deductions, taxable income, cost of goods sold, and balance sheet information. Of particular importance for this study, the form indicates whether 50 percent or more of the voting stock of a corporation is owned by foreigners and, if so, requests the owner's country. This information allows us to classify U.S. companies as either foreign or U.S. owned. Companies referred to as foreign controlled in our analysis are the ones that actually identified a specific foreign country.

The data from these forms were used to construct two basic data sets, a cross section and a panel. The cross section was constructed using 1987 data and was formed by first restricting the companies only to those in the corporate files that had been sampled with a probability of one. It was further truncated by excluding all companies with assets less than $50 million. All companies in finance, insurance, or real estate were also eliminated. In addition, the analysis was restricted to consolidated returns only. This left approximately 600 foreign-controlled companies and 4,000 domestically controlled companies. The foreign companies in the sample account for 68 percent of the total assets of nonfinancial foreign-controlled companies in 1987, and the domestic companies in the sample account for 72 percent of the total assets of domestic nonfinancial companies.

The panel data set was constructed from the basic 1120 data for the years 1980 to 1987. To be included in the panel data set, a company had to file the 1120 tax form and be sampled by SOI every year from 1980 to 1987. This effectively limits the panel to firms with assets of $50 million or more each year. To increase the sample size, we included in the panel nonconsolidated as well as consolidated firms. The panel data set includes about 1,300 domestically controlled firms and 110 foreign-controlled firms. Although the panel has many fewer companies than the full 1987 cross section, it is valuable in identifying the role of start-up costs and exchange rates.

In addition, we used two other data sets. The first of these links 291 foreign-controlled companies on the 1987 data files with information on their parents. The parent corporation was obtained from the *International Directory of Corporate Affiliations* and *Who Owns Whom;* financial and tax information for the parent was obtained from *Moody's International.* Finally, we used a sample of foreign acquisitions linked with Compustat financial information to study the preacquisition profitability of the target companies. In all cases, we focus only on nonfinancial companies in the United States.

7.1.2 Other Issues

The principal measure that is used in this paper to compare the profitability of foreign-controlled and domestic companies is the ratio of taxable income (total income less total deductions on line 28 of Form 1120) to total assets. Note that taxable income is before net operating loss (NOL) deductions due to carryforwards from earlier years and also before special deductions, mainly dividends-received deductions. The NOLs are excluded because we wish to focus on the activity of a particular year unaffected by carryforwards. As far as dividends are concerned, the investment in the stock of another company will be reflected in the assets in the denominator, so the income should not be excluded from the numerator. In any case, the data can be examined to see whether dividends are more important for domestic companies.

Total assets, rather than sales, are used in the denominator because of the conceptual expectation that rates of return on assets, but not necessarily the ratio of income to sales, should be equalized. The assets reported on Form 1120 are those used for financial reporting purposes, not tax basis. They are based on historical valuations. The relationship between the current market value of assets and their book value depends, in part, on the time pattern of the company's investments. Probably more important is their involvement in mergers and acquisitions, because it is then that assets are likely to be adjusted to market value. Because of these valuation problems, it will sometimes be convenient to use sales as an asset proxy. But when the taxable income to sales ratio is the profitability measure, it will be necessary to adjust for sources of systematic error such as the company's degree of dependence on outside suppliers.

In the analyses in the later sections, domestic companies are used as the natural control group. After all, the well-publicized difference between foreign and domestic companies shown in table 7.1 is the starting point for the inquiry. Nevertheless, domestic companies may have some shortcomings as a control group. It might be claimed that the comparison is unfair to foreign-controlled companies because the intangibles developed by U.S. companies will produce U.S. taxable income while intangibles created by foreign parents, presumably by home-based R&D, will yield taxable income in the home country. We will be in a better position to deal with this issue at the end of the next section, where we will see that it is not likely to be quantitatively very significant.

A number of alternative control groups might be considered. One suggestion is to restrict the comparison only to U.S.-controlled multinational companies on the grounds that they are more comparable to foreign-controlled multinationals. This greater comparability is not completely obvious, because U.S. domestic companies may be the frequent target of foreign acquirers. Further, it might be argued that the taxable income reported by U.S. multinational companies is itself distorted because of the income they shift out of the United States. In any case, as described more fully below, the results are not changed significantly when U.S. multinational companies are used as a control group. In general, the foreign differential is even larger because U.S. multinational companies are somewhat more profitable than purely domestic companies.

Some have suggested using foreign affiliates of U.S. companies as a control group because there may be something distinctive about being a company in a foreign location. That would result in a foreign differential much larger than is shown in table 7.1. The Department of Commerce 1982 benchmark survey

Table 7.1   Taxable Income as a Percentage of Total Assets and Sales in Foreign- and U.S.-Controlled Companies (1987 aggregate data*)

	Taxable Income/Assets		Taxable Income/Sales	
	Foreign	U.S.	Foreign	U.S.
All Industries	.58%	2.14%	.89%	4.37%
Nonfinancial	1.01	3.79	1.00	3.51
Manufacturing	1.60	4.94	2.39	4.21
Wholesale trade	.68	3.24	.29	1.41

Note: Taxable income is total income less total deductions (line 28 on Form 1120) before net operating loss and special deductions. Sales refer to gross receipts or sales (line 1 on the Form 1120). Data may differ slightly from tables in *SOI Bulletin* 10 (Summer), 1990, because of differences in definitions.

*Based on tabulations of 1987 corporate tax file.

on foreign direct investment indicates that foreign affiliates' pretax income was 8.76 percent of total assets, while their parents earned only 4.76 percent on total assets. But there are many problems with using U.S. affiliates abroad. First, they do not mirror foreign companies in the United States, which are much more likely to be the result of acquisitions than of start-ups. Second, it would be necessary to deal with the different economic environments and incentives to shift income in each foreign location. Accordingly, we stick with all domestically controlled U.S. companies, including both multinational and strictly domestic companies, as the control group, both because the public controversy has started on that basis and because the alternatives seem less valid. We will also report results when other control groups are used.

7.2   Evidence from 1987 Corporate Cross Section

We begin by using the 1987 cross-section data to analyze five issues: start-up or acquisition effects, debt and earnings stripping, variations across foreign countries, the use of income over sales as a dependent variable, and the potential use of various types of expenses as transfer pricing mechanisms.

7.2.1   Start-up or Acquisition Effects

The first column of table 7.2 gives the benchmark first regression for the relationship between the ratio of taxable income and total assets, denoted by r_t, and dummies indicating industry and foreign-controlled status. The results mirror the aggregate data in table 7.1 and reveal a very large negative and statistically significant foreign effect of 3.57 percentage points.[4] (The overall

4. In the 1987 sample, the mean r_t for domestic companies is 4.07, and .87 for foreign-controlled companies. These are very close to the aggregate 3.79 and 1.01 for nonfinancial companies in table 7.1 even though the 1987 sample means are unweighted and the sample is restricted

Table 7.2   **Alternative regressions for Taxable Income to Asset Ratio (1987 file—nonfinancial corporations)***

Intercept	.0286	.0500	.1437
	(9.73)	(12.67)	(28.54)
Foreign	− .0357	− .0267	− .0259
	(− 7.46)	(− 5.48)	(− 5.73)
Manufacturing	.0280	.0227	.0136
	(6.86)	(5.52)	(3.55)
Wholesale	.0105	.0056	.0073
	(1.89)	(.01)	(1.42)
Transportation and utilities	− .0098	− .0114	− .0079
	(− 1.81)	(2.11)	(1.57)
Food	− .0088	− .0063	− .000
	(− 1.12)	(− .80)	(− .00)
Electronics	− .0201	− .0187	− .0318
	(− 3.10)	(− 2.90)	(− 5.31)
Chemicals	.0320	.0297	.0186
	(4.03)	(3.77)	(2.55)
Age 1: ≤ 5 years		− .0411	− .0176
		(− 9.62)	(− 4.29)
Age 2: >5–≤10		− .0252	− .0123
		(− 4.73)	(− 2.47)
Age 3: >10–≤15		− .0217	− .0112
		(− 3.49)	(− 1.94)
Age 4: >15–≤20		− .0218	− .0110
		(− 3.87)	(− 1.92)
Age 5: >20–≤30		− .0142	− .0066
		(− 2.61)	(1.32)
Debt-assets			− .1461
			(− 26.01)
Intangible plus other assets			− .0299
			(− 3.03)
R^2 adjusted	.033	.052	.186

*Regressions are unweighted; t-values in parentheses.

mean of r_t in the sample is 3.69 percent.) The importance of other variables will be identified by the extent to which their inclusion reduces this foreign-domestic differential.

The next column of table 7.2 shows how the results change when dummy variables based on the company's date of incorporation are added. The age

---

only to companies with assets in excess of $50 million. As we will see in comparing the ratio of taxable income to sales, table 7.1 understates the difference in sales margins because of the large number of small, low-margin domestic companies included in the aggregate data.

Incidentally, for companies in electronics, food, and chemicals, both the specific-industry dummy and the manufacturing dummy apply. The specific-industry coefficient, therefore, reflects the industry's return net of the average manufacturing return.

dummies are all significant, with the expected pattern of younger companies having lower profits, and reduce the foreign effect by 25 percent. Does the significant effect of age reflect the start-up costs of new companies? This is unlikely because the average size of companies in the sample that were incorporated in the past five years is very large, $919 million in total assets, which is not much smaller than the average of $1,046 million for all companies in the sample. Recently incorporated foreign-controlled companies average $662 million in total assets.

Rather than start-up costs of newly established companies, the date of incorporation dummies appear to reflect the revaluation of assets following mergers and acquisitions. Although reincorporation is not legally necessary as a result of a merger or acquisition, it seems a common consequence. As noted in the introduction, the revaluation of assets after an acquisition can affect the measured ratio of taxable income to assets in several ways. One is simply the direct effect of increasing the denominator in the taxable income to asset ratio. Depreciation expenses can also increase because of a step-up in basis (which has become more difficult after the Tax Reform Act of 1986). Finally, the value of assets interacts with leverage because, with a given debt-asset ratio, interest expenses rise as asset valuation increases.

The significance of asset revaluations is confirmed by the next table, 7.3, which gives the correlation of other variables with the age variables. The first column of table 7.3 gives the regression results for companies' debt-asset ratio on the age and industry variables. The sign and significance of the date of incorporation variables suggest that acquisitions and not start-ups are being identified. The next column is even more persuasive because it uses the ratio of intangible plus "other" assets to total assets as the dependent variable. If an acquiring company pays more for its target than the value of its tangible and financial assets, it would put the remainder, including goodwill, in this residual category. The age effect is highly significant and much larger for more recent dates of incorporation. Finally, as we will see later in this section when we use sales in the denominator and purge the profitability measure of all revaluation effects, profit margins are not significantly related to the date of incorporation.

Returning to table 7.2, we see that the regression in the third column includes as independent variables the ratios of debt and intangible assets to total assets. They are introduced to identify the role of debt and asset revaluations more directly. They are each highly significant, particularly the debt-asset ratios, but the foreign effect is not greatly reduced. Overall, the age, debt, and intangible variables reduce the foreign effect by about 28 percent.[5]

---

5. When a separate r_t regression is performed for foreign companies only, the coefficients are, in general, similar to the pooled ones. In particular, the coefficient for the debt-asset ratio is virtually unchanged.

Table 7.3   **Debt and Intangible Assets versus Age (1987 cross section)***

Dependent Variables	Debt-Assets	Intangible and Other Assets-Total Assets†
Intercept	.626	.077
	(63.2)	(13.72)
Manufacturing	−.062	−.000
	(−6.04)	(−.01)
Chemicals	−.075	−.001
	(−.381)	(−.07)
Food	.033	.046
	(1.70)	(4.14)
Electronics	−.086	−.017
	(−5.35)	(−1.82)
Transportation and utilities	.019	.027
	(1.39)	(3.45)
Wholesale	.021	−.040
	(.53)	(−5.09)
Age 1: ≤ 5 years	.143	.091
	(13.52)	(14.86)
Age 2: >5–≤10	.082	.037
	(6.28)	(4.83)
Age 3: >10–≤15	.068	.025
	(4.37)	(2.86)
Age 4: >15–≤20	.075	.028
	(5.30)	(3.49)
Age 5: >20–≤30	.049	.015
	(3.59)	(1.96)
Foreign		.004
		(.58)
R^2 adjusted	.080	.068

*t-values in parentheses.

†The numerator includes intangible plus "other" assets reported in Schedule L on Form 1120.

7.2.2 Debt and Earnings Stripping

The first column of table 7.4, which gives the regression results when the debt-asset ratio is the dependent variable, shows why the inclusion of debt-asset ratios in the earnings regression does not affect the estimated foreign differential substantially. There is virtually no difference between foreign and domestic leverage ratios, holding age and industry constant. In fact, even without adjustment for age and industry, the difference is small, with the average foreign debt to asset ratio in the 1987 cross section about 3 percentage points greater than the overall sample mean of 66 percent.

The next two columns of table 7.4 look further into the issue of debt and earnings stripping. They use information on loans from shareholders reported on tax returns. (We should caution that some taxpayers may not specifically identify shareholder loans on their tax return.) It is convenient to think of

Table 7.4   **Debt, Interest Costs, and Shareholder Loans (1987 cross section of nonfinancial corporations)***

	Debt/Asset Ratio	Debt/Asset Ratio	Interest Expense/ Asset Ratio
Intercept	.626	.621	− .0074
	(63.2)	(62.9)	(− 5.37)
Foreign	.005	.001	− .0035
	(.40)	(.09)	(− 2.66)
Manufacturing	− .062	− .063	.0034
	(− 6.05)	(− 6.12)	(3.22)
Wholesale	.020	.020	− .0009
	(1.44)	(1.45)	(− .66)
Chemicals	− .076	− .074	− .0035
	(− 3.83)	(− 3.79)	(− 1.76)
Food	.033	.031	.0022
	(1.70)	(1.60)	(1.11)
Electronics	− .086	− .085	− .0062
	(− 5.33)	(− 5.26)	(− 3.78)
Transportation and utilities	.019	.019	.0052
	(1.40)	(1.47)	(3.76)
Age 1: ≤ 5 years	.142	.140	.0075
	(13.25)	(13.11)	(6.80)
Age 2: >5–≤10	.081	.078	.0063
	(6.06)	(5.84)	(4.62)
Age 3: >10–≤15	.067	.066	.0025
	(4.27)	(4.24)	(1.57)
Age 4: >15–≤20	.075	.076	.0056
	(5.28)	(5.37)	(3.89)
Age 5: >20–≤30	.049	.050	.0023
	(3.56)	(3.66)	(1.68)
Loans from shareholders/ assets		.522	− .0118
		(6.67)	(− 1.47)
Loans from shareholders × Foreign		− .256	− .0159
		(− 2.01)	(− 1.23)
Debt-asset ratio			.0582
			(38.08)
R² adjusted	.080	.090	.288

*t-values in parentheses.

shareholder loans as having two effects. One, they may increase the overall level of the company's debt rather than simply substituting for third-party debt. Second, for a given debt-asset ratio, loans from shareholders may provide the opportunity for the company to make excessive interest payments to related parties offshore.

The first effect is examined in column 2 of table 7.4. The results show that loans from foreign shareholders increase debt-asset ratios only modestly. In view of both the coefficient for all shareholder loans and the coefficient for loans from foreign shareholders, a one dollar increase in loans from foreign shareholders increases debt by about 25 cents. Because the average foreign shareholder loan-asset ratio is only 3.7 percent, the overall effect is small.

The third column of table 7.4 looks at the impact of shareholder loans on interest payments as a percentage of total assets, holding the debt-asset ratio constant. It indicates that, if anything, loans from foreign shareholders reduce the ratio of interest payments to assets for a given debt-asset ratio. More important, the coefficient of the foreign variable is negative and significant; foreigners' interest expense, holding the debt-asset ratio constant, is significantly lower than for domestic companies. The interest cost differential, in view of the average debt-asset ratio of about two-thirds, seems to be about fifty basis points.

Summing up, even though loans from shareholders may not be well reported on corporate tax returns, the similarity between foreign and domestic leverage ratios and foreign companies' low interest costs suggest that debt and earnings stripping are not important in explaining the foreign differential.

7.2.3   Country Effects and the Cost of Capital

To this point, we have estimated a pooled foreign coefficient. In order to determine whether the pooling is supported or whether finer country characteristics are at work, we create country dummies for the twelve parent countries with the most foreign affiliates in the United States. Table 7.5 modifies the basic taxable income to assets and debt to assets regressions by including parent country dummies instead of the general foreign dummy. The first column indicates generally small differences in debt-asset ratios among the major investing countries, although the debt-asset ratio of Japanese-owned companies is almost 10 percentage points higher than that of domestically controlled companies and the debt-asset ratio of companies whose parents are based in the Netherlands is 6 percentage points higher.

In the regression reported in the second column of table 7.5, the debt-asset ratio is held constant. What stands out in the second column is the relative uniformity of the country profitability differentials where there are more than a small number of observations. The Japanese differential is by no means unusual, being about the same as that of the United Kingdom and substantially smaller than that of West Germany.

One question is whether the pattern of country differentials is consistent with the differences that might be expected in countries' cost of capital. There is continuing controversy about how to measure differences in the cost of capital across countries (see Poterba 1991). A consistent set of cost-of-capital estimates is also not available for the countries listed in table 7.5. Accordingly, we chose a simple indicator that suggests itself, namely the extent to which a country is a capital exporter. This is measured by the size of the country's current account surplus in the balance of payments as a percentage of gross domestic product (GDP). Countries presumably export capital because they have lower returns at home than they can earn abroad on world

Table 7.5   **Country Effects for Debt and Taxable Income to Assets (1987 cross section)***

Country (Number of Companies)	Debt/ Assets	Taxable Income/ Assets
Canada (75)	−.011	−.018
	(−.35)	(−1.60)
Japan (86)	.097	−.025
	(3.31)	(−2.32)
United Kingdom (122)	−.064	−.026
	(−2.62)	(−2.85)
Netherlands Antilles (26)	.015	−.038
	(.29)	(−2.01)
Netherlands (65)	.059	−.014
	(1.78)	(−1.18)
West Germany (42)	.009	−.048
	(.23)	(−3.15)
France (35)	−.075	−.027
	(−1.68)	(−.64)
Sweden (20)	−.008	−.031
	(−.14)	(−1.40)
Switzerland (30)	−.037	−.029
	(−.78)	(−1.61)
Bermuda and Panama (10)	.062	.019
	(.74)	(.62)
Australia (14)	−.069	−.049
	(−.99)	(−1.88)
Italy (3)	.362	−.155
	(2.39)	(−2.06)
Other foreign	.034	−.024
	(.93)	(−1.74)
Debt-asset ratio		−.149
		(−26.8)
R^2 adjusted	.084	.184

*Industry and age variables not displayed; t-values in parentheses under coefficients.

markets (assuming relatively neutral treatment for foreign and domestic income). However, when the capital-exports variable is added instead of the country dummies, it has no explanatory power.

7.2.4 Ratio of Income to Sales as the Dependent Variable

Up to this point, the basis for the comparison of foreign and domestic companies has been the ratio of taxable income to assets, r_t. The age dummies were used to control for the revaluation of assets following acquisitions, but the date of incorporation is an imperfect acquisition measure. Some companies reincorporated in recent years because certain states have advantages in defending against a takeover. Conversely, acquisitions can take place without a reincorporation. Therefore, sales are convenient to use as an alternative denominator because they are free from asset valuation problems. In other words, sales may be a good proxy for the market value of assets.

But, because of the effect of revaluations on taxable income, a simple ratio of taxable income to sales is itself not free from the consequences of asset revaluations after an acquisition. First, as noted earlier, interest expenses can increase with a given debt-asset ratio. Also, depreciation expenses can increase after acquisition because of the potential step-up in basis. Accordingly, we construct an adjusted sales margin in which interest expenses and depreciation are added to income.

In a final sales margin variation, we attempt to get closer to an operating earning concept by starting with the adjusted margin and taking out interest, dividends, and royalties received. The use of sales as a capital proxy presumably applies only to operating assets, not to financial investments. This operating income adjustment might be particularly relevant for foreign dividends, which may be much more important for domestically controlled multinationals than for foreign companies.

Table 7.6 presents results for each of the three sales margin concepts. There are two regressions for each margin. The first has just the foreign and industry variables. The second adds age, the debt-asset ratio, the ratio of purchases to total expenses, and the inverse of total assets as independent variables.[6] The purchases to total expenses ratio is intended to control for the possibility, which in fact turns out to be true, that foreign-controlled companies are more dependent on outside suppliers—that is, they are less integrated than domestic companies. Foreign companies would then be expected to have lower profit margins because any sales level corresponds to a smaller amount of capital investment. Finally, the inverse of total assets is used as a size variable.

The results in table 7.6 reveal that there is still a large significant foreign differential even when all of the revaluation consequences of acquisitions are taken out of the comparison. When the adjusted margin, including depreciation and interest expenses, is used, the foreign differential in the first regression is 5.6 percentage points and highly significant. If anything, this differential is greater than is apparent in the aggregate data in table 7.1, which may be distorted by the presence of a large number of small, low-margin domestic companies. When the other variables are added, the foreign differential becomes 5.0 percentage points, a reduction of about 11 percent. The reduction in the differential, using the pure profit margin (before adjustment), is much larger, about 30 percent, in part because of the debt and age variables. But this result may be somewhat suspect because of the positive sign on the purchases variable. One notable feature of these results is that the age variables are small and insignificant when interest and depreciation expenses are added

---

6. Purchases are taken from Schedule A on Form 1120, describing the components of costs of goods sold. Total expenses are revenues less net income.

Table 7.6   **Sales Margins***

Independent Variable	Taxable Income/Sales		Adjusted Income/Sales†		Operating Income/Sales‡	
Foreign	− .043	− .030	− .056	− .050	− .051	− .044
	(− 5.02)	(− 3.54)	(− 6.19)	(− 5.48)	(− 6.00)	(− 5.06)
Manufacturing	.057	0.28	− .014	− .012	.013	.007
	(7.77)	(3.95)	(− 1.83)	(− 1.56)	(1.74)	(1.00)
Wholesale	.036	.012	− .053	− .008	− .023	.003
	(3.67)	(1.20)	(− 5.03)	(− .67)	(− 2.32)	(.31)
Transportation and utilities	.008	.018	.098	.067	.109	.090
	(.86)	(1.92)	(9.50)	(6.40)	(11.21)	(9.05)
Food	− .016	− .011	− .026	− .012	− .021	− .010
	(− 1.15)	(− .81)	(− 1.74)	(− .79)	(− 7.47)	(− 0.73)
Electronics	− .013	− .031	− .015	− .026	− .024	− .034
	(− 1.08)	(− 2.79)	(− 1.25)	(− 2.19)	(− 2.12)	(− 2.96)
Chemicals	− .034	.011	.035	.024	.024	.013
	(2.36)	(.86)	(2.36)	(1.65)	(.73)	(.93)
Purchases/to-tal expenses		.055		− .113		− .066
		(5.21)		(− 9.73)		(− 6.06)
Debt/assets		− .223		− .091		− .108
		(− 21.97)		(− 8.21)		(− 10.27)
1/total assets		− 1170		− 2809		− 1847
		(− 2.55)		(5.57)		(− 3.87)
Age 1: ≤ 5 years		− .032		− .011		− .004
		(− 4.33)		(− .16)		(− .55)
Age 2: >5–≤10		− .020		.004		− .005
		(− 2.17)		(.46)		(− .52)
Age 3: >10–≤15		− .023		− .000		− .018
		(− 2.15)		(− .9)		(− 1.59)
Age 4: >15–≤20		− .006		.012		− .005
		(− .060)		(1.11)		(− .46)
Age 5: >20–≤30		− .006		.006		− .005
		(.66)		(.94)		(− .48)
R² adjusted	.002	.047	.052	.090	.047	.080

*t-values of the coefficients in parentheses.

†Adjusted income is taxable income plus interest expense and depreciation deductions.

‡Operating income is adjusted income less dividends, royalties, and interest received.

to the numerator, in contrast to the unadjusted net income regressions, rein-
forcing the view that the date of incorporation variables reflect asset revaluation rather than operating start-up losses.[7]

    In the final two regressions in table 7.6, using the ratio of the operating
income to sales as the dependent variable, the foreign differential is reduced
slightly. It is 5.1 percent with the industry dummies only, compared to 5.6

    7. It might be argued that start-ups have higher depreciation expenses, but the data indicate that
the depreciation-sales ratio is correlated with the age variables, although the depreciation-asset
ratio is not, which is consistent with the asset valuation interpretation.

percent before the investment income is removed. This reduction is consistent with the difference between the two groups in the ratio of aggregate investment income to sales, which is 2.73 percent for domestic companies and 2.17 percent for ones that are foreign controlled. The foreign effect falls to 4.4 percent when the age, debt, and purchases variables are introduced. Combining the adjustment both for investment income and for purchases and the other independent variables (i.e., going from the initial foreign effect of 5.6 percent for the adjusted margin to the 4.4 percent in the last column) achieves a reduction in the foreign effect of about 22 percent.

The size variable turns out to be significant in these profit margin regressions. A similar size variable, the inverse of sales, is sometimes significant in the taxable income to asset regressions. (The reason for the switch from assets to sales is to remove any spurious correlation with the denominator in the dependent variable.) In neither case does its inclusion significantly alter the foreign effect. All the regressions in this section are unweighted. When the observations were weighted (by total wage costs), the results were not significantly altered. The main effect of weighting was to remove some anomalies in the results, such as the significant positive coefficient for the purchases variable in the unadjusted-margin regression.

7.2.5   Expense Patterns

The 1987 cross section can also be used to see whether foreign-controlled companies have a pattern of expenses different from that of domestic companies and whether any difference is related to reported taxable income. This may provide evidence on the potential degree of transfer pricing abuses. The first issue is the dependence of the company on purchases from other firms. It might be expected that foreign companies that rely more on purchases have a greater opportunity to shift income abroad, because many of these transactions could be with offshore related companies. Also, a higher ratio of purchases to total expenses may itself reflect excessive prices paid to affiliates. "Other" expenses, which include royalty payments, management fees, and other overhead charges by affiliated companies, are another interesting category. Accordingly, the regressions in table 7.7 include variables formed by interacting the foreign dummy with the ratio of purchases to total expenses and the ratio of other expenses to total expenses. For each variable, there is both a taxable income to asset regression and an adjusted-margin regression.

Columns 2 and 4 of table 7.7 do not reveal any consistent relationship between foreign companies' reliance on purchases and their profit margins or rates of return. In the r_t regression, the coefficient of the interaction of the foreign and purchases variables is basically zero. In the adjusted margin regression, the foreign purchases variable is positive and significant, not the pattern expected if there is income shifting.[8]

---

8. The lack of significance of the foreign purchases variable demonstrates that including the ratio of purchases to total expenses in the regressions in table 7.7 did not "overadjust" for the

Table 7.7   **Purchases and Other Expenses (1987 cross section)***

Independent Variable	Taxable Income/Assets		Adjusted Income/Sales	
Foreign	−.020	−.027	−.010	−.116
	(−3.25)	(−3.35)	(−.79)	(−6.28)
Debt/asset ratio	−.150	−.150	−.078	−.083
	(−27.2)	(−27.1)	(−6.49)	(−.68)
Other expenses/total expenses	.001		.120	
	(.33)		(15.8)	
Foreign × Other expenses	−.054		−.337	
	(−1.64)		(−4.71)	
Purchases/total expenses		.023		−.147
		(3.74)		(11.56)
Foreign × Purchases		.0003		.134
		(.02)		(4.03)
R^2 adjusted	.187	.190	.123	.075

*Age and industry dummies not shown; t-values in parentheses.

Columns 1 and 3 of the table, which give the results for the ratio of "other" to total expenses, are more indicative of the possibility of income shifting. The interaction of the foreign and other-expenses variable is negative with borderline significance in the r_t, taxable income to asset regression, and again negative and highly significant in the adjusted margin regression. Foreign companies do not on average have a higher share of other expenses than domestic companies, but the ones that do will have lower profit margins and rates of return.

7.2.6 Foreign and Domestic Intangibles and Other Control Group Issues

Finally, we can return to some of the control group issues raised earlier. One is the possibility that a comparison of the U.S. profitability of foreign-controlled and domestic companies is intrinsically unfair because each company's intangibles tend to be developed in its home base. Thus, a U.S.-based company's income will include a return on its intangibles, including income derived from exports and foreign operations (through royalties), whereas a foreign company will have to pay royalties back to its parents. This asymmetry in the source of intangibles does not, however, seem to be a significant factor in explaining the foreign differential. First, it applies only to start-ups, not to acquisitions of U.S. companies, which are a quantitatively much more significant vehicle for foreign ownership. Second, the foreign differential is

---

difference between foreign and domestic companies. For it might be claimed that foreign companies' measured dependence on outside suppliers just reflects their overpaying for their materials. If that were the case, one would expect a large negative coefficient for the foreign purchases variable in the profit margin equation because the purchases variable would indicate more than a simple adjustment for the capital actually used by the company. Similarly, the foreign purchase coefficient should be negative in the taxable income to assets regression.

not larger in high-technology industries such as chemicals or electronics. Along the same lines, the foreign differential is not much affected when the ratio of R&D to assets or sales is added as an explanatory variable. In addition, to the extent that foreign income and royalties bias any comparison of foreign and domestic companies, we have already abstracted from this effect in creating the operating earnings concept in table 7.6. Finally, nontax data on royalties published in the *Survey of Current Business* indicates that they do not significantly alter the profitability measures. U.S. parents received $7.0 billion of royalties in 1987, while U.S. affiliates of foreign companies paid $1.0 billion to parents. If royalties received were taken out of domestic companies' income and royalties paid were added back to foreign-controlled companies' income, the average domestic-foreign income differential would be little affected.

Earlier we also discussed the use of U.S.-based multinational corporations (MNCs) as the control group rather than all U.S. companies. The extent to which the results are altered was examined either by adding an MNC dummy as another variable or by restricting the analysis only to MNCs and foreign-controlled companies.[9] We added an MNC dummy variable to the profitability regression reported in the third column of table 7.2. Although the coefficient for the MNC variable is positive, it is small and insignificant. The MNC variable is larger and significant when only the foreign and industry dummies are included in a regression corresponding to the first column of table 7.1. Accordingly, adding the age, debt, and other variables explains a somewhat larger percentage of the initial foreign-MNC differential, about 40 percent compared to the 28 percent referred to earlier. But the differential between foreign-controlled companies and MNCs is substantially larger to start with, so the unexplained differential is slightly larger.

When sales margins are used as the profitability measure, as in table 7.6, the MNC dummy remains positive and significant for the taxable income margin and the adjusted margin regressions even when other explanatory variables are included. This may reflect the larger foreign investment income of multinational corporations, because the MNC coefficient is much smaller and insignificant in the operating margin regression where investment income has been removed. Thus, apart from any asymmetry in the importance of foreign investment income when sales margins are used, using MNCs as the control group does not affect the results much. The unexplained foreign-domestic differential is generally slightly larger because of the somewhat greater profitability of multinational companies.

To sum up the analysis of the basic control group in section 7.2, adding explanatory variables such as the date of incorporation and the debt-asset ratio

---

9. A U.S.-controlled company was designated as an MNC if it received a foreign tax credit in excess of $1 million or any gross-up credit for foreign dividends (indicating at least 10 percent ownership of a foreign company) or had filed a Form 5471, the information return for foreign-controlled companies.

reduces the foreign-domestic difference in profitability by about 25 percent. The results are robust across countries and are not affected much by using taxable income over sales rather than taxable income over assets as the dependent variable. Further, expense patterns of foreign- and domestically controlled companies do not by themselves indicate large transfer pricing problems.[10] Still, we are left without about 75 percent of the initial difference in foreign and domestic returns to explain.

7.3   Exchange Rate and Trend Effects in the Panel

The 1980–87 panel is made up only of companies that filed a corporate tax return in each of the eight years. Because no new entrants during the period are included, it can be used to identify any maturation or learning effects as foreign companies grow from start-up status or begin to benefit from the up-front investments in their acquisitions. This maturation effect might be expected to be particularly notable in manufacturing because of the greater significance of economies of scale and investments in technology.[11]

The panel can also be used to identify any effects of exchange rates on the relative profitability of foreign-controlled companies. As noted in the introduction, because foreign-controlled companies use a disproportionate amount of imported components, their profits relative to domestic companies may be affected by fluctuations in the price of the U.S. dollar. The year 1987 may therefore give an inaccurate picture of foreign companies because by then the U.S. dollar had fallen by about 30 percent in real terms from its peak in 1985. If there is an exchange rate effect on rates of return, it should be particularly visible in foreign-controlled wholesaling companies because they import proportionately much more than manufacturing and other companies.

Any relationship between the price of the dollar and foreign-controlled companies' rates of return need not necessarily reflect "pricing to market," or the attempt to maintain long-term market share by absorbing higher costs. Even in a conventional model, an increase in costs will reduce rates of return if the importer has made investments on the expectation of lower costs and greater demand by ultimate consumers. There may also be a very short run exchange rate effect to the extent that importers have trade credit extended to them by exporters denominated in foreign currency. In any case, the exchange rate effect should not last indefinitely, because in the long run the importer's capital should adjust to any new, permanently lower price of the dollar. Still, these short-run effects may be important for an extended period of time.

We attempt to identify any trend or exchange rate effects in a pooled regres-

10. As we will discuss more fully in dealing with the distribution of returns, there may be no correlation between purchases and profitability, because the intrinsically more profitable companies have more leeway in shifting profits from the United States.

11. Lichtenberg and Siegel (1987) found that total factor productivity in manufacturing plants tended to gradually improve after a change in ownership.

sion for 1980 through 1987. We interact foreign manufacturing and foreign wholesaling dummies in turn with a time trend and with an index of the real value of the dollar published by the Federal Reserve Board. The exchange rate and trend variables each take on a single value in all observations in a given year. As always, domestic companies are included in the pooled regression. A separate dummy variable for each year is also included to reflect changes in business conditions and tax provisions.

Table 7.8 presents regression results based on the panel. It indicates that the real price of the dollar has a highly significant effect on foreign wholesalers' taxable income. Their profits go up when the real value of the dollar increases. The impact is also large quantitatively. For example, the Federal Reserve Board index for the real value of the dollar went from 132.0 in 1985 (and 128.5 in 1984) to 90.6 in 1987, implying a decline of 4.7 percentage points in foreign wholesalers' taxable income to asset ratio. The exchange rate coefficient for foreign-controlled manufacturers is also positive, but it is predictably much smaller than the wholesale coefficient and is statistically insignificant.

The interaction of the time trend with the foreign manufacturing dummy indicates a highly significant positive-trend effect for foreign-controlled manufacturers. There is no comparable trend for U.S.-controlled companies over the period. (The foreign wholesaling trend coefficient is negative but statistically insignificant and smaller in magnitude). The improving foreign manufacturing return over time is also quantitatively large, with the taxable income to asset ratio increasing by .68 percentage points each year. Thus, at the beginning of the period in 1980, the foreign-domestic differential for manufacturing companies in the panel was very large, but it declined substantially from 1980 to 1987.

These exchange rate and trend effects are also clearly visible if each year in the panel is looked at separately. The negative differential for foreign manufacturers was about 10 percentage points in 1980 and fell quite consistently until it was about 3.5 percentage points in 1987. Foreign wholesalers in the panel had a *positive* 6.5 percentage point differential in 1984 (the peak in the dollar being in early 1985) and moved to a negative differential of about 3 percentage points in 1987.

How much should the exchange rate and trend effects evident in table 7.8 change our view of the foreign differential in 1987? First consider the exchange rate. The extent to which foreign wholesalers' 1987 profitability is distorted by exchange rates depends on the expected long-run exchange rate on which the foreign importers based their investment decisions. Surely it was not the extremely high value of the dollar in 1984 and early 1985. If we use the average real value of the dollar from 1980 through 1989 as a more realistic norm, the coefficient in table 7.8 suggests that foreign wholesalers' real return in 1987 was 1.6 percentage points less than the long-run average. Because foreign wholesalers account for 17.5 percent of total nonfinancial foreign-

Table 7.8   **Exchange Rate and Trend Effects in Taxable Income over Assets Regression (1980–1987 panel)***

Independent Variable	Coefficient
Foreign × Manufacturing	− .063
	(− 1.93)
Foreign × Wholesale	− .063
	(− 1.64)
Foreign manufacturing × Trend	.0068
	(3.33)
Foreign wholesale × Trend	− .0035
	(− 1.47)
Foreign manufacturing × Exchange rate	.00026
	(.88)
Foreign wholesale × Exchange rate	.00113
	(3.25)
Foreign	− .0249
	(− 2.88)
Debt-asset ratio	− .189
	(− 53.4)
R^2 adjusted	.24

*Year, age, and basic industry dummies not displayed; t-values in parentheses.

controlled assets, the overall 1987 foreign return would be .28 percentage points higher under "normal" circumstances. In terms of our sample, foreign wholesalers account for 24.4 percent of the foreign observations, so the estimated foreign differential in the regressions would be .38 percentage points smaller under normal circumstances.

Let us now turn to the quantitative significance of the trend effect. The improving profits of foreign-controlled manufacturers in the panel suggest that the 1987 differential may be distorted by the presence of recent entrants in the form of start-ups or acquisitions. The precise significance of the improving profitability of foreign manufacturing companies over time in explaining the overall 1987 differential is a difficult issue. A company would be willing to take an initial lower return if it can expect to see its rate of return increase steadily in the future. But how long can this profitability improvement be expected to continue? Also, where is the typical 1987 foreign manufacturing company in its growth process? Some long-established companies should have returns above comparable domestic companies.

One way we attempt to evaluate the approximate significance of the manufacturing trend effect is to start with hypothetical domestic and foreign investments and construct the different time paths of taxable income. The domestic company is assumed to have a constant real return of 10 percent on total assets. After deducting interest payments based on a debt-asset ratio of .6 and a 10 percent interest rate, its taxable income to asset ratio is .04, close to the mean in the 1987 cross section. Taking the present value of the respective income streams, we find that investors would be indifferent between this constant return and the foreign prototype with an initial 5 percent return on total assets that grows by 6 percentage points per year for twenty years and is constant at that level thereafter. After interest deductions, the foreign investment will initially have negative taxable income.

Next, it is necessary to match the time path of the foreign company's taxable income with the time distribution of foreign investment. The Department of Commerce data on acquisitions and start-ups, available since 1979, can be used to calculate the distribution of 1979–87 vintages. Data on the stock of foreign direct investment at the end of 1978 and 1987 suggest that about one-third of 1987 foreign-controlled assets were in foreign hands at the beginning of 1979. If we assume that this pre-1979 investment has a mean vintage of fifteen years, we find that the average foreign taxable income to asset ratio was .030 in 1987, compared to .04 for domestic companies. These estimates do not seem very sensitive to the assumptions made.

Another way of gauging the significance of the manufacturing maturation effect is using the regression equation in table 7.8 to calculate the 1987 taxable income to asset ratio of foreign manufacturing companies, including the adjustment for the exchange rate. That yields a domestic-foreign differential in 1987 of − .013, or about 1.3 percentage point less than had remained in the 1987 cross section after the age, debt, and intangible asset variables were added. Thus, both methods of evaluating the manufacturing trend seem to yield approximately the same 1 percentage point difference.

Manufacturing companies account for 63 percent of total nonfinancial foreign-controlled assets and for 47 percent of the companies in the 1987 cross section. A manufacturing return 1.0 percentage point higher would, therefore, reduce the domestic-foreign differential by .5 of .6 percentage points.

In summary, it appears that the exchange rate and growth effects discussed in this section can explain about 1.0 percentage point of the 1987 domestic-foreign difference in the ratio of taxable income to assets. When this is combined with the amount of the differential explained by the age, debt, and other variables in section 7.2, approximately one-half of the initial differential remains.

7.4   Distribution of the Ratio of Taxable Income to Assets—Extreme Losses or Concentration around Zero

The distribution of foreign-controlled companies' taxable income can provide evidence on how likely it is that manipulation of income is taking place. Persistent large losses in relation to assets or sales would not suggest (very successful) tax planning, because the foreign company could lower its worldwide tax bill by shifting some of its losses to other jurisdictions. If foreign companies' low average profitability were due to a relatively small number with extreme losses while the remainder resembled domestically controlled companies, it would be difficult to claim that foreign companies are engaging in widespread income shifting.

On the other hand, what distribution would be consistent with earnings shifting? First, the value of shifting large profits to low-tax locations and the value of shifting large losses to other high-tax locations would lead one to expect a concentration of companies around zero taxable income (in relation to assets). If shifting were costless, all companies would be at exactly zero taxable income at all times. In the general case, bookkeeping costs, potential penalties, and legal scruples prevent perfect shifting, but a concentration near zero would still be the expected pattern. In particular, if there is widespread income shifting, there would be a large disparity at the very high profitability part of the distribution. Companies with intrinsic high profitability could shift substantial profits from the United States and still leave income large enough not to attract the suspicion of tax auditors. It is presumably difficult for tax administrators to attack "normal" or average profitability levels.[12]

7.4.1 Description of the Distribution

Table 7.9 shows the 1987 distribution of the ratio of taxable income to total assets for foreign-controlled and domestic companies. The three components of table 7.9 apply, respectively, to all nonfinancial companies in the 1987 cross section, all wholesaling and manufacturing companies, and all nonfinancial companies with assets in excess of $250 million. In each case, data in the table reveal a very clear concentration of foreign companies around zero. For the most comprehensive group in the first two columns of the table (displayed in figure 7.1), about 37 percent of the foreign companies are in the interval from $-.025$ to $+.025$. In contrast, the domestic distribution not only has a higher mean but is much flatter in the central range. Furthermore, the frequency of very profitable companies, with r_t in excess of .20, is three times greater for domestic companies than for foreign ones. In contrast, the difference in the frequency of extreme losses is not very large, with 3.4 percent of the foreign companies versus 2.0 percent of the domestic ones having r_t less than $-.15$.

If anything, the remaining columns of table 7.9 strengthen this picture of foreign taxable income concentrated around zero. In the case of manufacturing and wholesaling companies (which account for more than 70 percent of the foreign observations), the foreign distribution remains about the same while the domestic distribution is flatter. The discrepancy in the high profitability range is even greater. In the last two columns, which restrict the analysis to only the companies with total assets in excess of $250 million, the concentration of foreign companies around zero is even more evident, with

---

12. Shifting large profits out of the United States may be easier than eliminating losses. In the latter case, the company may already have worldwide losses. The incentive to shift losses may be reduced because of their value as carryforwards or carrybacks. It may also be easier to justify charges for services by the parent of the affiliate than the reverse.

Table 7.9   **Distribution of Taxable Income over Assets for Foreign and Domestic Companies (1987 cross section)**

Taxable Income/Assets	All Nonfinancial Companies		Manufacturing and Wholesale Only		All Nonfinancial > $250 Million	
	Foreign	Domestic	Foreign	Domestic	Foreign	Domestic
≤ − .15	.034	.02	.030	.018	.013	.012
> −0.15 to − .10	.0445	.025	.040	.022	.022	.017
> − .10 to − .075	.029	.025	.028	.016	.018	.012
> − .075 to − .05	.055	.040	.044	.032	.045	.033
> − .05 to − .025	.098	.068	.082	.062	.071	.057
> − .025 to 0	.185	.116	.187	.104	.232	.118
> 0 to .025	.183	.149	.185	.139	.223	.178
> .025 to .05	.122	.144	.143	.133	.129	.175
> .05 to .075	.087	.120	.089	.124	.080	.143
> .075 to .10	.058	.080	.061	.086	.058	.077
> .10 to .15	.053	.106	.061	.133	.067	.091
> .15 to .20	.036	.054	.033	.067	.022	.043
> .20	.015	.048	.016	.061	.018	.046

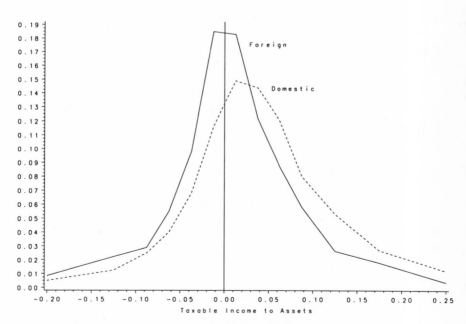

Fig. 7.1   Distributions of the ratio of taxable income to assets

more than 45 percent in the $-.025$ to $+.025$ interval, and the frequency of foreign and domestic companies with extreme losses is virtually identical.[13]

The more concentrated nature of the foreign distribution is confirmed by statistical tests. For companies with assets in excess of $250 million, the standard deviation of foreign-controlled companies' taxable income to asset ratio is .070, compared to .095 for domestic companies. Given the number of companies in each group (223 and 1,383), the difference is highly significant using a standard F-test. When various nonparametric tests for the difference in two distributions are applied, such as the Wilcoxon rank-sum test, the scores are always highly significant.

Is the concentration of foreign-controlled companies around zero taxable income a fortuitous outcome in a single year, 1987, or is it apparent in other years as well? The 1980–87 panel can be used to answer this question. The left part of table 7.10 gives the distribution of r_t in the panel with each year counting as a separate observation. (Broader income categories are used because of the relative sparseness of the companies in the panel). The concentration of foreign companies around zero is virtually identical to the 1987 cross section, which is remarkable in view of the large changes in tax laws and economic conditions over this period. As would be expected, averaging over the eight years concentrates both foreign and domestic companies around their means, but the difference in the distributions seems, if anything, more striking.

7.4.2   Persistence near Zero

If a significant number of foreign companies make an effort to remain close to zero taxable income, their behavior over time can also be expected to differ from domestic companies. They would be more likely to persist in the area around zero. Also, foreign companies finding themselves above the region near zero might be expected to reduce their taxable income in succeeding periods.

Table 7.11 shows that this behavior over time that would be consistent with income management seems to take place. The table gives the probit results for the probability that a company will be in a given profit interval *given* its position in the previous year, after controlling for industry, age, and year effects. The lagged profit range dummies are interacted with the foreign dummy to see if foreign-controlled companies behave differently from domestic ones.

Of particular interest are firms whose returns center around zero. The third column of table 7.11 gives the coefficients for the probability of being in the $-.025$ to $.025$ interval. The coefficient of the interaction of the foreign dummy with the variable indicating presence in the central interval in the previous year is positive, large, and highly significant. In other words, foreign

---

13. In the less than $-.15$ category, average foreign profitability exceeds domestic profitability. The aggregate differential is therefore not due to extreme foreign losses.

Table 7.10 **Taxable Income Distribution from 1980–87 Panel**

Taxable Income/ Assets Ratio	Each Year as a Single Observation		Average from 1980 to 1987	
	Foreign	Domestic	Foreign	Domestic
≤ − .075	.104	.052	.068	.048
> − .075 to − .025	.157	.075	.068	.051
> − .025 to + .025	.375	.242	.475	.249
> − .025 to .075	.149	.270	.112	.336
> .075 to .15	.115	.208	.103	.202
> .15	.101	.152	.075	.114

Table 7.11 **Probit Results for Probability of Being in a Given Income-Assets Interval (1980–1987 Panel)***

Position in Previous Year	Prob. ≤ − .075	Prob. > − .075 to − .025	Prob. > − .025 to .025	Prob. > .025 to .075	Prob. > .075 to .15	Prob. > .15
> − .075 to − .025	− .586	.061	.281	.326	.281	− .117
	(− 7.41)	(.75)	(3.45)	(3.36)	(2.31)	(− .72)
> − .025 to .025	− 1.472	− .442	.356	.586	.345	.241
	(− 19.60)	(− 6.31)	(11.95)	(6.96)	(2.95)	(1.75)
> .025 to .075	− 1.872	− .918	.088	1.29	.854	.064
	(21.77)	(− 11.92)	(1.25)	(15.54)	(7.55)	(.49)
> .075 to .15	− 1.941	− 1.231	− .587	.644	1.767	.876
	(− 20.64)	(− 13.99)	(− 7.62)	(7.58)	(15.66)	(7.01)
> .15	− 2.124	− 1.571	− 1.11	− .260	1.075	2.38
	(18.21)	(13.53)	(11.58)	(− 2.71)	(9.27)	(18.96)
≤ − .075 × Foreign	− .032	.307	− .230	− .262	− .111	− .351
	(− .21)	(1.93)	(− 1.25)	(− 1.05)	(− .35)	(− .86)
> − .075 to − .025 × Foreign	− .132	.289	− .136	− .173	− .164	− .043
	(− .93)	(2.27)	(− 1.04)	(− 1.08)	(− .75)	(− .16)
> − .025 to .025 × Foreign	− .031	− .090	.226	− .195	− .269	− 4.90
	(.22)	(− .83)	(3.19)	(− 2.03)	(− 1.78)	(− .00)
> .025 to .075 × Foreign	.534	.135	.227	− .495	.237	− .005
	(2.62)	(.67)	(1.69)	(− 3.61)	(1.60)	(− .02)
> .075 to .15 × Foreign	.325	− .050	.232	− .151	− .064	.136
	(1.25)	(− .16)	(1.29)	(− .91)	(− .44)	(.81)
> .15 × Foreign	.105	.023	− .222	.302	− .076	.068
	(.26)	(.06)	(− .71)	(1.44)	(− .44)	(.43)

*Industry, year, and age dummies not displayed; *t*-ratios in parentheses.

companies are much more likely to persist in the − .025 to .025 area. Furthermore, the fourth column, giving the probability of being in the interval just above (.025 to .075), indicates that foreign companies are much *less* likely to persist there than domestic companies. (They are also less likely to move into this interval from the central region.) some of the foreign-controlled companies leaving the .025 to .075 interval move up, but more move to lower profitability levels, including the central area. Particularly notable is the fact, as shown in column 1, that foreign companies in the .025 to .075 interval are much more likely to move down to the lowest profitability category, below − .075, than domestic companies.

The probit coefficients can be used to illustrate the quantitative difference between foreign and domestic firms. For example, the probability that a manufacturing company in 1987 with a date of incorporation five to ten years earlier will persist in the − .025 to .025 range is .10 (or 22 percent) greater if it is foreign. If the company had been in the .025 to .075 interval, the probability of its remaining there is .19 (or 38 percent) lower if it is foreign.

The first and sixth columns of table 7.11 indicate that foreign and domestic companies are about equally likely to persist at the extremes of profitability, below − .075 and above .15. Foreign companies are much more likely to persist in the − .075 to − .025 interval, which generally seems a relatively temporary state for all companies.

7.4.3   Relationship to Previous Results

It appears appropriate at this point to attempt to integrate the results in this section with the earlier ones, or at least to resolve any apparent contradictions. For example, the previous section indicated that exchange rates were significant in explaining the profitability of foreign wholesalers. Foreign manufacturers were shown to have rising profitability over time. Are the persistence results in table 7.11 affected by the inclusion of these exchange rate and trend variables? The major conclusions are not altered. The strong persistence of foreign companies near zero remains, and the exchange rate and trend variables are insignificant for this central state. Similarly, the nonpersistence of foreign companies in the interval just above zero is also essentially unaffected, but the trend is almost significant in causing foreign manufacturing companies to be more likely to be in this state. Furthermore, the exchange rate and trend variables, for wholesalers and manufacturers, respectively, are also significant in some of the probits for the other states. For example, the exchange rate is significant in reducing the probability that foreign wholesalers will be in the lowest profitability interval. Also, the trend significantly increases the probability that foreign manufacturers will be in the interval from .075 to .15.

Is the distribution of profitability distorted by the asset revaluation effects discussed in section 7.2? One way of judging this is by looking only at companies incorporated in the past five years. Although the mean return for domestic companies decreases, the large difference between the foreign and domestic distributions is still notable. The foreign distribution remains much more concentrated in the − .025 and .025 interval. The foreign and domestic distributions are very similar at the low end up to − .025, when the foreign distribution jumps up sharply and then falls rapidly above .025. In contrast, the domestic distribution is much flatter in the region above − .025. Our interpreting the difference in distributions as suggesting income shifting is therefore not contradicted by the earlier results.

It may also be of interest to see how the results in section 7.2 are affected if the 1987 cross section is limited only to companies with positive taxable income. Some might argue that companies that show losses must actually be losing money, because they do not have any incentive to reduce taxable income below zero. (Because of loss carryovers and prospective audits, this is not strictly correct.) When only companies with positive income are included, the foreign differential reported in section 7.2 remains significant but is somewhat reduced in magnitude. For example, the 2.59 percent differential for r_t in the last column of table 7.2 becomes 1.96 percent with a t-value of almost four. The differential in sales margins is reduced somewhat more but remains highly significant. (The r_t and the operating income to sales margin differentials, in fact, become virtually identical.) The significance of some of the other variables changes. For example, the age dummies are much smaller and largely insignificant in the r_t regression, while purchases become much more significant in the sales margins regressions.

To summarize this section, both the distribution of r_t in 1987 and its changes over time revealed by the 1980–87 panel are consistent with the pattern expected if income shifting by foreign companies is prevalent. Foreign companies tend to concentrate near a zero ratio of taxable income to assets and persist there. The low average taxable income of foreign-controlled companies does not seem to be attributable to any large extent to the greater frequency of extreme losses. On the other hand, there is a very large domestic-foreign discrepancy in the frequency of highly profitable companies.

7.5 Affiliate Taxable Income and the Characteristics of the Parent Company

Financial information on the foreign parent company may provide insight on the financial incentives of the affiliate as well as on its ability to manipulate income. For example, if the affiliate is small relative to the parent, it may be more likely that the affiliate is able to incur losses for a long time before becoming successful. The small relative size of the affiliate may also indicate that it is at an early stage in its growth process. Other aspects of the parent's activities may also be relevant. Information on the parent's U.S. acquisition activity would indicate whether the subsidiary is more likely to have been a start-up rather than the result of an acquisition. In addition, the presence of an affiliate in a tax haven may enhance the parent's ability to shift income from the U.S. to low-tax jurisdictions.

The relationship between the parent's (book) income and the affiliate's taxable income is also of interest. Admittedly, taxable income and book income may differ substantially. Furthermore, accounting standards vary across countries, particularly with respect to affiliates' inclusion in the parent's "consolidated" financial reports. Still, common products and management would lead one to expect a positive correlation between parent and subsidiary profitability. Further, this correlation could increase as the affiliate becomes large relative to the parent, for two reasons: first, the affiliate becomes a larger component of the parent's worldwide profit; second, it is more likely to be included in the parent's consolidated financial reports.

To investigate these issues, we linked a subsample of the foreign-controlled companies in the 1987 cross section with financial information on their controlling parent. *Who Owns Whom* and the *International Directory of Corporate Affiliations* were used to identify the owners of the corporations filing U.S. tax returns. On this basis, approximately 400 parent firms were identified. The sample size was reduced to 291 because some did not have financial information listed in *Moody's International.*

Table 7.12 gives regression results for the U.S. subsidiaries' taxable income to asset ratio when variables based on the parent's characteristics are included as explanatory variables. The size variable is the ratio of the affiliate's total sales to the parent's. The haven variable is a dummy set equal to one if *Moody's* lists a subsidiary in a tax haven. The acquisition data are derived from *Mergers and Acquisitions* magazine and include acquisitions by the parent from 1974 through 1987. (These acquisition data are described more fully in section 7.6.) The acquisitions variable is the ratio of the reported total value of acquisitions by the parent to the total assets of the subsidiary. Profit rate is the ratio of the parent's pretax net income to its total assets. The profit-size variable is the interaction of the parent profit rate with the size variable.

The only new variables that are consistently significant are the ones based on the parent's profit rate. In the first column of table 7.12, the parent's profit rate has a significant positive coefficient. But when the profit rate to size variable is introduced in the second regression, the simple profit rate is no longer significant. As expected, the affiliate's profitability is more closely related to the parent's when the affiliate accounts for a large share of the parent's worldwide operation. The coefficient for the profit-size variable tends to be close to one. Furthermore, when the leverage ratio is not included as a variable, the constant term in the regressions is small and not very significant. Thus, it appears that when the affiliate is so large that it virtually represents the parent's entire worldwide operation, the affiliate's taxable income to asset ratio tends to approximate the parent's profit rate. But it is also necessary to consider the negative coefficient on the relative size variable. A negative coefficient would be expected in this case because there must be an offset to the increasing weight of the parent's profit rate as the affiliate's size increases relative to the parent.[14] But the negative coefficient is much larger than expected. Accordingly, the coefficients indicate that if the affiliate constitutes the parent's entire

---

14. In other words, the relationship is of the form $r_A = r_p.S + (1 - S)r$, where r_A is the affiliate profit rate, r_p is the parent's, S is relative size, and r is some average affiliate profitability.

Table 7.12   **Affiliate Taxable Income to Assets and Parent Characteristics (1987 parent-affiliate link)***

Constant	.054	.085	.074	.011	.002
	(2.00)	(3.08)	(2.95)	(.52)	(.10)
Subsidiary sales/parent	.036	−.084	−.061	−.079	
sales	(1.80)	(−2.20)	(−2.06)	(−2.61)	
Haven	.001	.000	−.000	−.002	−.002
	(.12)	(.19)	(.10)	(−.30)	(−.20)
Acquisitions/affiliate	.022	.037	.033	.028	.026
assets	(1.06)	(1.82)	(1.66)	(1.35)	(1.23)
Parent pretax	.250	−.132			
income/assets	(2.78)	(−.97)			
Size × Parent profit		1.51	1.21	1.34	.81
rate		(3.66)	(4.54)	(4.91)	(4.39)
Affiliate debt-asset	−.104	−.106	−.103		
ratio	(−4.10)	(−4.30)	(−4.21)		
R^2 adjusted	.113	.156	.156	.098	.077

*Age and industry dummies not displayed; t = values in parentheses.

operation, its profitability only approximates the parent's when the parent is highly profitable. Also, as indicated by the .25 coefficient for the parent's profit rate in the first column, the relationship between parent and affiliate profitability seems in general much weaker.

Turning to the other independent variables in table 7.12, the affiliate's size relative to the parent is of borderline significance and positive in column 1, when the sign is not affected by the presence of the size to profit rate variable. The positive sign is consistent with some type of start-up effect. (The parent's absolute size is never close to being significant, which casts doubt on any cost of capital or long horizon interpretation.) The value-of-acquisitions variable is sometimes close to being significant, although the coefficient is positive and not easy to interpret. It may suggest that acquisitions are more profitable than start-ups or that they become profitable more quickly than start-ups. Finally, the tax haven coefficient is virtually zero in all specifications. This may reflect a problem in methodology alluded to in earlier sections. It is possible that only the most profitable firms incur the costs of establishing tax haven affiliates, if the presence of supernormal profits is required to justify the haven expenditure. If these highly profitable foreign firms shifted income until their profit rates were identical with less profitable foreign subsidiaries in the United States, no effect would be noted on the tax haven variable, even though the haven was responsible for the subsidiaries' reduction in U.S. taxable income.

Even though accounting rules are not standardized across countries, it is of interest to compare the profitability of foreign parents with similar companies based in the United States. Using the data from *Moody's International,* we find that the average parent's pretax profit rate is 8.49 percent (and 4.99 after provision for tax). This compares with 5.97 percent pretax for the average

U.S. nonfinancial company in the 1987 Compustat. To the extent that U.S. and foreign accounting data are comparable, foreign parents seem *on the average* to be more profitable than the average U.S. company. This superior profitability does not suggest a lower required return on capital, although the role of the cost of capital is clouded by the fact that we would expect multinational companies to have better economic prospects.

Further, even in view of the difference between the taxable and book income concepts, the discrepancy appears very large between the parents' average 8.49 pretax profit rate and the 2.28 percent taxable income rate reported on the average by their subsidiaries. In contrast, the average 5.97 percent profit rate for domestic nonfinancial companies in Compustat is only modestly greater than the 4.07 percent taxable income rate in the 1987 sample. Among major investing countries, the largest discrepancy between parent and affiliate profitability is in companies from the United Kingdom. Affiliates from Japan had low relative returns before adjusting for leverage, but their parents also were relatively unprofitable compared to parents from other countries; the discrepancy between parent and affiliate returns was therefore close to the average.

7.6   Profitability of Companies prior to Foreign Ownership

Acquisition of U.S. assets has prevailed as the primary means of foreign entry into U.S. business. Foreign activity in 1987 proved no exception. According to Commerce Department data, new foreign operations in 1987 comprised 543 acquisitions and 435 establishments. Despite the approximate numerical equality of these two methods, acquisitions accounted for 84.2 percent of the $40.4 billion spent on foreign entry into the United States. In light of the prominence of foreign merger activity, it seems important to see whether characteristics of the acquired firms themselves are responsible for the relatively low foreign earnings.

To assess the possibility that the low profitability of foreign-controlled companies is caused by the low profitability of the U.S. targets they acquired, we turn to a sample of 118 foreign acquisitions that were completed between the years 1980 and 1987.[15] The regressions in table 7.13 involve not only those U.S. firms that were subject to foreign takeover but also U.S. firms from the Compustat industrial file. In order to replicate the general regression form presented in earlier sections of this paper, we use the ratio of book income to total assets as the dependent variable in the first two columns of table 7.13. The foreign target dummy is set at a value of one for U.S. companies in the year prior to being acquired by a foreign owner. The results indicate that for-

15. This sample of foreign mergers is a subset of those analyzed in an event study by Swenson (1991). The larger sample includes all foreign acquisitions that occurred between 1974 and 1987 and were listed in the quarterly rosters of the publication *Mergers and Acquisitions* as well as having Compustat information on the financial characteristics of the target.

Table 7.13   **Profitability and Growth of U.S. Companies prior to Foreign Ownership***

	Dependent Variable			
	Book Income/ Assets	Book Income/ Assets	4-Year Sales Growth	4-Year Asset Growth
Constant	.050	.050	0.402	0.485
	(19.69)	(16.57)	(20.25)	(24.54)
Foreign target dummy	− .0033	− .0040	0.25	0.071
(yes = 1)	(− 0.48)	(− 0.70)	(0.37)	(1.45)
Food		.0066		
		(1.67)		
Chemical		.0050		
		(1.58)		
Electronics		.005		
		(0.130)		
Year dummies	Yes	Yes	Yes	Yes
R² adjusted	0.007	0.012	0.010	0.018

**t*-values in parentheses.

eign targets were, on average, less profitable than comparable U.S. companies but that the difference is small and not statistically significant. Hence, the low profitability of foreign-controlled companies does not seem to be attributable to the low quality of the assets acquired. The second regression includes dummy variables for each year, as well as for selected industries. Once again, there is no indication that foreign firms purchase abnormally low profit firms.

The fact that foreign-controlled companies have a very low ratio of taxable income to sales even though they earned normal profits prior to being acquired suggests several possibilities. Foreign owners may have made large investments after acquiring their U.S. companies, which depresses their earnings in the initial years of operation, or foreign firms may have been willing to take lower profits in the short run while operations were modified. Alternatively, the low profitability subsequent to takeover may arise from the diversion of profits to foreign locations.

Rates of return are not the only dimension on which the performance of targets of foreign acquisition may deviate from the performance of domestic companies. As indicators of differences in the time path of firm activity, columns 3 and 4 of table 7.13 consider the four-year growth rates of sales and assets. Again the sample includes industrial firms from the Compustat files, and the foreign target dummy variable indicates those U.S. firms that become the target of a foreign acquisition in the subsequent year. The results show that prior to their acquisition, foreign targets were growing somewhat faster than comparable U.S. companies. In the case of asset growth, the foreign target coefficient is of borderline statistical significance. This is consistent with the finding in Swenson (1991) that foreign targets tended to have higher price-earnings ratios than did the targets of domestic acquisition, as this is an indicator that future earnings are expected to grow.

This evidence on the growth of firms targeted for foreign acquisition may give some confirmation to the trend effect described in section 7.3. But the trend or maturation effect may reflect other factors as well. As suggested above, foreign owners may, after they acquire a company, make large initial investments in order to better utilize the assets. In addition, the 1980–87 cross-section data involve foreign operations that started prior to 1980. To the extent that foreign investment activity before 1980 may have involved a larger share of start-ups than was true in the 1980s, the acquisition data will not provide a complete picture.

7.7 Summary and Conclusions

Aggregate statistics indicate that foreign-controlled companies in the United States report strikingly less taxable income than do their domestically controlled counterparts. Although many possible explanations have been proposed, their validity has not been established in previous work. We have examined firm-level data to evaluate the relative merit of these explanations.

Of the initial foreign-domestic differential, we find that about 50 percent is definitely attributable to the special characteristics of foreign-controlled companies and not to transfer pricing. First, the revaluation of the book value of assets following acquisitions can distort the comparison of the ratio of taxable income to assets. Second, a maturation process is indicated by the fact that profitability of foreign-controlled manufacturing companies rises over time relative to comparable domestically controlled firms. Foreign investors may, therefore, accept lower initial returns in exchange for high long-run profits. Third, the taxable income of foreign-controlled wholesale companies relative to their domestically controlled counterparts is found to rise as the real value of the dollar increases relative to other currencies. In particular, the large drop in the dollar since 1985 has depressed recent returns of foreign investors in wholesaling.

Other commonly suggested reasons for the foreign-domestic differential have less explanatory power. First, we find that debt and earnings stripping do not appear to be major reasons for the low taxable income of foreign-controlled companies. In general, the debt-asset ratio of foreign-controlled companies is not notably different from that of domestically controlled companies, and their interest expense for a given level of debt is significantly lower. Although foreign-controlled companies have an apparent preference for operations with rising profit profiles, there is not much evidence that any advantage in the cost of equity capital explains the foreign income differential. Neither parent size nor whether a parent is from a capital-exporting country is important. Furthermore, foreign parents seem in general to be more profitable than the typical U.S. company.[16] Additionally, we find that the evidence does not support the hypothesis that foreign firms tend to acquire relatively unprofitable firms. Low profitability is a characteristic of foreign-controlled companies irrespective of their country or origin. It is not restricted to companies based in only a few countries or operating in a narrow range of industries.

The distribution of foreign rates of return between 1980 and 1987, however, does provide indirect evidence that income shifting is partially responsible for the low rate of return of foreign firms. Not only were foreign firms heavily concentrated around a zero rate of return but they also tended to persist in the zero region, and they were more likely to transit back to the zero region from a higher profit range. This phenomenon seems remarkable when placed in the context of ongoing tax reforms, economic cycles, and large exchange rate fluctuations and seems indicative of foreign company efforts to reduce U.S. taxable income through earnings manipulation. While the degree of transfer pricing distortions is perhaps smaller than might be feared, income shifting seems to be at least partially responsible for the remaining gap in taxable income.

References

Graham, Edward M., and Paul R. Krugman. 1989. *Foreign direct investment in the United States*. Washington, D.C.: Institute for International Economics.

Lichtenberg, Frank, and Donald Siegel. 1987. Productivity and changes in ownership of manufacturing plants. *Brookings Papers on Economic Activity,* 643–73.

Poterba, James M. 1991. Comparing the cost of capital in the United States and Japan: A survey of methods. *Federal Reserve Bank of New York Quarterly Review* 15:20–32.

Price Waterhouse. 1991. *U.S. international tax policy for a global economy.* Prepared for the National Chamber Foundation.

Swenson, Deborah L. 1991. International mergers and acquisitions in the U.S.: Do foreign bidders pay more? Manuscript.

Comment   Jeffrey K. MacKie-Mason

Foreign-controlled corporations report lower taxable profit rates than do U.S.-controlled corporations. To no one's surprise, there has been suspicion that

---

16. The unexplained differential in the ratio of taxable income to assets is almost 2 percentage points. In view of debt-asset ratios of about two-thirds, this would imply that the cost of equity capital would have to be more than 7 percentage points lower for foreign companies to explain the remaining differential. An equity cost of capital advantage of anything resembling this magnitude seems highly implausible.

Jeffrey K. MacKie-Mason is associate professor of economics and public policy at the University of Michigan and a faculty research fellow of the National Bureau of Economic Research.

foreign corporations are hiding their profits and not paying their "fair share" of taxes. Of course, it may be true that foreign-controlled corporations are simply less profitable. Before this paper by Grubert, Goodspeed, and Swenson, there was precious little evidence to help us distinguish between these (and other) explanations for the well-known difference in profit rates.

What we learn from this paper is that almost every plausible hypothesis finds some support in the data as a partial explanation for the profit rate difference. There is not one simple, dominant story. On the central hypothesis— that the profits are being hidden, presumably through transfer pricing—the authors suggest that as much as 50 percent of the difference in reported profits may be due to transfer pricing.

On the other hand, it may be that none of the profit rate difference is due to transfer pricing. The authors provide no direct evidence either way. Their research design is to use the "residual method." They attempt to explain the puzzle with every story they can, and then, as they write in their introduction, "This still leaves us with a significant difference that we are unable to explain by forces other than transfer pricing."

The extent to which we can believe the importance of transfer pricing depends on how convinced we are that (1) a complete list of alternatives was considered and (2) the full extent of the alternative effects was measured. I find myself convinced that they have done a fine job in identifying many different effects, but there are some plausible effects left untested. Further, several of the stories they do consider are measured with low-power, indirect tests. Thus, I am not very confident in the magnitude of the residual nor whether the extent of transfer pricing is cause for more policy effort than is already under way.

I do not think that it was a mistake for the authors to use the residual method for investigating the importance of transfer pricing. Indeed, they have little choice. By their nature, transfer pricing activities are guarded as private information. Direct measurement is not feasible. This paper represents a careful and thoughtful effort to learn what we can from available data, and we learn much from it. We must be cautious, however, about drawing stronger inferences than the residual method can support.

Even if we do not learn the final word on transfer pricing, there is much to be learned on the importance of the other stories. For the remainder of my comments, I will focus on the measurements the authors do undertake rather than on those they do not.

First, since the paper considers so many explanations, I think it would be helpful to organize them. Each of the stories in the paper falls into one of four categories:

1. "True" economic profits *are* different for foreign- and domestic-controlled firms, because there is some incentive for foreigners to own low-profit firms.

2. *Ex ante,* expected true profits are the same, but shocks lead to different *ex post* realized profit rates.

3. True profits are the same, but some accounting rule difference or anom-aly in the data leads to different reported profits.

4. True profits are the same, but foreign owners arrange to *report* lower profits through transfer pricing and other income-shifting techniques.

1. Foreigners own lower-profit firms. Foreign investors might systematically own lower-profit firms if, for example, they face a lower real cost of capital. The authors test this point only indirectly, by assuming that being a capital exporter proxies for a low cost of capital. Entering the ratio of current account surplus to gross domestic product as an explanatory variable has no explana-tory power in the profit rate regressions, but that is not a very convincing rejection of the possibility of capital cost differences.

The authors note that a disproportionate number of foreign-controlled firms are recent acquisitions. They do not provide an equilibrium explanation for this[1] but observe that the different ownership composition could bias foreign firms toward low reported profit rates. In particular, a step-up in asset basis upon acquisition would increase the denominator of a profit-assets ratio.[2] In-deed, the profit rate differential drops from about 3.6 percent to 2.6 percent when age-of-incorporation dummies are introduced. This result seems quite strong and important.

The apparently important differences between the types of firms that are foreign- and domestic-controlled suggest that carrying the analysis one step further would be useful. The authors use age of incorporation as a proxy for acquisitions (and possibly other sources of real profit differences), but it is possible to identify actual acquisitions by year, using, for example, the data in *Mergerstat*. If the authors did that, they could really sharpen the test of acquisition effects by changing the control group, comparing foreign-acquired firms to only domestic-acquired firms rather than to all domestic-controlled firms. That would help us determine whether the profit rate difference is due to the fact that the firm was acquired or to the fact that foreigners own the firm.

2. Expected profits the same, but foreigners had bad stochastic realizations. The analysis in the first half of the paper is based on a cross section of reported profit rates in one year (1987). Was that just a bad year for foreign owners? The authors use a 1980–87 panel to investigate the possibility that exchange rate movements are the culprit. Exchange rates seem important for wholesal-ers, but the authors do a good job of showing that this effect has a rather small

1. Tax policy seems to provide some incentive for a higher rate of foreign acquisitions, espe-cially in recent years. See Gordon and MacKie-Mason (1991) and Scholes and Wolfson (1988).

2. No typology is perfect: the step-up in basis is really an accounting artifact, or one of my type 2 stories. But it also seems plausible to think that for other reasons the *true* profit rate of recently acquired firms may differ from stable, mature firms.

effect on the aggregate profit rate difference. Of course, a number of other possible sources of unexpectedly bad foreign performance are not tested, such as changes in trade and tax policies.

3. Accounting rule artifacts. With one exception, the authors do not discuss the possibility that the profit rate gap is due simply to differences in reporting rules. (The exception is the step-up in basis upon acquisition, as discussed above.) Perhaps it is obvious that the reporting rules are blind to location of ownership. Even if there were a smoking gun, I am not conversant enough in international tax reporting rules to identify it. One thing I have learned, however, is that the U.S. rules for multinationals are sufficiently complex that I would believe almost anything. If there is a simple reason why the data cannot be explained by accounting rule differences, I would have liked the authors to at least briefly educate the rest of us.

4. True profits are the same, but foreign firms do more income shifting to avoid U.S. taxes. Although the authors have no direct tests that reveal income shifting, they do provide some intriguing evidence to support interpreting the residual as due in part to shifting. They hypothesize that if foreign firms were more aggressively managing their taxable income, we should expect to see their profit rates concentrated around zero. Indeed, this appears to be the case. Unfortunately, the authors choose to present the results with graphs and tables and eschew presentation of any nonparametric tests of the hypothesized differences between the distributions of foreign- and domestic-controlled profit rates, making it difficult to be sure how convincing the differences are. The weight of the evidence clearly is consistent with the presence of some income shifting, however.

The authors test a number of other, mostly lesser explanations that fall into the above four categories. Their exposition of the results is clear and interesting and does not need repeating by me. Instead, I would like to close with three concrete suggestions that I think would increase the overall effectiveness of the paper.

First, I would find it quite helpful to have a better sense of the *target* of analysis. The paper is motivated by table 7.1, which shows a difference in profit rates. Since the authors have income statements and balance sheets, it would be a simple matter to provide a decomposition of the profit differences into revenue and cost elements. Suppose we found that the difference was mostly due to differences in depreciation deductions but not in revenues? Or perhaps that the assets denominator was the culprit, largely due to differences in intangibles rather than in plant and equipment? We could then design tests that were more narrowly focused and powerful. Also, our thinking about alternative explanations would likely be stimulated. Simply saying that profit rates are different is too vague.

Second, I think we might learn quite a bit from attention to a different control sample. Nearly all of the foreign-owned firms are presumably parts of multinationals. Comparing these firms against only domestic-controlled multinationals (rather than all domestic firms) would focus the investigation of the sources of profit differences. Just as with my proposal to compare foreign and domestic *acquired* firms, we could learn about the extent to which it is *foreign* firms that are different, versus *multinational* firms.[3]

Last, the authors could have learned more from another nice, near-experiment available in their data. They investigate the phenomenon of low-profit foreign-acquired firms by studying the profits of the target firms *before* acquisition. In these analyses, in the last part of the paper, they compare foreign acquisition targets to all U.S. corporations and discuss a number of reasons that might explain their finding that targets have insignificantly different profits before but significantly lower profits after the acquisition. The much more informative and relatively clean analysis would be to compare the before-and-after profitability of foreign targets that were later acquired by *domestic* firms. Even a simple two-way analysis of the following sort could be revealing:

Profit Rate

	t	$t - 1$
U.S. acquirer		
Foreign acquirer		

Does the profit rate fall after acquisition, regardless of the acquirer's location? Is the decrease larger for foreign acquisitions? The same simple calculations could be done with a further restriction of the U.S. acquirer group to multinationals, an even more closely comparable control group.

This is a long paper but very rich with informative analysis. At the end, however, we are still left without a strong sense of the importance of transfer pricing. And there is still much that can be learned about the causes of profit rate differences from the data the authors have collected. Nonetheless, my critical remarks should not obscure the fact that this paper provides a number of new and interesting results, and we now know much more than before about the profit rate differences between foreign- and domestic-controlled corporations.

3. In response to my earlier comments, the authors did include a paragraph reporting that their main results continue to hold when the control group is restricted to domestic MNCs; I am glad to see that. However, they do not go beyond affirming their initial analysis. They could take advantage of this natural control group to improve our understanding of the sources of profit rate differences.

References

Gordon, R. H., and J. K. MacKie-Mason. 1991. Effects of the Tax Reform Act of 1986 on corporate financial policy and organizational form. In *Do taxes matter? The impact of the Tax Reform Act of 1986,* ed. J. Slemrod. Cambridge, Mass.: MIT Press.

Scholes, M. S., and M. A. Wolfson. 1988. The effects of changes in tax laws on corporate reorganization activity. Working Paper. Stanford Graduate School of Business.

8   Income Shifting in U.S. Multinational Corporations

David Harris, Randall Morck, Joel Slemrod, and
Bernard Yeung

By their very nature, multinational corporations trade goods, services, financial capital, and intangible assets across national borders within their enterprise. By using artificial transfer prices in these transactions and concentrating debt financing in highly taxed subsidiaries, a multinational can shift taxable income within its group of companies to reduce its overall tax burden and to achieve other objectives, such as bypassing capital controls. From a country-policy perspective, such behavior can affect tax revenues and the level and location of investment and employment. From a firm-policy perspective, questions arise as to the mechanics, costs, benefits, and thus optimality of such behavior.

Surprisingly little evidence on income shifting based on firm-level data is available. In this paper, we present such evidence. We find that U.S. manufacturing firms with subsidiaries in low-tax countries have relatively low U.S. tax payments per dollar of assets or sales. Furthermore, having a subsidiary in a high-tax region is associated with higher U.S. tax payments. These results suggest that U.S. manufacturing companies do engage in this sort of income shifting.

After reviewing the limited existing empirical literature in section 8.1, we

David Harris is a graduate student at the School of Business Administration, University of Michigan. Randall Morck is professor at the Faculty of Business, University of Alberta. Joel Slemrod is Jack D. Sparks Whirlpool Corporation Research Professor of Business Administration and professor of economics at the University of Michigan and a research associate at the National Bureau of Economic Research. Bernard Yeung is professor at the School of Business Administration, University of Michigan.

The authors are grateful for helpful comments by Harry Grubert, Jack Mutti, James Wheeler, Peter Wilson, and seminar participants at the University of Michigan's Workshop on Tax Policy Research, the University of California–Los Angeles, the University of Michigan, l'Université de Montréal, the Northern Finance Association, and the NBER Summer Institute's International Taxation Workshop. The authors also thank the Center for International Business Education at the School of Business Administration, University of Michigan, for providing financial support.

present our empirical framework and data in section 8.2. In section 8.3, we report cross-firm regression results that are consistent with the notion that multinational firms shift income from high-tax locations to the United States and from the United States to low tax locations, thus reducing their overall tax liabilities. In sections 8.4 and 8.5, we discuss statistical and economic issues that might affect our results. In section 8.6, the economic significance of our results is addressed. Section 8.7 concludes the paper.

8.1   Review of the Literature

There is a substantial literature on the extent to which the internal pricing policies of multinationals are influenced by tax factors. Alworth's (1989) review of this literature suggests the importance of tax considerations but also points to the impact of market structure, the nature of product markets, and limitations on profit repatriation.

Considerable anecdotal evidence suggests that tax-motivated income shifting by U.S. multinationals occurs. Wheeler (1988) describes U.S. tax court cases where income was apparently shifted for tax reasons. In one example, G. D. Searle in 1975 had an average return on employed assets of -42.3 percent in the United States and 119 percent in Puerto Rico—a zero effective tax rate jurisdiction. Of course, anecdotal evidence does not establish the economywide prevalence of income shifting.

There have been two recent empirical attempts to uncover systematic evidence of income shifting by examining observable variables that should be affected by it. Grubert and Mutti (1991), using cross-country aggregate data on U.S. multinationals' affiliates, regress two measures of affiliate profitability in 1982 against the host country's statutory corporate income tax rate (or tax holiday rate if one was generally available). They run similar regressions on a measure of the average tax rate: the ratio of foreign taxes paid to book income of U.S.-controlled corporations with positive profits. The growth of the host country's gross domestic product is included as a proxy for economywide pretax profitability.

They find a significant and large negative relationship between either measure of foreign taxes and either measure of foreign affiliate profitability. In other words, firms declare more income in low-tax jurisdictions. This is consistent with income shifting. The magnitude of the estimated effect is noteworthy. In their favored regression, a drop in the statutory tax rate from 40 percent to 20 percent implies an increase in the ratio of after-tax profits to sales from 5.6 percent to 12.6 percent and an increase in the after-tax rate of return on equity from 14.2 percent to 20.7 percent. Clearly, these results imply that a lower tax rate is associated with a higher pretax rate of return and do not simply reflect a smaller slice taken by taxation out of an unchanging level of profitability.

Hines and Rice (1990) also analyze country-level aggregate data from 1982 on U.S. nonbank majority-owned foreign affiliates. They investigate the effect of host-country tax rates[1] on the location of U.S. multinationals' pretax non-financial profits, pretax financial profits (i.e., net interest income), total profits, and factors of production. Using regression analysis, they find a negative relation between all of these variables and host-country average tax rates.

The results in both Grubert and Mutti (1991) and Hines and Rice (1990) are consistent with the hypothesis that the reported income of U.S. multinationals' foreign affiliates tends to appear in countries with low corporate income tax rates. Moreover, Hines and Rice argue that the apparent success of tax haven countries in attracting taxable income is not obviously a bad thing for U.S. welfare. Because the U.S. taxes its resident multinationals on a residual basis, moving the location of their income from a high-tax foreign country to a low-tax foreign country may increase the total taxes paid that are received by the U.S. Treasury. However, to the extent that taxable income migrates from the United States to a foreign country, the U.S. Treasury is a clear loser. In any case, neither Grubert and Mutti nor Hines and Rice directly address the extent of income shifting between the United States and other countries. Both focus on income shifting between foreign affiliates. A more complete picture of income shifting by U.S. multinationals requires an assessment of income shifting to and/or from the U.S. parent. That is the issue we address in this paper.

7.2   Methodology

Our objective is to uncover systematic evidence of income shifting, using firm-level data. Because shifted income is by nature difficult to observe directly, we attempt to predict its impact on observable variables, a methodology not different from that in Grubert and Mutti (1991) or Hines and Rice (1990).

We start with a firm's current U.S. tax, denoted as $T_U = \tau_U R_U$, where τ_U is the U.S. statutory corporate tax rate and R_U is reported U.S. taxable income. For simplicity of exposition, we assume a linear tax function. R_U can be decomposed into

$$R_U = Y_U - Y_{UL} + Y_{HU} ,$$

where Y_U is actual U.S. income, Y_{UL} is income shifted from the United States to subsidiaries in low-tax jurisdictions, and Y_{HU} is income shifted from subsidiaries in high-tax regions to the United States. Total U.S. tax liability, $T_U = \tau_U(Y_U - Y_{UL} + Y_{HU})$, unlike its component parts, is reported by most firms and is therefore readily observable. The relationship between

---

1. They define the average tax rate as the lesser of the benchmark survey tax rate and the statutory rate. For some tax-haven countries where these data are unavailable, they obtain the tax rate from the *Economist*'s *Tax Havens and Their Uses*.

$\tau_U(Y_U - Y_{UL} + Y_{HU})$ and a firm's presence in locations with tax rates different from the U.S. tax rate reveals information about Y_{UL} and Y_{HU}. Hence, we attempt to use regression analyses to uncover the relation between a U.S. firm's U.S. tax payment and the firms' presence in foreign locations with different tax rates.

As a starting point, we assume that the choice of where to operate is exogenous and unrelated to the income shifting decisions with which we are primarily concerned. This is meant as a simplifying assumption, not as a statement about how we think the world works. The empirical implications of it not holding are discussed in sections 8.5 and 8.6.[2] This assumption allows us to treat the location of foreign operations as independent variables in the following regression:

$$\left(\frac{T_U}{S_U}\right)_{ft} = g^H d_{ft}^H + g^L d_{ft}^L + b z_{ft} + \varepsilon_{ft} \, ,$$

where T_U is U.S. tax liability, S_U is a scaling factor; f and t are firm and time subscripts, respectively; d_{ft}^H and d_{ft}^L are vectors of dummy variables indicating firm f's presence in various high-tax and low-tax regions, respectively, in period t; z_{ft} is a vector of control variables; g^H, g^L, and b are vectors of regression coefficients; and ε_{ft} is an error term.

The hypothesis we test is that the elements of g^H are positive, while those of g^L are negative. This hypothesis presumes that operating in a high-tax country induces income shifting *to* the United States and that operating in a low-tax country induces income shifting *from* the United States.

Our sample consists of two hundred U.S. manufacturing firms selected randomly from the SIC 3000 industries of the primary, supplementary, and tertiary industry file listing of Compustat. Compustat data from 1984 through 1988 are supplemented with data from company annual reports.[3]

The dependent variable is the firm's current taxes payable to the federal government net of investment tax credits. It is retrieved from Compustat (item 63) and then verified by cross-checking with annual reports and tax notes.[4]

---

2. Our empirical investigation focuses on the relationship between income shifting and the locations of a firm's foreign affiliates. Investment decisions are based mainly on very long run considerations such as expected future input costs, the availability of infrastructure, nontax government policies, and expected product market growth. There are long lags in formulating and implementing investment plans, and there are also large adjustment costs to altering ongoing investment strategies. Thus, decisions about the location of foreign direct investment are arguably only tangentially related to income shifting opportunities. Our future research is aimed at exploring this issue.

3. Data obtained from annual reports are dated according to the Compustat dating convention, as described in the *Industrial Compustat User's Manual* published by Standard and Poor's Compustat Services, Englewood, CO 80112.

4. Raw Compustat data and cross-checked data generate similar results. Note that current U.S. federal taxes as reported in a company's annual report are an estimate of the actual tax liability made at the time the report is published (usually January). Dworin (1985) finds that this estimate is generally greater than the actual tax payment. The principal causes of this discrepancy are the inclusion of a "cushion" in the financial tax provision for possible audit adjustments and differ-

We drop observations where the firm's current U.S. federal tax liability is zero, because firms in this situation may face different income shifting incentives from those described above.[5] After excluding these cases and observations with missing data, we obtain a sample of 486 firm-years that are quite evenly distributed over the five sample years.

A firm's U.S. income is likely to be roughly proportional to the size of its U.S. operations. We want to explain income shifting, $Y_{HU} - Y_{UL}$, using total U.S. federal taxes, $T_U = \tau_U(Y_U - Y_{UL} + Y_{HU})$. Dividing the latter variable by the size of U.S. operations allows us to interpret variations in the resulting ratio (after controlling for other obvious predictors of U.S. taxable income) as due to income shifting. This procedure also reduces the potential for heteroscedasticity problems. The scaling variables used, total U.S. sales and the total book value of U.S. assets, are obtained directly from financial statements. A company must report a rough geographic breakdown of its sales and assets if foreign sales or assets exceed 10 percent of U.S. sales or assets. If a geographical breakdown is not reported in a given year and the firm has no foreign subsidiaries at that time, its total sales and assets are treated as U.S. sales and assets. If foreign subsidiaries exist but no geographical breakdown of sales and assets is presented, we exclude the observation on the grounds of missing data.

In some specifications, we include seven independent variables to control for differences in firm characteristics that may have direct or indirect effects on a firm's pretax profitability and tax position. The variables are research and development spending, advertising spending, depreciation and amortization, rental expenses, investment tax credits, interest expenses, and number of employees. The last variable is meant to capture wage expenses, which are unavailable in Compustat for over 90 percent of our observations. All the control variables are obtained from Compustat[6] and are worldwide consolidated fig-

---

ences in the extent of consolidation in financial reports versus IRS tax reports. To the extent that the audit cushion is larger for firms that are more aggressive tax minimizers, it should reduce our chances of finding evidence of income shifting. Consolidation for financial reporting is more extensive than for IRS tax reporting. Important affiliates included in the former but not in the latter are foreign affiliates with U.S. income, domestic international sales corporations (DISCs), Puerto Rican corporations, and some financial affiliates such as insurance, investment, and real estate companies. Given our objective, the more extensive consolidation for financial reports is appropriate. Note that provisions for future repatriated income in financial statements are considered deferrals and thus are not included in estimated current tax expenses.

5. In this panel, 68 percent of the firm-years have positive U.S. federal taxes, 13 percent have negative U.S. federal taxes, and 19 percent have zero U.S. federal tax. Our results are similar for the full sample, for the subsample without observations with zero U.S. federal tax, and for the subsample including only observations with positive U.S. federal taxes. For the subsample that includes only observations with negative U.S. federal taxes, the results are similar to those we report but are less significant.

6. These variables are assumed to be zero if the Compustat reports 0.0001 (unavailable observation) or 0.0008 (insignificant observation) and all other financial data are available. The number of employees is considered missing if Compustat reports 0.0001 or 0.0008.

ures.[7] These control variables are scaled by either the firm's worldwide sales or its worldwide assets to match the scaling factor used in the dependent variable.

All of these independent variables have a tax shield effect and should therefore be related to lower U.S. tax liabilities. However, some of them may also capture other effects that increase tax liability. Research and development spending or advertising spending may proxy for the presence of intangible assets that increase the return to foreign direct investment (Morck and Yeung 1991, 1992).

Finally, in certain specifications, we introduce industry dummies based on three-digit standard industrial classification (SIC) codes to control for interindustry differences in profitability and tax burdens.

The independent variables that we focus on are the elements of d_{ft}^H and d_{ft}^L. They are categorical variables indicating a firm's presence in high-tax and low-tax jurisdictions. To operationalize this notion, we divide the non-U.S. world into thirteen regions (for descriptions, see table 8.1 footnotes), which we place in one of five groups according to how readily they can be classified as high- or low-tax jurisdictions:

1. *Regions with a statutory tax rate higher than that of the United States:* Canada, Japan, Australia and New Zealand, and high-tax countries in Western Europe

2. *Regions with a statutory tax rate lower than that of the United States:* low-tax countries in Western Europe, the "Four Dragon" Asian countries, and other noncommunist Asian countries

3. *Extremely low-tax regions:* Ireland and tax havens

4. *Regions affected by capital controls or other political concerns:* South Africa and Latin America

5. *Others:* Africa and OPEC countries

Subsidiaries in communist countries are ignored both because they are very rare and because they are subject to idiosyncratic policies on earnings repatriation.

We determine the multinational structure of each firm in each year, using various issues of the *International Directory of Corporate Affiliations.* The vectors d_{ft}^H and d_{ft}^L consist of ones and zeros indicating the presence or absence of any subsidiaries in the high-tax and low-tax regions, respectively.[8] For example, if a firm has two subsidiaries in Hong Kong, one in Japan, and three

---

7. Geographic breakdowns of these variables are not available.

8. We count only subsidiaries in measuring a firm's presence in overseas locations. Branches and representative offices are not included. For tax purposes, branch income is consolidated with that of U.S. operations. Thus, income shifting among branches is likely much less effective, if not totally ineffective, in reducing a firm's tax burden. The definition of a subsidiary is that in the *International Directory of Corporate Affiliations* (1985/1986): "A chartered business whose shares are owned, in whole or in part, by another company. The level of ownership is generally greater than 50%."

in England; the vectors contain ones in the three columns for Four Dragons, Japan, and high-tax Western Europe and zeros elsewhere.

We use indicator dummies rather than the tax rates themselves, for several reasons. First, as Hines and Rice (1990) point out, calculating a representative tax rate for a country is notoriously difficult.[9] Second, income shifting may be motivated by reasons other than tax minimization, such as risk avoidance, bypassing capital controls, or reducing tariff payments. Moreover, the effect of tax differentials on income shifting depends critically on the regulatory environment. These effects lead to nonuniform relations between tax rate differentials and shifted income and make it difficult if not impossible to devise a manageable empirical approach along these lines. By using carefully designed regional dummies, we can capture a net income shifting effect due to tax minimization and these other factors.

If the amount of income shifting depends on the size of a firm's operations in the various jurisdictions involved, our use of indicator dummies could render our results noisy and therefore less reliable. On the other hand, if income shifting requires only the firm's presence in the various jurisdictions, our specification is preferable. Since a detailed geographic breakdown of the extent of non-U.S. operations is not available in general, the point cannot be resolved here.

In table 8.1 we list the regions, their representative corporate tax rates, and the expected signs of the regression coefficients of the regional dummy variables.[10] The corporate tax rates are reported merely to provide a glimpse of the differences between the tax rates in these regions and the U.S. tax rate. In general, we expect the regression coefficients of the dummies indicating a firm's presence in higher-tax regions to be positive and those indicating a firm's presence in lower-tax regions to be negative.

The extent of income shifting is affected by its cost, holding tax rate differentials constant. Hence, our explanatory variables should include measures of this cost. Income shifting is usually conducted via artificial transfer prices[11]

9. According to Hines and Rice, "No single measure of the corporate income tax rate can accurately capture the precise difference in tax burdens corporations face in different countries. For one thing, the complexity of tax codes (including different provisions for tax deductions, depreciation rules, loss carry forwards and carry backs, and nonstandard income concepts) precludes the possibility of distilling a well-defined tax rate for each country. In addition, a single tax rate cannot capture industry and firm specific tax holidays or other features" (p. 42).

10. We calculate the corporate tax rates using data from *Price Waterhouse Corporate Taxes: A Worldwide Summary* (1984, 1988). For the countries in each region, we collect the corporate tax rate applicable to foreign-owned subsidiaries. The tax rates chosen apply to income arising from the manufacture and sale of goods in the host country. If progressive tax rates are provided, the highest rate is used. If there are dual rates on repatriated and retained earnings, we record the lower rate. State and local income taxes are included in the reported rate, net of federal tax deductions allowable. If more than one state tax rate is provided, a simple average is used. Value-added taxes, tariffs, and withholding taxes on dividends, royalties, and rents are excluded. Also excluded are tax holiday rates and other specialty tax rates.

11. These transfer prices include accounting prices used for intracompany exchanges of goods as well as services from intangibles, tangibles, and financial assets.

Table 8.1   Regions and Their Mean Statutory Corporate Tax Rates

Region	Mean Statutory Corporate Tax Rate[1]		Comparison to the U.S. Rate	Expected Sign[2]
	1984	1988		
Canada	47%	41%	Higher	+
Japan	50	50	Higher	+
Four Dragons[3]	30	26	Lower	−
Rest of Asia	48	49	Higher	− ?[4]
Low-tax Western Europe[5]	31	29	Lower	−
High-tax Western Europe	49	47	Higher	+
Ireland[6]	50	50	Lower	−
Australia/New Zealand	48	47	Higher	+
Latin America	38	39	Lower	?[7]
South Africa	46	50	Higher	+
Africa	43	43	Lower	?[7]
Tax havens[8]	22	21	Lower	−
OPEC	47	47	Lower	?[7]
United States	46	34		

[1]These are average corporate tax rates based on *Price Waterhouse Corporate Taxes: A Worldwide Summary* (1984, 1988). See text footnote 10 for details.

[2]Expected signs of regression on coefficients for dummy variables indicating presence of subsidiaries there.

[3]Hong Kong, South Korea, Singapore, and Taiwan. Tax holidays are available in all except Hong Kong, so statutory rates overstate the tax burden.

[4]India and Pakistan skew the mean upward. Most countries here have lower rates than the United States.

[5]Switzerland, Luxembourg, and Malta. Tax holidays are not factored into the rate reported.

[6]A rate of 0 percent applies if the firm qualifies for a tax holiday.

[7]While the tax differentials for these regions appear to be negative, these regions are well known to have significant political risks or capital controls. Hence, the sign for the regression coefficient of these regions is uncertain.

[8]Tax havens include Andorra, Antigua, Bermuda, Bahamas, Barbados, British Virgin Islands, Cayman Islands, Channel Islands, Cyprus, Gibraltar, Grenada, Kiribati, Liechtenstein, Netherlands Antilles, other Caribbean, St. Kitts–Nevis, St. Vincent, and Vanuatu. Substantial tax holidays are available, so statutory rates greatly overstate the actual tax burden.

that deviate from true economic prices. Caves (1986, ch. 8, 246–47) argues that there are two constraints on such behavior. First, the use of artificial transfer prices and multiple books can lead to internal confusion and suboptimality in a firm's operation. Second, income shifting is constrained by tax collectors' monitoring efforts. While the validity of the former is an empirical issue, the second constraint is undeniable.[12]

In dividing the world into regions, we attempt to control for differences in

12. Wilson (ch. 6 in this volume), in a case study of nine firms with sophisticated tax planning procedures, finds that some firms do use multiple sets of books and that tax collectors' efforts to restrict transfer pricing have been stepped up in recent years.

the cost of income shifting. We bundle together countries that have similar business climates and tax enforcement regimes, as well as similar statutory tax rates. The SIC code dummies introduced to control for interindustry differences in tax burdens may also control, to some extent, for interindustry differences in the cost of income shifting.

Still, substantial differences in income shifting costs might exist within industries. The presence of intangible assets may reduce the cost of income shifting. Intangible assets, by their very nature, do not have readily available arm's-length prices, and therefore the usual regulatory guidelines for establishing transfer prices are not easily enforceable. Furthermore, the prices applied to transferring intangibles can often be set as lump sums (e.g., patent fees) so that no wedge is driven between marginal costs and benefits related to production. Some of our independent variables capture the presence of intangible assets. Research and development spending proxies for the presence of technological expertise, while advertising expenditure proxies for marketing skill.

Debt financing may also facilitate income shifting. Tax deductions relating to interest expenses can be concentrated in highly taxed subsidiaries. Thus, interest expenses may also proxy for a low cost of income shifting.

We therefore investigate the interaction effect of these measures of the cost of income shifting with the location dummies. We expect that indicators of low-cost income shifting should increase the absolute values of the regression coefficients of the regional dummies.

8.3   Empirical Evidence

Table 8.2 contains univariate statistics for the variables described above. The ratio of U.S. federal tax to U.S. assets has a mean of .0314, while the ratio of U.S. federal tax to U.S. sales has a mean of .0231. Both have sizable standard deviations of about 1.5 times their means. Negative values of these variables exist because of tax refunds.

In 50.6 percent of our observations, the firm is multinational, having at least one foreign subsidiary. In 49.8 percent of the observations, there is at least one subsidiary in high-tax European countries—the most popular location for foreign direct investment. Canada is the second-most popular host country: 41.6 percent of the observations record at least one subsidiary there. Following Canada are Latin America (27.8 percent), Japan (26.1 percent) and Australia/New Zealand (24.5 percent). Among the low-tax regions, the Four Dragons are the most popular (19.8 percent), followed by low-tax European countries (15.8 percent), with the noncommunist Asian countries being the least popular (9.3 percent). Ireland (13.0 percent) appears to be more popular than the other tax haven countries (9.1 percent). The least popular location overall for subsidiaries is Africa (2.7 percent).

Table 8.3 reports unweighted average U.S. federal tax liabilities (scaled

Table 8.2   Descriptive Statistics

Variable	Sample Size	Mean	Standard Deviation	Minimum	Maximum
Dependent Variables					
U.S. tax/U.S. assets	475	0.0314	0.0445	−0.1673	0.2799
U.S. tax/U.S. sales	486	0.0231	0.0347	−0.2212	0.1922
Multinational structure dummies					
Multinational dummy	486	0.5062	0.5005	0.0000	1.0000
Canada	486	0.4156	0.4923	0.0000	1.0000
Japan	486	0.2613	0.4398	0.0000	1.0000
Four Dragons	486	0.1975	0.2985	0.0000	1.0000
Asia	486	0.0926	0.2902	0.0000	1.0000
Low-tax Europe	486	0.1584	0.3655	0.0000	1.0000
High-tax Europe	486	0.4979	0.5005	0.0000	1.0000
Ireland	486	0.1296	0.3362	0.0000	1.0000
Australia/New Zealand	486	0.2449	0.4304	0.0000	1.0000
Latin America	486	0.2778	0.4484	0.0000	1.0000
South Africa	486	0.0967	0.2959	0.0000	1.0000
Africa	486	0.0267	0.1615	0.0000	1.0000
OPEC	486	0.0576	0.2333	0.0000	1.0000
Tax havens	486	0.0906	0.2873	0.0000	1.0000
Control variables scaled by worldwide sales					
R&D/sales	486	0.0342	0.0387	0.0000	0.1804
Advertising/sales	486	0.0137	0.0263	0.0000	0.1705
Depreciation/sales	486	0.0382	0.0222	0.0030	0.1372
Employee/sales	480	0.0116	0.0045	0.0027	0.0315
Rent/sales	486	0.0132	0.0116	0.0000	0.0690
ITC/sales*	486	0.0019	0.0035	0.0000	0.0338
Interest expenses/sales	486	0.0182	0.0173	0.0000	0.1256
Control variables scaled by worldwide assets					
R&D/assets	475	0.0381	0.0388	0.0000	0.1659
Advertising/assets	475	0.0193	0.0391	0.0000	0.2949
Depreciation/assets	475	0.0436	0.0188	0.0093	0.1407
Employees/assets	469	0.0146	0.0073	0.0023	0.0625
Rent/assets	475	0.0162	0.0149	0.0000	0.0841
ITC/assets*	475	0.0022	0.0034	0.0000	0.0226
Interest/assets	475	0.0210	0.0175	0.0000	0.1396

Note: The multinational firm indicator and regional dummies are zero or one. Their means are the fraction of firms that are multinational and the fraction of firms that have at least one subsidiary in the indicated region. The countries included in each region are listed in the footnotes to table 8.1.

*ITC = Investment tax credits.

separately by U.S. assets and U.S. sales) for firms grouped by the locations of their subsidiaries. For instance, the first row reports these two values for the firms in our sample with at least one subsidiary in Canada. These first-pass results generally conform to expectations. Compared to the average tax ratios of purely domestic U.S. firms (reported in the last row), the average U.S. tax ratios of firms with subsidiaries in higher-tax locations are higher,

Table 8.3   **Unweighted Average U.S. Federal Tax per Dollar of U.S. Assets and of U.S. Sales, by Location of Foreign Subsidiaries***

Location of Subsidiary	U.S. Taxes U.S. Assets	U.S. Taxes U.S. Sales
Canada	0.03493	0.02271
Japan	0.03658	0.02784
Four Dragons	0.02812	0.01768
Asia	0.02807	0.01894
Low-Tax Europe	0.03733	0.02476
High-Tax Europe	0.03308	0.02392
Ireland	0.02751	0.01756
Australia/New Zealand	0.03204	0.02102
Latin America	0.03502	0.02171
South Africa	0.04574	0.02782
Africa	0.02289	0.01211
OPEC	0.01832	0.01109
Tax havens	0.01278	0.00947
All multinationals†	0.03300	0.02401
Purely domestic firms‡	0.02991	0.02232

*Note that a firm with several subsidiaries may be included in more than one group.
†Overall means for firms with any foreign subsidiary anywhere.
‡Overall means for firms without any foreign subsidiaries.

while those of firms with subsidiaries in lower-tax locations are lower. The average tax ratios of firms with tax haven subsidiaries are by far the lowest. One exception to this pattern is that average tax ratios of firms with subsidiaries in low-tax European countries are higher than those of domestic firms. Note also that the average U.S. tax ratios of firms with South African subsidiaries are higher than those of domestic firms. This suggests income shifting from South Africa to the United States.

Table 8.4 presents our key regression results. In regressions (1) through (4), the dependent variable is U.S. federal taxes paid per dollar of U.S. assets; in (5) through (8), the dependent variable is U.S. federal taxes paid per dollar of U.S. sales. Even-numbered regressions include three-digit SIC code dummies. Regressions (3), (4), (7), and (8) include the seven control variables described above.

The results are almost uniformly consistent with income shifting. The dummy variables for the three most unambiguously low-tax regions—labeled Dragon, Ireland, and tax havens—all have significant negative coefficients, suggesting that U.S. multinationals operating there shift income out of the United States to these regions. The dummy variables for the two most unambiguously high-tax regions—Japan and high-tax Europe—are positive and significant, suggesting that U.S. multinationals operating there shift income from these regions into the United States. Furthermore, multinationals operating in South Africa have increased U.S. tax liabilities, suggesting that non-

Table 8.4   OLS Regressions Explaining U.S Federal Taxes Scaled by U.S. Assets or U.S. Sales

	U.S. Federal Tax per $ of U.S. assets				U.S. Federal Tax per $ of U.S. Sales			
	(1)	(2)	(3)	(4)	(5)	(6)	(7)	(8)
Canada	.0031	−.0147	.0013	−.0107	−.0096	−.0215	−.0072	−.0173
	(0.36)	(1.53)	(.15)	(1.17)	(1.49)	(3.04)	(1.19)	(2.66)
Japan*	.0161[a]	.0152[b]	.0113[b]	.0083	.0184[a]	.0169[a]	.0117[a]	.0100[b]
	(2.53)	(2.21)	(1.82)	(1.22)	(3.76)	(3.18)	(2.50)	(1.95)
Dragon*	−.0090[a]	−.0139[b]	−.0139[b]	−.0218[a]	−.0102[b]	−.0193[a]	−.0126[a]	−.0216[a]
	(1.33)	(1.78)	(2.14)	(2.88)	(1.96)	(3.26)	(2.26)	(3.91)
Asia	.0011	−.005	−.0019	.0028	.0055	.0017	.0080	.0029
	(0.11)	(0.05)	(0.21)	(0.26)	(0.74)	(0.19)	(1.16)	(0.37)
LT Eur.	.0129[c]	.0094	−.0167[b]	.0153[b]	.0082	.0024	.0024	−.0008
	(1.85)	(1.23)	(2.37)	(2.02)	(1.52)	(0.41)	(0.46)	(0.13)
HT Eur.*	−.0017[d]	.0130[a]	.0047[d]	.0259[a]	.0084	.0195[a]	.0102[b]	.0255[a]
	(0.23)	(1.44)	(0.65)	(2.96)	(1.49)	(2.97)	(1.91)	(4.10)
Ireland*	−.0135[b]	−.0109[a]	−.0141[b]	−.0145[a]	−.0116[b]	−.0155[a]	−.0143[a]	−.0186[a]
	(1.84)	(1.32)	(2.01)	(1.81)	(2.05)	(2.42)	(2.72)	(3.10)
Aus./N.Z.	−.0110	−.0089	−.0161[b]	−.0144[c]	−.0067	−.0077	−.0059	−.0050
	(1.43)	(1.12)	(2.16)	(1.88)	(1.12)	(1.25)	(1.06)	(0.86)
L. Amer.	.0059	.0101	.0051	.0070	−.0005	.0035	−.0024	.0011
	(0.85)	(1.39)	(0.75)	(1.00)	(0.09)	(0.64)	(0.48)	(0.21)
S. Afr.*	.0344[a]	.0318[a]	.0363[a]	.0307[a]	.0207[a]	.0277[a]	.0222[a]	.0271[a]
	(3.71)	(3.11)	(4.12)	(3.15)	(2.87)	(3.46)	(3.33)	(3.68)
Africa	−.0179	−.0308	−.0140	−.0383[b]	−.0110	−.0062	−.0136	−.0106
	(1.15)	(1.70)	(0.94)	(2.22)	(0.90)	(0.44)	(1.20)	(0.81)
OPEC	−.0068	.0006	.0090	.0136	−.0060	.0021	−.0002	.0039
	(0.69)	(0.05)	(0.93)	(1.08)	(0.77)	(0.21)	(0.03)	(0.41)

	(1)	(2)	(3)	(4)	(5)	(6)	(7)	(8)
Havens*	−.0340[a1]	−.0439[a1]	−.0315[a1]	−.0391[a1]	−.0244[a1]	−.0286[a1]	−.0177[a1]	−.0180[a1]
	(3.67)	(4.06)	(3.54)	(3.71)	(3.38)	(3.44)	(2.63)	(2.21)
R&D			.0018	.0032			.1475[a]	.1162[c]
			(0.03)	(0.04)			(2.67)	(1.74)
Adv.			.1815[a]	.1748[a]			−.0313	−.1267[c]
			(3.45)	(3.00)			(0.53)	(1.88)
Deprec.			−.2649[b]	−.3217[b]			−.0173	−.0128
			(2.31)	(2.55)			(0.20)	(0.13)
Empl.			−.2880	.2521			−1.165[a]	−.8221[b]
			(1.01)	(0.73)			(3.59)	(2.01)
Rent			−.0836	−.4234			−.4655[a]	−.7086[a]
			(0.51)	(2.32)			(3.08)	(4.11)
ITC†			.2134	−.1083			.9114[b]	.5847
			(0.34)	(0.18)			(1.99)	(1.28)
Interest			−.7471[a]	−.6694[a]			−.5767[a]	−.5786[a]
			(5.94)	(5.10)			(5.93)	(5.50)
Intercept	.0299[a]		.0580[a]		.0224[a]		.0461[a]	
	(10.8)		(8.39)		(10.4)		(9.24)	
SIC dummies	No	Yes	No	Yes	No	Yes	No	Yes
Sample	475	475	469	469	486	486	480	480
R²	.0867	.2587	.2041	.3605	.0814	.2487	.2459	.3944

Note: Numbers in brackets are *t*-ratios. Control variables are scaled by worldwide total assets in (1) through (4) and by worldwide total sales in (5) through (8).

*Regression coefficients are significant and consistent with hypothesis.

†Investment tax credit.

[a, b, c]Significant at 1%, 5%, and 10%, respectively.

[a1, b1, c1]Significant at1%, 5%, and 10%, respectively, in one-tailed tests.

[d]High-tax Europe is significant in (1) and (3) if firms with subsidiaries in only one region are excluded.

tax reasons such as avoiding capital controls or political instability may also drive income shifting.

The existence of subsidiaries in other Asian countries, Latin America, Africa, and the OPEC countries does not significantly affect U.S. tax liabilities. Multinationals operating there face conflicting incentives. On one hand, they have tax incentives to shift income from the United States into these regions, which generally have lower statutory tax rates than the United States does. On the other hand, multinational firms also have incentives to shift income out of these regions into the United States because of currency risks, political risks, capital controls, and so on.

One initially surprising result is the negative coefficient for Canada, which had statutory rates comparable to but slightly higher than the U.S. rate during the sample period. However, Glenday and Mintz (1990) point out that a large and increasing proportion of Canadian firms were in surplus tax loss situations during the early 1980s—as high as 61.4 percent in 1984—so their effective marginal tax rates were lower than the statutory corporate rates. The same explanation applies to Australia and New Zealand in this period. Finally, the coefficient for low-tax Europe is positive and is significant in regressions (1), (2), and (4). Tax rates there are lower than in the United States because of generous tax holidays and other provisions. This result is puzzling, and we can only speculate that firms may be so constrained in using these schemes that their effective tax rates are actually not lower than in the U.S.

As discussed above, the presence of both intangibles and debt financing make income shifting easier. We examine this idea by introducing a cross-term between the regional dummies and a dummy indicating the presence of these cost-reducing factors. Research and development spending per dollar of total sales, or of total assets, is used to proxy for production-related intangibles. Similarly, advertising spending per dollar of total sales, or of total assets, is used to proxy for marketing-related intangibles. A firm with high interest expenses per dollar of total sales or assets has more opportunities to shift income by concentrating its debt financing in highly taxed subsidiaries. To capture these effects, we create a dummy variable equal to one for observations in which any of these three variables is in the highest quartile of the whole sample, and zero otherwise.[13] This dummy indicates that the cost of income shifting may be low.[14] We repeat regressions (4) and (8), adding cross-terms between this "low-cost" dummy and the thirteen regional dummies in our regression analyses. The results are reported in table 8.5.

These factors do appear to facilitate income shifting. Indeed, the movement of income to the United States from high-tax Europe and Japan seems to rely solely on them. The regional dummies themselves have insignificant coeffi-

13. We experimented with other definitions of this interactive dummy variable and obtained results similar to those reported below.

14. Of the multinational firms in our sample, 69 percent are classified as having low cost in income shifting, while 63 percent are classified as such in the full sample.

Table 8.5   **OLS Regressions Explaining U.S. Federal Taxes Scaled by U.S. Assets or U.S. Sales: Cross-term Indicating Low-Cost Income Shifting Channels**

	U.S. Federal Tax per $ of U.S. Assets		U.S. Federal Tax per $ of U.S. Sales	
	Dummy	Cross-term[1]	Dummy	Cross-term[1]
Canada	.0071	−.0255	.0038	−.0284[c]
	(0.39)	(1.23)	(0.29)	(1.191)
Japan*	−.0199	.0352[cl]	−.0138	.0312[al]
	(0.87)	(1.48)	(0.98)	(2.14)
Four Dragons*	−.0083	−.0117	−.0143	−.0092
	(0.52)	(0.67)	(1.15)	(0.68)
Rest of Asia	.0546[a]	−.0654[al]	.0117	−.0156
	(2.69)	(2.93)	(0.85)	(0.95)
Low-tax Europe	.0224	−.0107	.0027	−.0049
	(1.21)	(0.54)	(0.20)	(0.34)
High-tax Europe*	−.0063	.0348[bl]	.0112	.0144
	(0.43)	(2.11)	(1.11)	(1.29)
Ireland*	.0094	−.0274	.0012	−.0245[cl]
	(0.35)	(0.99)	(0.09)	(1.60)
Australia/N.Z.	−.0120	.0193	−.0094	.0164
	(0.56)	(0.85)	(0.58)	(0.95)
Latin America	.0036	−.0075	−.0029	−.0028
	(0.25)	(0.47)	(0.25)	(0.21)
South Africa*	−.0139	.0454[cl]	.0100	.0206
	(0.45)	(1.38)	(0.67)	(1.22)
Africa*	−.0168	−.0797[bl]	−.0084	−.0257
	(0.64)	(2.27)	(0.42)	(0.93)
OPEC	−.1634[a]	.1668[a]	−.0276	.0359
	(4.12)	(4.39)	(1.20)	(1.56)
Tax havens*	−.0394[bl]	−.0123	−.0025	−.0170
	(1.78)	(0.51)	(0.13)	(0.87)
Control variables	Yes		Yes	
SIC code dummies	Yes		Yes	
Sample size	469		480	
R^2	.4695		.4304	

Note: Numbers in brackets are *t*-ratios.
*Results are consistent with hypothesis.
[1]Regional dummy × dummy indicating low-cost income shifting channel.
[a,b,c]Significant at 1%, 5%, and 10%, respectively.
[al,bl,cl]Significant at 1%, 5%, and 10%, respectively, in one-tailed tests.

cients, while the cross-terms are positive and significant. Similar regression results for South Africa imply that income is shifted from there to the United States via these same factors. Our results also indicate that firms shift income to the United States from Africa, Ireland, and the Four Dragon countries (although the Four Dragon coefficient is insignificant) via these channels. The income shifting from the United States to Canada detected in table 8.4 also appears to involve intangibles and/or debt-related channels. Note, however, that these factors may play a less critical role in income shifting to tax havens. The cross-term for the tax haven dummy is insignificant.

The results in table 8.5 are not, however, nearly as statistically strong as those in table 8.4. The results for Australia and New Zealand, Latin America, and the low-tax European countries are not significant at all. The weakness of these results may be due to the inevitable collinearity between the cross-term and the regional dummies themselves.

8.4   Statistical Issues

In this section, we examine the robustness of our results, focusing on the regressions reported in table 8.4, especially (4) and (8), and their statistical reliability.

First we investigate the possibility that our results might be driven by outliers. Using regressions (4) and (8), we identify a firm as an outlier if its studentized residual is greater than three.[15] There are four outliers in regression (4) and seven in regression (8).[16] Both regressions were repeated without the outliers. The coefficient for the Japan dummy in (8) becomes insignificant but is still positive. In (4) with no outliers, Japan remains positive and significant. Other regression results are not changed materially. We conclude that our results are probably not driven by outliers.

There may be heteroscedasticity and missing-variables problems in our regression. Heteroscedasticity could be caused by less than perfect scaling of the dependent variable or by missing variables. However, heteroscedasticity-consistent t-statistics (see White 1980) are not materially different from the simple t-statistics we report.

Missing variables can also bias the coefficient estimates. Recall that the numerator of our dependent variable can be expressed as $\tau_U(Y_U - Y_{UL} + Y_{HU})$, where Y_U is a firm's U.S. income and both Y_{UL} and Y_{HU} are shifted income. The problem of missing variables may arise if we do not adequately control for variations in Y_U. Indeed, given the simple specification of our regression equations, it is likely that we do not capture all relevant control variables.

We examine the missing-variables issue by repeating regressions (4) and (8), using a fixed-effects model. In other words, we regress the deviations of firms' U.S. tax ratios from their sample period means (1984–88) on the deviations of the independent variables from their respective sample period means. This procedure eliminates the impact on the dependent variable of firm-

15. In (8), one of the identified outliers actually has a studentized residual of 2.975 and a Cook's D statistic of 0.084. No nonoutliers have Cook's D statistics greater than 0.025, and all but two have Cook's D's below 0.02.

16. Two of the four outliers in regression (4) are multinational firms, as are four out of the seven outliers in regression (8). For the multinational firms, the prediction errors are all positive. Of the five uninational firms, three have positive prediction errors.

specific but time-invariant missing variables that affect the dependent variable additively.

Using this fixed-effects model, we obtain a positive coefficient for Canada, high-tax Europe, Australia/New Zealand, and Latin America; we obtain a negative coefficient for Japan, Four Dragons, other Asian countries, low-tax Europe, Ireland, South Africa, Africa, and tax havens.[17] No estimate is very significant. This is not surprising; we are suppressing much information with this technique, and it ignores any lags between incorporation of an affiliate and the onset of income shifting. Except for Japan and Latin America, the sign of a coefficient is positive when the corresponding region's tax rate is higher than in the United States and is negative when its tax rate is lower than in the United States. These results are consistent with the hypothesis that multinational firms shift income out of high-tax countries to the United States and into low-tax countries from the United States.

A subsidiary in Latin America increases U.S. tax liabilities in both the fixed-effects model and the simpler specifications reported in table 8.4. This again suggests that income may be shifted out of Latin America to avoid political risks and capital controls, even though tax rates there are generally lower than in the United States. The negative sign for the Japan dummy indicates that our previous estimates of the impact of having a subsidiary in Japan on U.S. tax liability may not be robust.

The coefficients for Canada and Australia/New Zealand now have positive signs, as our income shifting hypothesis predicts. This suggests that the negative effect subsidiaries in these regions have on U.S. tax liability may be due to tax losses carried forward by older subsidiaries. New subsidiaries owned by firms first entering these regions may not be in this situation and thus face the actual higher statutory tax rate.[18] As a consequence, these firms shift income out of these regions to the United States.

The fixed-effects model does not completely eliminate the problem caused by not fully controlling for a firm's profits, because of nonadditive or time varying effects. This is not just a statistical problem but also an economic issue. We therefore defer a more complete discussion to the next section.

We conclude that the regression results reported in table 8.4 do not appear to be driven by heteroscedasticity or missing-variables problems. The effect that having Japanese subsidiaries has on U.S. tax liabilities is not, however, very robust.

8.5 Economic Issues

We now turn our attention to the economic interpretation of our results. The question we address is whether or not there are sensible economic interpretations for our findings other than income shifting.

17. A dummy for OPEC is not included, because no firms have changed their presence there.
18. This is certainly true of greenfield expansions. However, Canadian tax law allows the transfer of some tax losses under some circumstances following acquisitions.

Our dependent variable is a firm's current U.S. federal tax liability divided by either its U.S. assets or its U.S. sales. Due to repatriated income from foreign subsidiaries, this tax ratio may be higher for a multinational firm than for a domestic firm. U.S. tax laws imply that income repatriated from a subsidiary in a low-tax location increases federal taxes net of foreign tax credits, while income repatriated from a subsidiary in a high-tax location does not. Hence, income repatriation alone should lead to a positive, rather than negative, regression coefficient for the lower-tax regional dummies, while the higher-tax regional dummies should have a nonpositive impact on our dependent variable. However, we obtain negative regression coefficients for the low-tax regional dummies and positive coefficients for the high-tax regional dummies. Thus, our results are clearly not due to income repatriation.

Our results might be driven by macroeconomic factors such as regional economic performance and changes in exchange rates. It is conceivable that such changes in the economic situation of a foreign host country might have a significant impact on the firm's U.S. profits and, thus, on its U.S. taxes. To ascertain that our results are not due to transitory macroeconomic changes, we repeat regressions (4) and (8) in table 8.4 using year-by-year data. The results are reported in tables 8.6 and 8.7.

The year-by-year regressions generate very consistent results. The signs of the regression coefficients for the separate years are identical and are also identical to the full-sample estimates except for Japan, low-tax Europe, and Latin America. However, as should be expected given the much smaller sample sizes, the statistical significance of the coefficients is attenuated. The lack of consistency in the coefficient estimates for low-tax Europe and Latin America is also not particularly surprising given that we do not obtain significant results in the pooled sample analysis. Japan aside, our findings do not appear to be driven by transitory regional macroeconomic factors.[19]

Another possible problem is that there might be a relationship between firm

---

19. Because our data include years before and after the Tax Reform Act of 1986 (TRA86), it is also potentially instructive to look at any differences in the estimated relationships across the two periods. TRA86 lowered the corporate statutory tax rate from 46 percent to 40 percent in 1987 and to 34 percent in 1988 and thereafter. This change by itself should increase the amount of income shifting from high-tax countries into the United States and decrease the amount of income shifting from the United States to low-tax countries. TRA86 also increased the likelihood that a firm will be in excess foreign tax credit status. This development increases the payoff to income shifting, because it reduces the likelihood that changes in taxes paid to foreign governments will trigger offsetting changes in the amount of foreign tax credit granted by the U.S. government. In the aggregate, then, following TRA86 there should be more income shifted out of high-tax foreign countries, while the change in income shifted into low-tax countries is less certain. No such pattern is apparent in table 8.7. However, two further considerations make the story more complicated. First, TRA86 also restricted the ability to average foreign taxes in the calculation of foreign tax credits. Second, because of the gradual phase-in of the tax rates, there were important incentives to change the timing of income realizations. This renders data from 1987 and 1988 somewhat suspect as an indicator of steady-state behavior and makes 1986 data suspect as a sample of typical pre-TRA86 behavior. For a more detailed discussion of TRA86, see Slemrod (1990). Harris (1991) analyzes the effect of TRA86 on income shifting.

Table 8.6   **Year-by-Year OLS Regressions of U.S. Federal Tax/U.S. Assets, 1984 through 1988.**

	Year				
	84	85	86	87	88
Canada	−.0616[c]	−.0119	.0004	−.0113	−.0103
	(1.99)	(0.34)	(0.01)	(0.44)	(0.54)
Japan	−.0018	.0193	−.0148	.0111	.0043
	(0.10)	(0.76)	(0.73)	(0.63)	(0.29)
Four Dragons*	−.0421[b1]	−.0274	−.0241	−.0220	−.0058
	(1.82)	(0.97)	(1.06)	(1.11)	(0.35)
Rest of Asia	.0036	.0063	.0163	−.0017	.0091
	(0.11)	(0.17)	(0.59)	(0.06)	(0.34)
Low-tax Europe	.0137	.0336	.0110	.0270	.0094
	(0.73)	(1.03)	(0.46)	(1.28)	(0.55)
High-tax	.0469[b1]	.0311	.0386	.0207	.0253[c1]
Europe*	(1.82)	(0.92)	(1.51)	(0.87)	(1.47)
Ireland*	−.0158	−.0337	−.0354[c1]	−.0158	−.0091
	(0.76)	(1.21)	(1.36)	(0.74)	(0.53)
Australia/N.Z.	−.0099	−.0540[c]	−.0156	−.0118	−.0175
	(0.46)	(1.95)	(0.64)	(0.57)	(1.08)
Latin America*	.0354[c]	.0023	−.0023	.0088	.0051
	(1.75)	(0.10)	(0.91)	(0.43)	(0.30)
South Africa*	.0581[b1]	.0626[b1]	.0372	.0438[c1]	.0125
	(2.01)	(1.87)	(1.22)	(1.60)	(0.42)
Africa*	−.0223	−.0364	−.0865[c1]	−.0483	−.0514
	(0.41)	(0.59)	(1.64)	(1.10)	(1.42)
OPEC	.0399	.0069	.0113	.0144	.0359
	(0.83)	(0.11)	(0.31)	(0.49)	(1.31)
Tax havens*	−.0452[c1]	−.0344	−.0257	−.0307	−.0404[c1]
	(1.53)	(0.81)	(0.72)	(1.07)	(1.58)
Control variables	Yes	Yes	Yes	Yes	Yes
SIC code dummies	Yes	Yes	Yes	Yes	Yes
Sample size	97	92	93	93	94
R^2	.6530	.5873	.5887	.5985	.5616

Note: Numbers in brackets are t-ratios.
*Sign of coefficient is significant with hypothesis in all years.
[a, b, c]Significant at 1%, 5%, and 10%, respectively.
[a1, b1, c1]Significant at 1%, 5%, and 10%, respectively, in one-tailed tests.

profitability and the location of subsidiaries. If affiliate locations and actual U.S. profits are both related to unobservable differences in a firm's profitability, then the estimated coefficients of table 8.4 will be biased estimates of the magnitude of income shifting made possible by multinational operation. The ideal procedure for dealing with this problem is to construct a structural model of the joint decisions of where to locate and how much income shifting to do, estimated perhaps by a two-stage least squares procedure where, in the equa-

Table 8.7   Year-by-Year OLS Regressions of U.S. Federal Tax/U.S. Sales, 1984 through 1988.

	Year				
	84	85	86	87	88
Canada	− .0737[a]	− .0165	− .0193	− .0224	− .0091
	(2.89)	(0.64)	(1.03)	(1.54)	(0.95)
Japan	.0172	.0209	.0040	.0042	− .0048
	(1.09)	(1.12)	(0.27)	(0.38)	(0.57)
Four Dragons*	− .0303[cl]	− .0259[cl]	− .0215	− .0137	− .0210[al]
	(1.52)	(1.28)	(1.26)	(1.17)	(2.51)
Rest of Asia	.0130	− .0140	.0128	.0050	.0194
	(0.44)	(0.52)	(0.60)	(0.27)	(1.32)
Low-tax Europe	− .0173	− .0147	− .0002	.0097	.0033
	(1.13)	(0.61)	(0.01)	(0.72)	(0.32)
High-tax	.0495[bl]	.0292	.0248[cl]	.0259[bl]	.0252[al]
Europe*	(2.31)	(1.24)	(1.35)	(1.93)	(2.85)
Ireland*	− .0070	− .0142	− .0357[bl]	− .0236[bl]	− .0079
	(0.38)	(0.67)	(1.78)	(1.79)	(0.83)
Australia/N.Z.	.0023	− .0235	− .0098	− .0032	− .0072
	(0.12)	(1.14)	(0.55)	(0.26)	(0.81)
Latin America	.0310[c]	− .0011	− .0028	− .0020	− .0054
	(1.82)	(0.07)	(0.19)	(0.17)	(0.57)
South Africa*	.0446[bl]	.0451[bl]	.0376[cl]	.0327[bl]	.0089
	(1.76)	(1.83)	(1.61)	(1.95)	(0.52)
Africa*	− .0249	− .0058	− .0294	− .0202	− .0236
	(0.53)	(0.12)	(0.75)	(0.75)	(1.15)
OPEC	.0310	.0114	.0032	− .0072	.0099
	(0.75)	(0.24)	(0.12)	(0.40)	(0.64)
Tax havens*	− .0283	− .0196	− .0303	− .0058	− .0137
	(1.11)	(0.59)	(1.16)	(0.32)	(0.94)
Control variables	Yes	Yes	Yes	Yes	Yes
SIC code dummies	Yes	Yes	Yes	Yes	Yes
Sample size	99	93	94	95	99
R^2	.6796	.5726	.5728	.6918	.7163

Note: Numbers in brackets are t-ratios.

*Sign of coefficient is consistent with hypothesis in all years.

[a,b,c]Significant at 1%, 5%, and 10%, respectively.

[al,bl,cl]Significant at 1%, 5%, and 10%, respectively, in one-tailed tests.

tion for reported U.S. tax paid, actual location is replaced by a predicted-location variable which is purged of the unobservable influences that may be correlated with actual U.S. parent profitability. Although ideal, this procedure is difficult, fraught with its own problems and data difficulties. It is therefore left for future research. We employ simpler techniques.

One simple approach is to repeat regressions (4) and (8) in table 8.4, including consolidated before-tax income (scaled by either worldwide total assets or worldwide sales) as an additional control variable. While this procedure is statistically problematic because it induces a correlation between the regression residual and the added explanatory variable, it nonetheless sheds light on the robustness of the coefficient estimates for the regional dummies. The regression result is that the dummy for Japan becomes insignificant in the analog of regression (8) and negative in the analog of (4). The other coefficient estimates do not change materially, and significance levels actually increase slightly.[20]

If a firm's profitability is related to the location of its subsidiaries, the relationship should also be captured in a regression of a firm's global after-tax income on the regional dummies. Results of this procedure are reported in the left panel of table 8.8. Regressions (1) and (2) explain global after-tax income, using the regional dummies and control variables including industry dummies. The dependent variable in the former is scaled by worldwide assets and in the latter by worldwide sales. The dummy for Japan in (1) has a significant positive coefficient.[21] Those for Canada, Europe, and South Africa are positive and insignificant. Subsidiaries in Asia, the Four Dragons, Ireland, Australia/New Zealand, Latin America, OPEC, Africa, and the tax havens are insignificantly related to lower U.S. taxes (the Four Dragons group borders on significance). We conclude that a relation between profitability and subsidiary location does not explain away our results.

Our results might also be capturing scale economies embedded in multinationals. An important explanation for the existence of multinational firms, the *internalization theory* (see Caves 1986), posits that having subsidiaries in *any* large foreign market leads to higher returns on certain intangibles. According to this view, multinational firms possess information-based intangible assets with public good properties. Technological know-how, marketing expertise, and exceptional management could be such goods. Due to well-known problems stemming from the economics of information, normal markets for these goods may not exist. Because of their public good properties, these assets should be applied on as large a scale as possible to maximize firm value. The solution is to expand the firm's scale: *internalizing* markets for these intangibles. Including R&D spending and advertising expenses (proxies for technology- and marketing-related intangibles, respectively) as independent variables is intended in part to control for this effect. If internalization is not entirely controlled for, however, our results could be affected.

Internalization could thus imply that having generic foreign subsidiaries increases profits and therefore taxes—especially if the subsidiaries allow access to large markets. While the positive coefficients on high-tax area dum-

20. The procedure discussed in the text does not eliminate the potential simultaneity bias but instead changes the nature of the bias and, under certain assumptions, changes its sign. Thus, the fact that the qualitative nature of the results is not altered by including the worldwide profitability variable implies that they are not an artifact of this sort of simultaneity bias.

21. Given the alleged entry barriers in Japan, it may not be surprising that successfully entering that market is correlated with high earnings.

Table 8.8   Regressions of Global After-Tax Income and Global Taxes on Regional Dummies and Control Variables

	Global Income		Global Tax	
	Assets (1)	Sales (2)	Assets (3)	Sales (4)
Canada	.0103	−.0034	−.0051	−.0064
	(1.19)	(0.36)	(0.83)	(0.98)
Japan	.0209	.0149	.0163	.0130
	(2.13)	(1.37)	(2.36)	(1.76)
Four Dragons	−.0171	−.0124	.0054	.0105
	(1.66)	(1.10)	(0.75)	(1.37)
Rest of Asia	−.0074	−.0040	.0018	−.0020
	(0.48)	(0.24)	(0.17)	(0.17)
Low-tax Europe	.0170	.0136	.0027	−.0013
	(1.58)	(1.12)	(0.35)	(0.16)
High-tax Europe	.0056	.0159	−.0002	−.0012
	(0.61)	(1.55)	(0.03)	(0.18)
Ireland	−.0166	−.0204	−.0127	−.0197
	(1.36)	(1.51)	(1.48)	(2.16)
Australia/N.Z.	−.0043	.0051	.0048	.0076
	(0.38)	(0.41)	(0.60)	(0.90)
Latin America	−.0049	−.0077	.0094	.0134
	(0.54)	(0.76)	(1.46)	(1.95)
South Africa	.0065	.0202	.0040	.0081
	(0.43)	(1.21)	(0.38)	(0.72)
Rest of Africa	−.0105	−.0102	−.0442	−.0377
	(0.37)	(0.32)	(2.20)	(1.77)
OPEC	−.0015	−.0113	−.0146	−.0145
	(0.09)	(0.60)	(1.21)	(1.13)
Tax havens	−.0112	−.0001	−.0231	−.0152
	(0.81)	(0.01)	(2.37)	(1.46)
Control variables	Yes	Yes	Yes	Yes
SIC codes	Yes	Yes	Yes	Yes
Sample size	475	469	475	469
R^2	.3244	.3023	.2882	.2523

Control variables are scaled by worldwide total assets in regressions (1) and (2) and by worldwide total sales in (3) and (4).
Note: Numbers in brackets are *t*-ratios.
[a, b, c]Significant at 1%, 5%, and 10%, respectively.

mies could be due in part to internalization-related profits, the negative coefficients on low-tax region dummies are unambiguous evidence of income shifting. Moreover, the low-cost income shifting indicator variable in table 8.5 also serves as an indicator of some of the assets likely to lead to internalization profits: technology and marketing ability. Internalization theory implies that the cross-product terms should all be positive. Again, this is so only for high-tax countries. Intangibles are associated with lower U.S. taxes when the firm has a subsidiary in a low-tax region. This result is consistent with income shifting. We conclude that while our results for high-tax areas may be affected by internalization, those for low-tax regions unambiguously imply income shifting from the United States to low-tax countries.

Finally, an alternative approach to testing for income shifting is to run regressions explaining total worldwide taxes. In the absence of income shifting, dummies indicating a firm's presence in high-tax regions should have positive coefficients, while dummies indicating a presence in low-tax regions should have zero or negative coefficients, depending on how much income is repatriated. Income shifting should reduce the positive coefficients of high-tax region dummies. Indeed, enough should render them insignificant. Furthermore, income shifting implies that low-tax region subsidiaries should be associated with a reduction in worldwide tax, as does the absence of income shifting. Thus income shifting implies insignificant coefficients for high-tax regions and uninterpretable results for low-tax regions. Although we feel that this is not an ideal hypothesis for statistical verification, we present the results of such regressions in the right panel of table 8.8.

Regressions (3) and (4) explain global taxes, using regional dummies and control variables including industry dummies. The scaling factor in (3) is worldwide assets and that in (4) is worldwide sales. The general insignificance of the high-tax region dummies is consistent with income shifting. Again Japan does not fit the pattern. Also, consistent with income shifting, the coefficients of the low-tax region dummies are either negative or insignificant. We conclude that the lack of results in regressions of this form is consistent with income shifting.

In summary, our regression results are most readily interpretable as evidence for income shifting. The estimated impact of having a subsidiary in Japan on a firm's U.S. tax may, however, be due to factors other than income shifting.

8.6   Economic Significance

So far, the focus of this paper has been entirely on whether or not the pattern of signs obtained in the regression analysis is consistent with the hypothesis that multinational firms engage in income shifting. In this section, we reflect on the magnitude of the estimated coefficients and the implied economic effect. We concluded above that the various statistical and economic problems inherent in this study cannot explain away the basic result that income shifting occurs. We do not, however, deny that some of them may adversely affect the precision of our point estimates. In particular, if the scale of affiliate operations, which we are unable to control for, is related to the magnitude of income shifting, the precision of our estimates may be diminished. We therefore must proceed into the following discussion with this caveat in mind.

A second caveat is that this analysis compares the U.S. taxes of firms with various multinational structures against those of uninational firms. The internalization theory suggests that multinational operations enhance profitability. A multinational structure therefore *should* be related to higher U.S. taxes—due to higher profits—even in the absence of income shifting. On average, as table 8.3 shows, multinational firms in our sample do have higher U.S. tax liabilities than uninational firms do. The average multinational has a U.S. tax bill equal to 3.3 percent of its assets and 2.4 percent of its sales. The average uninational's tax bill is only 3.0 percent of assets and 2.2 percent of sales. Since we use uninational firms' taxes as our benchmark rather than what the multinationals' taxes would be absent income shifting, all of our estimates understate the tax reduction due to income shifting.

We use the regression results reported in table 8.4 to estimate the effect of income shifting on overall U.S. corporate tax revenues. The dot product of the vector of regression coefficients on the regional dummies with the vector of regional dummies for a firm is an estimate of the effect of income shifting on that firm's U.S. tax ratio. Multiplying this by the scaling variable gives a dollar estimate of the change in the firm's U.S. tax liability due to income shifting. Results from this calculation suggest that income shifting does reduce U.S. tax revenue. This happens even though the average tax ratios of multinationals in table 8.3 are higher than those of uninational firms. This is because multiplying through by the scaling factor reveals large dollar value tax reductions for the biggest firms in our sample. These dominate the dollar value sums. The size of the reduction in U.S. tax revenues depends on whether table 8.4's regression (4) or (8) is used. The overall reduction is 3 percent of U.S. tax liability based on regression (4) and 22 percent based on regression (8). Obviously, the difference between these two estimates shows that this exercise is not very precise.[22]

Whatever the reduction in U.S. tax receipts, it appears to be due to income shifting by very large multinationals. Firms with subsidiaries in more than five regions show lowered U.S. tax bills. Based on (4) in table 8.4, the average multinational firm with subsidiaries in more than five regions uses income

---

22. The individual coefficients of specific regional dummies can also be interpreted. As an example, the estimated coefficient from table 8.4's regression (4) on the regional dummy for Ireland is −0.0145. This implies, ceteris paribus, that having an affiliate in Ireland is associated with a reduction in the ratio of U.S. income to U.S. assets of .0352 (.0145 divided by the average U.S. tax rate of .412). For a multinational firm with U.S. assets equal to five times its Irish assets, the implied jump in the Irish income to assets ratio is 0.176. The aggregate income to assets ratio in 1982 for U.S. affiliates in Ireland was 0.23. This rather large estimate is consistent with the qualitative findings of the previous studies discussed in section 8.1. Of course, these estimates are for an average firm. For a multinational with a very small presence in Ireland, this technique probably produces far too high an estimate of the actual amount of income shifting. In an oral communication to the authors, Peter Wilson has suggested that firms with Irish or tax haven subsidiaries may be more likely to have Puerto Rican subsidiaries as well. Our data sources do not include Puerto Rican operations in the lists of foreign subsidiaries. It is therefore possible that the Ireland and tax haven dummies are picking up the effects of income shifting to Puerto Rico. Also in an oral communication, James Hines has suggested that firms that are more aggressive in saving U.S. taxes are more likely to have subsidiaries in Ireland and other tax havens; part of the large negative effect of these regional dummies may be explained by this.

shifting to reduce its U.S. taxes to 51.6 percent of what they would otherwise be. Based on (8), this falls to 50.6 percent. This implies that when the various control variables and industry effects are taken into account, large multinationals have lower U.S. tax bills than comparable uninational firms do.

In contrast, multinationals with subsidiaries in five or fewer regions show elevated U.S. tax bills. While the simple sums of the regression coefficients for the regional dummies are negative, $-.0352$ for regression (4) and $-.0215$ for (8), weighting the sums by the means of the regional dummies turns them positive: .0116 for (4) and .0016 for (8). This implies that when the various control variables and industry effects are taken into account, a multinational with subsidiaries everywhere has a reduced U.S. tax ratio, while the average multinational has a higher U.S. tax ratio than a comparable uninational firm.[23]

Although the uncertainties inherent in our methodology make estimates of the dollar value of income shifting imprecise, we can draw some qualitative conclusions about economic significance. First, income shifting probably reduces overall U.S. tax receipts. Second, this is largely due to the *largest* multinationals using income shifting to substantially lower their U.S. tax bills. Third, the *typical* multinational has a higher U.S. tax liability than does a similar uninational firm. The last finding could be due either to higher earnings stemming from internalization or to a net inflow of shifted income to the United States. The ability of the largest multinationals to reduce their U.S. taxes is, however, most likely due to income shifting.

8.7   Conclusions

We examine five years of data from the annual reports of two hundred U.S. manufacturing corporations. We find that U.S. tax liability, as a fraction of either U.S. sales or U.S. assets, is related to the location of foreign subsidiaries in a way that is consistent with tax-motivated income shifting. Having a subsidiary in a tax haven, Ireland, or one of the Four Dragon Asian countries (all jurisdictions with low tax rates) is associated with lower U.S. tax ratios. Having a subsidiary in a high-tax region is associated with higher U.S. tax ratios. These results suggest that U.S. manufacturing companies are able to shift income out of high-tax countries into the United States and from the United States to low-tax countries. This behavior reduces U.S. taxes substantially only for firms with an extensive multinational structure. For multina-

---

23. Regressions (3) and (4) in table 8.8 generate similar results. Morck and Yeung (1991, 1992) find that multinational structure and expansion increase firm value only if intangibles are present. Since firms with intangibles may be able to engage in income shifting more easily, a naïve interpretation of their results is that the increased value is due to reduced taxes. However, the average multinational pays more worldwide taxes than does a similar uninational firm, presumably because it is more profitable. The increased value must therefore be due to factors such as the internalization of foreign markets rather than to reduced taxes. Reduced taxes might explain increased value only for the largest multinationals.

tional firms as a whole, income shifting leads to a moderate reduction in aggregate U.S. tax payments. Finally, our results support the idea that multinational firms conduct income shifting for non-tax-related purposes, such as avoiding capital controls and reducing political risks.

References

Alworth, Julian. 1989. *The financial, investment, and taxation decisions of multinationals.* Oxford: Basil Blackwell.

Caves, Richard E. 1986. *Multinational enterprise and economic analysis.* Cambridge: Cambridge University Press.

Dworin, Lowell. 1985. On estimating corporate tax liabilities from financial statements. *Tax Notes.* December 2. 965–71.

Glenday, Graham and Jack M. Mintz. 1990. The nature and magnitude of tax losses of Canadian corporations. Harvard Institute for International Development Working Paper. Cambridge, Mass.

Grubert, Harry, and John Mutti. 1991. Taxes, tariffs, and transfer pricing in multinational corporation decision making. *Review of Economics and Statistics* 73 (May): 285–293.

Harris, David G. 1991. The association of corporate multinationality with United States tax rates. Working Paper, University of Michigan.

Hines, James R., and Eric Rice. 1990. Fiscal paradise: Foreign tax havens and American business. NBER Working Paper no. 3477. Cambridge, Mass.: National Bureau of Economic Research.

International directory of corporate affiliations. Various issues. Skokie, Ill.: National Register Publishing; Macmillan.

Morck, Randall and Bernard Yeung. 1992. Internalization: An event study test. *Journal of International Economics* 33 (August): 41–56.

———. 1991. Why investors value multinationality. *Journal of Business* 64 (April): 165–87.

Slemrod, Joel. 1990. The impact of the Tax Reform Act of 1986 on foreign direct investment to and from the United States. In *Do taxes matter? The impact of the Tax Reform Act of 1986,* ed. J. Slemrod. Cambridge, Mass.: MIT Press.

Wheeler, James. 1988. An academic looks at transfer pricing in a global economy. *Tax Notes.* July 4.

White, Halbert. 1980. A heteroskedasticity consistent covariance matrix estimator and a direct test for heteroskedasticity. *Econometrica* 48:817–38.

Comment   John Mutti

This paper is a welcome addition to the literature on income shifting by multinational corporations (MNCs). Most previous work has been based on in-

John Mutti is the Sidney Meyer Professor of International Economics at Grinnell College.

come reported by U.S. affiliates abroad, aggregated by country location. The authors instead use microdata for individual U.S. parent firms. Thus, their work does not remassage a well-used data set but introduces another perspective from which to assess the extent of income shifting. Furthermore, this approach allows explicit consideration of the extent of profit shifting out of the United States, something which could only be acknowledged implicitly in previous studies.

The paper is controversial because it finds very strong income shifting effects, not just from affiliates in high-tax countries to affiliates in low-tax countries but from the U.S. parent to affiliates in low-tax countries. This latter finding particularly might cause the policy-oriented reader to ask whether IRS enforcement of current transfer pricing regulations is ineffective. Critics of current policy might suggest that the United States should abandon its traditional reliance on arm's-length transfer pricing to determine the international allocation of income and instead should adopt some worldwide apportionment formula or otherwise impose some minimum presumptive corporate income tax.

While the authors avoid any sweeping calls for reform, they clearly want us to take their results seriously. Their central thesis, that substantial income shifting occurs, is supported in several alternative formulations of the dependent and independent variables. Also, the authors confirm that outlier observations are not driving their results. Such a focus on individual observations is always a useful check on data entry and on subsequent inferences that can be misleading when a few extreme entries account for the significance of particular variables.

In short, the authors make good use of their data set to suggest the scope and form of tax-motivated income shifting behavior. Nevertheless, there are several additional issues that merit attention with respect to the authors' methodology and the inferences to be drawn from their results.

One question rests on a simple issue of definition. Are the subsidiaries reported by the authors majority-owned subsidiaries, or do they use a lower degree of control, such as the 10 percent ownership figure used in the benchmark survey? If the latter is true, do the same costs and benefits of income shifting apply? If the former is true, do the authors lose important information regarding the way business is conducted in certain countries? For example, according to the 1982 benchmark survey, majority-owned affiliates account for less than a quarter of all U.S. affiliate sales in Japan, and less than 10 percent of all U.S. affiliate sales in Korea. Given the lack of robustness of the Japanese country dummy in the empirical results, this ownership distinction may be relevant.

A second data question involves the sample of firms considered. The choice to use parent firms in SICs 30 to 39 means that pharmaceuticals are not included in the data set. The strength of any Irish relationship is likely to be understated by this omission, and any projected effects on manufacturing parents in the aggregate should be recognized as contingent on this particular subsample.

Another important issue involves the authors' estimation technique. Regressions (4) and (8) in table 8.4 are based on OLS estimates from panel data covering five years and roughly 95 firms. The authors recognize that alternative approaches may be preferable. They refer to estimates from a fixed-effects model, which does not impose the constraint implicit in the OLS framework that the intercept term is the same for all firms. However, the authors never report the corresponding F-statistic to test whether imposing such a constraint in regressions (4) and (8) is consistent with the data or not.

As noted by the authors, in the fixed-effects framework, the relevant observations are the deviations from the sample period means for each firm. For a parent firm that has an Irish affiliate in all five years of the sample, there is no deviation from the sample mean; the only nonzero country dummy observations that will appear in the regression are those where affiliates are established or disposed of within the sample period. The authors might usefully note from the raw data whether that sort of activity is observed for a large proportion of the firms included. Also, what countries have seen the biggest changes in the numbers of affiliates located there? Do these trends primarily suggest a growing attraction of tax haven operations, as noted by Hines and Rice (1990) over the 1977–82 period, or is expansion into other countries just as common and therefore just as likely to be reflected by within-firm dispersion over the sample period?

Another variable whose performance in the fixed-effects formulation would likely be affected is the dummy to show a low cost of transferring income. Because this dummy is created from those firms in the upper quartile of R&D intensity or those firms in the upper quartile of reliance on debt finance, we again must ask whether such firm rankings are likely to change over the five-year panel or whether little within-firm variation will be observed.

Analysis of panel data by Gordon and Jun (ch. 1 in this volume) includes another potentially preferred alternative to OLS estimation, a random-effects model. Such a model would take into account the likely correlation of error terms across years for a single firm; that is, if a firm's tax-sales ratio is underestimated in one year due to omitted firm-specific information, it is likely to be underestimated in other years, too. Attention to this firm-specific variance might be warranted in generalized least squares estimates.

At a more general level, the estimates of regressions (4) and (8) rely upon a dummy variable to indicate the presence of an affiliate within a country, because the authors have no data on the scale of affiliate operations. By implication, just being in a tax haven allows the firm to shift enough income to eliminate practically its entire U.S. tax liability. Such an interpretation is not very convincing; otherwise, we would expect all firms to follow this pattern and operate in a tax haven. Ideally, we would like to know more about each firm's costs of shifting income to a tax haven, since the decision to establish an affiliate also is an endogenous tax strategy choice. The authors address this concern in part by interacting country dummies with another dummy, based on firm intangibles and interest payments, that represent a low cost of transferring income. The results from this exercise are reported in table 8.5, and I regard them as potentially relevant in addressing the larger issue of how much income shifting occurs and who does it most successfully.

The size of the estimated coefficients carries strong implications for policy. At one level, the authors assess whether the opportunity to establish foreign affiliates allows U.S. firms to reduce their U.S. tax liability. Based on table 8.4 estimates, the authors conclude that the largest MNCs seem most able to reduce their U.S. payments through profit shifting. In this context, "largest" implies MNCs with six or more foreign affiliates. From information in a more complete version of the paper, firms with six to nine affiliates did not seem that much different in terms of total U.S. tax due, after correcting for income shifting behavior, than firms with four or five affiliates. The first group, though, did more aggressively reduce their U.S. tax liability. This observation indicates that the U.S. tax disparity might be regarded as much a matter of horizontal equity as it is vertical equity.

The fact that two companies may be the same size but one takes a much more aggressive stance than the other to minimize its U.S. taxes suggests that accurate identification of these aggressive minimizers is important in projecting both the aggregate fiscal effect and the proper characterization of those able to reduce their U.S. tax. A potential way of presenting this perspective would be to make calculations comparable to those reported above but based on the table 8.5 estimates rather than the table 8.4 estimates. Such a procedure would be another indication of the robustness of the possible policy inferences.

Specific country dummies are intriguing as well, and the authors devote a footnote to explaining their Irish coefficient. They note that *if* U.S. parent firms maintain about five times as many assets in the United States as they do in Ireland, then the estimated coefficient of shifting of income out of the United States to Ireland indeed explains most of the income declared in Ireland. While this example may suggest that the coefficient estimate is plausible, it also raises a more basic question: how many U.S. parents keep such a high proportion of their assets in Ireland?

Although we have no precise survey data to address this question, two indications are possible. One is based on the 1982 benchmark survey, from which we can tell the total assets of manufacturing parents, the amount held overseas, and the amount held in Ireland. Calculate the assets held in the United States by MNC parents and multiply that number by the percentage of firms the authors report as having Irish affiliates. By that procedure, U.S. parents of Irish affiliates held $98 billion of assets in the United States, while their holdings in Ireland were $4.5 billion. Thus, the authors' one to five ratio appears to be too large by a factor of four. Assuming the same income-asset relationship reported in the benchmark data, the much smaller proportion of assets in Ireland implies that all of the income declared in Ireland is too small to account for the reduction in U.S. income tax that we would infer from the estimated coefficient.

An even more extreme judgment comes from examining the assets declared by parents that repatriate income from Irish affiliates. According to Form 1118s filed in 1986, U.S. parents claimed assets of $2.4 trillion, while Bureau of Economic Analysis annual survey data indicate the corresponding Irish assets that year were $11.2 billion. If, instead, the authors' one to five ratio of Irish to U.S. assets were to hold, U.S. assets in Ireland would have to exceed $350 billion, a very significant figure in a country with a gross domestic product of less than $25 billion. As a consequence, we again question whether the Irish coefficient shows too great a reduction in U.S. income.

The authors note a suggestion from G. Peter Wilson that their Irish variable may be highly collinear with an important omitted variable: does the parent also have a possessions corporation (an entity regarded as a domestic corporation) in Puerto Rico? Income shifting to reduce a firm's U.S. tax liability clearly occurs, but the estimated coefficient captures both the portion of income that goes to Ireland and the portion that goes to Puerto Rico. This plausible line of reasoning preserves the authors' contention that their results demonstrate significant income shifting ability of U.S. MNCs.

However, a large Irish coefficient cannot be interpreted as a sign that greater audit resources ought to be devoted to investigating the transactions of the Irish affiliate or that existing regulations are deficient in limiting the types of tax-saving strategies possible in Ireland. Rather, the policy implication may be to leave provisions affecting Ireland unchanged and instead to overhaul the possessions corporation provisions. From an alternative perspective, several changes have been made in U.S. tax law and administration that would be expected to raise the cost of shifting income to Ireland. For example, Internal Revenue Code section 367 was changed in 1984 to restrict the transfer of intangibles to foreign corporations. More recently, modifications were made in section 482 transfer pricing regulations, which established the expectation that foreign corporations must pay appropriate royalties to the U.S. parent, and Wilson reports substantial penalties assessed under section 6662 against firms found guilty of transfer price infractions. In spite of these changes, regression estimates of the Irish coefficient may show little of this effect, because of the continued ability of the parent to shift income to Puerto Rico.

A second country effect of interest is found in the case of tax havens. A key question becomes what tax benefits U.S. firms gain from shifting income to tax havens if that income generally will be subject to immediate taxation by the United States under subpart F of the Internal Revenue Code. One possibility is that the U.S. parent has excess foreign tax credits from other foreign-source income, so any additional foreign-source income declared in a low-tax country will be free of U.S. tax. Altshuler and Newlon (ch. 3 in this volume) report the likelihood that U.S. parent firms fell into that position during the 1980–86 period. Of additional interest as that data series is extended would be a distribution showing the *extent* to which firms have either an excess or deficit of foreign tax credits. For small variation around a norm of zero excess credits, we might surmise that transactions with the tax haven affiliate reflect a low cost of implementing a tax-minimizing strategy, whereas a consistently large surplus position suggests much higher costs of shifting income.

In conclusion, these comments are intended to indicate that drawing conclusions from the authors' study is not straightforward. They have done commendable work in assembling a panel of firms for whom foreign affiliates can be identified, and their results clearly support the view that income shifting occurs. The location of affiliates in Ireland, the Four Dragons, and tax havens seems to account for lower parent tax payments in the United States; whether this relationship is changing over time, responsive to U.S. tax policy reforms, or stable and independent of U.S. measures in the international arena cannot be established. The authors' alternative empirical perspective for analyzing the question of income shifting is an excellent base for further analysis, which awaits the accumulation of more years of data and more-specific information regarding the parents' reliance on other tax strategies such as possessions corporations.

Contributors

Rosanne Altshuler
Department of Economics
New Jersey Hall
Rutgers University
New Brunswick, NJ 08903

Alan J. Auerbach
Department of Economics
University of Pennsylvania
3718 Locust Walk
Philadelphia, PA 19104

Neil Bruce
Department of Economics
Mail Stop DK-30
University of Washington
Seattle, WA 98103

Alberto Giovannini
Graduate School of Business
622 Uris Hall
Columbia University
New York, NY 10027

Timothy Goodspeed
Department of Economics
Florida International University
Miami, FL 33199

Roger H. Gordon
Department of Economics
University of Michigan
Ann Arbor, MI 48109

Harry Grubert
International Tax (OTA)
Department of the Treasury
Main Treasury Building, Room 5121
1500 Pennsylvania Ave., NW
Washington, DC 20220

Bronwyn H. Hall
Department of Economics
611 Evans Hall
University of California
Berkeley, CA 94720

David Harris
School of Business Administration
Department of Accounting
University of Michigan
Ann Arbor, MI 48109

Kevin Hassett
Department of Economics
Columbia University
101 Uris Hall
New York, NY 10027

James R. Hines, Jr.
National Bureau of Economic Research
1050 Massachusetts Avenue
Cambridge, MA 02138

Roy D. Hogg
Arthur Andersen & Co.
P.O. Box 29
Toronto-Dominion Center, 19th Floor
Toronto, Ontario M5K 1B9
Canada

R. Glenn Hubbard
Graduate School of Business
Columbia University
Uris Hall 609
New York, NY 10027

Joosung Jun
Department of Economics
Yale University
28 Hillhouse Avenue
New Haven, CT 06520

Jeffrey MacKie-Mason
Department of Economics
University of Michigan
462 Lorch Hall
Ann Arbor, MI 48109

Jack M. Mintz
Faculty of Management
University of Toronto
246 Bloor Street West
Toronto, Ontario M5S 1V4
Canada

Randall Morck
Faculty of Business
University of Alberta
3–23 Faculty of Business Building
Edmonton, Alberta T6G 2R6
Canada

John Mutti
Sidney Meyer Chair
Department of Economics
Grinnell College
P.O. Box 805
Grinnell, IA 50112

T. Scott Newlon
Department of the Treasury
Main Treasury Building, Room 5117
1500 Pennsylvania Avenue, NW
Washington, DC 20220

James M. Poterba
Department of Economics/E52–350
Massachusetts Institute of Technology
50 Memorial Drive
Cambridge, MA 02139

Joel Slemrod
Office of Tax Policy Research
School of Business Administration
University of Michigan
Ann Arbor, MI 48109

Deborah Swenson
Fuqua School of Business
Duke University
Durham, NC 27706

G. Peter Wilson
Graduate School of Business
    Administration
Harvard University
Morgan 415, Soldiers Field
Boston, MA 02163

Bernard Yeung
School of Business Administration
University of Michigan
Ann Arbor, MI 48109

Author Index

Adler, Michael, 13n1, 14
Albert, Steven H., 155n8
Altschuler, Rosanne, 155n8, 306
Alworth, Julian, 78, 79, 84, 278
Auerbach, Alan J., 125, 129t, 138, 154n6
Ault, Hugh J., 47n1

Bank of Canada, 50t
Bartholdy, Jan, 61nn20,21
Battese, G. E., 38n35
Bernstein, Jeffrey I., 183n43, 189
Bhattacharya, Sudipto, 21
Boskin, Michael, 78, 120n1
Bradford, David F., 29, 47n1
Brown, James K., 183n43
Bruce, Neil, 47n1, 60n17

Canada, Department of Finance, 47n1
Carolin, R., 209
Caves, Richard E., 184n45, 284, 297
Cohen, Wesley M., 151n3, 170n30
Coopers and Lybrand, 27t, 28t

Deutsch, Antal, 76
Devereux, M., 3
Dixit, Avinash, 149n1
Dumas, Bernard, 13n1, 14
Dunning, John, 23n19
Dworin, Lowell, 280n4

Easterbrook, Frank H., 21
Eisner, Robert, 155n8

Feldstein, Martin S., 29n28
Fisher, Gordon, 61nn20,21
Flaherty, M. Therese, 181n38
French, Kenneth R., 13n1, 14
Frisch, Daniel, 47n2, 78, 79, 95n23
Froot, Kenneth A., 120n1, 137
Fuller, W. A., 38n35
Fullerton, Don, 3, 29, 154n6

Gale, William, 78, 120n1
Glenday, Graham, 290
Goodspeed, Timothy, 28n27, 47n2, 78, 79, 95n23
Gordon, Roger H., 21n17, 29, 272n1
Graham, Edward M., 239
Griliches, Zvi, 30n29, 149n1, 154n5, 166, 170n30, 171n31
Grubert, Harry, 28n27, 60n17, 278, 279

Hall, Bronwyn H., 170n30, 184n45, 189
Halpern, Paul, 61n18
Harris, David G., 22, 294n19
Hartman, David G., 62n22, 78, 82n7, 119, 123, 157n13
Hausman, J. A., 39
Hayashi, Fumio, 184n45, 189
Himmelberg, Charles P., 189
Hines, James R., Jr., 19n12, 21, 60n17, 63nn23,24, 64, 78, 79, 81n4, 84, 104, 106, 108, 129t, 155n10, 156n12, 157n14, 169n29, 278, 279, 283, 304
Horst, Thomas, 60n17

311

Hubbard, R. Glenn, 19n12, 21, 60n17, 61n21, 63nn23,24, 64, 78, 79, 84, 104, 106, 108, 157n14, 169n29

International Directory of Corporate Affiliations, 282n8
International Financial Bureau, Japan, 46
International Monetary Fund (IMF), 45

Jaffe, Adam B., 166, 171n31
Jenkins, Glenn, 76
Jog, Vijay, 47n1
Jun, Joosung, 60n17, 78

King, M., 3
Kmenta, Jan, 37n32
Kopits, George F., 78, 181n39
Krugman, Paul R., 239

Lach, Saul, 184n45, 189
Lawlor, William R., 163n21
Leechor, Chad, 60n17, 61n19, 62–63n22, 81n4
Levin, Richard C., 151n3, 170n30
Levy, David M., 184n45
Lichtenberg, Frank R., 184n45, 255n11
Lyon, Andrew B., 154n6

Machlup, F., 45
McIntyre, Robert S., 182
MacKie-Mason, Jeffrey, 61nn20,21, 272n1
Mairesse, Jacques, 154n5, 170n30, 171n31
Mansfield, Edwin, 155n9, 166n24, 180n37, 181n38, 183n43
Meron, Amos, 184n45
Mintz, Jack M., 47n1, 60n17, 61nn18,19,20,21, 62–63n22, 81n4, 290
Morck, Randall, 282, 301n23
Mose, Vergie, 165t
Mowery, David C., 170n30
Mutti, John, 60n17, 78, 278, 279

Nadiri, M. Ishaq, 183n43, 189
National Science Board, 152t, 191n2
National Science Foundation, 151n3, 181t
Newlon, T. Scott, 78, 106, 120n1, 306

Organization for Economic Cooperation and Development (OECD), 28, 31t

Pakes, Ariel, 154n5, 178n35
Pearson, M., 3
Pechman, Joseph A., 26n26
Petersen, Bruce C., 189
Porter, Michael E., 195, 196n2
Poterba, James M., 13n1, 14, 21, 248
Price Waterhouse, 83n10, 165t, 238n2
Price Waterhouse Corporate Taxes: A Worldwide Summary, 283n10, 284t
Prucha, Ingmar R., 183n43

Quijano, Alicia M., 121

Ravenscraft, D., 154n5
Razin, Assaf, 13n2
Redmiles, Lissa, 77n1
Reinganum, Jennifer F., 149n1
Reishus, David, 125
Rice, Eric M., 56n12, 278, 279, 283, 304
Romeo, Anthony, 166n24, 180n37, 181n38

Salant, W. S., 45
Schankerman, Mark, 154n5, 166–67n25, 178n35, 184n45, 189
Scherer, F. M., 154n5
Scholes, Myron S., 120, 124, 137, 156n12, 195, 196n2, 232, 272n1
Scott, John T., 184n45
Siegel, Donald, 255n11
Sinn, Hans-Werner, 106
Slemrod, Joel, 13n2, 29, 36, 60n17, 78, 110, 120n1, 123, 124, 130n11, 294n19
Stein, Jeremy C., 120n1, 137
Sullivan, Martin A., 155n8
Summers, Lawrence H., 21
Swenson, Deborah L., 15n3, 28n27, 120, 123, 124, 267n15, 269
Switzer, Lorne, 166n24

Tarshis, L., 45
Teece, David, 180n37
Terleckyi, Nestor E., 184n45
Tillinghast, David R., 83n10

U.S. Congress, 149n2
U.S. Congress, Joint Committee on Taxation, 47n1
U.S. Department of Commerce, 181t
U.S. Department of the Treasury, 82, 159, 176n34, 183

U.S. General Accounting Office, 155n9, 183n43

Wagner, Samuel, 181n38
Wheeler, James, 278
White, Halbert, 292
Wilson, G. Peter, 284n12

Wolfson, Mark A., 120, 124, 137, 156n12, 195, 196n2, 232, 272n1
Wozny, James A., 155n9

Yeung, Bernard, 282, 301n23
Yoffie, D., 208nn16,18

Subject Index

Accelerated cost recovery system (ACRS), 59–60

Acquisitions: cost of, 141–42; debt arrangements for, 56; effects on foreign-controlled companies, 243–46; methods in foreign direct investment, 119, 123–30; new direct investment in U.S., 238–39, 267; revaluation of assets after, 242, 245; worldwide and territorial, 130–37. *See also* Mergers and acquisitions

ACRS. *See* Accelerated cost recovery system (ACRS)

Advance corporation tax (ACT), 87, 111

ALADI agreement, 205, 207

Aluminum Co. of Canada v. *The Queen*, 54n13

Argentina, 205

Branches, foreign (of multinationals), 79n3, 80, 156–57

Capital: differences in countries' cost of, 248–49; tax treatment of new and old, 6–7, 125–30, 137. *See also* Acquisitions; Cost of capital; Mergers and acquisitions

Capital controls: effect and use of, 14, 42–43; measuring for presence of, 25–34; as risk, 290

Capital-export neutrality, 2, 82, 109

Capital flows: among high- and low-tax countries, 24; data for analysis of, 45; with foreign direct investment, 36, 121–22;

portfolio and foreign direct investment as, 13–15; test for composition of international, 25–36. *See also* Cost of capital; Investment

Carryovers. *See* Cross-crediting

CFCs. *See* Controlled foreign corporations (CFCs)

Chemical industry, 201, 213–14, 229

Competitive advantage: gaining firm, 198; of greater R&D, 149

Controlled foreign corporations (CFCs): calculating tax rate for dividends remitted, 112–13; definition and data, 89–90; dividend remittances of, 95–96, 100–103; with excess credit and excess limitation, 92–95. *See also* Cross-crediting; Dividend payments; Remittances

Coordination frictions: conditions for, 199; in firms' sourcing decisions, 218–20; linked to transfer prices, 222–23

Cost of capital, 3; for acquisitions, 141–42; in analysis of foreign-controlled firm income, 248–49; for capital exporter, 272; for foreign-controlled companies, 239–40

Country frictions: defined, 198–99; effect on manufacturing location decisions, 201; related to pharmaceutical industry, 203, 205–6; in semiconductor industry location decisions, 209–13

Coupling frictions: effect on manufacturing location decisions, 201; related to chemical industry location decisions, 213; re-

Coupling frictions (*continued*)
lated to materials industry, 216; related
to pharmaceutical industry, 205; related
to semiconductor industry, 209, 212–13;
types of, 198
Coupling restrictions: effect on pharmaceutical manufacture, 206–7; in manufacturing sector, 201; in software industry, 215
Credit. *See* Cross-crediting; Deemed-paid foreign tax credit; Excess credit; Foreign
tax credit; Tax credit
Cross-border charges: after Tax Reform Act
(1986), 5; effect of U.S.-Canadian tax
reforms on, 5, 61–62, 68–69, 72–73;
U.S.–Canadian, 50–51, 54–55; use of,
62, 68; to U.S. parent companies, 49
Cross-crediting: occurrence and effect of, 82,
94–100, 109; over time, 97–98; under
Tax Reform Act (1986), U.S., 83, 109;
using excess credits and limitations, 81.
See also Capital-export neutrality; Excess credit; Excess limitation; Jurisdictions, high- and low-tax

Data sources: for analysis of Canadian-U.S.
tax reforms, 5, 47, 49; in analysis of income repatriation, 79; in analysis of income shifting, 10, 280–81, 282n8,
283n10, 303; for analysis of remittances
and tax payments, 5–6, 89–90; for analysis of tax and nontax factors, 4–5; for
capital flows, 45; for foreign-controlled
companies analysis, 9, 240–41; for foreign investment model, 138; for tax
treatment of foreign equity ownership,
14; for tax treatment of portfolio versus
direct investment, 25–26, 29–30,
35–36, 45; for U.S. firm response to
R&D expense allocation,
168–71, 191
Debt and earnings stripping, 238, 240, 246–
48, 269
Debt finance: effect of U.S.-Canadian tax reform on, 61, 72–73, 75; effect on U.S.
firm subsidiaries of, 5, 60–61; for
foreign-controlled companies, 238; in income shifting, 277, 285, 290–92; use
of, 21, 55
Debt flows (United States to Canada), 55
Deemed-paid foreign tax credit: of dividend
payments, 83, 95; tax before, 81
Deferral. *See* Tax deferral

DISC income. *See* Domestic international
sales corporation (DISC) dividend income
Diversification, international, 13–15
Dividend payments: as channel for remittance
of foreign income, 83, 95; derivation of
tax prices for, 110–12; effect of nontax
considerations on, 64; effect of U.S.-
Canadian tax reform on, 62–64, 68,
72–73; from high- and low-tax CFCs,
113–14; increased, 49; as percentage of
foreign corporate income, 95; rate for direct foreign and portfolio investment,
20–21; as remittances from CFCs, 95–
96, 100–103. *See also* Jurisdictions,
high- and low-tax
Dividends: deemed-paid foreign tax credit
for, 83, 95; imputation system for, 20,
86t, 87–88; incentives to deter repatriation of, 63; under split-rate foreign tax
systems, 86–87; tax price of remitted,
84–88, 103–10
Domestic international sales corporation
(DISC) dividend income, 83
Dominion Bridge Co. Ltd. v. *The Queen*,
54n13

Earnings and profits: of foreign-controlled
firms, 237–38; look-through rules for,
56–57, 75; tax treatment for U.S. subsidiaries, 58–59, 62. *See also* Debt and
earnings stripping
Economic Recovery Tax Act (1981), 7,
158–59
Enforcement, tax, 2, 13, 15–16
Excess credit: creation of, 95–97; in cross-
crediting, 97–100; in foreign tax credits,
156; global tax price with, 88; to offset
residual U.S. tax, 81–83, 88; to reduce
tax liability, 18; tax law effect on debt finance with, 61, 72–73. *See also* Cross-
crediting
Excess limitation: in cross-crediting, 97–100;
in foreign tax credits, 81–83; global tax
price with, 88
Exchange rates: effect on income of foreign-
controlled companies, 255–58; effect on
U.S. foreign firm R&D, 152–54; link
between FDI and, 146
Expense allocation: of foreign-controlled
companies, 252–53; under U.S. tax system for foreign income, 57–58

Factor prices, 23

Foreign-controlled firms: acquisitions as foreign direct investment, 119, 123–37, 238–39, 243–46, 267; factors influencing earnings and tax payments by, 9, 237–40

Foreign direct investment (FDI): acquisition of existing capital assets, 6, 13, 119, 123–37, 238–39, 243–46, 267; analysis of TRA86 effect on, 124–30; consequences for acquisitions in U.S., 238–40; effect of capital controls on, 25; factors favoring, 80; model of, 138–43; net tax rates of, 22–23; possible incentives for increased, 146–47; tax treatment of, 16–22, 120; of territorial and worldwide firms, 130–37, 145–46; in United States, 120–22

Foreign sales corporation (FSC), 83

Foreign-source income. *See* Income, foreign-source

Foreign tax credit: averaging, 56–57; carryover to offset U.S. tax, 83, 95–100, 103; direct and indirect, or deemed-paid, 80–81; to eliminate liability on royalty income, 164; limitation on, 78; reinvoicing as determinant of, 225; tax price depends on, 83; in U.S. tax law, 57, 156. *See also* Deemed-paid foreign tax credit; Excess credit; Excess limitation; Tax prices

France: evidence of capital controls in, 30–31; tax treatment for foreign-source income, 19

Frictions (in tax planning), 196–97. *See also* Coordination frictions; Country frictions; Coupling frictions

FSC. *See* Foreign sales corporation (FSC)

Functional currency method, 58

GAAR. *See* General antiavoidance rule (GAAR), Canada

General antiavoidance rule (GAAR), Canada, 54

General limitation income, 83

General Utilities doctrine, 124–25, 142

Global strategy theory, 196, 198

Imputation systems: corporate dividend remittances under, 86t, 87–88; effect on personal tax advantage of dividend, 32–33; effect on personal tax rate of dividend, 20; tax prices under U.K., 111–12

Incentives, financial, 211

Incentives, tax: capturing effects of, 78; for foreign direct investment, 145–46; in tax deferral of foreign income, 156–57; in tax deferral policy, 80; for U.S. R&D, 149–50, 158–65; in U.S. tax law, 120

Income, capital: residence-based tax on, 2; tax discrimination between domestic- and foreign-source, 2

Income, domestic: deduction of R&D expense against, 157–60; R&D undertaken for, 160–62; without tax liability, 18–19

Income, foreign-source: baskets, or pools, 56–58, 82–83; reports of U.S. corporation, 77; residence principle applied to repatriated, 122–23; surtax on repatriated, 33–34; taxation of territorial or worldwide, 122–24; with tax deferral, 80; tax liability of multinational firm R&D, 156–60; tax on and credit allowances for, 78–79. *See also* Excess credit; Excess limitation; Foreign tax credit; General limitation income; Profits; Tax deferral

Income, taxable: changed tax treatment of U.S. firm, 58; effect of macroeconomic factors on multinational, 294; flow of U.S. multinational, 83–88; foreign-controlled company shifting of, 8–9, 21, 258–64; generated by foreign-controlled companies, 269–70; reporting by U.S. multinationals of, 279; of U.S. multinational and uninational firms, 330–31; U.S. policy to credit payments of, 78; U.S. tax credit policy for withholding, 80. *See also* Income shifting; Profits

Income shifting: among U.S. manufacturing firms, 277–78; conditions for, 252; effect on revenue, 3; evidence of, 258–64, 270, 287–92, 299. *See also* Jurisdictions, high– and low-tax

Intangibles: in comparison of domestic- and foreign-controlled companies, 253–55; in cost of income shifting, 285, 290–92; returns on certain multinational firm, 297–99

Interest: as channel for remittance of foreign income, 82–83, 93t, 94–95, 157; cross-border charges for, 54–55; deductibility of expense under TRA86, 57, 238; look-through rules to detect, 56; from U.S. subsidiaries, 88

Internalization theory, 297–300
Internal Revenue Service, Statistics of Income Division (SOI), 89n18, 240
Investment: abroad for corporate and individual, 4; characteristics of R&D, 188–89; cross-border, 3; different methods used by foreign multinationals, 119; factors discouraging domestic, 80; factors influencing, 35; factors influencing foreign, 23–35; model to analyze effect of TRA86 on foreign, 125–30; U.S. tax law incentives for foreign, 120; worldwide and territorial in United States, 130–37. *See also* Acquisition; Foreign direct investment (FDI); Portfolio equity investment; Reinvestment

Joint ownership, 24
Jurisdictions, high- and low-tax: capital flows among, 24; classification of, 282–92; in cross-crediting, 95–100; dividend payments from firms in, 113–14; income shifting among, 21, 277–80, 301–2; tax ratios of firms in, 286–87

Location decisions: factors influencing manufacturing, 201–13; shift in rationale for, 230. *See also* Jurisdictions, high- and low-tax
Look-through rules, 56–57, 75

Management and administration fees, 54–55, 58
Manufacturing sector: coupling and country frictions in, 201; factors influencing location decisions, 201–13; income shifting in, 277–78; tax and nontax considerations in, 213–14, 219, 229, 232–33. *See also* Chemical industry; Materials industry; Pharmaceutical industry; Semiconductor industry; Software industry
Materials industry, 201, 216
Mergers and acquisitons: as form of foreign direct investment, 120, 242, 245; tax treatment under TRA86, 124–25. *See also* General Utilities doctrine
Minimum tax, alternative, 59
Multinational firms: implementation of residence-based taxation for, 2; internalization within, 297–99; investment in foreign countries, 18; research activities of,

160; shifting of taxable income by, 21; tax treatment of foreign investment, 13
Multinational firms, foreign: investment methods of, 119–20, 123–24; tax treatment in United States of, 122–30. *See also* Foreign direct investment
Multinational firms, U.S.: effect of tax credit position of, 82; foreign and domestic research and development of, 151–54; predictions of responses to tax system changes, 60–73; response to R&D tax incentives, 149–50; subsidiary location decisions, 277–302; tax payments and income remittance of, 90–100; tax policy for branch and subsidiary, 80. *See also* Controlled foreign corporations (CFCs); Foreign-controlled firms; Income shifting; Jurisdictions, high- and low-tax; Parent firms, U.S.

1986 TRA. *See* Tax Refort Act (1986)
Nontax considerations: characteristics of, 232; in firm location and sourcing decisions, 8, 196–99, 201–16, 229; in income shifting, 290, 302; for location of manufacturing firms, 232–33; in maximizing firm's value, 196–97; in portfolio and direct foreign investments, 23–25, 45; in portfolio and foreign direct investment, 14, 45, 137–38, 146–47; potential effect on dividend payments, 64; in R&D expenditures, 152–54; in sourcing decisions, 218–21. *See also* Frictions; Restrictions; Tax considerations

Omnibus Budget Reconciliation Act (1989): R&D expense allocation under, 159; R&E credit under, 155

Parent firms, U.S.: controlled foreign corporations of, 89–90, 92–96, 100–103, 112–13; cross-border charges to, 49; effect of Canadian tax system changes on, 5, 51–55; subsidiaries and branches of, 156–57. *See also* Controlled foreign corporations (CFCs)
Performance evaluation systems: determinants of after-tax, 226–28; pre- and after-tax, 220–23

Pharmaceutical industry, 201–8

Portfolio equity investment: criteria for, 35; effect of foreign, 23, 36; net tax advantage of, 31–33; net tax rates, 22–23; tax treatment of, 13, 15–16. *See also* Capital controls

Profits: effect of exchange rates on foreign-controlled, 255–58; foreign-controlled and domestic firm, 161n19, 241–43, 269–70; prior to foreign ownership, 267–69, 272, 274; related to multinational firm internalization, 297–300; shifting by foreign-controlled companies, 219–25, 270; shift to low-tax locations, 259; tax policy of United States toward foreign, 79–83; U.S. tax policy for foreign branch and subsidiary, 80, 156–57

Public policy. *See* Tax policy, U.S.

Puerto Rico, 106

Regulation: influence on pharmaceutical industry location, 201–4, 207; U.S. Treasury 1.861–8 and 1.954.3(a)(4), 149–50, 158, 160–65, 215n28

Reinvestment, 62–64, 68, 75

Reinvoicing (in transfer pricing), 224–25

Remittances: different channels for U.S. firm foreign income, 83, 94; effect of tax avoidance on pattern of, 109; tax effects of dividend, 100–110; tax price of dividend and tax-deductible, 84–88; withholding tax by foreign-source income country, 79. *See also* Repatriated income; Repatriation

Rents: as channel for remittance of foreign income, 83, 93t, 94–95; cross-border charges for, 54–55; as income, 58; from U.S. subsidiaries, 88

Repatriated income: corporate surtax on, 33–34; disallowance since 1986 of some pooling, 19; effect on tax ratio of multinational, 294; exemption of part of foreign-source, 19; pooling of multinational, 18–19; royalty income as, 164, 188; taxation of U.S. subsidiaries', 156–57. *See also* Remittances

Repatriation: behavior of U.S. subsidiaries in Canada, 74–76; effect of tax deferral on U.S. firm, 80, 221; incentives for, 82; of income by U.S. multinational firms, 78–79; residence principle application to in-

come, 122–23; use of tax deferral for foreign income, 156–57. *See also* Cross-border charges; Debt finance; Dividend payment; Reinvestment; Remittances

Research and development (R&D): for domestic and foreign sales and income, 160–65; domestic and foreign targeting of U.S. firm, 181, 188–89; expense allocation rules, 149–50, 158–65, 188–89; offshore U.S. multinational, 151, 160, 165; proposed changes in tax treatment for, 182–85; R&D/GNP ratio for five industrialized countries, 151–52; U.S. firm response to allocation rules, 165–81; by U.S. multinational firms at home and abroad, 151–65. *See also* Income, domestic; Income, foreign; U.S. Treasury

Research and experimentation (R&E) credit. *See* Tax credit

Residence-based taxation: advantages and limitations of, 2; of foreign-source income, 122–24; of U.S. tax system, 156, 279; worldwide approach, 122–38

Restrictions: effect on manufacturing location decisions, 201; impeding tax minimization, 196. *See also* Coupling restrictions

Rhythm method, 59, 63–64, 68, 75

Royalties: as channel for remittance of foreign income, 83, 93t, 94–95; cross-border charges for, 54–55; as foreign income, 88, 157; as income, 58; as intangibles, 253–54; withholding tax rates on U.S. firm, 164–65, 188

Sales corporations. *See* Domestic international sales corporation (DISC); Foreign sales corporation (FSC)

Sales tax, 79n3

Semiconductor industry, 209–13

Signaling, 21

Software industry, 215

SOI. *See* Internal Revenue Service, Statistics of Income Division (SOI)

Sourcing decisions: as element of worldwide tax planning, 226–28; tax considerations in, 218–19. *See also* Performance evaluation systems; Transfer prices

Split-rate corporate tax system: in analysis of capital flows composition, 29; defined, 26; tax prices under, 110–11

Spur Oil Ltd. v. *The Queen*, 54n13

Subsidiaries, foreign (of multinationals): interest, royalties and rents from, 88; repatriated income of, 19, 156–57; U.S. tax policy for, 58–59, 80

Surtax: Canadian corporate, 52–53; in portfolio and corporate investment analysis, 24, 31, 33–34

Takeovers, 125

Tax, foreign. *See* Income, foreign-source; Income, taxable

Tax avoidance: effect of incentives for, 109; influence of tax deferral on, 80; of tax on dividends, 20

Tax avoidance, Canada. *See* General anti-avoidance rule (GAAR), Canada

Tax base, 59, 61, 62

Tax benefits. *See* Tax considerations

Tax considerations: for foreign firms investment, 119–120; for location of manufacturing sector plants, 201–13, 229; in location of marketing and distribution facilities, 216–18; in manufacturers' sourcing decisions, 219, 229; in multinational internal pricing, 278; in portfolio and direct investment analysis, 45–46. *See also* Incentives, tax; Jurisdictions, high- and low-tax; Nontax considerations

Tax credit: Canadian investment and R&D, 53–54; conditions for pooling repatriated income for, 19; under double-taxation conventions, 16–18, 109; with foreign direct investment, 16–17; under imputation tax system, 87; for multinationals with repatriated income, 18–19; for research and experimentation (R&E), 149–50, 154–55; rhythm method for, 59, 63–64, 68, 75; U.S. foreign tax credit limitations, 56–57; under U.S.-U.K. tax treaty, 87–88, 111. *See also* Deemed-paid foreign tax credit; Excess credit; Foreign tax credit

Tax deferral: on foreign income of U.S. companies, 6, 78, 80; for subsidiaries of U.S. parent firms, 156

Tax Equity and Fiscal Responsibility Act (1982), 206n14

Tax exemption: foreign country rules for, 17; for repatriated income, 19

Tax havens, 46, 238

Tax law, Canada, 47–55. *See also* Tax policy, Canada

Tax law, U.S.: effect on income repatriation patterns, 78; foreign tax credit in, 57, 156; incentives in, 120; proposed (H.R. 5270), 2, 9; related to R&D, 157–65. *See also* Tax policy, U.S.

Tax minimization, 196

Tax planning: coordination of worldwide, 226–28; government rules restricting, 196, 198. *See also* Frictions; Nontax considerations; Performance evaluation systems; Restrictions; Sourcing decisions; Tax considerations; Value chain considerations

Tax policy, Canada: statutory and nonstatutory changes in, 51–55; for U.S. subsidiaries, 74–76

Tax policy, foreign: with conflicting incentives, 290; related to R&D, 165, 182–84

Tax policy, U.S.: differentiated domestic and foreign R&D, 157–58; for foreign branches of U.S. parent firms, 156–57; for foreign multinationals, 119–20; issues in design of R&D policy, 150–55; related to foreign direct investment, 124–30; for research and experimentation, 149–50; statutory and nonstatutory changes in, 51–55

Tax prices: calculation of controlled foreign corporation, 90; decision to shift R&D spending, 7, 189–93; defined, 83; of dividend and tax-deductible remittances, 84–88, 103–10; for income remittances, 79; response to R&D expenditures of U.S. firms, 171–81, 188. *See also* Tax rates

Tax rates: calculating dividend remittance, 112–13; changes in U.S. and Canadian statuatory, 50–54; effect on R&D, 154; excess credit and limitation with foreign, 81; on multinational firm foreign income, 156–57; on portfolio and corporate investment, 22–23, 25–36. *See also* Tax prices

Tax Reform Act (1986): baskets of foreign income under, 83, 109; corporate investment tax changes of, 124–25; effect on investment incentives, 6, 137; foreign tax credit limitation in, 56–57; income shifting incentives under, 294n19; issues related to R&D investment, 159n18; R&D and R&E credits under, 155; tax base broadening under, 59

Tax systems: changes in U.S. and Canadian, 49; international aspects of U.S., 156–60; look-through rules in U.S., 56–57, 75; predictions related to reform in, 60–73. *See also* Foreign tax credit; Income, foreign; Tax deferral

Tax systems, foreign: dividend remittances under imputation system, 86t, 87–88; remittance under classical, 84–86; split-rate, 86–87

Tax transfer prices. *See* Transfer prices

Tax treaties: Canada-U.S., 50n4; U.S.-U.K., 87–88, 111

Tax treatment: with joint ownership, 24; partial section 946 method, 58; of portfolio and foreign direct investment, 13–14, 25–36; pre-1984 U.S., 56; proposed changes for U.S. R&D, 182–85; territorial and worldwide approaches to, 122–38, 142–43; U.S.-Canadian reforms in corporate, 47

Technical and Miscellaneous Revenue Act (1988): R&D expense allocation under, 159; R&E credit under, 155

Technology transfer, U.S., 181n38

The Queen v. *Irving Oil Ltd.*, 54n13

TRA86. *See* Tax Reform Act (1986)

Trade agreements. *See* ALADI agreement

Trade barriers, 23

Transfer prices: expenses as mechanisms for, 243–55; gain from setting; 33, 45; location and sourcing decisions effect on, 196–97, 218–20, 229; role in firm location decision, 199; role in shifting profit and income, 8, 219, 221–25, 283–84; setting in Canadian tax system, 54; to shift taxable income, 237–38, 271, 274; tax and nontax considerations in setting, 8, 221–25; use in income shifting of artificial, 277, 283–84

Transportation costs, 23

U.S. Treasury: regulation § 1.861-8, 149–50, 158, 160–65; regulation § 1.954-3(a)(4), 215n28. *See also* Internal Revenue Service, Statistics of Income Division (SOI)

Value-added tax (VAT), 79n3

Value-chain considerations, 198–99, 228. *See also* Coordination frictions; Country frictions; Coupling frictions; Coupling restrictions